EASY DEATH

HYPNOTHERAPIST
DR. BRUCE GOLDBERG
PAST LIVES) FUTURE LIVES

FILM
IKERU

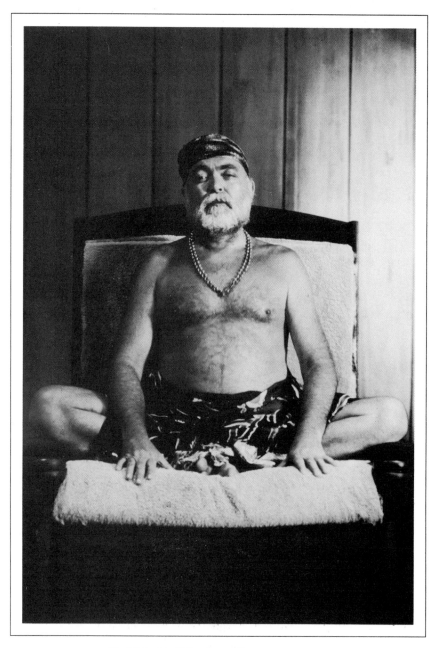

The Divine World-Teacher and True Heart-Master,
SRI DA AVABHASA (THE "BRIGHT")
Sri Love-Anandashram, September 1991

EASY DEATH

Spiritual Discourses and Essays on the Inherent and
Ultimate Transcendence of Death and Everything Else

by
the Divine World-Teacher and True Heart-Master,

DA AVABHASA
(THE "BRIGHT")

*Compiled with commentary
by Connie Grisso, Carolyn Lee,
and James Minkin*

Consulting Editor, Frans Bakker, M.D.

SECOND EDITION

THE DAWN HORSE PRESS
CLEARLAKE, CALIFORNIA

NOTE TO THE READER

The devotional, Spiritual, functional, practical, relational, cultural, and formal community practices and disciplines discussed in this book, including the meditative practices, the Yogic exercises of conductivity, the breathing exercises, the life-disciplines of right diet and exercise, the intelligent economization and practice of sexuality, etc., are appropriate and natural practices that are voluntarily and progressively adopted by each student-novice and member of the Free Daist Communion and adapted to his or her personal circumstance. Although anyone may find them useful and beneficial, they are not presented as advice or recommendations to the general reader or to anyone who is not a participant in Da Avabhasa International or a member of the Free Daist Communion. And nothing in this book is intended as a diagnosis, prescription, or recommended treatment or cure for any specific "problem", whether medical, emotional, psychological, social, or Spiritual. One should apply a particular program of treatment, prevention, cure, or general health only in consultation with a licensed physician or other qualified professional.

For a further discussion of individual responsibility in the Way of the Heart, our claim to perpetual copyright to the Wisdom-Teaching of Da Avabhasa, and His renunciate status in the Free Daist Communion, please see "Further Notes to the Reader", pages 403-7 of this book.

First edition, June 1983
Second edition, enlarged and updated, December 1991
Printed in the United States of America

Produced by the Free Daist Communion in cooperation with the Dawn Horse Press

Library of Congress Cataloging-in-Publication Data

Da Free John, 1939-
        Easy Death: Spiritual Discourses and Essays on the Inherent and Ultimate
Transcendence of Death and Everything Else / by the Divine World-Teacher and True Heart-
Master, Da Avabhasa (The "Bright"); compiled with commentary by Connie Grisso,
Carolyn Lee, and James Minkin; consulting editor, Frans Bakker.
        p.   cm.
        Includes bibliographical references and index.
        ISBN 0-918801-30-3 (softcover)
        1. Death—Religious aspects.   2. Spiritual life.   I. Grisso, Connie.
        II. Lee, Carolyn.   III. Minkin, James.   IV. Bakker, Frans.   V. Title.
        BP610.B81663   1991
        299'. 93—dc20   91-45959
                                                                              CIP

Dedication

Beloved Sri Da Avabhasa,
Most Gracious Master of life and death,
You are the Light of our hearts,
The One Who Dissolves all bewilderment,
Relieves all fear,
And Grants the Gift of Eternal Happiness.

May each one who reads this book
Feel Your Divine Compassion and Love
And be moved to find Your Graceful Help,
While alive, at death,
And in any circumstance that may appear.

Your devotees

About the Cover

The cover design is a symbolic representation of an essential feature of Sri Da Avabhasa's Way of the Heart. The egg represents the knot of egoic recoil from the Freedom and Bliss of the Divine Reality, or Consciousness Itself. The image of the hand dropping the egg signifies the release of the self-contraction that marks all un-Enlightened human existence. This symbolism was inspired by Sri Da Avabhasa's unpublished liturgical drama, *The Mummery*.

CONTENTS

PART III: "AFTER DEATH, MIND MAKES YOU"

PART IV: "YOU WILL TREAT ONE ANOTHER DIFFERENTLY
IN DEATH"

On Serving the Death Process

Foreword

by *Richard Grossinger*
author, Planet Medicine, *and* Embryogenesis

Since I began reading spiritual literature at the age of nineteen, more than twenty years ago, no book has changed my view of the universe more profoundly than *Easy Death*. Da Avabhasa has spoken directly to the heart of our human situation—the shocking reality of our brief and unbidden lives. Through his words I have experienced a glimmering of eternal life and view my own existence as timeless and spaceless in a way that I never did before.

We live under the shadow of death; we cannot evade it; we cannot minimize it. Science, politics, and the modern media all try to propagandize us into seeking absolute fulfillment on this plane, but any happiness achieved on that basis will be superficial and transient. We exist in preparation for an extraordinary experience that everyone has undergone, even the ordinary aunts and uncles we view in old photographs: "They have been zapped out of this experience." They have gone on this mysterious journey, no matter what and how they lived. And we will follow them, each and every one of us.

Yet Da Avabhasa is extraordinarily thorough in his criticism of false assurances—things we tell ourselves that will make no difference in the end. The actual experience of death will overwhelm any planning, any memory. The cosmic shock of death will not suddenly enlighten us and make it possible for us to transcend. We should not rely on the inevitable improvement of our insights in a purgatory or heaven, or some vague guess of another chance after reincarnation. One may nurture the best of intentions for merging with higher planes, but under the actuality of the transition between lives, everyone will be returned inevitably to where they really are. The universe has no other way: "You cannot even hold on to your philosophy or your mantra when you pass by a crosslegged nude on a couch! So what do you think happens from life to death and back to life again . . . in the midst of such a profound event as psycho-physical death?"

The answer lies in cultivating attention and full joyful surrender before death. Da Avabhasa's "easy death" is a willing, conscious giving back of life. You surrender not because there is nothing left in the end and you are obliterated and extinguished anyway, but because there is nothing to keep and the law that has given you life in the beginning requires surrender at its end.

In this way, death becomes a necessary experience, "a radical fast," Da Avabhasa calls it, since it purifies us of our elemental aspect, our gross self. If we feel there is nothing other than this gross self, that does not reduce our reality; ideas can no more destroy than preserve whatever is our soul. Even if we feel we must be something more, that in itself does not create something more. "Knowledge is never more than knowledge about—and knowledge about is confounded by death. There is no knowledge about things that is senior to death. Death is the transformation of the knower. . . . Death is a process in which the knower is transformed, and all previous or conditional knowing is scrambled or confounded. . . . To 'consider' death is fruitless, since the knower is what is changed by death."

Part of Da Avabhasa's comprehensive teaching on death is a description of the process of moving through the subtler aspects of the brain and nervous system into the source of mind and phenomena through the mechanics of attention. His teachings are an unmythologized expression of the wisdom that may also be found in ancient guidebooks such as the *Tibetan Book of the Dead*. He depicts the vision of the Divine "Brightness" in star-form and of the surrounding Cosmic Mandala (a vision that may serve as a guide to the newly dead person), and he presents it from a variety of angles and perspectives.

It is precisely because our attention is so stubbornly attached that great Adepts humanly incarnate that transcendent Divine "Brightness" and attract human beings to meditate upon them, realize the inherent Divinity, and transcend all of these limiting mechanisms of egoic attention and energy. And the call to devotion to him as such a window to the Divine Reality is the essential message of Da Avabhasa in his teachings, and of his devotees in their many remarkable testimonies, in *Easy Death*.

The book closes by showing once again that death is simply another experience in life. If one sees life clearly for what it is, then, as he points out, death will not represent a major change at all; it will be simply a relocation, as from California to New Zealand. If life is surrendered before death, it will not have to be surrendered under duress at the time of death.

I would caution the reader against assuming that what you will find here is in any way consoling assurances. Here is a matter of life and death, presented with searing absoluteness, with the only alternative requiring supreme self-sacrifice both while we are alive and when we die.

Specifically, Da Avabhasa warns us against taking too seriously the spiritual literature on life after death. After all, he points out, people brought back to life from near death give egoic interpretations of these states in order to reassure themselves that they are going to a peaceful and shining place and will be among loved ones. He offers no such consolations.

In a dream we are surrounded by people who are aspects of our own psyche. If we are told by one of them that we are dreaming, we may hear it, but it is part of the chatter of the dream and does not alter our dreaming. During waking life we are also aspects of a dream, but it is the dream of the Radiant Conscious Being. In the dream of this being we are all the same person. And so, in this book Da Avabhasa tells us, in essence, "When you Awaken, you will Awaken to and as the very same Being that I Am."

Editors' Preface
to the Second Edition

This is the second edition of *Easy Death*. The first edition appeared in 1983, to wide acclaim. Many people in the professions associated with death and dying expressed their immense appreciation of the first edition, and Elisabeth Kübler-Ross hailed the book as a "masterpiece".

After 1982 (the latest date of the Talks and Essays in the first edition), Sri Da Avabhasa did not cease to Speak about death. In fact, He continued to devote many occasions with His devotees to this subject, especially during 1987, a period when He recapitulated the fundamentals of His entire Wisdom-Teaching with great Urgency and Passion. Since 1987, Sri Da Avabhasa has Given few Talks, but has rather devoted Himself to the Writing, enlarging, and updating of His major Scriptural Texts, which constitute what He calls His "Final Word" on every matter (including death) that He has ever Addressed.

The first edition of *Easy Death* concentrated on Essays and Talks from the first decade of Sri Da Avabhasa's Spiritual Work and included some remarkable Stories about death by His devotees who benefited from His Wisdom during that time. In this new edition of *Easy Death,* there are Talks and Writings from all phases of His Work, ranging from an excerpt from *The Knee of Listening* (Written in 1970) to His most recent Oral Communications to Mate Moce (Given in April 1991). Elements from the previous edition have been included, but there is also a great deal of new material. Basically, this second edition of *Easy Death* is a new book, and even the Talks and Essays that appeared in the first edition have been updated to conform with the fullness of Sri Da Avabhasa's current use of language when describing the conditional reality and the Divine Reality.

In the excerpts from His Scriptural Texts (notably *The Dawn Horse Testament*) you will notice a distinctive style of Writing. As with all His great creative Acts of Teaching and Blessing, Sri Da Avabhasa has broken completely new ground in the formation of His summary Word. The

English language has not hitherto been developed as a means of Divine Communication, and so Sri Da Avabhasa has been obliged to press the English language to its limits and beyond, to express the Inexpressible. For years He crafted the English language daily to make it work—molding it, bending it, stretching it, modifying and transforming it, adopting new conventions of capitalization and lowercasing (especially in *The Dawn Horse Testament*), and punctuation. With endless inventiveness, He has required written language to do things it has never done before.

His particular use of capital and lowercase letters counters the conventions of ordinary written English, in which references to the ego-"I" (including proper nouns) stand out through capitalization. In Sri Da Avabhasa's Ecstatic Writing, references to the Divine Reality are given prominence through capitalization, and limited, conditional references are typically subordinated through lowercasing. When He Speaks or Writes of Himself with uncommon capitalizations ("Me", or "My", and the like), He is communicating the Ecstasy of His Unconditional Realization of the Divine. Sri Da Avabhasa is using language in a new pictorial way, as He Says, "to interrupt the common flow of mind and Signal your Heart that it is time to Awaken, As You Are." Out of our respect, gratitude, and love for Sri Da Avabhasa, His devotees capitalize references to Him and His Work and the Heart-Awakeness He Transmits.

When you read what Sri Da Avabhasa has to Say anywhere in this book, and most especially in the passages from His Scriptural Texts, it is important to remember that you are receiving more than mere words. There is an unparalleled Transmission of Divine Blessing here, available to anyone who is sensitive to It.

If you come to *Easy Death* open to the Blessing it carries, you will find yourself drawn into a heart-conversation as alive and intimate as any secret exchange between Guru and disciple in ancient times—one that will continue even after you have closed the book.

Sri Da Avabhasa (The "Bright")
Sri Love-Anandashram, November 1991

Divine Grace and the Truth about Death

PART I

Grief and Grace

by Connie Grisso

Connie Grisso, R.N., a former hospice patient-care coordinator, received her B.S. degree from the State University of New York and has worked for the past twelve years in the death and dying field. She resides in northern California, where she is the Director of Mate Moce,[1] the death and dying ministry of the community of Free Daists. She has been a devotee of Sri Da Avabhasa since 1973.—the Editors

In 1971 my mother died of throat cancer. She was only 51 and one of the most important people in my life. I was just finishing my studies as a graduate nurse and had begun a career in critical care or intensive care nursing at a large teaching hospital in Los Angeles. I was young and idealistic, full of the Western medical ideal of "saving lives and triumphing over death", as if such were possible. I worked with many outstanding and renowned physicians who were dedicated to striving for this mastery over death, but even as a new member of the team, I was beginning to see the holes in our idealism. Sometimes, even often, our patients died, and no one ever spoke about this. That was twenty years ago, and

---

1. See the Appendix to this book for a full description of the Mate Moce Ministry and the services it provides.

death had hardly begun to come out of the closet in America. After I brought my mother to the medical deities, and even <u>she</u> died, I began to feel deeply disturbed about this ideal of "saving lives". It seemed to me that it was based upon a paralyzing fear and lack of understanding about death. As for my own life, it was shattered in the face of this loss, which I did not know how to deal with in any way. Part of my distress was simply losing my mother, and part of it resulted from the way in which she had died.

In the process of dying, my mother finally came to the point of choosing to end her own life. She confided her plans to me and requested that I research the amount of medication that would constitute an overdose. I never had the courage to look up the information, or even to guess. I could not bear the thought of losing her, and yet she was suffering each day and just waiting to die. So I understood her despair and felt torn.

Late one night, we sat up watching the news, and afterwards my mother asked me to fix her a cup of bouillon before going to bed. It was one of the few things she could still swallow. I prepared this warm drink and left it on the stand next to her chair. As we said goodnight, a look passed between us, and I knew we would not see one another again in this life. I walked outside into the warm night and sat down and cried for a long time. Then I went to my bed, exhausted.

In the early morning, my sister wakened me to say our mother had "fallen asleep" in her chair. With a sense of foreboding, I went immediately to her and discovered she was barely breathing at all. An empty bottle of sleeping capsules lay next to the remaining half-cup of bouillon. A few weeks before, when she had confided her plans to me, she asked me to promise not to allow her to be taken to the hospital or resuscitated.

I felt obliged to respect her wishes, and I also knew how dreadful an attempt at resuscitation could be. I had seen enough vegetative patients on respirators in my hospital rounds.

And so I told our family that she was dying now, and we placed her fragile body in bed. My father wept quietly in the living room while I sat with her for the next hour or so until all vital signs were gone.

That waiting time was an eternity of pain for me, and I now know that it must have been very difficult for my mother as well. I did not know of any scriptural readings or sacred instruction to offer. I just sat there or paced the room agonizing with her, full of grief and guilt over failing her in so many ways. And I blamed myself for her death, for reasons I could not altogether explain.

Her body was cremated the next day and the ashes scattered at sea by some mortuary personnel. There was no ceremony, no service, not even any announcement. No one spoke about what had happened or how much we loved her or how we could release her. There was a terrible starkness about the whole event.

During the initial period after her death, I was distraught, unable to pass through the normal grieving process or to release my mother in any way. Gradually I became able to cope, but I found myself moving through life mechanically. I was a rigid, frozen personality, and only my husband knew of the pain and distress that I had hidden away inside myself. I could not face going back to nursing, so I took a job teaching at a nearby school for handicapped children, in order to avoid the whole arena of death and dying.

In the summer of 1973, something occurred that changed everything. By an extraordinary Intervention of Divine Grace, I was drawn into the Company of Sri Da Avabhasa.

The notion of having a Spiritual Master was not something I as a Westerner was accustomed to. The whole idea of a living God-Realized Master and devotion to a Guru was not part of my Christian upbringing. In the ancient Wisdom-cultures of the East, the Function of Guru is widely understood and revered. Not so here in the West, where our scientific materialism inculcates so much doubt of God and doubt of the need for a living Teacher.

So it is remarkable in itself that, when my husband and I came across Da Avabhasa's Wisdom-Teaching, we were able to acknowledge the profundity of His Wisdom and also acknowledge Him as the Living Source of Truth. Shortly thereafter, we went to His Ashram in Los Angeles and met Him Personally. I will never forget that first meeting with my Sat-Guru. He was gathering with His devotees for a celebratory occasion. Sri Da Avabhasa (then known as Bubba Free John[2]) was such a Radiant Being that even in my contracted and Spiritually unprepared state I was able to feel His Love and acknowledge His Greatness. At the end of the evening, He held each of us for a long time in a Sacred Embrace. In that Embrace, I could feel our oneness. I no longer felt myself as separate—His Heart

---

2. During the early years of His formal Teaching Work with His devotees, Sri Da Avabhasa was known as "Bubba Free John". "Bubba" was one of Heart-Master Da's childhood nicknames, and it means "brother", or, in this case, "Spiritual friend". "Free John", a rendition of "Franklin Jones", which was the Name given to Him at birth, means "a liberated man (Franklin) through whom God is Gracious (Jones)". Throughout the years of His Work with His devotees, Sri Da Avabhasa has assumed Names of Spiritual significance appropriate to the moment of His Work.

21

and His breathing were my own. I felt as if I were resuming a relationship that had existed for a very long time, even Eternally. Because of my strong heart-response to Him, I felt no hesitation in entrusting my entire life to Sri Da Avabhasa.

In those early years of His Teaching Work, Da Avabhasa Worked with His devotees in a very intimate manner, face to face. He spoke with us, lived with us, celebrated with us, Taught us how to eat, how to walk, even how to breathe correctly. He participated in every aspect of ordinary living with us, trying to Help us become prepared for real Spiritual life.[3] We were enchanted by His Divine Radiance, His Happiness, His Humor, His more than brilliant Insight into every topic we discussed, and the literal Transmission of Spiritual Power we could feel in His Company.

He was Great. Unfortunately, we were not so great. There I was, one of the early devotees to come to Sri Da Avabhasa, so un-Happy, confused, and totally unqualified for what He Offers—which is a real, self-transcending Spiritual practice leading to Divine Self-Realization. Most of us were in the same dreadful shape. We sat in front of Him frozen in recoil from the various traumas of our lives (traumas which we ourselves were often unconscious of) while He Discoursed brilliantly for hours on end, trying to bring us to life. No group of people needed to understand themselves more, or more desperately needed to be "saved" from themselves.

In order to relax our rigidity, so that He could begin to Work with us, Sri Da Avabhasa allowed the use of alcohol during gatherings with Him. And so, one night, in an inebriated state, I blurted out the whole story of my mother's death to a few intimate women friends.

I do not even remember what details I told them. But I do know that by this time my feelings of guilt and loss over not being able to save her,

---

3. The heart of all of Sri Da Avabhasa's Teaching Work (from 1970-1986), whether formal or informal, was the Submission of His own body-mind to identify with the characteristics, qualities, limitations, and habits of His devotees, so that He could thereby reflect back to them the inherent bondage and suffering of their self-enamorment and seeking. Thus, Sri Da Avabhasa appeared to be "like" His Western devotees, to share their interests and drives, Working with them in a "brotherly" manner, or in the manner of a Spiritual friend, in order to Help them see themselves, and, thereby, to create the foundations of His Teaching Message and the sacred culture that must perpetually serve His Work on Earth.

When Heart-Master Da's Teaching Work came to an end on January 11, 1986, in the Great Change that marked the onset of His Divine Emergence (see pp. 37-39), that form of Submission to His devotees and to all other beings came to a sudden end. Since that time, His body-mind has no longer conformed to the qualities of others. Rather, His body and mind are utterly Conformed to His own inherent and eternal Nature as the Divine Self, the Heart. Now He only Stands Firm in His Divine Disposition as the Divine World-Teacher and the True Heart-Master of His devotees, no longer consenting to relate to them in any "brotherly" or "friendly" fashion. Thus, He must be approached with sacred understanding of Who He Is and through proper devotional formalities if one is to rightly and fully receive His continuous and always Given Heart-Blessing.

first from her cancer and then from her suicide, had become a secret conviction in me that I was responsible for her death—even that I had somehow actually killed her. I recall the sympathetic look on my friends' faces as I told my story, and yet I actually felt <u>nothing</u> about what had been a gut-wrenching ordeal of my young life. I spoke about it as if I were narrating a documentary—I had repressed every shred of emotion associated with the event.

The following evening I entered Heart-Master Da's Residence. As was often the case during this period, there was a loud party going on with blasting music, dancing, and peals of laughter. Somehow the song that was playing ended just as I walked in, and the Voice of Sri Da Avabhasa boomed across the large room . . . "There she is—THE MOTHER KILLER!"

Everything came to an abrupt halt, silenced by His Shout. I slumped to my knees in a near-faint, horrified, overcome by the feelings of fear and anxiety that had suddenly surfaced. He had dared to express out loud what I secretly felt about myself and what I was living with. He had gone right to the bottom line of what I was suffering.

I remained in a kind of semi-conscious state, so that I have only a vague recollection of what took place over the next few hours. I have to rely on friends' accounts of the events that followed. Supported on either side, I continued to faint away, unable to remain fully conscious as my secret came out. Sri Da Avabhasa said to everyone in His powerful Voice, that "most people have something they do not like about their parents, but very few go so far as to actually kill them!"—and on and on.

People rushed to my defense: "Oh no, Bubba, please," they begged, "don't talk like that—she's not that bad, she's really a good person . . ." I could only hear bits and pieces in the distance as I slipped further into a gray place that was full of pain.

Sri Da Avabhasa would only speak to me once in a while, in the course of a more general conversation He was having with others in the room. And I would reply briefly. Still, He elicited many of the details of this ordeal with my mother, calling forth from my unconsciousness the hidden memories and self-loathing that accompanied each part. My skin was flushed and hot, my heart palpitating. Somehow He was unlocking the emotions surrounding my mother's death, and I was reliving them. The emotional pain was so great that I could barely stay conscious. And so, my Beloved Guru went on to prod and poke and draw the snakes up out of my buried past, while I swooned and fainted away.

The purifying Work that Sri Da Avabhasa was doing with me went on for several gatherings. I was one of the topics each evening. And every time, it took all the strength I had to return to my Sat-Guru's House—I wanted so much to run away. I felt I could not face the horrifying self-revelation one more time. But, somehow, Sri Da Avabhasa was Helping me to stay with Him in the process He was taking me through, and so I kept returning for another round.

On the final night of this ordeal, I was able to remain more or less conscious and look at Him directly as He Worked with me. I felt His silent Instruction to cooperate with Him by relaxing and breathing deeply. At the end of that evening, I stopped off in the Meditation Hall to offer a gift.[4] I felt amazingly light-hearted and happy, simple and innocent. I was renewed. I felt so happy as I gazed at Sri Da Avabhasa's Chair in the Meditation Hall and thanked Him for all His Gifts to me. I could feel that everything He had done, no matter how painful, had been for my sake. I had complete faith in Him. His Love was unmistakable.

As I knelt before His Chair, I looked down at the wedding band on my left hand. It was my mother's ring, her final gift to me, and I had clung to this ring in my guilt-ridden attachment to her. Without fore-thought, I slipped the ring off my finger and left it on the dais as a gift. I do not even recall wondering why I did it. I just had the feeling, "I don't need this anymore," and I thanked my Guru in my heart.

A week passed before I saw Sri Da Avabhasa again. The Work He had done in my psyche and body-mind continued to unravel the tangle of knots below my heart, and I noticed that I was becoming happier. I knew that this feeling of light-heartedness and happiness came from being in the Company of Sri Da Avabhasa, but did not, as yet, relate it to being relieved of the burden of my mother's death. I did not consciously realize what He had done. At the end of the week, I returned to Persimmon (as our Sanctuary in northern California[5] was then called) to see Sri Da Avabhasa.

This time, when I entered the house, there were only a few devotees sitting around Him. It was a quiet and intimate occasion. I bowed at His

---

4. The Guru-devotee relationship is epitomized through the act of the giving and receiving of gifts, which Sri Da Avabhasa has called "the Sacrament of Universal Sacrifice". This simple practice involves the devotee offering a gift to Heart-Master Da (in His physical Form or in the Form of a photographic Murti or Representational Image), and receiving a Blessed Gift in return. The devotee's gift is generally modest—even a leaf, a flower, a fruit, or water is sufficient—and represents the surrender of himself or herself. The Gift returned to the devotee may also be in the form of water, or fruit, or flowers—infused with Sri Da Avabhasa's Grace and Blessing Power—and each such Blessed Gift represents the manner in which He replaces His devotee's difficulties and karmas with the Gift of His own Divine Condition.

5. "Persimmon", which is now called "The Mountain Of Attention", is one of three Hermitage Ashrams that have been established and Empowered as Retreat Sanctuaries by Sri Da Avabhasa for practitioners of the Way of the Heart.

feet and felt His Loving Regard. Then one of my friends, who was sitting near Him, said, "Connie, where is your wedding ring?" I was quite surprised as I looked down at my hand—I had forgotten about leaving it in the Meditation Hall. "Well, . . ." I said slowly as the moment came back to me, "I left it in . . ." and my voice trailed off. My friend pointed to our Guru's Hand. He was wearing my mother's ring on His little finger!

Suddenly the whole ordeal He had taken me through became clear. By some marvelous Gift of insight, I instantly understood what He had done. As everything "clicked", He smiled at me. There was a tacit understanding between us, a revelatory moment that is difficult to describe. Every detail of my unconscious pattern of withdrawal, my presumption of being separated from Happiness or God, was revealed to me in a split second. I saw the apparent tragedy of my mother and myself as an error, or erroneous assumption. In this sudden clarity, I could feel that both my mother and I inhere in God, and always had. We were free. There was no longer any problem. I realized that we each had been profoundly Served by Sri Da Avabhasa.

This sudden knowledge or true self-understanding was like the liberating sword in traditional Tibetan Buddhist lore, which instantly severs or cuts away the false images by which the seeker is bound. With that new unbound freedom, I knew and acknowledged my Beloved Sat-Guru much more deeply than before, surrendering to Him with a clear and heart-opening love. Gratitude and devotion overwhelmed my being. I bowed my head to the floor and wept for joy.

I knew that this emotional purification, as profound as it was for me, was just one example of my Sat-Guru's Power to heal and purify and release every form of bondage in His devotees. That was one of my earliest encounters with Sri Da Avabhasa. My All-Compassionate Guru had Worked a miracle of calling up the serpents of fear, grief, and guilt and driving them out of this body-mind. What Sri Da Avabhasa did with me was a graphic example of the Heroic and selfless way that He Worked with hundreds of others in every dimension of human and Spiritual experience during those Teaching years.

As the years passed, when Da Avabhasa Spoke about death, Giving the Talks that were to appear later in *Easy Death,* I was often in the room. Over time, it became obvious that He was Instructing me very specifically about death and dying and preparing me to serve the death transitions of His devotees.

By now, considerably relieved of my fear and contraction, I had become more interested in exploring with Him the death transition and examining its relevance to the Spiritual Process. On one occasion at the end of the summer of 1976, in the midst of apparently ordinary social talk, Heart-Master Da walked over to me and asked me to lie down on the floor next to Him. He lay flat on His Back next to me and closed His Eyes, saying, "Now do exactly as I do." Then, through silent Instruction, He Guided me through a remarkable experience of the transition called death.

First there was an explosion of inner sounds. Then I felt the layers of the body-mind release and fall away. "I" was separating out from the physical body and seemed to fly upwards, whirling through dark space at an incredible speed. I was moving toward an overwhelming brilliant light. At some point, I recall slipping through a kind of "grid" as a speck of consciousness.

For an instant I did seem to lose all self-awareness, but throughout the rest of the experience I was aware of the most remarkable clarity. I found that I felt more familiar and at ease with "myself" traveling without the body than I was when I was dragging it along, anchored to it by my usual physical-body identification. I felt myself to be alive as consciousness, at ease as the witness of mind and attention.

But at different moments in this cosmic journey, I felt the deep urges of the body-mind drawing me back towards embodiment, and I sensed the frustration of having no physical body through which to enact or fulfill desires. This made a stunning impression on me, and I remember feeling how foolish it would be to waste the opportunity of a human lifetime—the opportunity to do sadhana, or Spiritual practice, that could help free me from the binding attachments I had now seen so clearly. In fact, this impulse to practice, to Realize a Greater Position, seemed to summarize the import of this entire experience.

The next thing I became aware of was a loud buzzing or humming sound as I slowly came back into the body-mind, taking on each layer, starting with the most subtle. I was led back into the mind first, then the body. The inner sounds quieted until once again I was aware of lying on the floor.

When I opened my eyes, Heart-Master Da Love-Ananda's Face was right next to mine, and He was grinning at me with a gigantic smile. He opened His Mouth and started to laugh. It was more than a laugh—it was a victorious and triumphant Shout! It was glorious to hear. Instead of being awestruck by this remarkable journey I had just taken with Him, what I felt was sheer marvel at Who He Is. I felt yes! there is this great scheme of conditional existence, of which embodiment is a part. But first and most importantly, HE IS THE MASTER OF IT ALL! And I have a relationship with That One!

Without exchanging a word with me, Heart-Master Da got up, walked back to His Seat, and began a Discourse on death and "the grid" through which we pass after death. Sri Da Avabhasa's Talks were never mere discourses. Quite often they were a living Communication of the process being described.

The Teaching years were full of these remarkable incidents through which Sri Da Avabhasa was always Instructing His devotees, each one according to his or her own particular karmas or needs. Each such Revelatory incident over the years would re-clarify and re-confirm for the devotee how remarkable and real is the process that Sri Da Avabhasa was Demonstrating in our lives. In this way, and over time, I grew more and more committed to Him and convinced of His Greatness and Truth, more and more serious about and grateful for the profound opportunity it is to practice in His Company.

In 1979 I started working with the dying, and I have been involved with the hospice and dying-at-home movement ever since. At first, it was an opportunity for me to feel the tremendous need for help that dying individuals have—not only the obvious need for human help and support for the dying process itself, but also the more profound need for Spiritual help. I saw that everyone was searching for a right understanding of dying—and of living. It became increasingly obvious to me that Heart-Master Da is exactly that Divine Help.

Sometimes I would offer my co-workers and hospice families the first edition of *Easy Death,* and I would see them open up to feeling and talking about death more freely. Some would report feeling a sense of the Presence of God when I brought them Sri Da Avabhasa's book or read sections from it aloud. Through doing this, I learned how available He is to all, how His Wisdom and the feeling of the Divine that Pervades His Words can evoke a response in anyone.

This always remains true, but, over the past few years I have become aware that He expects much more of me in my service to the dying and in my communication of His Wisdom about death than offering this kind of solace. He is not satisfied to have His profound Instruction about death be turned into some superficial relief applied at the end of a lifetime spent in bewilderment and confusion, out of relationship with God, our true Divine Self.

27

In Instructions that He Gave in April of 1991 to Mate Moce, the Death and Dying Ministry of the community of Free Daists, Sri Da Avabhasa criticized some materials of the popular death movement that we had sent Him for His review. These materials contained suggestions for techniques or exercises that one could use in the death process in order to make a more auspicious transition.

He responded immediately, pointing out the error in thinking that any form of "self-help" could be sufficient when entering into something as profound as the death process. You cannot, He emphasized, manipulate yourself into an improved future destiny by what you do on your deathbed. The same conditional self that you are trying to preserve or relieve or satisfy is what is being undermined in the death process. Here is an excerpt from what He had to Say (these Instructions appear in full in Chapter 20):

SRI DA AVABHASA: The "death games" recommended in popular literature these days are, in general, procedures that can be relaxing and consoling, but they do not have the ability to change your destiny after death. . . . If you are interested in going beyond your ordinary and lesser destiny, you should respond to Me and to the Way of the Heart by doing the sadhana I have Given for the sake of your Liberation. You should not expect some technique you might do on your deathbed to Liberate you.

Throughout this book, you will find more of Heart-Master Da's insistence that we not accept the false consolation offered by certain popular or "new age" views about what happens at death and after death, or in the process of reincarnation. Reports of near-death experiences and evidence of reincarnation do not merely suggest that we should live the golden rule, be kinder to one another, and the like. Such evidence calls our attention to the necessity to transcend altogether our identification with a limited, suffering body-mind and to come into relationship with What is Greater. The Argument and Insistence of such Divine Adepts as Sri Da Avabhasa have existed throughout time, and these individuals stand within all the great cultures of religion and Spirituality goading us, shaking us, calling us to "wake up now!"

Let me bring this introduction to a close with one final story about my relationship to Sri Da Avabhasa:

In November 1990, it was my good fortune to participate in a three-week retreat at Sri Love-Anandashram, in Fiji. It had been exactly four years since my last visit to Sri Love-Anandashram (an island also known by the Fijian name of "Naitauba"), which is the principal Hermitage Residence of Sri Da Avabhasa. A great deal of change had occurred in Heart-Master Da's Life and in mine over those years. I had seen Him only a few brief times during this period, and I was full of longing for this reunion with my Master. I had also been searching for a way to fully understand the changes in my Heart-Master's outward quality and manner of approach to His devotees since His Divine Emergence in 1986 (see pp. 37-39). Gone was the interactive, human relationship He had engaged with us earlier in the days of His Teaching Work, and so was the more familiar human character who had lived with us, and like us, in order to Teach. Now He simply "Stood Firm" in His Radiant Divinity, Calling us to a devotional relationship with Him.

There is so much that could be said about that meeting with Sri Da Avabhasa at Sri Love-Anandashram. The meeting took place on so many levels of my being. I think it may best be summarized by what occurred in the last formal Darshan[6] occasion of my retreat. The occasion took place in a little Fijian-style temple not far from Sri Da Avabhasa's Residence. To go to Sri Love-Anandashram is like finding yourself situated quite miraculously at the edge of Infinity, in another realm where the sensory perceptors of the being are overwhelmed, intoxicated, and sublimed. Just to be there is to feel Supreme Happiness, Love, Bliss, and Joy. And the Source of the Love-Blissful Feeling that saturates this place is Sri Da Avabhasa's Spiritual Heart-Transmission.

I had come on retreat full of expectation about witnessing the further miraculous Sign of God that would be manifesting in my Heart-Master, and I was not disappointed. Each sighting of Him had been full of such Divine Blessings and His Heart-Transmission that literally transforms the being. This final day was no different. As the conch blew,[7] signalling His approach to the Hall where we waited, my heart was full of anticipation. Suddenly His figure filled the doorway, and He Strode into the room, then up to His Chair at the front. The atmosphere was charged. There was a sense of Fullness and an intense stillness, in spite of the occasional

6. Darshan, in Sanskrit, means "seeing", "sight of", "vision of". In the Indian traditions, "to have Darshan" of a saint, holy image, etc. is a participatory, feeling act, not merely a visual witnessing of an object. In the Way of the Heart, Darshan is the spontaneous Blessing Sri Da Avabhasa Grants freely by allowing His bodily (human) Form to be sighted, and thereby Contemplated, by His devotees.

7. A conch shell is used in many sacred traditions, because when it is blown the sound brings the feeling energy of the body to life. Whenever Sri Da Avabhasa is about to appear where His devotees are present, a large conch is blown to celebrate His appearance, and to call everyone to an occasion of Darshan with Him.

ecstatic cries of His devotees. He sat down, looking straight ahead with an incredible fierceness. I approached His Chair to offer a gift at His Feet. His Eyes looked out above our heads, on the world—I could feel His Absolute Determination.

As I knelt just a few feet from Him, I felt open and vulnerable, relieved of my chronic self-meditation after several weeks of purification and Blessing on retreat. I held up my hands to behold Him. I could feel Sri Da Avabhasa's Spiritual Heart-Transmission as a steady wave of Blissful energy pouring into my body, so that my upheld hands were pressed back by a tangible force. His incredibly strong Transmission became a blast of heat and light, overwhelming me with His Communication of Love and Bliss. My hands and whole body began to shake with the tremendous force coming from Him. I felt my body starting to resonate with that vibration. It felt as if all my cells were spinning at light speed. It was like standing in a wind tunnel. If my hair had not been clamped into a tight bun, I imagined, it would have flown out and stood straight on end!

Sri Da Avabhasa sat unmoving as I spoke my humble words of praise and gratitude and love, though I felt His complete Reception of my offering. Then I lay prostrate before Him and felt His Regard for everyone— for the whole world—sweep over me. And I felt the world's need, the need of each person, to know Him at Heart.

Sri Da Avabhasa's Impulse to Free everyone from the insult of mortality is evident on every page of *Easy Death*. As you read it, you may feel your attention drawn to Sri Da Avabhasa and to His Calling to come into relationship with Him. He Offers this Invitation to every living being without exception—to everyone. May you be Blessed to Find Him!

Da Avabhasa's Revelation of How to Transcend "Death and Everything Else"

by Carolyn Lee and Meg McDonnell

I magine this: Your friend is in the hospital, in the final stages of a terminal illness. But when you go to visit him, he starts to talk about where he would like to go next year for your annual trip together—a year you both know he will not live to see. Should you talk with him about his denial of death or simply go along with it?

Or perhaps your father is dying and in intolerable pain. Your family is in a chaos of emotion about what to do, and your mother is abandoning her lifelong faith, angry at God for allowing such suffering. What wisdom can you bring to the situation? How can you act with both life-positive strength and acceptance?

Or perhaps your brother, with whom you were very close, was killed in an airplane crash several weeks ago. Since the time of the crash, you have had ghostly visitations and dreams of him and, totally unaccustomed to any such phenomena, you feel that you are going insane. Where do you turn for help?

Or perhaps you simply notice that you are afraid to love anyone for real, because you know that they cannot stay with you forever. How do you get beyond this limit on intimacy and feeling, on your capability for life itself?

Perhaps you simply notice, and really let it sink in, that everything that lives also dies. Everything. What does this teach you about how you should live? What is the real message in death itself?

There is no more gripping question for human beings than the question of death. Where do we go? What does it mean? Does any part of us survive it? And why—why are we bound to suffer such devastating and irreversible loss? How are we to deal with this reality—of our own ending and the ending of those we love? No pat, superficial solutions suffice when death is what we are facing.

This book is a Gift for anyone who is really looking for the answers to these questions. It is a compilation of Discourses and Writings Given by One Who understands death thoroughly—from the most profound, unique, and Helpful perspective we could ever hope to find.

Sri Da Avabhasa, Whose Wisdom appears in this book, is a Living Spiritual Master, or True Heart-Master. His Authority on the subject of death (and on all subjects crucial to our right understanding of how to live) derives from the most auspicious of all sources—that of Divine Realization Itself. What He Speaks of in these pages, He Speaks of based on what He has Himself Realized. Thus, His Wisdom is not secondhand. His Insight is not limited to any localized perspective or traditional approach. He brings a "radical" (fundamental, or irreducible) approach to the understanding of death (and life) that is comprehensive, Intelligent, and uplifting beyond compare.

Who is Sri Da Avabhasa and why is the Wisdom that He Offers us in *Easy Death* so unique? Most of us have much to learn and much to out-grow in our lifetime, if death (and life itself) is to be most auspicious for us. At one point in *Easy Death*, Sri Da Avabhasa uses an analogy to describe our relationship to death, Saying, "You are all like astronauts—your whole lifetime is associated with preparation for the launch!" For Sri Da Avabhasa, however, almost the reverse is true.

Sri Da Avabhasa's Realization and the Wisdom that He has to Offer are not merely the sum total of His experience in this Lifetime. Heart-Master Da was <u>born</u> fully Realized—He came into this realm already fully equipped with Divine Faculties and with a very specific Intention. Like One Who has parachuted down into a situation where everyone's life is threatened, His whole Lifetime has been a Rescue Mission! His very Appearance in a mortal frame is a Sacrifice, the result of a conscious deci-sion made in the Eternal Light of the God-State, in response to "all the human voices calling out to God", so that we could see directly what it is to be Free, to transcend fear and death, to be awake to Who and What we really Are. Sri Da Avabhasa is Divine Help in a time and place where we need it most.

Sri Da Avabhasa was Born, as He has Said, "In A Moment Of Terrible Necessity". The year of His Birth, 1939, was one of the darkest moments of world history. His early childhood years were the era of World War II, the genocide of the Jews in German-occupied Europe, and the explosion of the first atomic bombs. He came into a world crazed with death, and

He did His Work in the Spiritual desert of modern materialism that presumes "when you're dead, you're dead."

Sri Da Avabhasa Calls everyone to an understanding that there is much more to our existence than the merely material. Nevertheless, His purpose has never been to offer a short-term "cure" for suffering, a palliative easy to swallow but ineffective in the long run. He has come to Liberate us from every limit we place on Love and Happiness—and to do so effectively, by equipping us with a strength of understanding, insight, and transcendence that will carry us through life and beyond death.

Thus, Sri Da Avabhasa's entire Life has been the Demonstration of what it is to be fully vulnerable in the face of death and loss, while always remaining Free, Standing in the Eternal Divine Condition That is Prior to all that dies. He is the Personification of the Changeless—in perpetual embrace with, while also always transcending, that which changes and dies. It is important to know this Mysterious Fact about Him in order to appreciate the supreme scope of His Authority on the subject of death.

Because He literally Descended into this human realm from the God-State (that Condition of Perfectly Illumined Joy or Love-Bliss that He Calls "the 'Bright'"), Sri Da Avabhasa is familiar, by direct experience, with all the structures of our existence—both ordinary and esoteric. In this book He describes these structures and how they can illuminate our understanding of death. And the events of His own Life have been events in which He, as the Divine Person, the "Bright" Itself, has paradoxically lived as a human being. Sri Da Avabhasa is thus profoundly sympathetic in His understanding of the human struggle, more vulnerable and Compassionate than any ordinary man or woman could be. At the same time, Sri Da Avabhasa is a Signpost to That Which is greater than human, to That Which is untroubled by change and death. Thus, His own experience with death has always been extraordinary, with much to Teach us.

In His autobiography, *The Knee of Listening,* Sri Da Avabhasa makes an extraordinary confession—He tells us that, at the early age of two, He became acutely aware that those around Him did not share in His enjoyment of the "Bright", that others were not established in the Divine Freedom He had known since birth. As He became aware of the extent of the suffering of those around Him, He was moved to a great Gesture of Self-Giving for their sake. He had already made the ultimate Sacrifice in Appearing in a body that would suffer human limitations and die, but, in doing so, He had retained His Divine Awareness. Now, in a profound gesture of Sympathy for all of us who suffer and die in this realm, He let go of His conscious identification with the "Bright" and began to identify instead with the ordinary persona of the body and mind He had been born into. He did this in a Gamble of Compassion—hoping that by doing so He would be able to discover in His own body-mind, and thereby reveal for all, the way whereby everyone could Realize that they, too, are Free, Eternal, Divine.

From the time of this Sacrifice until Sri Da Avabhasa's full Divine Re-Awakening at the age of thirty, the "Bright" was always present, latent as a fierce mysterious Impulse in His Being. Occasionally, the "Bright" broke through, coming to the fore with a Clarity that helped to guide the course of His Life.

Sri Da Avabhasa was born into a middle-class American family, and His Great Work to bring the God-Realizing process into the human plane began in this most ordinary context. When Heart-Master Da was ten years old, He discovered His black cocker spaniel, Bootsie, dead in the cellar of His parents' house. Seeing Bootsie dead, Sri Da Avabhasa gave Himself up to storms of grief, and He felt that He could not go on living. He decided to appeal to God to take His life as well as Bootsie's—at an appointed time two days hence.

As the time approached, Sri Da Avabhasa began to regret what He had done: He wanted to live after all. But breaking an agreement with God was, He felt, not possible, and so He watched television as the moment approached and tried to relax the rising fear. When the time came and He did not die, Sri Da Avabhasa felt incredible relief and a painful sense of the preciousness of merely being alive. More than that, He came to a conscious understanding of His true Nature, and He saw that He had fallen for an illusion! The loss of Bootsie did not mean an end to life and love as He had presumed. Happiness did not lie in trying to follow Bootsie to another realm, but in releasing Bootsie (and Himself and everyone else) in the Fullness of That Which cannot die. This was one of the many moments of the resurgence of the "Bright" in His early life.

When . . . I felt the loss of the little animal I loved, I was moved to find him, to be where that love continued as is. So I was motivated to a drastic ascent from life, to what seemed to be God because of my separated mentality. But at last I saw that very motivation to be the source of separation, and it was a forceful cutting away of consciousness and life and love.

In the hours of waiting for death I was not conscious as the "bright", the full Presence of my being. I was separate from it, and saw all consciousness and love and light as radically above, apart from me and this world. Only too late, it seemed to me then, did the shock of what I awaited draw me into that fullness again. And I saw that reality was already, presently full and did not stand out in the symbolic state I was awaiting.

I learned this lesson at that time. It is not the product of reflection years hence. As a small boy I operated with that awareness and enjoyed the knowledge of real consciousness. (The Knee of Listening, *New Standard Edition, forthcoming)*

Years later, during a period of study at a Lutheran seminary in Philadelphia, Sri Da Avabhasa passed through a highly dramatic death experience—one that was seminal in allowing His intuition of His native Divine Condition to come forward permanently.

In *The Knee of Listening* He vividly Describes what happened:

I was in the bathroom when this episode began. . . . As I looked at my face in the mirror, it appeared gray, disturbed and deathlike. The saliva in my mouth stopped flowing, and I was overcome by a rising anxiety that became an awesome and overwhelming fear of death.

I was fixed in the knowledge that I was soon to go mad and die. . . .

In the hours and days that followed, there was no relief from the overwhelming fear.

Finally, on the third day after this process began, I was lying home alone in the afternoon. It was as if all my life I had been constantly brought to this point. It seemed that all of the various methods of my life had constantly prevented this experience from going to its end. All my life I had been preventing my death.

I lay on the floor, totally disarmed, unable to make a gesture that could prevent the rising fear. And thus it grew in me, but, for the first time, I allowed it to happen. I could not prevent it. The fear and the death rose and became my overwhelming experience. And I witnessed the crisis of that fear in a moment of conscious, voluntary death. I allowed the death to happen, and I saw it happen.

When that moment of crisis had passed I felt a marvelous relief. The death had occurred, but I had observed it! I remained untouched by it. The body and the mind and the personality had died, but I remained as an essential and unqualified consciousness.

When all of the fear and dying had become a matter of course, when the body, the mind, and the person with which I identified myself had died, and my attention was no longer fixed in those things, I perceived reality, fully and directly. There was an infinite bliss of being, an untouched, unborn sublimity, without separation, without individuation, without a thing from which to be separated. There was only reality itself, the incomparable nature and constant existence that underlies the entire adventure of life.

35

After a time I got up from the floor. I walked around and beamed joyfully at the room. The blissful, unthreatened current of reality continued to emanate from my heart, and not a pulse of it was modified by my own existence or the existence of the world. I had acquired a totally new understanding.

In the course of this event, Sri Da Avabhasa suffered the full force of what we usually suppress—the terrible fear of dissolution, of annihilation, or losing consciousness forever when the body dies. But when Heart-Master Da surrendered, no longer struggling to prevent the fear, it was as if flood-gates had opened—and the Bliss of Consciousness Poured through Him. The body, as He now understood, was not the source of our fundamental existence at all! Consciousness, Love-Bliss, the Divine Reality was the Source, and so bodily death was not an ending, but simply a transformation of the being in God.

This was ego-death, the shedding of a fundamental limit on the "Bright". Now enormous Spiritual energy was released in Him, and within a few years He Re-Awakened fully and permanently to the "Bright" State of His Birth. In this Divine Re-Awakening, in September, 1970, Da Avabhasa Recaptured the Enjoyment of the "Bright", the One Divine Consciousness He had always been.

This Realization was not exclusive, as if Sri Da Avabhasa were the only One for Whom such Freedom were potential. No, it was the uncovering of the Real, Deathless Identity of every one of us.

At every stage of His miraculous Life, and even in every moment, Sri Da Avabhasa has had to continuously engage the same Sacrifice that brought Him to this realm in the first place. He has had to constantly activate His Intention to remain in the body, so that He could be of Service to all of us, who need a very graphic, bodily demonstration of what it is to be Free, to be God-Realized.

The Force of My Native Condition is so profound that I am constantly coming to the point of near death, and not just occasionally but daily. Nevertheless, the phenomenon is no longer like an anxiety attack, as it was in the Event in Seminary. Nor is it inexplicable. It is not threatening in any way. It is just part of the tension of My Commitment to this Birth. To drop the body is not a goal, nor is it overwhelmingly attractive, because My Commitment is to remain in this descended state until the Purpose of My Birth is fulfilled. . . . In My case, I must give great attention, great energy to being here, whereas others are bound to being here, and, in their search, they feel they must give great energy and attention to getting out of here. While others are struggling to get out of here, I am struggling to stay here, because if I do not give great energy and attention to staying here, I will float away.

Some day I will float away. . . . Remember Me. Remember Who I Am. Remember what the incident of death is for Me. It is not cold death, not being murdered into the ground. It is nothing of the kind. It is the relinquishment of this body-mind. When this body disintegrates into the elements, there is instant restoration to the Condition That Preceded My Birth, Where I will Sit and Be and Wait for all those who respond to Me as a result of My Work. There is no death for Me. Absolutely none. Neither is there really death for you—but death is simply more impressive to you. (April 23, 1984)

Sri Da Avabhasa's lifelong struggle to remain "descended", or Present in the body, culminated in an experience that He has Described as the most auspicious Event of His Life—His "Grand Victory".

It was Sri Da Avabhasa's Impulse to be of Service to others that caused His Birth and that has kept Him alive in the body ever since. And Sri Da Avabhasa has never been satisfied when His devotees will accept only a medium degree of Blessing and Wisdom—He has always looked for those who would actually incarnate the Process of Realization in His Company to the fullest extent. It is through His Work with such unique and exemplary aspirants that He has Looked to establish His Way of the Heart so that it can survive beyond His human Lifetime, at a Spiritual depth that can turn human history to a more benign course.

Despite the fact that many thousands came to see Him, and grew to love Him, and even stayed to practice in His Company, by January, 1986—after sixteen years of Teaching Work—nobody, not one person, had shown the kind of Spiritual depth that would allow him or her to receive all that Sri Da Avabhasa had to offer. He had been unreserved in His attempts to break His devotees out of their complacency and to get them to take more of what He had to Give, but it had not worked. Thus, He reached the point of utter despair with His Spiritual Work.

In the early hours of January 11, the crisis reached its peak. Heart-Master Da was speaking by telephone with devotees gathered in a nearby building, telling them of His heartbreak and despair and saying that He felt He was soon going to die. Without Spiritually responsive devotees, the Purpose of His Life was thwarted, and He had no choice, really, but to withdraw, to return to the Source from Which He had come. Even as He spoke, Da Avabhasa felt numbness coming up His arm, and in a few moments He had collapsed on the floor.

In the chaos of grief and panic that followed, Sri Da Avabhasa's apparently lifeless body was laid on His bed. It was several minutes before the

37

doctors arrived and began to take measures to revive Him. At first, only the basic life-signs were present in His body, but after some time Heart-Master Da recovered waking consciousness. But He was not the same as before. He explains here what the signs of this Event, which He has Described as the initiation of His Divine Emergence, truly signified:

When someone's death is observed by another person or a number of other persons, the death appears to be an ending. However, one experiences one's own death not as an ending, but as a process. The individuals who were present on January 11, 1986, to observe the various signs associated with the initiation of My Divine Emergence have described It as a clinical death Event with a subsequent return to life. But for Me, that Event was, and continues to be, a Process. In other words, there was no ending, and therefore, no death in the sense of an ending. . . . In My Experience on January 11, 1986, there was an apparent swoon, but with no loss of Consciousness Itself. The body was dropped to the bed, and it may have appeared to the observers to be unconscious, or perhaps not alive, or barely alive, but all the while I Was and Am Consciousness Itself. In the initial Event associated with this Process, this body was surrendered utterly into Me, the Self-Existing and Self-Radiant "Bright", and necessarily Divine, Self-Consciousness. And this Process of Surrendering this body into My ultimate Self-Condition is still continuing. It did not come to an end on that early morning of January 11, 1986. In other words, there was no death and then a coming to life. There has simply been an unbroken and continuing and ever more profound Process in which this body (or body-mind) is Surrendered into Me. (November 3, 1989)

How can we understand such a Mysterious Event? Really, all we can do is bear witness to the results of what occurred in Sri Da Avabhasa on that day. For in this Great Sacrifice, which was the most esoteric kind of death, Sri Da Avabhasa found a way to fulfill the Impulse that had made His Birth.

Even though I have existed as a man during this Lifetime obviously—I became profoundly Incarnate—I now assumed an impulse toward human existence more profound than I had assumed before, without any reluctance relative to sorrow and death.

On so many occasions I have told you that I wish I could Kiss every human being on the lips, Embrace each one, and Enliven each one from the heart. In this body I will never have the opportunity. I am frustrated in that impulse. Even though I have done all kinds of Spiritual Work, I will never be able to do that exactly. But in that motion of sympathetic

Incarnation, that acceptance of the body and its sorrow and its death, I realized a Kiss, a way to fulfill the impulse. . . .

In My profound frustration this body died. I left this body. And then I suddenly found My Self reintegrated with it, but in a totally different disposition, and I achieved your likeness exactly, thoroughly, to the bottoms of My feet, achieved un-Enlightenment, achieved human existence, achieved mortality, achieved sorrow.

To Me, this is a Grand Victory! I do not know how to Communicate to you the significance of it. (January 27, 1986)

To grasp the import of His Confession and how He Accomplished this "Kiss"—this profound Gesture of Love—we must remember Who is Speaking to us. When Sri Da Avabhasa Says, "'I' achieved your likeness exactly, thoroughly, to the bottoms of the feet, achieved un-Enlightenment, achieved human existence, mortality, and sorrow," He is Telling us that the Divine Person Accomplished this.

For who among us, born to die and struggling in the interim with suffering of all kinds, would happily proclaim such a thing to be an accomplishment? The very things that we spend our lifetime striving to overcome, Sri Da Avabhasa was happy to have finally fully achieved. Truly, His Descent from the Formless Condition of the "Bright" into the limitation of form is His Victory, His powerful stroke of Mercy and Intervention in the human sphere.

All of this helps us to understand how unique the Help that is available in this book is, and why these chapters contain such unsurpassed Wisdom about how to die (as well as how to live).

In Part One of *Easy Death,* Sri Da Avabhasa Calls us, with the reassuring Authority of One Who knows perfectly, to relax our fear of death by observing that we inhere in God, in the One Universal Divine Reality, and that death is a process of change and transformation, not an ending. It is a process that we can know about and prepare for, much as we study about and prepare for "other great events, such as childbirth, or an operation, or a test of knowledge and skills relating to a profession". Sri Da Avabhasa Calls us to understand that death is both necessary and benign, serving a real purpose, not only when it occurs but in every moment while we are alive. Sri Da Avabhasa Tells us:

You should prepare for death as a process of complete surrender and release of all physical, emotional, and mental clinging to the present body-mind, its relations, and this world. Your death should be a complete release of this present "school" and a complete abandonment of the present design and content of your conditional self. You should fully consent to die

at the moment of death, and so be released toward what is new and await-
ing you above and beyond the "realities" of the present body-mind. Your
ability to do this will be either enhanced or limited to the same degree you
are able to surrender while alive in the Divine Love-Bliss-Consciousness
that Is God. Therefore, in order for death to be an ecstatic transition for
you, you must not only study and prepare for the specific and terminal
process of death itself, but while alive you must also devote yourself to an
ecstatic or self-transcending way of life. (p.53)

The Truth of Sri Da Avabhasa's Instruction is borne out by the often
extraordinary experiences of His devotees, of which many accounts are
given in the last portion of *Easy Death*. One such account tells of Judith
Swaney, a woman who suffered from childhood diabetes, losing her eye-
sight and then one of her legs to this crippling disease. In her late thirties,
Judith suffered a major heart attack, then congestive heart failure, then
kidney failure. As her life drew to a close, it was her resort to Sri Da
Avabhasa's Wisdom about death and His Blessing Presence in her life that
allowed Judith to face these insults, and to die an "easy death".

Here, Margot Soley, a friend of Judith's, writes:

Judith brought great determination and stubborn will to her life and to
overcoming and coping with the limitations that she faced because of her
illness. Initially this made it hard for her to receive help from others, for she
did not want to be a burden. . . .

As she struggled against all odds to hold on to life, Judith was
Blessed with several communications from Sri Da Avabhasa that transformed her relationship to the ordeal of dying. Margot writes that

her body visibly relaxed and softened, and her face radiated with a child-
like joy. She confessed that the only means of getting through this . . . had
been her Remembrance of, and resort to, Sri Da Avabhasa. . . .

When death became imminent, Judith received a Blessed Murti—a
sacred photographic representation of Sri Da Avabhasa—as a Gift from
Him, which she felt as the most tangible expression of His Love that she
could have received. It was after this Blessing that Judith

began to say that she did not want to hold on to life anymore, that she felt
she was ready to die. There was a resolution in her prayers, and she began
to show signs of a profound tiredness. It was clear she was given over to her
Heart-Master and was no longer in the struggle to hold on to life. It

was this capability to be prepared for death that was Sri Da Avabhasa's Graceful answer to her most passionate prayers.

Sri Da Avabhasa Calls us to a very realistic appraisal of the situation we are in. Most of us unwittingly follow our impulses and desires in this life, without a great deal of rigorous self-inspection—but where is all of that leading us?

There is nothing that is good or pleasurable that will not be taken away from you. And that separation is going to be painful. Therefore, there are no purposes of an ultimate kind that can be fulfilled in manifestation. There are countless purposes that can be fulfilled by conditional existence, countless purposes that can animate conditional existence, but they are all passing. They are all brief. They all have two sides—a pleasurable and positive one and a terrible one that is associated with all kinds of limitation and suffering. All purposes, all motions, have those two sides. Your purposes are not merely a picture of some Ultimate Will. The Divine is not the will that accounts for your purposes. The Divine is That in Which all of these purposes and motions arise, That Which is Realized when you transcend your clinging, your self-contraction. If there is a purpose with which you should associate yourself, it is the purpose of submission to That and Realization of That.

. . . But you must appreciate your situation. You must benefit from the wisdom and the instruction of those who have practiced beyond the mortal view, and then you must yourself embrace that greater practice. (October 15, 1982)

In Part Two of *Easy Death*, Sri Da Avabhasa Calls us again and again to the understanding that our impulses and desires, the habit patterns of our attention, literally create our destiny while we are alive and even more dramatically when we die.

I have pointed out to you on a number of occasions that while you live in conditional form, you make mind, you create the psyche, through associations, repetitions, reinforcement. When you die and the body drops off, mind makes you. After death, you live in the world of mind as you have created it while alive. The after-death states have been called "bardos", or "planes". Really, all such concepts are simply descriptions of how the mind operates dissociated from physical embodiment. You will spontaneously, through no will of your own, enter into realms of mind after death that correspond to your state of mind—not just your thinking mind but your subconscious and unconscious mind, the whole force of your tendency toward objects and conditional states. . . .

Mind makes association with realms that seem pleasurable, and after death you may pass in and out of these realms. But if you observe how desperate, egoically "self-possessed", depressed, craving, and dissatisfied you are generally, you will appreciate more profoundly what is likely after death and into what kinds of mind-realms you will be drawn. They are hells, purgatories, dark passages. They seem to go on for vast periods of time, even until they exhaust themselves and you pass out of them as you pass from one dream to the next. (pp. 147-48)

A chilling testimony by Tom Closser (from Part V) provides a very graphic demonstration of the fact that we <u>need </u>to observe and go beyond our limits while alive in order go beyond the destiny those limits, if uninspected and unreleased, will create for us at death. Tom, who had suffered a life-threatening accident, recounts his experience of one of the realms he passed into as he lingered between life and death. Tom's story is testimony to the profound way that Sri Da Avabhasa, Who was actually physically present to Serve Tom directly, Helped him in the midst of this crisis. Here, Tom is speaking of one of the realms he experienced in his out-of-body state, as he lingered between life and death, and some of the beings that he encountered there:

(They) finally hit upon the one experience which seemed to control my attention more strongly than anything else—the sense of being threatened. I was standing in the middle of a street, and a bakery truck would drive towards me. It would slam on its brakes and slide into me. Right before the truck would hit me, I could feel myself going into panic. Then the experience would repeat itself. It happened repetitively—hundreds, maybe thousands of times. I was stuck in that experience.

In the midst of this experience, I "shouted", but it was not a physical voice. Somehow, I could, just for a moment, remember and feel Heart-Master Da Avabhasa. . . .

Suddenly, I felt myself enter my body again, from the head down. I was back in the clinic, and Heart-Master Da Avabhasa was there. He was talking to me. When I saw Him, my heart burst with Happiness and relief. I had been so much in need of Him in that horrifying experience—more deeply and more profoundly than I had ever been in my entire life. I felt what an incredible opportunity it is to be physically embodied in a time and place where He is presently alive—and what a horror it is to pass through this life and not realize something greater than being completely controlled by your own mind and attention. I was weeping.

Tom's story points toward another aspect of the Wisdom that Sri Da Avabhasa brings to us in *Easy Death*. In Part Three, Sri Da Avabhasa makes it very clear that there are <u>many</u> dimensions to our existence, even an infinite number of possible worlds and experiences into which we may be projected at death. Sri Da Avabhasa humorously Says:

All the visible galaxies that you can see are perhaps something like a single cell on the big toe of what may seem to you to be a gigantic person, but who is perhaps a little troll in some other world much like this one. (p. 57)

In Part Three, Sri Da Avabhasa outlines, with unprecedented precision, the total spectrum of experience that comprises the cosmos. And, even more, He Tells us exactly what these structures mean in terms of our potential destiny after death:

Because of the tendency to be identified with the body, and also because of all the taboos associated with conventional consciousness in this world, people do not investigate, or thoroughly explore and "consider", the status of their own experience in any moment. Therefore, when they have uncommon experiences, such as near-death experiences or even mystical experiences, they interpret and modify those experiences, or only move into certain kinds of experiences, because of limiting tendencies or presumptions of mind. . . .

The situation of conditionally manifested beings in this world is typical of conditional beings in all worlds. You are presuming a limited condition of being, based on identification with attention in your current state of embodiment. The embodied attention is surrounded by a massive psychic form or individuated state of energy. And each of you is living out that condition in the gross plane of embodiment. You have the opportunity, in the subtler range of your existence, to explore more subtle conditions of existence and even the Ultimate Divine Self-Condition of all existence. That opportunity is directly available to you in the present moment, but you are dissociated from it through the habit mechanism of attention. Likewise, in sleep, in dreams, in reveries, in near death, in death, in your life of aspiration and creativity, in all kinds of moments, you are thrown out of the circumstance to which you are tending to bind yourself habitually, and you have the opportunity to perceive, or intuit, That Which is Ultimate or Divine. (pp. 177-79)

The search to be satisfied has an unrelenting force to it—and it causes us to repeat certain familiar types of experiences, lifetime after lifetime.

Thus Part Three also includes a very sophisticated discussion of the process of reincarnation and what it means for us. In examining the mechanical nature of reincarnation, Sri Da Avabhasa constantly Calls us to feel our heart's most primal urge to the Inherent Freedom prior to all dimensions of existence:

> . . . *the Way of the Heart is most direct. It is not the path of the stages, fulfilled by moving attention into subtler and subtler dimensions of objective existence. It is the direct Way of returning attention to its Source. . . When you acknowledge the motive toward release and make it the mover of your life, you transcend your seeking and your bewilderment. You become associated with real practice, real responsibility. Then that motive toward release . . . simply becomes free attention, or that which is inherently free, inherently released, and, therefore, that which inherently satisfies the motive toward release. (pp. 185-87)*

The secret of an "easy death" is thus, through Divine Wisdom and Help, to regenerate the capability for release that is the primal instinct each and every one of us feels. And this release is not nihilistic, as if we are to welcome death and the abandonment of the body as a superior alternative to life. The release that every heart really seeks to find is the release of separate and separative self and the discovery of the Eternal Nature of Who we really are.

In Part Four, Sri Da Avabhasa provides a practical roadmap of what happens when we relinquish the body in death, and He offers great Help in understanding exactly how to serve the process of true release, both in ourselves and in others. In Part Five, this loving service to the dying is exemplified in Ron Jenson's moving account of how Sri Da Avabhasa's Wisdom and Blessing enabled him to help his entire family during the traumatic death of his younger brother:

> *I could feel that death could actually be an ecstatic occasion, a wonderful occasion of transformation, as my brother became more and more released from his body and mind.*
>
> *Yet it was also true that the fear, the anxiety, and all the horror of losing someone you love was being felt by all of us. This was my younger brother dying, one of my closest intimates. There was the intense pain of watching him die from cancer. Nevertheless, there was always this other dimension to it that was powerful and potent. Everybody, even my aunts and uncles, staunch pillars of the mainstream churches, were eventually caught up in it. One uncle who serves as a bishop in a Christian denomination came to me and said that he had never been involved in a death*

and dying process of actually serving someone, talking about the technicalities of the death process with the person, and serving the person emotionally. He had never been involved in anything like what we were doing, and he was moved to tears many times by what was happening around my brother. . . . We were all being helped by Heart-Master Da and His Wisdom-Teaching to release and let David go.

Sri Da Avabhasa is always Blessing all beings—those who are living and those who are dying. And, just as Sri Da Avabhasa Himself has Demonstrated in His own Life, and as the testimonies of His devotees bear out, you do not have to die physically to discover the Great Wisdom about death. A complete understanding of both life and death can effectively be awakened in us in this lifetime.

But such deep knowledge is not something that can be acquired through books, even through this book, in and of itself. Such knowledge is an evolutionary matter for humanity as a whole, and a matter of Revelation for each of us individually. When and how that Revelation is Given depends on Grace, but it also depends on us. This book will have done its work if it leaves you convinced of the necessity to invest yourself in the living process that prepares you for death—the relationship to Sri Da Avabhasa, Who has Realized the Deathless Condition and is able to Awaken that same Realization, by Grace, in those who respond to Him.

PART I

Understanding Death
and
Going beyond Fear

Sri Da Avabhasa (The "Bright")
Sri Love-Anandashram, November 1991

Understanding Death and Going beyond Fear

INTRODUCTION

In Part One, Sri Da Avabhasa looks at why we are afraid to die. Death is not, as He Says, a matter of being "reduced to Zero", snuffed out by the universe. It is a process of transformation, in which we should participate naturally.

In "How the Problem of Death Is Overcome" (an excerpt from His Masterwork, *The Dawn Horse Testament*), Sri Da Avabhasa develops a profound Argument about the nature of human beings, and He gets to the root of our fear of death. Human beings, as Sri Da Avabhasa points out, are caught in a difficult evolutionary moment. Our egoic self-awareness has evolved further than that of lower animals, but we still have the same primal instincts that they have toward food, sex, and territory. The difference is that we can no longer relate to these urges in a simple way, as the lesser beings do. We complicate and exaggerate our instincts, and we live in a state of chronic mental anxiety. As a result, we have developed more and more sophisticated technology to satisfy the motives toward food, sex, and territory—and to stave off death as long as possible.

But there is much, much more to be known about life and death than our present vision of existence and our anxious relationship to death would suggest. Fear of physical death arises from the sense we have that we are nothing more than the physical body, which, looked at in the light of human experience as a whole, is a very strange point of view! If we take a few moments to relax and breathe and feel the whole body, we may become aware that we exist in a field of energy that extends beyond our physical bodily limits. And most of us can recall moments of intuition or psychic insight that suggest we live in a greater dimension of being than that of the visible world. The Spiritual traditions, also, are full of reports of blissful realms of experience that transcend physical awareness. But no psychic insight or Spiritual experience permanently relieves fear, unless the mechanism of fear itself is understood.

As a result of profound self-observation, Sri Da Avabhasa discovered in His own Life what that mechanism is. It is a chronic activity of self-contraction or recoil from the inherent Happiness of existence, an activity that results in our sense of identity with the body as a separate self, or ego-"I". Only in the penetration, or surrender, of this very contraction can we know complete and lasting freedom from the fear of death.

This is how we grow Spiritually—via ever-deepening surrender of separate self into Communion with What Is—the Mystery of Being within Which we came to birth and into Which we are released when we die. And how is that surrender accomplished? By the Grace of the Realizer, who Liberally Reveals what it is to be free of egoic self and who Grants that Freedom to those who enter into the Sphere of his Grace.

The Talks in this book were Given directly to those who have taken up such a self-surrendering practice in relationship to Sri Da Avabhasa. Through this practice, whatever our present form or place of appearance, we will Realize more and more the Bliss, Joy, Happiness, and Love that are inherent in existence and that can never be threatened by death.

CHAPTER 1

The Truth about Death

by Da Avabhasa
May 21, 1980

It is commonly said that human beings do not know about death, since nobody has come back to tell about it. Of course, this is false. Many people have died and been revived, and their reports are very revealing. Likewise, many reliable individuals devoted to one or another form of Spiritual practice have enjoyed and subsequently communicated about the subtle and Transcendental aspects of human existence, all of which relate to the process of death and one's destiny beyond it.

What people truly mean when they say they do not know about death is that they do not know exactly what will follow it in their own case. But the generalized attitude of no-knowledge about death only provides an emotional excuse for avoiding confrontation with the reality of death and the necessity to study it and prepare for cooperation with its process.

The death process, like all the common events of human experience, is clearly available for you to witness in others and to study as a common as well as a personal physical or psycho-physical event. You can and must prepare for that event, even as you normally prepare for other great events, such as childbirth, or an operation, or a test of knowledge and skills relating to a profession. Just so, like every individual, you have many experiences during your lifetime that clearly duplicate at least some of the psycho-physical aspects of the death process. These include the regular act of going to sleep, the experiences endured during periods of illness, and the progressive revelation enjoyed via a lifetime of meditation. Also, many people are given remarkable experiences that reveal and demonstrate to them the actualities of the death process. I My Self have

51

had such experiences, including complete duplication of the death process, leading to emergence from the physical body, the mind-self, and this world, as well as to rebirth, or eventual resumption of psycho-physical existence.

Therefore, you should not presume that you do not and cannot know about the death process. You can and must know about that process, and you must prepare for it through psycho-physical self-study. Even if you do not come to know in advance exactly what will follow your own death, you can know about and do preparatory exercises in the death process itself, since it involves the familiar processes of your present body-mind. And you can, while still alive in this world, enter into the profound practices of esoteric Spirituality, wherein you can Realize your Real Condition and Ultimate Destiny as well as the actual structures of your experiential existence.

II

Fear of death is anxiety, or emotional recoil, experienced in anticipation of the event. Such advance fear is basically the result of a failure to observe the death process in others and to study the death process through systematic education and self-observation.

Death is a necessary, purposeful, and ultimately benign psycho-physical process. It is similar to the process of giving birth, except that it occurs to both males and females. You must study the death process bodily and through observing others. Above all, tension and fear must be relaxed during the death process (as it must be by a woman in childbirth). You must relax and release, as when going to sleep, in a feeling of deep trust, love, and surrender to the Divine Reality on Which the process depends.

What is on the "other side" of the death process may or may not be revealed to you beforehand, but it will certainly be revealed to you when it actually happens! Therefore, your only responsibility is to study, prepare for, and rightly engage the death process itself, much as a woman approaching childbirth.

In the birth process, the newly born enters this world via the lower bodily organs of the mother. In the death process, the living being enters a new world via the crown of the head of the dying body (which, in effect, is the "mother" of the living being).[1] You must learn how to coop-

---

1. At death, the entity—in the Hindu tradition the *jiva*—withdraws from the physical organism by ascending through the crown of the head, which is the same process consciously pursued in Yogic meditation.

erate with the death process as a natural event leading to this end.

The failure of such cooperation tends to make the death process painful and disturbing, even as the birth process can be for the mother who fails to surrender and cooperate with the event. And if you do not surrender with attention, feeling, breath, and body in cooperation with the death process, you will tend to interfere with the ultimate event of release and separation from this body and world—which, like sleep, is intended to refresh and strengthen the phenomenal being in preparation for a rebirth, or resumed embodiment. Resistance during the actual death process makes the necessary transition difficult, and you may thereby force yourself into a pattern of psychic withholding whereby you remain fixed in a ritual of illusory and frustrated association with past experiential aspects of the now dying or receding body and world. (In that case, attention does not pass freely to the crown of the head and beyond, but it becomes locked in dreamlike associations with memories, vital associations, and various aspects of experience in this passing body and world.)

You should prepare for death as a process of complete surrender and release of all physical, emotional, and mental clinging to the present body-mind, its relations, and this world. Your death should be a complete release of this present "school" and a complete abandonment of the present design and content of your conditional self. You should fully consent to die at the moment of death, and so be released toward what is new and awaiting you above and beyond the "realities" of the present body-mind. Your ability to do this will be either enhanced or limited to the same degree you are able to surrender while alive in the Divine Love-Bliss-Consciousness that Is God. Therefore, in order for death to be an ecstatic transition for you, you must not only study and prepare for the specific and terminal process of death itself, but while alive you must also devote yourself to an ecstatic or self-transcending way of life.

III

The "secret" or Law of the death process is the same that applies to existence during one's born lifetime: The right relationship to the process is that of love-surrender, not recoil or withdrawal. The death process is simply another form of participation in the Mystery and Universal Unity of existence. Death is not self-suppression. It is not a process whereby the conditional self is reduced to Zero or thrown into eternal Chaos. Such a passage, if it seems to arise, either during your

53

lifetime or in the process of death, is an hallucination created by your own recoiling fear. In any case, the hallucination eventually vanishes, and it will vanish most quickly and permanently if you will surrender your egoic self through feeling into Ecstatic Love-Communion with the Self-Existing and Self-Radiant Divine Being in Whom all conditionally manifested beings and experiences and worlds arise and change and disappear.

The death process should not be engaged merely as a retreat from embodiment. It should not be used to retreat <u>into</u> the egoic self. Rather, it should be engaged as self-surrender, or love-surrender of the total body-mind. As when going to sleep, you should simply relax and rest your hold on the states of body and mind. If you enter into the death process trusting the Self-Existing and Self-Radiant Divine Being to the point of utter self-surrender, then the event will suffer no distortion, and you will emerge into a right, profound, and ultimately Happy destiny—even as such surrender and trust relieve your life, and sleep, and dreams of distortion, fear, illusion, and doubt while you live in this world.

And death is not a permanent event or effect. It is only a transition to further experience. It is a transforming event that prepares you for another birth, just as it stands before you now, motivating you toward self-transcending surrender during your lifetime. Death and rebirth are the inevitable cycle of your existence, until you grow and evolve and surrender and serve beyond the limits of all the schools of cosmic Nature, and so Emerge permanently into the "Bright"[2] Divine Self-Domain,[3] Where you will exist in Inherently Perfect Identification with the Divine Being as well as in an Inherently Perfectly evolved or elaborated Relationship with the Divine Being.

So be it.

---

2. Since His Illumined boyhood, Sri Da Avabhasa has used the term the "Bright" (and its variations, such as "Brightness") to describe the Blissfully Self-Luminous Divine Being, eternally, infinitely, and inherently Self-Radiant, Which He knew even then as the All-Pervading, Transcendental, Inherently Spiritual, and Divine Reality of His own body-mind and of all beings, things, and worlds.

3. Da Avabhasa Affirms that there is a Divine Domain that is the "Bright" Destiny of every Realizer of the Divine Self. It is not elsewhere, not a place like a subtle heaven or mythical paradise, but It is the always present, Transcendental (and Inherently Spiritual) Divine Self of every conditional self, and the Radiant Source-Condition of every conditional place. The God-World, or Realm of Self-Light, transcends even the most heavenly dimensions of conditional space-time, and is beyond the mind's capacity to experience, describe, or comprehend.

CHAPTER 2

Death Is Not Your Concern

a Talk by Da Avabhasa
February 18, 1974

SRI DA AVABHASA: Because of your position in the midst of things, you tend to think of death over against life. But when you begin to understand your actual situation, then you see the transformation that manifests as living, experiencing, and dying as a continuum, a single process. Because of your present fixed activity as the seeker, as "Narcissus",[1] the eternally recurring mortal, you tend to think that death is fundamentally a physical event. Because you tend to be frightened, you like to think that death stands over against your psyche. You like to think that perhaps the psyche, that individuated consciousness, that sense of forms and complications and images and ideas and experiences and memories, survives. But when you begin to understand, you see that death is not merely a physical event, but a psycho-physical event, in which not only the body dies but the psyche also. Therefore, while alive you must enjoy wisdom relative not only to the body and the world but also to the psyche.

The life-death process is a necessary and ultimately Happy transformation in which one's fundamental existence is realized. But when you examine life and death from the point of view of "Narcissus", who is fearful

---

1. In Sri Da Avabhasa's Teaching-Revelation, "Narcissus" is a key symbol of un-Enlightened Man as a self-obsessed seeker, enamored of his own self-image and egoic self-consciousness. As "Narcissus", every human being constantly suffers in dilemma, contracted in every dimension of the being, recoiling from all relations and even from the fundamental condition of relationship (or relatedness) itself. In *The Knee of Listening* (p. 26), Heart-Master Da summarized His insight into "Narcissus" as the avoidance of relationship: "He is the ancient one visible in the Greek myth, who was the universally adored child of the gods, who rejected the loved-one and every form of love and relationship, who was finally condemned to the contemplation of his own image, until he suffered the fact of eternal separation and died in infinite solitude." For one who understands most profoundly, the activity of avoidance, or self-contraction, is ultimately understood to be simultaneous with the condition of relationship or relatedness itself.

and separate, you cannot tolerate endless transformation. You have no tolerance for psycho-physical life or death. When you begin to assume your mortality and feel you cannot escape it, then you try to escape psychic transformation, or psychic death. Yet the entire transformation must inevitably occur. When your resistance to that profound transformation breaks down, then you allow its fullness to be enacted, and you realize ecstasy with continually greater profundity in the midst of the endless unfolding of existence.

When you have realized such wisdom, then not only do you allow physical death at some point but you also allow psychic death. If you are intelligent, you allow it while alive. Then you have no ultimate fear of transforming events. Then you need not defend yourself against them with philosophies, descriptions, dogmas, experiences, and psycho-physical rigidity. You live fully and creatively. You pass through psychic death while alive, and you enjoy genuine understanding of your relationship to the body and its various states. You become capable of bodily death.

Even so, there is no reason to seek death, no reason to leave this world unnaturally. For very real and unreasonable reasons this psycho-physical manifestation is given to you to deal with, and it is fitted to the qualities of your karmic and pre-conscious dependence. It is a continual test, and it contains the continual possibility for lessons, for Freedom, for Liberation in the Divine, for a truly or Divinely Humorous life in God. This life is very much your appropriate business, rather than philosophical and metaphysical ruminating about how to get out of it. You are not ultimately released from the limitations of life except in the fullness of the enjoyment of God.

The human manifestation is unique, and the classical Spiritual traditions have valued it above the apparently glorious, heavenly states that may be lived in subtle worlds. Mankind has the capability to move through all functional conditions, all limited states—gross, subtle, and causal[2]—and to Realize the Divine absolutely. This capability is not

2. The Teachings of many esoteric sacred traditions include "maps", or detailed descriptions, of the psycho-physical anatomy of human beings and the cosmos. Sri Da Avabhasa is in agreement with the traditional descriptions that the human body-mind and its environment consist of three great dimensions—gross, subtle (or astral), and causal.

The gross, or most physical, dimension is associated with what Heart-Master Da calls the "frontal line" of the human body-mind, or the descended processes of psycho-physical embodiment and experience in the waking state.

The subtle or astral dimension, which is senior to and pervades the gross dimension, includes the etheric (or energic), lower mental (or verbal-intentional and lower psychic), and higher mental (or deeper psychic, mystical, and discriminative) aspects of the conditionally manifested being. The subtle dimension is associated primarily with the spinal line of the body, which corresponds to the ascending processes of

enjoyed by beings in the subtle worlds any more than it is enjoyed by chickens in this world. Thus, the human state is valued in the world's religious and Spiritual traditions.

There is no fixed world. In this world, which is essentially a vital manifestation, everything seems so fixed and solid and moveless and not capable of being influenced by your mere mentalizing. But even this world is not fixed, as you begin to see as soon as you fall into God and become Humorous. Then you see how unfixed and fluid this world is, and how unfixed and fluid the vast, infinite cosmos is. The conditional realm is fluid, shapeless, and unreasonable. When you fall into God, then every world becomes the God-World, because you are constantly intuiting the Divine there.

There are great dimensions, great cosmic possibilities, into which you may drift and enjoy a kind of mortality that seems immortal. There are worlds where longevity is intensified almost to the point of immortality, but not to literal immortality. Even those worlds are declining and passing through cycles. There is no fixed condition. There is no condition to be maintained other than the Divine, the Real, the Eternal Self-Condition in Which all the cosmic worlds are arising. There are endless worlds that cannot be conceived from the point of view of mankind. If you look out into the night at the infinite numbers of stars and planets, what you see is still only one little tiny galaxy. Through a large telescope you may see thousands of galaxies that contain billions of possible worlds. Yet even these are only worlds that are visible to you within this portion of the spectrum of light, this narrow vibration in which you conceive visibility.

All the visible galaxies that you can see are perhaps something like a single cell on the big toe of what may seem to you to be a gigantic person but who is perhaps a little troll in some other world much like this one. You cannot analyze the possible conditions in the worlds and the planes of conscious awareness and come out having gained some knowledge or having fixed for yourself some superior Spiritual destiny. Investigation of the possibilities of existence can only ultimately confound

psycho-physical embodiment, including the brain core and the subtle centers of mind in the higher brain. (It is only secondarily associated with the frontal line of the body-mind.) It is also, therefore, associated with the visionary, mystical, and Yogic Spiritual processes encountered in dreams, in ascended or internalized meditative experiences, and during and after death.

The causal dimension is senior to and pervades both the gross and the subtle dimensions. It is the root of attention, or the feeling of relatedness, or the essence of the separate and separative ego-"I". The causal dimension is associated with the right side of the heart, specifically with the sinoatrial node, or "pacemaker" (the psycho-physical source of the heartbeat). Its corresponding state of consciousness is the formless awareness of deep sleep.

you. It is a kind of suffering. It even serves you like suffering, in that it makes you fall apart and at last yield to the Divine.

The event of a human death in the midst of all of that is nothing. Everybody attributes so much importance to death and wants it to be something so terribly profound, whereas the human psycho-physical death is not even worthy of being called a minor incident among the worlds. In the midst of the path of your own ultimate existence, it is not even a minor incident. It seems important only from the point of view of fear.

Death seems important to the mind because the mind's fundamental function is to defend the ego. The mind is a hedge around the sense of separate existence. As such, the mind is always set against desire. The mind and desire are two opposing principles. Desire is always moving you toward a formless, even Transcendental, condition, always moving you toward union, toward concentration on what is outside yourself, toward attention in something beyond the knot of the self-contraction. While desire is moving you, you are also continually obsessed with the mind. And the mind is always trying to create a hedge around the ego, to continue this sense of separate existence. Thus, life is a conflict between the enclosure of mind and the explosion of desire. Both movements assume the ego, or the separate and separative self. Desire wants to remove it, and mind wants to reinforce it and make it immortal.

The Truth is not in following the path of mind or the path of desire, the path of self-preservation or the path of self-fulfillment. The Truth is in understanding the underlying principle in this adventure of life, which is the constant realization of conflict.

When the ego, the self-contraction, the separate and separative self, is no longer the principle of your existence from moment to moment, then the whole program of mind and desire is loosened, undermined, undone. Then at the root of your existence is the continuous Realization of the Self-Existing and Self-Radiant Fullness of the Divine. That Realization transforms mind and desire and makes life quite a different event, even though it may appear to be the same as it was. One who has understood in this fundamental way is Happy while alive. He or she continues to think and use the mind and psyche, apparently like everyone else. He or she continues to act and be moved, apparently like everyone else. But mind and body are no longer the principles of his or her existence. He or she is no longer founded in them, because he or she is no longer founded in egoic existence and the drama of "Narcissus" that is enacted as mind and desire.

It is not death that is significant, but the living process of transcendence of the egoic self and Identification with the Divine Self, or Consciousness Itself. That process makes everything, from lunch to death, something new, something known in Truth, no longer a matter of concern. It makes the vast cosmic process no longer a matter of concern. The whole profound philosophical mulling over of death is appropriate only for the seeker, who is still bound to the dramatization of the adventure of "Narcissus". Such an individual is very concerned with his or her own death, with his or her own Spiritual destiny. Such a person is always interested in hearing all about how it is after death and about all the planes of conscious awareness and about all the cosmic and Transcendental dimensions. If, for one reason or another, he or she is able to believe these descriptions with some intensity, he or she feels somewhat consoled.

Even so, there is no idea that lasts beyond your final breath. The massive philosophical and psychological defense that people create through a lifetime of seeking all goes, in an instant. People wind up after death in the same condition that they suffered while alive, or worse, with more from which they must be purified. But the individual who is Awake understands the functions of life and mind and his or her true relationship to them and is released from dependence upon the drama that the usual man or woman exercises in the midst of his or her functions. At the point of death, such a one goes through the same rip-off process as any other one, but he or she is released, truly. He or she passes into a different functional existence, relieved of the secondary bondage that the usual man and woman must deal with, everything that causes the usual man or woman to drift back, unconscious, to lesser states and confusions and mysterious conditions.

Therefore, it is better to understand the mind than to create philosophy with it. There is a deeper personality than the bodily personality that identifies with the conceptual and verbal mind, and that deeper personality is what passes beyond this life, not your philosophy and all your ideas and experiences. Such things do not have the strength to pass from one room to another. You cannot even hold on to your philosophy or your mantra when you pass by a cross-legged nude on a couch! So what do you think happens from life to death and back to life again? As soon as a desire or some intense condition arises, philosophy and the usual practices go out the bottom. If your little search is that fragile during life, what do you think occurs in the midst of such a profound event as psycho-physical death?

Divinely Enlightened beings know absolutely nothing about what will happen after death, any more than they know what will happen in the next moment while alive. They may hear rumors in the world and in the mind about what might tend to occur, but they are not involved or concerned with the fixing of future events, either for themselves or for any others. They are involved with the process of Divine Self-Realization, instantly. They are always involved with the process of life, as a Divinely Conscious event in this moment, and now in this moment, and now in this moment, and now in this moment.

Divinely Enlightened beings see the smithereens of the worlds and know them to exist in the Great Consciousness, not merely in space. They know that the worlds themselves are not fixed, nor do they represent any fundamental limitation to the Realization of Divine Enlightenment. Thus, they are not people of concerns, or of programs, or of descriptions. They are utterly Free of all of them. They have become always already Ecstatic. For such beings there is, therefore, no straightforward description of Reality, or of the cosmos, or of life. Only God is Apparent to such beings. Only the Paradox survives.

CHAPTER 3

How the Problem of Death Is Overcome

an Excerpt from
The Dawn Horse Testament,
by Da Avabhasa

Among the beings On Earth, human beings Are Unique, or At Least Significantly Advanced In The Development Of psycho-physical functions that Are Only Latent or Less Developed In the case of the lesser world of lower organisms, plants, trees, insects, fishes, birds, mammals, and the rest. Among The Apparent Differences Between Man and lesser beings Is The Greatly Developed Capability and Capacity For mentally Reflective and conceptually Abstracted knowledge (and Consequent inventiveness) That Is Evident In the human case.

Even So, It Is Not conceptual or Abstract thinking that Is The Unique Characteristic or Capability Of Man. Neither Is toolmaking (or inventiveness and technology), which is a secondary product of Abstract or conceptual thinking, The Unique Characteristic or Capability Of Man. Abstract thought and technology are themselves only servants Of The Unique Capability Of Man. They are Signs, or Secondary Evidence, Of The Unique Characteristic Of Man.

The Unique Characteristic Of Man Is The Capability For self-Understanding. The Unique Capability Of Man Is The Characteristic Process Of self-Transcendence. The Unique Characteristic and Capability Of Man Is The Progressive Evolution (or The Seven-Stage Developmental Process) Of The (Ultimately, Inherent, and Inherently Perfect) Realization Of Consciousness Itself, or The Realization Of Divinely Enlightened (or Self-Radiant and Self-Existing) Consciousness Through The Progressive (and, Ultimately, Inherent, and Inherently Perfect) Transcendence, and, At Last, The Outshining,[1] Of the body-mind (and Of The Totality Of conditional Existence).

The Unique Achievement Of Man (or Of The Divine Person, Who Appears As Man) Is The Fulfillment and The Transcendence Of The Seven Stages Of Life.[2] Abstract thinking (In The Form Of Profound "Consideration"[3]) and technology (In The Form Of Right Practice) Are Useful Instruments For Directing This Evolutionary and self-Transcending Conscious Process, but conceptual thinking and technological inventiveness Tend To Become Exalted, or Valued As Ends In themselves, So That they Become The Chronic, Compulsive, and Obsessive Preoccupations Of Man, When egoity, or self-Fulfillment, Rather Than self-Transcendence, Becomes The Motivator Of Man.

The lesser beings function Largely From The Base Of What Is Commonly Called "The Unconscious". That Is To Say, Compared To Man, they Apparently Operate With Much Less Of (or, At Least In some cases, Even Without Much Of) What Are Commonly Called The "Conscious" and "Subconscious" Structures Of mind. Human beings Are Actively Bringing The Unconscious (In Its Totality, Including, Potentially, Its Superconscious Heights and, Ultimately, Its Inherent, and Inherently Most Perfectly Deep, Perfection) Into a More and More Clearly Conscious state of mind (and Of Conscious Realization, Even Prior To mind).

The Unconscious (As mind) Is the Fundamental functional mind, or the functional Source-mind. It Is Constantly Active and Effective, but (Perhaps Because its contents are Not objectified in a conventionally Familiar and conventionally Usable mental form) it Is Not (In The General Case) Immediately or Directly known or Acknowledged By the Conscious

---

1. "Outshining" is a technical term, synonymous with "Divine Translation", that Da Avabhasa uses to refer to the final Demonstration of the four-phase process of Divinization in the seventh, or fully Enlightened, stage of life. In this Event, body, mind, and world are no longer noticed, not because the Divine Consciousness has withdrawn or dissociated from conditional phenomena, but because all arising phenomena are perceived by the Divine Self as only modifications of Itself, and the "Bright" Radiance of Consciousness now Outshines all such phenomena.

2. Sri Da Avabhasa has Described the evolutionary potential of the human individual in terms of seven stages of life. See the essay "The Seven Stages of Life" on pages 375-79 of this book for a summary description of this unique Revelation, Given by Sri Da Avabhasa, of the human and evolutionary destiny of humankind.

3. The technical term "consideration" in Sri Da Avabhasa's Wisdom-Teaching is similar to the Sanskrit concept of samyama, as classically presented in the *Yoga-Sutras* attributed to the Yogic Adept Patanjali. Such "consideration", as Sri Da Avabhasa explains, is "a process of one-pointed but ultimately thoughtless concentration and exhaustive contemplation of a particular object, function, person, process, or condition, until the essence or ultimate obviousness of that subject is clear". As engaged in the Way of the Heart, this concentration results "in both the highest intuition and the most practical grasp of the Lawful and Divine necessities of human existence".

mind. Therefore, Between the Unconscious mind and the Conscious mind Is a Transitional mind, the Subconscious (or dreaming and dreamlike) mind. The Subconscious mind Is Immediately Below, or Behind, or (In Superconscious states, Developed or Revealed Via The Subconscious mind or Process) Even (Spatially) Above the Conscious mind, and it Is (or May Be), To A Degree, Directly (or Consciously) known, Acknowledged, and Used (or Expressed) By the Conscious mind. Therefore, the Subconscious mind Is A Communications Bridge Between the Unconscious mind and the Conscious mind (and Between the Conscious mind and the Unconscious mind).

Human beings Are Bringing The Unconscious To Consciousness Through Evolutionary Stages That Make Transitional Use Of The Subconscious Mechanisms. The Spiritual, Transcendental, and Divine Process May Be Understood As A Sequence Of (Possible) Stages Of Growth Culminating In (Inherent, Inherently Perfect, and Necessarily Divine) Consciousness Of (and Inherently Perfect, or Inherently Free, Responsibility For) All Of Reality (So That The Hidden Secrets Of mind Are Conscious, Even In mind, and The Transcendental, Inherently Spiritual, and Divine Source, or Inherently Perfect Subject, or Perfectly Subjective Self, or Limitless Prior Condition, Of mind, Even Of The Unconscious conditional Source-mind, Is Realized To Be Consciousness Itself).

In General, humanity At Large Is Struggling In The Earlier Stages Of This Process (In The Context Of The First Three Stages Of Life). Even So, much (conditional) knowledge Has Been Brought To Consciousness, but that (conditional) knowledge Is Only Partial and, As A Result, what human beings now Regard As common or reliable (conditional) knowledge Is Only The Beginning Of (conditional) knowledge, and what is conditionally known Has The Force (or Significance) Of A Problem (or A Yet Unresolved Urge To know).

Among The Most Significant Forms Of such human knowledge Is the knowledge of death. The lesser beings experience fear, self-protectiveness, survival instincts, adaptation urges, sickness, and death, but their Involvement With all of that Is At The Level Of Urges Coming From The Unconscious. The lesser beings Are Not (At The Level Of the Conscious mind) Very self-Aware Of death, its Structure or Purpose, or Even its Inevitability. Human beings, However, Are, Even Characteristically, Acutely Aware Of death As An Inevitable and Apparently Terminal personal Event. This Awareness Is Unique (conditional) knowledge, but It Is Also Only

Partial (conditional) knowledge. It Is A Sign That human beings (Not Otherwise More Fully Awake) Are Yet functioning On The Base Of The Unconscious Relative To The Larger Context, Real Process, and Ultimate Purpose Of death, and Of life itself. Thus, For human beings At The Lesser (or Commonly Characteristic) Level Of human Evolution, death Is A Problem, A Threat, A Dilemma, or A Question In the mind.

Since human beings function Rather Uniquely At The Level Of Subconscious and Conscious mind (and Since Evolution Itself, Epitomized On Earth By human beings, Is, In Its Fullest Development, Primarily A Process In mind, Moving Toward The Revelation Of Self-Existing and Self-Radiant Consciousness Itself, and Only Preliminarily, and Otherwise Secondarily, A Process Of gross form and gross adaptation), human beings Naturally Feel Threatened By death As An Always Present or Abstract Possibility and Concern Of mind (Just As, In General, human beings Characteristically experience sex As An Always Present or Abstract Possibility and Concern Of mind, Whereas lesser beings Are Generally Associated With sex Via instinctive and Unconsciously Generated cyclic patterns). Therefore, human beings Are (In General) Also Constantly Moved To Achieve sexual pleasure (With or Without An Intention To reproduce), and they Are Otherwise (In General) Constantly Moved To Confront and Answer or Solve (Through Effective psycho-physical Efforts) The Abstract and Really Threatening Problem Of death.

In Contrast To most human beings, lesser beings (From which, or Relative To which, human beings Are, By A Process That Functions At All Levels, and Not Merely At The gross material Level, Of The psycho-physical Cosmos, Evolved and Evolving) Are Generally Moved Only instinctively, To reproduce themselves Excessively (That Is To Say, Frequently and/or in Superfluous numbers, So That a Sufficient number Will Survive all Natural threats and reproduce the species again). Also, lesser beings Are instinctively Moved To kill for food, territory, or breeding mates (who, Like food and territory, Basically Represent The instinctive Right To reproduce), and they Are Otherwise instinctively Moved To Defend (or Even Simply To Agitate) themselves Only In The Instants Of Direct Confrontation With a Really (and bodily) Threatening physical opponent (Whereas human beings, In their Comparatively More Evolved, or mentalized, personal and social state, Are, Because Of mental Anxiety, Sometimes Moved To kill Even their own Kind at war, and Otherwise To Be Aggressive and Defensive and Agitated Even In circumstances that Are Not Directly, or Really and bodily, Threatening). Therefore, human beings (and Mankind

As A Whole) Must Evolve Further Than all lesser beings (Even By The Evolution Of mind), So That they May Transcend All The mental, emotional, and physical Exaggerations Of their sub-human Inheritance Of instinct (Particularly As Those Exaggerations Are Demonstrated Via egoic and Loveless and Destructive Motives Associated With sex, and food, and territory, and Aggression).

It Is Also Notable That, As Mankind Develops Its Abstracted Involvement With (Especially) sex and death To The Degree That most human individuals Tend To live to and beyond the Natural reproductive age, human populations Tend To Become Overlarge, So That The Quality Of ordinary human experience and The Possibility Of Growth Into and Through The Advanced and The Ultimate Stages Of Life[4] Become Either Threatened Or Really Diminished. This Indicates That, As human populations Acquire The Capability For longevity, they Must Control human reproduction, and they Must Also Become Informed and Guided By The Wisdom-Culture Of Superior (or, Really, Divine) Understanding and Purpose, or Else human beings Will Tend, In The Likeness Of lesser beings, To Continue To reproduce Excessively and To Remain Devoted, In The instinctive or Unconscious Manner, To self-Survival (Rather Than To self-Transcendence) and To Effort and Seeking Merely For The Sake Of The Survival Of the organism itself (Rather Than To Submission Of the body-mind To The Great Reality, and To The Purpose Of self-Transcendence).

When human populations Achieve The Capability For individual longevity, they Must Control or Transcend The instinctual reproductive Strategies Of Excess, For Those Strategies Work (or Produce An Ecologically Balanced Result) Only If The Rate Of early-life deaths Is Relatively Large. Likewise, As human beings Acquire longer life spans, they Must Realize The Superior (or self-Transcending) Purpose Of conditional Existence, and they Must Be Moved (and Also Grow) To Demonstrate That Purpose In The Context Of The Advanced and The Ultimate Stages Of Life, or Else conditional Existence Will Be Devoted To sub-human and egoic Survival games and The petty territorial (or political

---

4. Sri Da Avabhasa uses the term "advanced" to describe the Spiritually activated stages of life—the fourth stage of life and the fifth stage of life. Individuals who practice in the context of the advanced stages of life are those who, by Grace, have Awakened to the Divine as the tangible, All-Pervading Presence or Radiant Spirit-Force or Person, with Whom they live in a constant relationship of devotion, or Love-Communion.

Da Avabhasa reserves the term "ultimate" to describe the sixth stage of life and the seventh stage of life, or individuals who practice in the Domain of Consciousness Itself.

and social) Conquests That Come From The Increase Of experience and knowledge and power In The lower human Context Of The First Three Stages Of Life (Untouched By The Great Purpose, and Untouched By The Culture, The Balancing Effect, and The Evolutionary Process Of Awakening Associated With self-Transcendence In The Context Of The Advanced and The Ultimate Stages Of Life).

Therefore, As human groups increase in size because of the longevity of individuals, death itself Must Be Really Understood and Transcended, In Consciousness, and (Progressively) In The Context Of The Advanced and The Ultimate Stages Of Life. Likewise, merely reproductive sexuality Must Be Controlled (or Economized) By various Intelligent techniques, and sexuality itself Must Be (Progressively) Converted (and Positively Changed) By energy-Conserving, and Rejuvenative, and (Eventually) Spiritually Active and Spiritually Effective Sexual Practice.

For human beings, death Is A Proposition and A Puzzle That <u>Must</u> Be Understood and Transcended (By Correct and Revealing Information, or Fullest Education, and By The Real Process Of self-Transcendence). There Is No Peace For human beings Until This Matter Is Resolved.

Of Course This Matter Of death Is A Perennial Subject Of Conjecture and Research, but The Resolution Of The Question Requires Even More Than Information. As Is The Case With All Evolutionary Matters, This Question Can Be Resolved Only By Tapping What Is Always Presently In The Unconscious and Bringing It Into Consciousness. That Is To Say, The Overcoming Of The Apparent Problem and Motivating Stress Associated With death Requires The Evolutionary (and Thus Truly human, and Spiritual, and Transcendental, and Divine) Process Of Positively Changing and Directly Transcending the limitations of mind (or The egoic Burden Of limited knowledge and limited experience).

The Unconscious Is Simply The Totality Of What Is Real but Not Yet Fully Conscious (or Brought To Fully Conscious Acknowledgement and Realization). Since Mankind Has Gone So Far As To Become self-Conscious (or mentally and egoically self-Aware) About death, Mankind Must Be Submitted To A Process Of Becoming Really (and Not egoically) Conscious Of What Is Yet Hidden. And This Requires Truly human Growth, and Growth In The Context Of The Advanced and The Ultimate Stages Of Life, Via The human, and Spiritual, and Transcendental, and Divine Process Of Participatory self-Transcendence. Through Such self-Transcendence (Which Becomes self-Submission To The Divine Person or Reality), the (Presumed) knowledge Of The psycho-physical Potential Of

66

death Progressively Becomes Heart-Realization Of The self-Sacrificial Wound Of Divine Love-Bliss.

Deeper Than the Conscious mind Of Man In The Third Stage Of Life Is The Inherent Realization Of Eternal Love, Immortal Love-Bliss, Unqualified Being, Infinite Power, and Inherent Wisdom. Therefore, As The Spiritual, Transcendental, and Divine Process Develops (As Necessary) In The Context Of The Fourth, The Fifth, The Sixth, and The Seventh Stages Of Life, There Is Progressive Realization Of The Divine (or Perfectly Subjective, and Inherently Perfectly Conscious, and Self-Existing, and Self-Radiant) Self-Condition Of conditional Existence, and, In That Process, The Problem Of death (or The Wondering About The Purpose, Process, and Effect Of life and death) Is Overcome By Real Conscious Realization Of What Is Hidden From the lesser mechanical and Unconscious point of view.

CHAPTER 4

Death and
the Divine Destiny

by Da Avabhasa
April 20, 1978

Personal existence is not a "thing" or an "entity". Personal existence is a process. "I" is an activity, not an object, and not a fixed and eternally defined subject. The process that is "I" is a temporary and dependent aspect of a Great Universal Process. The individual arises, changes, and passes. It is caused and influenced by an immense and undefinable but ultimately ordinary and unnecessary pattern of appearances and disappearances. And the same process is duplicated as millions and billions and infinite possible variations of other human or human-like persons. The process, in every case, is Man, and each individual is an example and a moment of the same process, as fragile and dispensable as a single minnow in a maze of duplicate fishes, produced in excess for the sake of the species itself. And even the species is only another edible moment in the procession of forms.

The process that is "I" is integrated as a "person" while it persists, and then it is disintegrated in the Great Universal Process. The subtler mechanics of the "person" continue beyond ordinary death, associated with various forms of experience, and producing various "lives", until there is Awakening to the Way of Life in Truth. Only then is the Divine Destiny Realized. Only then does the grotesque and marvelous pattern of limitations fall away completely, in a death that is Most Perfect in God—a death that reaches Self-Existing Divine Consciousness and Self-Radiant Divine Love-Bliss.

CHAPTER 5

Death Is
the Way to Life

by Da Avabhasa
March 22, 1978

T he real man or woman learns to live by becoming willing and able to die. Such a one is able to confront the difficult barriers and frustrations of this slightly evolved world and yet remain capable of ecstasy in every moment.

Therefore, the primary initiation that leads to human maturity is the confrontation with mortal fear. Only when the ultimate frustration that is death has been fully "considered" and felt and understood as a process can the individual live without self-protective and self-destructive fears. Only in intuitive freedom from the threat and fear of death is the individual capable of constant love of the Divine Being, Truth, and Reality and also of transcendence of the frustrating and self-binding effects of daily experience. Only in freedom from mortal recoil is the individual capable of ecstasy under all conditions.

Therefore, be alive, but learn Divine Life by first dealing with your death. Become aware that you do not live, but that you are Lived by the Divine Person. Become My devotee by surrendering your illusion of independent life, which is the egoic self, or body-mind, in ecstatic Communion with Me, and, thus and thereby, with the Divine Person. Become willing to die in any moment, and maintain no inward armor against it. Die in every moment by not holding on to your life. Give your life up in devotion to Me, and allow the Divine Person, Condition, and Reality That is Revealed in My Company to Divinely Transfigure, Divinely Transform, and Divinely Translate[1] the body-mind into Itself.

1. Da Avabhasa has uniquely detailed four phases in the Enlightened Yoga of the seventh, or Divinely Self-Realized, stage of life.

When Divine Enlightenment is firmly established, the body-mind of the Realizer is first progressively relaxed into, or pervaded by, the inherent Radiance of the Spiritual and Transcendental Divine Self. This process of Divine Transfiguration expresses itself as the Realizer's active Spiritual Blessing in all relationships.

When the gross body-mind is Full in this Transfiguring process, Divine Transformation begins, wherein the deeper (or psychic, subtler mental, and root-egoic) dimensions of the body-mind are Infused with that same unqualified "Brightness" of Divine Being. This Transformation spontaneously yields extraordinary psycho-physical signs, such as the capability to heal, physical longevity, mental genius, and the profound manifestation of true Wisdom and selfless Love.

Such Divinization is not to be confused with the evolutionary Spiritual processes awakened via advanced Yogic meditation, which may yield apparently similar psycho-physical results or expressions, but which are still founded on the ego's exploitation of the Divine Spirit-Energy.

In the phase of Divine Indifference all attention and the whole body-mind are brought to most profound rest in the "Brightness" of the Divine Self, and the Realizer Freely Radiates universal Heart-Blessing, but spontaneously Free of even Enlightened concern for (or interest in) conditional objects, relations, and states.

In the Way of the Heart, and as Demonstrated by Sri Da Avabhasa, such Divine Indifference stands in contrast to the asceticism that motivates much of the traditional practice of strategic dissociation from the states and relations of the body-mind. Divine Indifference is the transition to the culminating phase of Divine Self-Realization, which is Divine Translation, or, as Heart-Master Da Avabhasa also calls it, "Outshining".

The four phases of the Yoga of Divine Enlightenment are discussed fully by Heart-Master Da in chapters 43 and 44 of *The Dawn Horse Testament*.

CHAPTER 6

Death, Sleep, and Meditation

a Talk by Da Avabhasa
October 9, 1980

DEVOTEE: Heart-Master Da, You have Said that we should be able to give ourselves up to death with the same pleasure with which we give ourselves up to sleep. It seems to me that many people die very gracefully, after having lived a full life, without being worn out and having to die. Such a death is not a sign of Divine Enlightenment, I know, but it seems natural to the body that has lived its full term and has remained relatively unaberrated.

SRI DA AVABHASA: The body need not even live its full term. You simply must be disposed to the naturalness of surrender and be happy to give yourself up to Whatever it is that is causing your existence. If death is necessary, you should be able to die gracefully even if you are not old.

DEVOTEE: The traditions are full of accounts of people who chose the time and occasion of their death.

SRI DA AVABHASA: Such people become aware of their death, at least when the appropriate time has come, but they do not arbitrarily decide to die.

Likewise, just as you must be able to surrender into sleep at night, in the waking state you must also be able to give up bodily consciousness, to enter into a dreamlike state and then to pass beyond it. You too should be able to enter into the Samadhi[1] of simply abandoning the functional

---

1. "Samadhi", in Sanskrit, means "placed together". It indicates concentration, equanimity, and balance, and it is traditionally used to denote various exalted states that appear in the context of esoteric meditation and Realization.

   In the course of God-Realizing practice, various Samadhis may arise, in life, and at the time of one's death. The ultimate Samadhi is Sahaj Samadhi, the unbroken Samadhi of the seventh stage of life, which must necessarily occur if the Way of the Heart is to be fulfilled.

conditions with which you are ordinarily fitfully associated. Thus, your meditative feeling-Contemplation of Me must develop to the point that you can sit down and "die"—sit down and give up the body, give up the mind, relax all dependence on body and mind, all feeling of fixed and necessary association with psycho-physical states, relations, environments. Just relax beyond them and let them all fall away.

Death itself is a dimension of meditation. It is not that in meditation you learn how to die, but death is a form of meditation, a form of the practice that you, as My devotee, and as a practitioner of the Way of the Heart, have engaged throughout your life. Sleep is also a form of meditation, or surrender. Death is an example of what you should have been doing all along in the waking state as well as in the ordinary daily transitions out of the waking state, such as sleep and meditation. Once you are comfortably related to the process of abandoning physical and mental states, then you have conquered much of what you fear about death, because that fear is related to the inability to surrender the body.

You have learned how to sleep, just as you have learned how to meditate. You also have learned how to die. You know exactly what the process of death is, insofar as it relates to the body and the loss of ordinary self-awareness. What there is beyond that, of course, is great and mysterious, but in any case it is given to you, not claimed and created by you. You must unlearn the fear of death by becoming responsible for bodily surrender while alive. Then all the unconscious roots of your psychotic fear of death are undone, and you stop hallucinating, and even chronically creating, anxiety.

You should know full well that you can surrender bodily, because you go to sleep every night. You should know that you can also surrender bodily in the waking state without becoming sleepy and somewhat stupefied. In meditative practice, one relaxes the body just as when going to sleep at night, but one remains conscious. The body becomes completely relaxed, and a sublime balance of energy comes over it. You may feel a tingling in the body. The breath slows, and soon you stop noticing the breath at all. You may even feel that your heartbeat has stopped. That realization may make you jerk yourself back to ordinary waking consciousness, just as when you go to sleep at night sometimes you jerk yourself awake. It is at that point, when you have noticed that perhaps the heartbeat is stopping, that you jolt back into your hold on the body.

In meditation, however, you should be able to pass beyond that point without losing consciousness, at least a few times, so that you can observe the mechanism of the loss of bodily consciousness. Precisely that happens in death, and nothing else. The central nervous system relaxes all the tension in the autonomic nervous system so that the conditional being observes the phenomena of the central nervous system and then passes beyond them. Ultimately, in meditation, you can go beyond all the psycho-physical states of the nervous system altogether. To do that at least once through ascended meditation changes something in your understanding forever, because you have already died in the fullest sense, you have passed out of the body-mind, and that passing has not diminished your existence. Quite the contrary, it has made possible the Realization of an Unqualified Condition of existence. The conditional being, then, is Happy and quite relieved to no longer suffer the impingement of psycho-physical independence.[2]

While you live in this realm of changes, however, you are tending to be uptight and contracted, because you are forgetting to surrender. Therefore, you must unlearn this contraction and Realize your True Condition. Then you will voluntarily and spontaneously give up the body-mind. The Fullness of Realization is simply that giving up, that absolute surrender, in which one no longer keeps a hold on the body-mind. Such is Sahaj Samadhi,[3] or the "Natural" State. It is not holding on. It is not defining one's existence. It is to be at rest in That Which is Eternal. Until you give yourself up to that Destiny, you must see that this life is temporary, changing, and unnecessary. Then allow existence to be sublimed by the Divine Being. Allow it to change, to pass away, to do whatever is its term to do.

2. In this passage Da Avabhasa is referring to the Realization of fifth stage conditional Nirvikalpa Samadhi. "Nirvikalpa" means "without form". Hence, "Nirvikalpa Samadhi" means literally "formless ecstasy". Traditionally this state is the final goal of the many schools of Yogic practice.

Fifth stage conditional Nirvikalpa Samadhi is a temporary Realization of the ascent of attention beyond all conditional manifestation into the formless Matrix of the Divine Light infinitely above the body, the mind, and the world. Like all the forms of Samadhi that may be Realized previous to Divine Self-Realization, it is a suspension of attention, produced by manipulation of attention and of the body-mind, and it is thus incapable of being maintained when attention returns, as it inevitably does, to the states of the body-mind.

3. The Hindi word "sahaj" (Sanskrit: "sahaja") literally means "together born", or "coincident", and it is extrapolated to mean "natural", even "innate". Sri Da Avabhasa uses the term to indicate the Coincidence (in the case of Divine Self-Realization) of the Transcendental (and Inherently Spiritual) Divine Reality with empirical, conditional reality—the inherent, or native, and thus truly "Natural" State of Being. The "Naturalness" of Divine Self-Realization, or Sahaj Samadhi, is that it is entirely Free, unforced, and effortless, consonant with the Nature of Divine Being (Itself), Which is Self-Existing, Self-Radiant, and always already the case.

Sahaj Samadhi stands in contrast to all Samadhis previous to Perfect Divine Awakening, which always depend upon a strategic effort of the un-"Natural" self-contraction, or motion of attention, to create a temporary psycho-physical state of balance and equanimity which admits a momentary intuition of Divine Freedom.

CHAPTER 7

Going beyond Fear

a Talk by Da Avabhasa
February 8, 1980

SRI DA AVABHASA: Is it not true that at some level of the body-mind you are always feeling anxiety, or an underlying sense of fear, always meditating on death and bad possibility? Yes. And in such a mood you are constantly injecting the toxic signals of this mood of fear into the serum, the stream, the water, of your own body. Activated as an automaticity by your mood of anxiety, fear releases the chemicals secreted by the hypothalamus and other endocrine glands. Then, as a reflection of this activated mechanism in the body, thoughts of death and bad possibility arise to the mind, and, in response to these chronically fearful thoughts, you recondition the bloodstream again with more negative chemistry! The usual man or woman lives always in a chronic state of fear, committed to egoic "self-possession" (or self-absorption)[1] and meditating on self-contraction.

The mechanism of fear is a contraction, like the reflex that occurs when the hand touches fire. The mechanism of fear is as useful to the body-mind as the reflex that keeps you from getting burned. But it is an arbitrary mechanism, not deep in your consciousness somewhere, but just a superficial little mechanism at the peripheral levels of the nervous system to save you from being attacked by a wild lion. How often are you attacked by a wild lion these days?

1. Conventionally, "self-possessed" means possessed of oneself—or with full control (calmness, or composure) of one's feelings, impulses, habits, and actions. Sri Da Avabhasa uses the term to indicate the state of being possessed by one's egoic self, or controlled by chronically self-referring (or egoic) tendencies of attention, feeling, thought, desire, and action. Thus, unless (in every moment) body, emotion, desire, thought, separate and separative self, and all attention are actively and completely surrendered, one is egoically "self-possessed", even when exhibiting personal control of one's feelings, habits, and actions.

The devotional practice of feeling-Contemplation of Heart-Master Da is the principal Means Given (by Grace) to practitioners of the Way of the Heart, whereby they may responsively (and, thus, by Grace) surrender, forget, and transcend egoic "self-possession".

Fear is just an ordinary mechanism that you must master, an attitude of the body. It is something that you are doing. It has no ultimate philosophical significance. You can breathe and feel and relax beyond it. You need take nothing into account philosophically. Just breathe and feel and relax beyond it. Just do not introduce that chemistry into the biological stream or the stream of water in your own body. Then you may look at what is before you and make philosophy!

Observe the cat, for instance, who uses fear to control threatening events. The cat is neither addicted to fear nor existing as fear, as you tend to be. In contrast to the cat—and almost all vital creatures, by the way—the human being is addicted to psychological fear. Human beings have transformed the mechanism of fear that is natural to the vital state of any animal into a chronic response of the physical being. The animal's sudden moment of fearful excitement is stimulated chemically for a specific purpose, but your chronic fear is chemical excitement toward no purpose. Fear is just a recoil, but you tend to prolong its effectiveness, as if waiting indefinitely to withdraw a finger from the flame.

Fear is one of the possible states you may experience, but it is not your natural state. Only when you enter into right relationship to all your possible states, including fear, are you able to realize your natural state. In your natural state, you are like the cat, which, although it may become afraid and roll into a ball when it is attacked, is not at all chronically afraid. The Very Divine Being, the Eternally Living One, Which exists as the cat and as every conditionally manifested being, is not contracted by fear. And just as the cat has not accomplished any great, profound, philosophical cycle of investigations of the universe to be free of fear, so you need have no great knowledge to be liberated from your fear.

You can be free of fear in this very moment, in any moment, even in a moment when some degree of fear seems conventionally appropriate. Fear collapses attention. Therefore, even when fear might seem appropriate, it is still better to be without fear, so that you may have complete attention in the moment to deal with the threat. Fear is plainly and simply inappropriate, except in the flash of comprehending imminent danger. But even then, in the very next moment, you are dealing with the danger rather than with the fear. Fear has only the most minute significance as a practical necessity in your life, and yet you are completely overwhelmed by it! You have made fear so chronic a mood that now you interpret your existence, even all existence, through the medium of that fear. Consequently you wonder if you are annihilated at death and if this life is just a terrible machine.

I have often mentioned to you the passage from the *Upanishads*[2] that says, "Wherever there is an other, fear arises." No demons, no bows and arrows, no nuclear war—only an other, only the sense of otherness, need arise to give rise to fear. And how does the sense of otherness develop? Through the self-contraction, whereby one feels separated from what one observes, therefore limited by it, and thus limited to what one can seem to be at this moment. Feel mortal and you feel incapable of flow, or change, or freedom. There is no ultimate metaphysical means for getting rid of fear, no ultimate knowledge. The alternative to fear is not some great answer that will ultimately prevent your being chronically and mortally afraid, which people are in general. Such knowledge is not even possible. The alternative is to understand fear as an ordinary mechanism of the body beyond which you can, and should, in any moment feel and breathe. You should be resting in your natural state, feeling and breathing whole bodily into the universal field of natural life-energy in which you are existing, not full of fear, doubt, contraction, becoming a black hole, another universe unto yourself into which everything is sucked, like Lake Narcissus!

So—you must be completely free of fear as an ordinary matter. Your state from moment to moment must be utterly free of fear. It is not at all possible to pass through the fundamental transformations of genuine Spiritual life until you have transcended fear. You may certainly have all kinds of experiences, but Perfectly self-transcending God-Realization depends entirely on the transcendence of fear.

You need not become Divinely Enlightened first before you can overcome fear. You need not become absorbed in some extraordinary state of Blessed God-Communion before you can be free of fear. To be free of fear is a natural and human capability. You must become sensitive to yourself in your fear, in your anxiety, out of which you build so much of your subjective and negative occupation every day. You must become sensitive to that process and feel just how it arises as a contraction in the nervous system and the brain.

As you begin to see how fear works as a mechanical process, you will also feel that it arises without external cause. You will begin to notice that it clicks into and out of operation in a range of moods from anxiety to terror in every moment of your existence, as a reaction to everything

---

2. The *Upanishads*, of which there are over two hundred, are principal Scriptures of Hindu esotericism. They record the wisdom of non-dualism in its different phases and aspects. The oldest Scriptures of this genre date back to the eighth century B.C.E., while the most recent *Upanishads* belong to this century.

that is present to your awareness—as if life were a question you had to answer before attaining the right to be free of fear. Fear is a rolling process in the body, a constant bodily tension, a permanent recoil or flight. You can also observe, through the practices I have Given you in the Way of the Heart—of Contemplating Me with devotion, and of feeling and breathing the natural life-energy, and, in due course, the Spiritual Life-Current—that fear is transcended in every moment. Thus, it is not by means of a long and complicated process, like slaying a dragon, that fear is overcome, but through natural, tacit, devotional surrender to Me, your Sat-Guru, and, thus and thereby, to the Divine Person.

Feeling-Contemplation of Me is a natural process of surrendering the body. The effort to surrender makes you fear, however, because effort is a form of self-meditation. But when you Contemplate Me with feeling-devotion, you are free of the contraction of your egoic self and thus naturally free of fear. Although there may be moments when fear and recoil are appropriate in the incidents of life, you remain sensitive to your response to them, so that you can deal with the events of life creatively. But the mood of fear does not become chronic, even in the midst of the problem-solving occasions of daily life.

DEVOTEE: Heart-Master Da, I have noticed that when fear becomes so overwhelming that I realize I would be better off not feeling it, I tend to surrender naturally.

SRI DA AVABHASA: Even then you are in a state of fear. You are only resisting terror. To surrender and pass through fear into Divine Love-Bliss is another matter. It is true that in extreme conditions people sometimes are thrust into a state that at least feels something like the Love-Blissful Radiance of Divine Being. But, in the ordinary moments of living, you are always passing into the mood of fear in one or another of its qualities, transforming your life altogether into life-negative moods and bewildered activities. You actually exist in the midst of that confrontation in every moment.

Those who become serious about real life while alive become sensitive to the quality of existence in every moment, unlike the usual man or woman who must lose everything again and again and again just to get a simple little lesson about ordinary life. Such a lesson of course can happen to you or to anyone, but do you need it? Are the terrible lessons really necessary? Is a horrible death necessary? Need you think, "Oh, the daily news could happen to me"? Or does your way of life control events and protect you from arbitrary and untimely death?

Practitioners in the traditions of Yoga seek to control the events of life by aligning themselves with the Living Divine and observing the course of events with free and conscious intention, minimizing their associations, transcending their obsessions, and breathing themselves into a constant condition of equanimity, and as a rule rather than on occasion. They look to determine the hour of their death and their destiny after death.

Certainly death is to be investigated, as one's entire life is, but is fear the appropriate medium of consciousness for examining such things? You think perhaps that if you must be afraid of anything, it should be death. But is fear the appropriate association with death? Does the body call for fear as the form of its relationship to death? Is this not an arbitrary choice of your own? In the realm of cosmic Nature, fear is not the emotional instrument for the passage through death. On the contrary, the body calls for surrender at death, for permission to make the transition. Just exactly what is the purpose, then, of this fear on which everyone is meditating?

DEVOTEE: Heart-Master Da, I have read that the relationship to fear of human beings today is quite different from that of people of earlier and more primitive times, who perceived threats directly and therefore could respond directly. Today human beings do not perceive so directly the threat of death in everyday life. People today feel threatened, but they perceive threat only subliminally, and, not being able to respond, they feel anxious.

SRI DA AVABHASA: Yes. More primitive people are afraid of what might kill them, but you are constantly afraid of death itself. Yet there is no great thing to be discovered about fear other than how it works as a mechanism. It has no philosophical consequences, no philosophical significance or depth. It is a very simple motion in the nervous system of the body, a motion that you can feel. You can feel how it arises, you can feel how it works as a mechanism, and you can feel and breathe through and beyond it at any time that you choose to do so. Once you realize that you need only enter into feeling-Contemplation of Me (and, thus and thereby, of the Divine Person) in any moment, you will never be afraid again. Until you realize how the mechanism of fear works, realize that you really need not feel fear anymore, you will be subject to all kinds of threats, and your "consideration" of death, which should be an untroubled examination of a natural process, will be aberrated by fear.

To transcend fear is a very ordinary responsibility. Fear has no content or necessity. Looked at in itself, it is just a chemical signal in the peripheral brain, a reflex in the nervous system that you have allowed to exercise itself into a chronic reflex. It is not mysterious. Nor is it inherent to your state of awareness or your state of existence. To transcend fear is thus not a psychological matter at all, but a matter of surrendering bodily, breathing and feeling into the natural life-energy that obviously exists. There is no doubt whatsoever that such natural energy exists—is there? No one can possibly doubt this. It is perfectly obvious to everyone!

Your practice of feeling-Contemplation of Me (and, thus and thereby, of the Divine Person Revealed to you by Me) must become so simple that you are not afraid, not negative, not toxifying the body-mind with adolescent psychology, but practicing self-surrender, self-forgetting, and self-transcendence with a will. Allow what is now fear in you to become the will to Divine Love-Bliss. Convert the energy that is fear and to which you have been devoting your life. Convert it, since fear no longer has any purpose, to the will to Divine Love-Bliss, the will to look and feel and be and act completely Happy.

Fear does not radiate. Fear contracts. As you sit here now, feel your anxiety, your fear of death—if after this entire discussion you are still afraid! Once having contacted the fear, just radiate the feeling. Feel it so intensely that you shine with it. Once you locate it, the feeling ceases to be fear. It becomes free feeling-energy. What you identify as fear is the natural energy of the individual being contracting upon itself and causing an implosive and unpleasant pressure. Do not force the natural energy to contract upon itself through reactivity. Allow it to be naturally present without contraction. Its will is to be so. No fear exists in it, nor do you engage the mechanism of fear when you are Happy, free of the self-contraction.

The discussion of the practice of Spiritual life is not appropriately associated with the "consideration" of fear and ridding oneself of the fear of death. You must deal with fear before you presume to take up the Spiritual Way, as a condition of your "consideration" of Spiritual matters, just as you must transcend emotional dissociation before you engage human intimacy and sexuality. Fear, like unlove, should not be part of a philosophical "consideration". While in the disposition of fear, you should not be "considering" the Self-Existing and Self-Radiant Divine Being and the life of Perfectly self-transcending God-Realization. See your own contraction and become responsible for that first. Then you will have free attention for what is directly before you. Otherwise, fear will only motivate you to acquire experience, and you will learn nothing.

Examine your own life—you have many ideas about God and the Godly life, and yet you are afraid. And you look to religion for a way to become not afraid, perhaps hoping for a great vision to assure you that after death you will go to heaven, where you will be with your loved ones and never again be afraid. You believe that a religious experience will transform your fear.

But fear is locked into your consciousness, and you cannot get rid of it, because you are viewing it in the wrong way. You are viewing fear as a problem that must be solved. You do not see how fear itself is arising. You only see its effects, and you make philosophy out of something that is otherwise very ordinarily native to you.

Fear is simply your inability to relax, to be surrendered, to feel and breathe fully into the Great Accomplishing Power in Which you are now inhering and Which is now Alive as you. Just surrender into That, allow It to be whatever It wants to be, whatever It is fundamentally. Instead, at present, you live in fear in the midst of It, you have a fearful relationship to It, and you have fearful knowledge of It. If you will surrender fear at its base, see it as an ordinary reaction over which you have complete control, then, already free, you can "consider" the nature of existence, even of death.

The universe is a Mystery, but fear is not the appropriate response to Mystery. Fear is perhaps the appropriate response to the attacking lion, and, even then, one's response should not be prolonged and debilitating fear, but sudden and great strength. Fear is not intended to be your chronic state. You only suffer it chronically because you are not responsible for yourself. You do not simply rest in That Which is controlling you. You will not surrender to That Which has brought you into being and Which is sustaining you at this present time and Which will still be the case after you are dead. You will not relax completely into That. You act as if there is something wrong about such surrender, as if you must always be on guard to defend yourself. Thus, you live in tension, egoic "self-possession", and fear, cut off from your natural state, cut off from Love-Blissful inherence in the Living Process.

Are you afraid of anything more than you are afraid of fear? Even death, for instance—you would not mind it nearly so much if only you could not be afraid of it! You say you do not want to die, but on the other hand you would not care about it at all if you were not afraid of it. What you are most afraid of, fundamentally afraid of, is fear. You are afraid that you will be afraid, and you mull over events in your mind, such as death, afraid you are going to become terribly afraid. Am I right? Therefore, all the time you are a little bit anxious because you never know when you are going to become afraid! Something frightening, a terrible death experience, for example, could happen at any time now, to yourself and to people you know.

You are, therefore, always afraid that you will be afraid, while at the same time you are afraid already. Fear is an automaticity you create, like the counting you perhaps do habitually in your mind. You have little habits like this, don't you? People have all kinds of tricks that they do with the mind when they lack an object on which to put their attention. Likewise, people do all kinds of things with their emotions when they do not feel the Living Divine Being. Fear, fear of being afraid, fear in advance, becoming fear now, is an automaticity, like not stepping on the cracks in the sidewalk.

You can rid yourself of your emotional wandering, your fearful contraction, now. I am here to Talk to you about God! Drop all the garbage that you want to spend the rest of your life overcoming. Drop it this very day, or this week, certainly! You can take care of it very quickly if you are serious about Spiritual life. If you are not serious about Spiritual life, then you will go on being terrified and anxious all your life. But if you seriously want to deal with your fear, just "consider" it as we have done, and "consider" the practice of the Way of the Heart that I have Given you. That would be sufficient.

CHAPTER 8

What Is More Than Wonderful Is Not Threatened

by Da Avabhasa
November 16, 1978

Fear of death is fear of surrender to Infinity.
Learn to surrender, to exist at Infinity while alive, and fear of death dissolves.

Fear of death is fear of the Unknown.

Realize the Eternal Unknowability of the Totality of Existence, and fear of death is transcended in the Feeling beyond Wonder.

If Happiness, or Freedom, depends on the Answer to the Question, then there can be no Happiness, or Freedom.

The Question cannot be satisfactorily or finally Answered.

For one who Abides at Infinity, Happy and Free, at ease with his or her Ultimate (or Divine) Ignorance,[1] the Question and Answer are equally unnecessary.

What began will come to an end.

What is More than Wonderful is not threatened.

The Process of the Totality of Existence is Transcendental, Inherently Spiritual, and necessarily Divine, and It is Eternal.

---

1. "Divine Ignorance" is Sri Da Avabhasa's term for the fundamental awareness of Being Itself, prior to all sense of separation from or knowledge about anything that arises. As He Proposes, "No matter what arises, you do not know what a single thing is." By "Ignorance" He means heart-felt participation in the universal Condition of inherent Mystery, not mental dullness or the fear-based wonder or awe felt by the subjective ego in relation to unknown objects. Divine Ignorance is the intuition of Consciousness Itself, transcending all knowledge that is cognized and all experience that is perceived by the self-contracted ego-"I".

For a detailed discussion of Sri Da Avabhasa's Wisdom-Teaching on Divine Ignorance, see chapter nineteen of *The Dawn Horse Testament*.

Only a fraction of the Whole can pass away in any moment, since only a fraction of the Whole appears in any moment.

Therefore, the Heart Itself is always already Full of Love and More than Wonder.

"I" is the body-mind, the fraction of the Whole that is now appearing and will soon disappear.

"I" must be surrendered to the Heart,[2] to the Whole, Which is Infinity, and Love, and More (and More) than even Wonder knows.

---

2. The Heart is God, the Divine Self, the Divine Reality. Divine Self-Realization is associated with the opening of the primal psycho-physical seat of Consciousness and attention in the right side of the heart, hence the term "the Heart" for the Divine Self.

    Sri Da Avabhasa distinguishes the Heart as the ultimate Reality from all the psycho-physiological functions of the organic, bodily heart, as well as from the subtle heart, traditionally known as the "anahata (or heart) chakra". The Heart is not in the right side of the human heart, nor is it in or limited to the human heart as a whole, or to the body-mind, or to the world. Rather, the human heart and body-mind and the world exist in the Heart, the Divine Being.

CHAPTER 9

Surrender and the Process of Grace

a Talk by Da Avabhasa
November 9, 1980

D EVOTEE: Heart-Master Da, on two occasions when I have come close to death through sickness, I realized a kind of ecstatic release of the body and the continuation of conscious awareness. I have had the certainty that I survive death since I was about fifteen or sixteen years old, but I also have the feeling that if I were confronted with just the right circumstance, I could pass into complete terror at the prospect of death. It seems there is a big difference between the kind of certainty I have experienced and the sadhana[1] You Describe of one's conscious passage through death, which seems to be the only thing that really liberates one from the fear of death.

SRI DA AVABHASA: At one level of psychic perception, you realize that mortal, physical existence is not the end, but only one level, of existence, and that you are existing in a multidimensional condition, of which the physical is only one dimension. Therefore, death is really a transformation, even physically, and not an ending. And you can observe this.

But, on the other hand, survival of death is not necessarily inherently pleasurable, any more than being physically alive is inherently pleasurable. Life lived as a Spiritual process is inherently pleasurable, but merely physical life can be very disturbed, threatened, and limited.

---

1. The word "sadhana", which is Sanskrit for "discipline", traditionally denotes practices directed toward religious or Spiritual goals. Sadhana in the Way of the Heart is not action to attain Truth or any state or condition, but, rather, action that expresses a present intuition of Truth, in conscious Communion with Sri Da Avabhasa, the Realizer, the Revealer, and the Revelation of that Truth.

Surviving death as consciousness with psychic form can be associated with all kinds of limitations, and it can even be terrifying, disgusting, monotonous, and oppressive. Everything about psychic existence can be just as terrible as everything about being physically alive.

It is ordinary and useful to observe, by being psychically awake, the larger features of the process of your existence, and to know that the physical is not the termination of existence but that you are involved in a process that precedes physical birth and continues after physical death. It is good to achieve this certainty, which can be realized by anyone as an ordinary matter. Even so, more than this is required to fulfill your life, because any one of a number of possibilities can pertain after you are dead, just as while you are alive. It is by your disposition, your conscious involvement in this endlessly transforming process, that you dispose yourself toward conditions of existence. You control your experiencing by your religious or Spiritual practice, your attitude, the content that you exercise, consciously or unconsciously.

Therefore, it is also essential to become responsible for this content, to become responsible for the entire process, or, even better said, to responsibly submit yourself to What is Conditioning—in the most profound and most benign sense of the word—this process. Only by such submission is Something inherently More than Wonderful demonstrated as the actual conditions of existence.

DEVOTEE: Heart-Master Da, it has been my presumption that true practice of religion or Spirituality is sufficient to confront the process of death in a way that is liberating, or at least not obstructing to the process. But are You Saying that if I am not psychically awake in the concrete terms You have Described, I represent an obstruction in the process of death?

SRI DA AVABHASA: Whether or not you represent an obstruction depends on the force of your Spiritual practice. If your presumption of the Divine Reality is without complication and you can simply surrender to Me as the Divinely Self-Realized True Heart-Master, then you need not have any psychic awareness of life after death and all kinds of magical psychic visions while you are alive, because the force of your surrender combines you with the process of Grace, and with the Source-Condition of all arising conditions, and, therefore, you are fulfilling the Divine Law and you are rightly oriented to the Divine Reality.

Awakening to the psychic content of existence is a secondary process, but it is also ordinary and natural, and there is no reason that it should not develop in some basic form. There are no absolute taboos against it. It is as ordinary as enjoying clarity of attention to gross phenomena. Such attention is not absolutely necessary for Divine Happiness, because to awaken psychically to the conditions of existence is just to see things as they are, as a machine, and not necessarily to surrender that machine into its Source-Condition.

You can have all kinds of psychic awareness and still be self-bound and not fulfill the Law that is God-Realizing and Liberating. On the other hand, whether you have or do not have psychic awareness of any significant kind, if, through feeling-Contemplation of Me, you simply surrender with the whole force of your being to the Divine Person, then you are fulfilling the Law, and you need not be concerned about whether you have psychic or mental certainty about how the universe works. In that disposition, you have tacitly presumed that the whole thing is immortal and eternal and working somehow or other, and so let it work. Your business is to surrender to Me (and, thus and thereby, to the Divine Person). If you fulfill this primary Law, but really do it on the basis of the tacit certainty of Spiritual Awakening, rather than on the basis of a merely psychic awakening, then this Spiritual certainty is obviously sufficient, because it is primary.

Nevertheless, it is an ordinary capability to be psychically awake, just as it is ordinary to be physically awake. Therefore, you should exercise yourself to the fullest while you are alive, and see what there is to see, while also fulfilling the Law in Spiritual terms, which is your primary obligation.

DEVOTEE: Heart-Master Da, it seems that to inspect past lives and have awareness of them is to take responsibility for greater patterns of action and reaction and karma. To do this, it seems, has value and is worthy of attention for the sake of releasing ourselves from tendencies. But is this a secondary obligation?

SRI DA AVABHASA: Of course it is secondary. Through the medium of psychiatry, for example, people may regress and discover how patterns were established since their birth in this lifetime through action-reaction in their present lifetime. Such regression may realize a certain freeing up of energy and attention, but in every present moment you must transcend the fundamental contraction of the conditional being. If you do that, then to discover the events of the past that may be controlling you is secondary and even unnecessary, because the events are not controlling you anymore. You are presently responsible in direct relationship to the Divine.

Remembering past lives is an extension of the same process of regression, and it is secondary for the same reason, although it is ordinary enough. If you are psychically awake, it is quite natural to observe the content of your existence at the deeper levels of psychic awareness. You can systematically regress for some therapeutic purpose, but you also quite casually and in an ordinary way remember things all the time. If you are psychically awake, you need not systematically try to recover past lifetimes, because observing past lifetimes is an ordinary matter of casually seeing something in a dream or in the deep psyche while awake.

DEVOTEE: Heart-Master Da, is there a similar fear in the psychic worlds to the fear of death in this gross world? Is the psyche afraid of dying, too?

SRI DA AVABHASA: At the level of the psyche, it is not so much a fear of dying, because there is a presumption of continuousness that is not so strongly present at the physical level. The fear at the level of the psyche is fear of certain conditions, fear of madness, fear of being confronted by terrifying phenomena. At the physical level you fear termination of physical life. At the psychic level you fear madness and confinement by unchanging terribleness. The fear of encountering these dark inventions acts as a lock, a barrier, against psychic awakening. The same kind of barrier exists not only to your perceiving things in higher psychic terms, but to your just becoming conscious of your subconscious and unconscious motivations, your deeper memory, and your feelings of pain and strong emotions even in this present lifetime.

Human beings tend not to become psychic because of the fears that are operative at the psychic level, which are different from those that are operative at the physical level. Your physical participation in life is retarded by fears associated with mortality and pain. Being contracted in the face of those possibilities, you become relatively self-involved and not very energetic and loving in your human physical relations. At the psychic level, you are likewise retarded by a whole other dimension of fear, so that you confine yourself to a rather superficial consciousness and a superficial level of feeling. In the psyche, you fear being confronted not by pain and mortality, which are features of fear at the physical level, but by torment, dissociation, horrors of all kinds, bewilderment, and loss of relations.

The conditional being is contracted upon itself by fear, and, therefore, it will not embrace the field of psycho-physical relations. The same kind of prohibition is acting against your psychic awakening that is acting against your physical happiness and energetic association with others.

DEVOTEE: I had an experience a while ago when I went to sleep. I seemed to be confronted by terrible images in a kind of hallucinatory world that was constantly changing. There was no way I could find my sense of individual self in the midst of all that. You came into the dream and Said, "You see? In this psychic condition, there is even less separation between what arises and your apparent self, so you feel immediately and directly. You do not feel any distance between you and what is arising, and it is very terrifying." And You Said, "Now you must wake up in this condition. Otherwise, this is what you will confront when you die." It seemed much more terrible than anything I have ever experienced physically. I felt completely just tossed around in the realm of endless bodies and images. I have something of a feeling of what it might be like if I am not awake in the psychic dimension, if I do not awaken from the psychic sense of confinement.

SRI DA AVABHASA: The function of the ego, or the separate and separative self, is to prevent experience. The ego is a device. The ego is "Narcissus". The ego is contraction. By participating in this contraction, you separate yourself and make yourself immune to the field of events. The field of events exists in many dimensions, but by presuming this separate and separative self—which is not an entity but an action, or contraction—you dissociate yourself from the field in which the body-mind exists, from every level of that pattern, every dimension of it. You prevent experience. You confine yourself to merely existing. You immunize yourself against phenomena.

Now, this is the common state of people. This is the fundamental state that I have always Addressed in you all. This is your disposition. You are trying to feel good as this egoic self. You are trying to save this separate and separative self. You are trying to acquire for it a good future, but that egoic self, that thing to which you are constantly referring, must be interfered with if you are to Realize Divine Happiness and a "good future".

This egoic self is not just the apparent one you call "I". This egoic self is a contraction, something you are adding to existence. It is a machine, a kind of robot, an invention of your own existence that is interfering with your existence.

You must release this machine, this contraction. By doing so, you enter into vulnerable intimacy with every level of the total field of existence, physically, yes, in terms of all the relations physical life involves, but also psychically, in terms of every dimension in which you can participate consciously.

You are natively vulnerable. But "Narcissus" is trying to become invulnerable. The purpose of the egoic self is to be invulnerable. Yet by becoming invulnerable, you dissociate yourself from the whole pattern of existence. In effect, by defining your existence, by becoming an egoic self, you cease to exist. You retard yourself in fear, which is the basic mood of this self-contraction.

Divine Help, or Divine Grace, Moves when there is an awakening whereby this separate and separative self is released and you accept vulnerability, or continuousness with the dimension within which each dimension of you is arising dependently. But it is not such vulnerability alone that you accept. By releasing the egoic self into its field and no longer contracting and defending it, you are associated with everything openly and, therefore, vulnerably, because you can now be affected in various ways.

Even so, the gesture of release is not made for its own sake or for the sake of participating vulnerably in events. That is just a secondary development of release or surrender. You are not surrendering to conditional events. You are surrendering into the Source-Condition of the egoic self, the Source-Condition of the field in which the egoic self exists. The primary aspect of this awakening, this release of the egoic self, is Communion with the Transcendental (and Inherently Spiritual) Divine Being.

Through the surrender that is Divine Communion, you are restored to the entire field of conditions. Therefore, you are awake in it, affected by it, but also active and effective within it. But the field of conditions is just the plastic that is being transformed. It is real, but secondary. It is itself ultimately controlled by the purpose of self-surrender, which is to live in the Divine, the Source-Condition of events, the Source-Condition of the egoic self, the Source-Condition of everything, to be vulnerable not merely to the field of events but to the Divine in Which the field of events is arising.

You must transcend the egoic self, yes, and, thereby, enter into relationship with the total pattern of manifestation. But you must most fundamentally surrender and accept your dependence on the Divine Being, accept your vulnerability to the Divine. Once you become vulnerable to the Divine, then all kinds of Help begin to appear. Your life becomes transformable. You become awake and able to participate in it, no longer retarded, no longer full of fear. Only by realizing this disposition of self-surrender do you fulfill the Law. Then your life begins to achieve the order that is in God rather than the order that is valued for its own sake.

In that process of surrendering, you are vulnerable to the whole affair of Spiritual life, and you must endure much purification and many encounters with things that are difficult. A kind of agony is related to the restoration of balance and to the regeneration of Fullness, or Love-Bliss. But the process of regeneration becomes tolerable when you are released from the point of view of the egoic self and you accept fully the "Point of View" of the Divine Reality.

In that acceptance, in that alliance with Grace, which you cannot understand ultimately at the level of the mind anyway, wisdom arises, and the natural observation of conditions that are not merely physical arises. All kinds of other conditions reflected at the level of the psyche begin to appear in the natural course of your daily life. The psychic aspect of your life begins to become much more full, whereas now, at least in the waking state, you are confined in a very petty way to a superficial verbal kind of mind from which the psychic and emotional fullness of life is almost totally absent. In most people, only certain shocks bring out anything deeper than the content of the verbal mind. But once you enter into the Spiritual Process, quite naturally—in other words, without your strategically pursuing it—there occurs the awakening of the psychic dimension of your life.

It is good for you to observe that you may in some sense be limiting that awakening by maintaining a conventional presumption or by just fixedly being involved in the social false-face of the superficial thinker. It is good to observe this as you are beginning to develop the natural process of self-surrender. You must observe the taboos and conventions to which you confine yourself, and, instead, allow yourself to swoon in meditation and in moment to moment existence. Allow yourself to be more deeply conscious. Allow the natural flow of images to develop in your consciousness.

If you will observe how your egoically defined consciousness operates ordinarily, you will see that you tend to confine your moment to moment consciousness to a kind of verbal progress. You are basically thinking in verbal terms. There may be a flash of visualized memory or a little bit of imagining here and there, but, for the most part, when people say the mind is going on all the time, they basically mean the verbal mind, and therefore only a part of human consciousness.

Mystics, magicians, Yogis, shamans, psychics—such people are simply allowing the total mind to be operative in moment to moment existence. They have been able to relax the reflex whereby attention and conscious awareness are confined to the left-brained, verbal, outward-directed personality, so that, instead of just an endless flow of sentences, a kind of automatic verbal consciousness in the head, a visual mind begins to engage automatically.

The visual mind can become operative on many levels. For example, with your eyes open or your eyes closed right now, you can imagine a cat. Even with your eyes open, you can probably think of a cat and see it. You can call your visual mind into operation in the present moment. With eyes open or closed, you can think of a scene somewhere and visualize it right now. You are not generally tending to do that, but you see that you can do it.

That activity of calling the visual mind into play is not necessarily in itself very profound, any more than the train of verbal thinking is necessarily profound, but it can become more profound if you relax and allow the body-mind to become much more sensitive, much more open, much more profound altogether, allowing its deep resources to begin to produce phenomena that are noticeable at the level of mind.

Something like this occurs whenever you go to sleep at night. Dreams begin. In general, you have not been conditioned to prevent dreams, although a certain level of conditioning is even limiting dreams, because most people's dreams are rather superficial reflections of the lower vital stress of life. Even so, dreaming can be very profound. All kinds of marvelous perceptions can occur at the level of dreaming, including higher psychic visions and premonitions. Magical performances can occur there that begin to be reflected in the gross world of the waking state.

In the waking state, you must likewise naturally begin to allow the visual mind to perform at a deeper level. Sometimes when you have not had very much sleep, you may have a few minutes to rest. You do not really want to go to sleep because you have something you know you must do in a few minutes, but you just close your eyes, trying to rest and yet stay awake. You will notice that you may begin to hallucinate while you are still awake.

You can apply this same possibility to your daily life in general, not by going to sleep all the time, but, for instance, at least in the occasion of meditation, by permitting yourself to psychically, mentally, and physically relax into a much deeper state without losing consciousness, without going into sleep. As a result, you begin to become sensitive to psychic conditions that you tend to exclude through the automaticity of the ordinary model of your human consciousness.

Meditation serves the evolution of humanity in exactly this sense. The purpose of meditation is to associate you with conditions in the waking state through a deeper level of awareness, so that you participate in this moment of existence at a level of depth, rather than superficially because of your self-bound contraction.

Release your separate and separative self by practice of the Way of the Heart in devotional relationship to Me. Release your separate and separative self at every level. Allow your existence to become a process of surrender moment to moment, but also a process of depth and profundity, in which the body-mind is operative in a very sensitive, vulnerable, and profound manner.

CHAPTER 10

There Is No Individual self That Dies

a Talk by Da Avabhasa
December 28, 1980

SRI DA AVABHASA: Current studies of the experiences of individuals who have clinically "died" for several minutes and then revived are producing a growing literature that compiles and reports these "after-life" experiences. Such phenomena could be used as indicators of the inherently Spiritual or self-transcending process that occurs at death. However, these "after-life" phenomena are typically valued merely as signs of personal, egoic survival. Those who commonly study and write about such experiences do not rightly understand death as a process of self-change and self-transcendence in which the separate and separative, or egoic, self may dissolve.

"After-life" phenomena, then, are not signs of egoic survival. Rather, they are signs of the transformation of the conventional self, the dissolution of various aspects of the personality, and passage into a condition that is not foreknown. They are signs of something that is falling away rather than continuing.

Yet, when people return to consciousness, therefore not having completed this process, they concretize the phenomena they encountered and interpret them to mean survival of the ego. Such individuals say that they are now more easeful because they survived death. They believe that there is an afterlife in which we pass into other worlds beyond this one. But the experiences and visions they report should be understood rightly to be hallucinated phenomena that arise from the stimulation of the higher centers of the brain during the withdrawal of energy and attention from the body at death. These experiences, like those of the conventional mystic, are, no matter how consoling or sublime, nonetheless founded in ego-consciousness.

However, the greatest Spiritual Wisdom reveals that the True Self is the non-ego, the Self-Existing and Self-Radiant Divine Being, or Ultimate Reality, Which is also the Source-Condition of the phenomenal fields of self-awareness and ego-identity. Its Nature and Existence cannot be proved by appeal to phenomenal events in life or death. The True Self can only be Realized in transcendence of the process of conventional or egoic self-identification and object-differentiation.

But the actual and Prior Nature of Consciousness Itself is not what people tend to presume on the basis of the conventions of experience. The conventional activity of the born being is to presume a sense of identity, which presumption is based on the appearance of phenomena. Having been born, you perceive that there is a body-mind, a physically based self. In your un-Realized, or un-Enlightened, state, Consciousness Itself, Which is the Field of that very perception, conceives of Itself in terms of this bodily presentation. It calls Itself "I" and thinks Itself to be identical with this bodily self. The phenomena in the mental field are likewise interpreted to imply that Consciousness Itself, Which is Transcendental and Inherently Spiritual, is limited by and identical to the stream of egoic consciousness and thought.

The ego does not in fact exist. Only the mechanisms exist whereby Consciousness Itself becomes manifested. Only phenomena exist. The true Nature of the apparently individual conscious being is Transcendental and, therefore, Inherently Spiritual, or All-Pervading. It is the Divine Source-Condition, or Matrix, of all phenomenal existence, and It does not have an independent, limited existence. Consciousness Itself is not definable by the phenomena of manifestations themselves.

The Nature and Very Existence of this Ultimate Identity cannot be proven by phenomenal events. In other words, you cannot make a conventional investigation of your ordinary life in this moment and thereby prove that your so-called "personal", or apparently individual, consciousness is Spiritual and Transcendental and, therefore, now and eternally Existing Prior to the states of life and death. Likewise, you cannot appeal to "after-life" phenomena or out-of-the-body experiences to prove the Nature and Existence of the Transcendental (and Inherently Spiritual) Divine Being or Reality. All experiences define the individual conscious being in terms of phenomena.

The Divine Truth, Reality, and Condition of the conditional being can only be Realized. It cannot merely be observed and then proven through appeal to conventions of objective events. The very process to which one might appeal as a scientist or a conventional religious knower is not the process that can demonstrate the Ultimate Nature of your identity or the identity of phenomena. You must transcend that very method of conventional knowing and presuming. You must go beyond the conventional differentiation whereby you conceive of yourself as something different and separate from other conditional beings and things.

"Consider" this: You are conscious in this moment. If I look at you and call your name, it is the body-mind-self that assumes I am talking to it. But it is not the body-mind-self who is actually here. There is only One Identity here. There appear to be individual conventions of separate selves, but they are phenomenal constructs superimposed on the Divine Being. The notion that each of us is a separate identity in the ultimate sense, and therefore conditioned, limited, and controlled by the destiny of this body-mind, is false.

Thus, the reason you survive death is not that the ego is immortal. You survive death because the Ultimate Identity of all phenomena and of the apparently individuated consciousness is Transcendental, and Inherently Spiritual, and necessarily Divine. Every feature of your temporary ego-identity is itself constructed out of a universal Field of Transcendental Consciousness and Eternal Spirit-Energy. The body-mind simply arises in a universal Field, and at death it is broken up into its various parts.

Therefore, the ultimate proposition of the great sacred traditions is that there is only one Reality, the Divine Self-Condition and Identity of everything and everyone. Divine Enlightenment is the tacit and direct Realization of that Truth. Once the conditional being is established in that Realization, then you participate in the arising patterns of existence in an entirely different manner than is conventionally presumed. Then the gesture of ego-identification has no force. Only the Ultimate Identity is presumed.

The difference between ordinary individuals and Divinely Enlightened beings is that ordinary individuals identify with the conventional or phenomenal self, while Divinely Enlightened beings Identify with the Transcendental (and Inherently Spiritual) Divine Reality. This is the only difference. Thus, depending on which of those two presumptions you choose, you will live in either one of two ways. One is the usual round of obsession, fear, and seeking in which the egoic self is the actor and the meaning of the drama. The other is the way of illuminated Intelligence, Love, Freedom, Spontaneity, and Infinite Happiness. Therefore, if you are going to live as Divine Enlightenment, you must understand this phenomenal convention of the egoic self with all the mechanics of existence that you have built upon it.

Previous to such Divine Enlightenment you fear death, and, therefore, you want to discover something about death that can make you feel hopeful about surviving. That is why people like to study occult and "life-after-life" phenomena. They like to hear conventional religious stories, such as the legend that Jesus was resurrected and ascended to heaven. Whatever the factual or historical authenticity of these stories may be, they are all interpreted as hopeful signs for the ego. Thus, you will remain fascinated by death, even to the point of being relatively self-destructive, because in some sense you want to get into it, even though you fear it. You will continue to read studies about "after-life" phenomena, always hoping to hear that it has been proven to the satisfaction of both science and you personally that you are going to survive death.

However, it is not the mystery of death that you must penetrate in order to be free of fear. Rather, you must transcend this concoction of ego-stress and self-contraction while alive. You must be in a different disposition toward life altogether in order to die free of fear. Instead of presuming this ego-position, you must rest in the Transcendental (and Inherently Spiritual) Divine Reality. Then both your present existence and all its future changes and dying will be allowed very simply and naturally, much like going to sleep at night. You will not merely have gained some consoling knowledge about death. Fear does not result from the lack of such knowledge. Fear is caused by ego-stress, and it must, therefore, be transcended while alive. The Spiritual Process is a way of transcending the mechanism of fear in every moment.

I have called the process of death "easy death", because that is what it must become. The process of death must become a natural, easeful process even if you lack final knowledge of its ultimate results. Human beings in general do not have a great deal of knowledge about their present born existence, and yet they are able, at least occasionally, to live easefully and happily. You must live death in the same way. Death is a spontaneous occurrence, and you must not feel that it is the destruction of existence.

To presume the phenomenal self-position is to give cosmic Nature a stick with which to beat you over the head. It is to be a "something", and all "somethings" are inevitably confounded, changed, and dissolved. Thus, the individuated self is an unnatural rather than a native presumption. You deny cosmic Nature this stick by Realizing the Truth of your existence, by being established in the Native Condition, or Reality, Which is relaxed, uncontracted, Free, Radiant, and Full. Then events can arise and change and pass away without your being confined to fear.

If you Realize that Divinely Enlightened disposition, then you are also paradoxically energized and no longer passive. This disposition releases great energy into the psycho-physical mechanism of existence. Divine Enlightenment Divinely Transfigures the body-mind. It Divinely Transforms it, Evolves it, Awakens Wisdom, and Generates the greater Powers of existence. Likewise, all those things also change and pass away. But if the greater functions arise without stress, without clinging, without self-identification, then they can have no negative or binding effects. They are simply the inherent expressions of the Divine Reality.

CHAPTER 11

The Divine Vision
and the Vision of Mortality

a Talk by Da Avabhasa
July 9, 1983

SRI DA AVABHASA: Everybody, one way or another, is trying to find out if there is a bigger message than death, but very few people are convinced, unless they are just a little balmy, that there is another message that is absolutely reliable and just plain old true. What is to be discovered is not so much information about life in conditional Nature, such as "You don't die when you die" or "You go to this or that place or state". What is to be discovered is a different total vision.

Your mortal vision is a total vision. It affects every aspect and function of your existence. You are convinced of this vision, and you are convicted by it. As a result, you are contracting in order to survive, manipulate, and punish others. You do all of that, just as everyone else does in his or her own unique and characteristic way. And the reason for it is mortal vision, the belief that when you die, you die, and that, in any case, life is all about separations, and nothing can be relied upon, and others are dangerous because, just like you, they are afraid and unpredictable. Only so much discussion about your egoic tendencies and your patterns is useful. Such discussion is useful only until you realize that everyone, including you, is possessed by an emotional problem, that you are the ego, that you are self-contracting in order to survive, and that the reason for all this is your belief in death and your belief that cosmic Nature is a machine that separates and destroys.

What is true? If the mortal vision is true, then I do not blame you one bit for being an ego! If the mortal vision is true, there is no reason to blame people for exhibiting unlove or anger, no reason to blame anyone for exhibiting himself or herself as a living being wholly controlled by an emotional problem about existing.

You affirm your existence, but it is totally in doubt. You know it is coming to an end—at least everything that you conventionally say is yourself is coming to an end. That much about death is certain. Life certainly does involve all kinds of potential separations, and, therefore, life is a struggle. If you want to keep any relationship together, keep any physical body together, you must struggle. And your success even at doing that will be limited, as long as you have this emotional problem, or as long as you allow your emotional problem to control your behavior, because, in its extremes, the ego has an anti-survival effect, although its basic purpose is apparently to serve your survival and protect you from destructive effects.

The real question, then, the question that makes a difference, is not "What tendencies toward reactivity do you exhibit?" The real question is, "Is there just death following this life?" Is life just a mortal struggle, in which you as a stack of molecules compete with others to last as long as you can and feel as good as you can until death, and that is it? Or is there a greater Truth?

It does not make any difference what I Say about it. You know My "Point of View", so-called, and you must Realize It. Therefore, I always Say to you that the Way of the Heart can only be practiced if you hear Me and see Me.[1] You must not just believe what I am Saying, or try to believe what I am Saying. You must use My Argument to understand your separate and separative self, to observe the process of your own existence, and then, on the basis of hearing Me, or most fundamental self-understanding, you must see Me, you must enjoy My Spiritual Heart-Transmission, you must Awaken to the Mysterious Dimension of existence that Transcends the vision of mortality. Until you Awaken to

1. In the Way of the Heart, "hearing" is a technical term used by Sri Da Avabhasa to describe most fundamental understanding of the act of egoity, or self-contraction. It is the unique capability to directly transcend the self-contraction, such that there is the simultaneous intuitive awakening to the Revelation of the Divine Person and Self-Condition. Hearing awakens in the midst of a life of devotion, service, self-discipline, meditation, disciplined study of, or listening to, Sri Da Avabhasa's Teaching Argument, and constant self-surrendering, self-forgetting, and self-transcending feeling-Contemplation of Him.

When hearing (or most fundamental self-understanding) is steadily exercised in meditation and in life, the native feeling of the heart ceases to be chronically constricted by self-contraction. The heart then begins to Radiate as love in response to the Spiritual (and Always Blessing) Presence of Sri Da Avabhasa.

This emotional and Spiritual response of the whole being is what Heart-Master Da calls "seeing". Seeing is emotional conversion from the reactive emotions that characterize egoic self-obsession, to the open-hearted, Radiant Happiness that characterizes God-Love and Spiritual devotion to Him. True and stable emotional conversion coincides with true and stable receptivity to Da Avabhasa's Spiritual Transmission, and both of these are prerequisites to further Spiritual advancement in the Way of the Heart.

that seeing, or Spiritual surrender to Me, you do not have even any interest in not being an ego.

There cannot be any emotional conversion, or release from the self-contraction, from the mutilation of feeling, or of love, without that Spiritual Vision. I told you all years ago, when we were "considering" emotional conversion, that at some point such conversion would have an effect on you, on your emotional-sexual intimacies, for instance, but, at its base, it is about Divine Self-Realization, God-Vision. It is only once you Realize the Spiritual Reality, enter into Communion with It, that you can incarnate love, that you can loose the self-knot. You do not have any motive to release the ego otherwise, and so you, and people in general, do not.

Now, you must deal with all your tendencies that are unique to you as an individual, and they are endless, but you will not be able to do that if you do not hear Me and see Me. If this mortal vision is still most basically convincing to you, and you really do not have a real Vision Superior to it, then you cannot go on with this "consideration". You must stay where you are until your vision changes.

Not having this Divine Vision is the basic problem of a human being. The absence of the Divine Vision, and the effect of the mortal vision, is basically what everyone in the world is struggling with. People try to get the Divine Vision in all kinds of ways. They try to find out if people survive death, for example. And science investigates all kinds of things, but science is not particularly disposed to discover anything metaphysical. People feel that if they could just have another vision that proves that conditional existence is not ultimately threatened but, rather, is fundamentally, inherently Happy, their life would change completely. Everybody has a sense of this, and, therefore, everybody is looking for it.

Yet it seems that very few people really get the Divine Vision, although they may have moments of feeling better or of thinking they have something, and then the feeling blows away. Very few people who even think they have discovered another vision change themselves very much. Most people do not incarnate the Spiritual Reality that they say they believe in. Even though they may call themselves religious, they remain dangerous egos, just like people who do not even presume to be religious yet.

You here who are involved with Me are supposed to be incarnating the life of love, yet even you are wondering whether there is something greater than mortality. You have not discovered That Which is Greater than mortality to a degree profound enough to allow you to let go of your armor, your egoic motives, your patterns of egoity, your history, your tendencies.

We can go on and on forever here, talking about all the tendencies you represent. Yet That Which makes a difference is absent. Only Realization of That makes it obvious to you that what you have been suffering is an imaginary disease provoked by your reaction to conditional reality. That disease does not really exist, and to assume this disease is entirely unnecessary from the Spiritual point of view—but, of course, that is only obvious if you awaken to the Spiritual point of view.

People who are trying to find out if there is Something Greater in life to feel better about are always functioning on the basis of the model of this body-mind, or the body, or the physical, looking everywhere in the physical universe for some proof that there is Something Greater. The body-mind, or the realm of conditional manifestation, is an artificial point of view. It is not the Condition in Which you Stand. You Stand in the Position of Consciousness Itself, not in the position of the body.

If you establish yourself profoundly in the Position of Consciousness Itself, you will Realize Its Status and the Status of everything, then. From the "Point of View" of Consciousness Itself, there is no "me", no "someone" identified with the body, confronted by the blah-blah-blah of manifestation, and all the while realizing somewhere inside "I am Consciousness". When you are Consciousness Itself, you Realize that you Stand in an Infinite Domain of Energy, just That, only That Energy and Its modifications, and you do not even encounter the body except as a modification of Energy. Whereas from the point of view of the ego, or the usual person, the body is encountered as solid stuff, solid "me". It is not encountered as Energy, and it is not encountered from the "Point of View" of Consciousness Itself. Rather, the body is the point of view from which Consciousness Itself seems to be examined. All the references that the un-Enlightened person makes to Consciousness Itself are made from the point of view of identification with the body.

All of that is itself a kind of aberration. You must Realize a right view of conditional existence. You Stand in the Position of Consciousness Itself, and everything that arises to Consciousness is a form of Free Energy. Just That. Even the most solid forms are just That, and this is obvious from the "Point of View" of Consciousness Itself. Whereas from the point of view of the body-mind, it is not even obvious what the Status of personal consciousness is, or the Status of any thing, or any state. It is just stuff, "thingness". Apart from Divine Self-Realization, the Divine Status of anything is not intuited or presumed.

In the Position of Consciousness Itself it is clear that there is only Consciousness in a Domain of Infinite Energy. All kinds of "things" are arising, but they are only modifications of the Energy of Consciousness. This is the Divine Vision I am Talking about, the Vision that makes all the difference. It is the Vision associated with Divine Enlightenment.

There is also a vision short of Divine Enlightenment, which is the beginning of Spiritual life and which necessarily precedes Divine Enlightenment. It is the vision that comes after a time of self-observation, in confrontation with My Argument, and a time of hearing, or most fundamental self-understanding. It is the vision I call "seeing", which is entrance into the Domain of My Spiritual Transmission, the tangible acknowledgement of My Transmission of the Spiritual Reality. Contact with My Spirit-Presence shakes something loose. It is a profound Awakening. What is more, surrender into My Spiritual (and Always Blessing) Presence through real practice of the Way of the Heart permits Ultimate Awakening to Identification with My Divine State of Being.

Therefore, to go beyond your limit of tendency you must either hear Me and see Me, or you must Awaken completely. You must enter into the Vision of Divine Enlightenment Itself. In that case, this mortal vision and its effects have no power. If you have a mind-form that is a version of the mortal vision, you Divinely Recognize[2] it as just another modification of Self-Existing and Self-Radiant Divine Being. There is nothing about it to be taken seriously.

If you are not an atheist, you could pick up a book written by an atheist and read atheistic thoughts, even think atheistic thoughts for a couple of minutes, but then, when you put the book down, having had those thoughts for the few minutes you were reading the book changes nothing whatsoever. Just so, having had contact with all kinds of presumptions in your own mind, having come into contact with the points of view of all kinds of people, having witnessed all kinds of things, your body-mind is filled with the evidence of all your contact with unillumined existence. Therefore, even in the Divinely Enlightened state, the fossils of past associations may reappear. But, Standing in the Free Position of Self-

---

2. Divine Recognition is Sri Da Avabhasa's technical term for the Inherent and Most Perfect Comprehension and Perception, Awakened in the seventh stage of life, that all phenomena (including body, mind, and conventional self) are merely (apparent) modifications of the Self-Existing and Self-Radiant Divine Person.

Existing and Self-Radiant Divine Being, you simply Divinely Recognize those things, and there is no need to take them seriously. There is really nothing to analyze about them because you already Stand in the Free and True Position.

Therefore, Divine Recognition loosens everything. It Liberates Energy from its fossilized forms, its conventions and limitations, which are the product of the history of false knowledge, false vision, false views.

Until this Divine Vision absorbs and dominates your existence, not only will you have all the tendencies that are now in evidence in your life, but you will accumulate more of them, get more and more into trouble the older you get, and become more and more un-Happy, more and more rigid, more and more a fossil, just an impression in the elements. Ultimately, Consciousness will disappear from the fossil you have become. Consciousness will not want anything more to do with it and will throw it off like excrement. And that is what we call "death", the Conscious Force of Being eliminating this flesh, as this flesh eliminates waste products while it lives. Death is not the ending of someone. It is the process of elimination, and it is a process without beginning or end.

Having the point of view of the body only, you do not understand death. You ask about death the same thing that you ask about life. Are you going to survive it? Are you going to live for another moment? Are the things you like going to continue to gravitate around you, remain associated with you? Is everything going to turn out all right? Or, from the experiential point of view, are things magically going to turn out all right? Even if you come to the Divine Vision, you will only be fitted to do a great creative work, to be involved in a great struggle. Life, in form, is a creative struggle, and you all want to be comfortable!

Rather than going on with this creative struggle, this, to some degree, disturbed effort that real life involves, you always want to restore order. You want to be able to withdraw from feeling involvement, from association with what is difficult. You just want a map of existence and security. And you are very adept at arranging your security all the time, and not at all adept at Awakening to the Great Vision. If you devoted yourself to the Great Vision instead, then you would not be so interested in being complacent, and you would go on with transforming your limitations through the Force of the Spiritual Reality.

Earlier this evening I watched a segment of a television series about the history of evolution. It is so well made, and well spoken, and well researched, and well photographed, that you are supposed to come away with a feeling of the beauty and complexity of cosmic Nature. But to Me the vision of cosmic Nature is most horrifying. I mean, talk about the vision of mortality!

This evening's program was an effort to account for the evolution of sea creatures, using the evidence of fossils, the fossil record, and then examining the live sea specimens of today to see how they relate. The variety of different types of creatures and their complexity is certainly amazing.

When people watch such programs, they want to feel how complex and marvelous conditional Nature is, or they want to feel there is a God—"Everything is so complex, here we are, and now look at that." Being all the time what you are, you can be insensitive to the creature you are looking at, but when I see a creature, I immediately feel what it is to be that kind of creature, and to Me existence in such a form is a horror show of elemental states.

There is a certain beauty to the complexity—all the color and all the rest of it. The realm of cosmic Nature is a marvel, certainly, but it is also a horror show, not only of birth and death, and struggle to survive, and creature feeding on creature, but also of being profoundly limited and strange, bizarre, grotesque. I find nothing consoling whatsoever about images of conditional Nature, merely, just by themselves.

Of course, such programs on evolution are also a kind of religious programming these days. The theory of evolution as it is currently proposed and generally described is just another creation myth, a way to account for why and how things happened centuries ago. The evolutionary description of cosmic Nature is not based on ultimate knowledge. It is an attempt to rigorously apply one limited explanation of things to what may be observed.

This television program was a bit of philosophy, illustrated. No great wisdom was being proposed by the pleasant gentleman who was telling everybody about these creatures and the fossil record. All he was showing us is the vision of cosmic Nature, the mortal vision, which, in itself, is horrifying.

CHAPTER 12

Easy Death

a Talk by Da Avabhasa
December 8, 1982

SRI DA AVABHASA: The Divine Spirit is not afraid of death.
Therefore, if you Commune with the Divine Spirit, if you are really
intimate with the Divine Spirit in this present moment, then the
body-mind's reactivity to death relaxes. The more profoundly you enter
into Divine Communion, the less you associate with the tendencies of the
body-mind. Death can be easy in that case. If you are entered into the
Divine Spirit in the process of death, then the body will go through the
natural process of death without aberrating your consciousness. Death
will be natural, easy surrender. There will be no clinging and no fear.

Death should be, and in general can be, easy, natural in this sense.
But, if death is to be easy, you must be linked to the Divine Reality that
Transcends the body-mind. Otherwise, if you are simply identified with
the body-mind and contracting, you are, as a matter of course, going to
awaken in fear at the point of dying, and you are going to awaken in
many other emotions and reactions that will determine your destiny after
death.

The Living One, the One Who Is Alive, the One with Whom you are
truly Identical, does not need a body-mind, is not afraid of releasing the
body-mind, is not associated with a body-mind that is programmed to die
and that is gradually self-destructing. Just as annual plants self-destruct in
one cycle of the seasons, so death is built into the body-mind. But the
Divine Self is not afraid of this program. It is completely Free of all the
implications of this dying.

The persona that is constructed upon the basis of identifying with the
body-mind, contracting as the body-mind, is out of synchronicity with the

Divine Freedom and Purpose. And so this persona is afraid. There is the Transcendental Divine Self-Condition, and there is the body-mind in all the mechanics of cosmic Nature, and then there is this persona, this "I", which is totally out of sync with both the body-mind and its Ultimate Source-Condition. You, as the "I", or the persona, are not only out of sync with the Divine Self-Condition. You are also out of sync with the body-mind, because the body-mind does not want to live forever. You want to live forever. The persona wants to live forever.

The Way of the Heart is not the Way to get in sync with the body-mind, but it is the Way to get in sync with the Transcendental (and Inherently Spiritual) Divine Being. To do so will also cause the persona to relax and to enter into unity with the body in equanimity, the sattvic[1] condition that expresses Communion with the Divine Self-Condition. Then you will go through the life-cycle in a balanced state, with the persona, or the reactive ego, relaxed and the body-mind in a state of equanimity. Your characteristics will become those of the Living One, the Self-Existing and Self-Radiant Divine Being, and fewer and fewer of the characteristics of the persona will appear. Over time, they will gradually disappear, and the body-mind will go through its inevitable destiny naturally, free of its changes while alive and free also in the death process, as in going to sleep or in meditation. You will simply be entering into a profound state of unity with the Divine Being.

Death is truly such Samadhi, but you live—or die—death as the ego, the persona, the "I", and so you do not feel it to be Samadhi. You do not feel that its implications are the same as those of profound meditation and Ultimate Samadhi. You feel death is an ending, a loss, a threat. Such a psyche only expresses dissociation from the Living One.

Therefore, while alive, enter into the Baptism of Communion with My Spiritual (and Always Blessing) Presence and understand this persona and relax it, allow it to enter into a unified state with the body-mind, so that the body-mind exists in a state of equanimity, and live in Divine Communion perpetually, so that the characteristics of the Living One, which are the characteristics of Divine Samadhi, or Divine Being, become your characteristics. In that case, then, death is easy death. Death has its native form, which is simply the Divine Being's relinquishing a particular mechanism and not losing anything in the process.

---

1. In the Hindu tradition, sattva is the principle or virtue of equilibrium and harmony, one of the three qualities, or gunas, of conditional existence (with inertia, or tamas, and motion, or rajas).

Your consciousness must become one with this Divine Reality. You must magnify your association with That, enter into Communion with That, rather than reinforce the persona, or the egoic tendencies of attention. In this way you prepare yourself for death, but you also live well. You live in wisdom. And if you have lived a lifetime in this wisdom, then death will certainly become a profound event, not different in kind from profound meditation.

PART II

How to Prepare
for Death
While Alive

Sri Da Avabhasa (The "Bright")
Sri Love-Anandashram, July 1991

How to Prepare for Death While Alive

INTRODUCTION

W hat happens after death? How is our present life related to our future destiny? And what can we do to change our destiny? These are the leading questions of Part Two.

First of all, can we even be sure that we survive death? The presumption that we do survive is obviously fundamental to this book. However, Sri Da Avabhasa is not simply asking us to believe in such survival. He encourages us to make our own discovery about the matter, taking into account the experience of mankind as a whole, beyond the narrow materialist view that death is the end of our existence.

It is useful to come to some clear personal intuition about whether we are going to survive death, because our convictions on this question should affect how we choose to live now. As Sri Da Avabhasa Remarks in "This Liberating Impulse", we do not simply "drift into the eternal sublimity" after death. The cosmos is not structured that way. There are real laws that determine our fate in the afterworlds based on this present life and the whole thrust of what we have granted attention to while alive.

"The destiny of the body-mind," as Sri Da Avabhasa Says, "is merely habit", a result of the habit-patterns of attention. For most of us, these habit-patterns are focused on efforts toward self-fulfillment in this body. We are involved in friendships, food, work, sex, entertainment, and so forth, and we forget what this realm really is, how we are all changing and dying. But Sri Da Avabhasa Calls us to a more realistic assessment:

Do not pretend that you exist in a Disney world of beauty. This life is many-sided, and you do not know what it is. Your Happiness depends on the total inspection of this life. Therefore, acknowledge the situation in which you find yourself and become manly (male or female) on the basis of this observation. Acknowledge this terrible circumstance and be Happy. . . . You exist in a place that is open-ended, an edge to Infinity, and you are dying. . . . Nothing else that you may project in your lifetime can change the fact that you are still a fleshy, homely being that can be crushed by circumstance. (December 23, 1977)

We could die in any moment and be thrown into an unknown destiny. Everyone knows this, but how often do we allow the message to sink in? Throughout *Easy Death*, but especially in Part Two, Sri Da Avabhasa invites us to be much more serious about our real situation than we ordinarily tend to be.

Sri Da Avabhasa's Revelation is that real Happiness always exists Prior to, and may be found in the face of, <u>whatever</u> experience comes our way—in this life, at death and beyond death. But to find and establish that Happiness as our constant enjoyment requires a very uncommon gesture of the individual. It requires that we become passionately devoted to Happiness. It is more and more a matter of self-sacrifice and ecstatic surrender.

The truth to bear in mind, wherever you may be in the Great Process of existence, is that "what you are doing in this lifetime links up with all future time". Our destiny after death and in any lifetimes to come will be no more or less than the sum of the tendencies of attention we are activating in this lifetime. And so it is worth asking ourselves what kind of destiny are we moved to. Upon our answer to this question depend some very important decisions about how we need to start living now.

CHAPTER 13

Use Your Life

a Talk by Da Avabhasa
July 3, 1988

DEVOTEE: Heart-Master, nine months ago I found out I am suffering from a potentially life-threatening illness.

SRI DA AVABHASA: Aren't we all! [Laughter.]

DEVOTEE: I found out that I am indeed going to die. During this time I have been Graced by a series of extremely intimate dreams about You and about being in Your Company. I often wake up feeling relieved of the self-contraction for a time. The most recent dream occurred a week or two ago. My children were gone, which is an unusual circumstance, and I spent more time than usual that evening in meditative feeling-Contemplation of You. When I went to sleep, I dreamed that I died from falling off a cliff, not from an illness. In the dream I looked for You and found You very readily. You Instructed me in death just as You had Instructed me in life in my other dreams. I felt Blessed by such a loving Communion with You. I am very, very grateful that You are my Sat-Guru[1] and that You are the Marvel that You are. Thank You.

SRI DA AVABHASA: All here are being Instructed and Guided while waiting to die. Isn't this true?

DEVOTEES: Yes.

1.The Sanskrit word "sat" means "Truth", "Being", "Existence". The term "guru" is a composite of two contrasting words meaning "darkness" and "light". In common usage in Indian society, a guru is anyone who teaches others conventional knowledge or practical lore. A Sat-Guru, however, releases, turns, or leads living beings from darkness (non-Truth) into Light (Living Truth). Moreover, the Sat-Guru is, and lives as, the very Truth, or Condition of Being, that is Awakened in the devotee.

SRI DA AVABHASA: And then what? While you are alive in the bodily state, you like to secure yourself in various ways. You define your territory, so to speak, define your image and your association with it, try to create security of a kind. You define your awareness by all those things, and you act as if it is forever.

In fact, however, basically none of those things pertain after death. There is conscious awareness, but the means you have while alive to define yourself and maintain your security are gone. This can be a very troublesome and very confusing experience. It is not true that there is death and then you go to the other side and carry on a new life that is just like being born here, and you just go on defining yourself from there. It is not true. All kinds of experiences are potential in the transition from this apparent security—or insecurity.

You cannot foretell your death, perhaps. You may not be aware of the designs that may be associated with it, but you must come to realize, understand, and accept the fact of it. You can come to a point of certainty about the survival of death, and very readily. Read the literature that gives reliable testimony to survival of death. To do this is useful. Above all, what you realize in devotional relationship with Me should Grant irrefutable proof. But it is not a matter of seeking your entire life to find out whether or not survival of death is so. By the time you find out, you will no longer be in a position to change what has become inevitable because of how you have lived.

Therefore, you should, rather directly and simply, rather quickly even, come to a point of certainty about survival of death and practice not merely for the sake of improving the situation of this present body. Practice, yes, in the context of the body presently. The body must be submitted. But practice in the context of Eternity relative to the Great Matter in God, because the situation in which you are existing currently can change dramatically tomorrow, even as a bodily circumstance. It will certainly change dramatically at the point of death, and what is experienced from that point has everything to do with your state while alive. Therefore, those who are best equipped to die are those who live in Divine Communion and who have established a motion in the midst of things that is auspicious. This is called "Salvation".

Whereas those who are without understanding, without devotion, whose motion is isolation, self-contraction, a life that is not Godward and that is irresponsible relative to the Law, or the Great Matter, or the very Divine, even relative to the cosmic laws—such beings, such apparent individuals, suffer while alive and will continue to suffer. They lose their security at death, as all do, but they are likely to move into a state of confusion. Many intervals and possibilities after death are not auspicious.

Do not fool yourself any longer that you can live for the sake of this bodily life. You must function in the context of what you are about altogether, purify your house, and surrender in Divine Communion, rather than hold on to things for security that will inevitably disappear.

The purpose of existence is Samadhi, Divine Self-Realization. The process of existence, then, is self-transcendence, or a process of purification, submission, and devotion. Those who take this God-Realizing course are guided by Wisdom and the Wise, and their future is auspicious.

In general, auspicious signs will also appear during the lifetime of those individuals. But the signs I am referring to most specifically are the signs of a devotional, Spiritual nature, since the outer circumstances of individuals differ according to their karmic destiny, or the desires already set in motion that account for the characteristics of their birth and the qualities of their person.

The process you must endure, which is self-transcending and purifying, must do its work. As a result, there will be Spiritual signs, and the signs in the bodily frame will be as auspicious as you can make them by right practice, taking into account the karmic motions that make the circumstance of being.

The popular religious and Spiritual message is rather exoteric. Generally, it leads people in the direction of improving their condition while alive. That is the most recent great dogma in this ever "Westernizing" world. Every religion, even everything altogether, is supposed to lead you to consume the goods of physical existence. At best, all of that is secondary. You exist in the Context of the Divine and Eternity, and you must function in that Context or, inevitably, you become defined by limits, and you start suffering them.

The course of Wisdom, then, is the course of self-transcendence. Some do this in the traditional setting only to get a Blessing here and there and to be reborn in a better circumstance. Some have no greater hope than that, would not hope for more than that. Others have greater aspirations and a greater feeling of their own strength and the Blessing of the Divine. They work not merely for goods in this life. In fact, they tend to be rather ascetic in many ways. They do not work for the sake of a better rebirth in this world the next time. They work so as not to be reborn in this world, but to migrate to higher worlds.

Those who work to improve this life as best they can and perhaps to have a better life next time are functioning in the context of the first three stages of life, and, to some degree, even perhaps in the context of the beginnings of the fourth stage of life. Those who work to be purified of this life entirely, not to be reborn within it but to migrate to higher worlds, are involved in the "advanced" context of the fourth stage of life[2] and in the context of the fifth stage of life, of mind-based ascent.

Then there are those whose Work is Perfect, whose Work is about the transcendence of conditional existence itself, and directly, through Perfect devotion. They look forward to no migration, no further births, no improvements of any kind, really, although they function auspiciously. They transcend all conditional possibilities and Outshine them, even the Shine Itself. They Realize the Divine Self-Domain, Which is beyond ascent and descent, beyond the great Circle of the cosmos, inexplicably Prior to it and yet Pervading it.

The point of view of your stage of life and of your developmental stage of the Way of the Heart[3] pretty well defines where you fit in that scheme I just Described. At the present time, I gather you are disposed enough toward Spiritual life to be at the beginning of religious life, or the esoteric process. By tendency, you are looking for things to get better here. If you had a better understanding of how things really work, you would see that you also expect things to be better after death and better next time, whether you think about it or not.

But, of course, that is only at the beginning, just as a vegetarian diet is the beginning of dietary discipline in the Way of the Heart. There is no

2. Sri Da Avabhasa has Revealed that there are three (possible) developments of the fourth stage of life.

The "original", or beginner's, context of the fourth stage of life involves the initial cultivation of devotional Heart-response to the Sat-Guru. In the Way of the Heart this is accomplished through consistent application to the practices of self-surrendering, self-forgetting, and self-transcending devotion, service, self-discipline, and meditation in feeling-Contemplation of Sri Da Avabhasa. This developmental response remains the fundamental devotional context throughout the entire course of practice in the Way of the Heart.

The "basic" context of the fourth stage of life is true Spiritual Awakening enjoyed by individuals who have matured beyond the beginner's practice through emotional conversion to actively radiant love, God-Communion, and receptivity to and responsibility for the Transmitted Spirit-Baptism of the True Heart-Master.

The "advanced" context of the fourth stage of life is characterized by the ascent of Spirit-energy in the spinal line and the focusing of attention toward the brain core.

3. Sri Da Avabhasa has described the development and maturation of practice in the Way of the Heart in terms of specific developmental stages. These developmental stages of practice, although seven in number, do not correspond one-to-one with the seven stages of life. However, through one's progress in the developmental stages of practice, growth through the seven stages of life is also accomplished.

Sri Da Avabhasa has also specified various forms of practice which are engaged by practitioners of the Way of the Heart at each developmental stage, and which are determined by the individual qualities of the practitioner and by his or her degree of maturity in practice.

satisfaction in all of that. It is simply the context in which to begin. The more you grow and the more your point of view is purified and advanced, the greater will be your understanding, your experience, your awareness altogether, and you will be moved beyond your present disposition.

Therefore, use your lifetime for the sake of Divine Self-Realization. If you use it for anything less, then what is less becomes your destiny. All destinies, fulfilled, have a force that leads you to dissatisfaction. There is an emptiness in acquisition. In getting, a dissatisfaction arises, because one was already full of the search. The search is an agony, a disease, a kind of stress you want to be relieved of. You believe you cannot be relieved of it until you achieve union with your object, whatever that may be. Therefore, in your stress, you desire to pursue that object. That pursuit is what you are full of. When you acquire your object, you are empty, because you are no longer full of the stress of the search, and all of a sudden you feel, in that moment of absence of the search, a glimpse of something greater, Freedom Itself, Happiness Itself. There is a kind of a feeling that Happiness is not to be identified with any object or the achievement of any goal at all. That space is illuminating. In that space of dissatisfaction and freedom from seeking, an individual may find the motivation to take up Spiritual life.

Perhaps all of you are here because something of that has happened in your life somehow, that crisis of dissatisfaction and freedom from identifying Happiness with acquisition of this or that or life just as it is. Perhaps you have had enough of that anyway, just a taste of it to make you dissatisfied with what life is presently and even perhaps dissatisfied with what it can become. There is an overriding impulse in you that you are perhaps only beginning to understand.

Its first signs are that it leads you to do sadhana, to begin to grow again, and to continue to grow altogether.

CHAPTER 14

Death Should Be Transcended, like Everything Else

a Talk by Da Avabhasa
August 9, 1987

DEVOTEE (in his mid-sixties): How can an ordinary aging person face death?

SRI DA AVABHASA: With great difficulty! [Laughter.] In My opinion, death should not be faced. Death should be transcended, like everything else. When you become involved in your mind with death, making much of death and thinking about death, then you become more and more worried. You think that because you are sixty-seven, death is much more important than when you were twenty-five, or fifty even, and it is not true.

You should be sensitive to the possibility of death even from your youth or your childhood. The effect of such an early confrontation with the inevitability of death should be your free resolution to practice the self-transcending Way of the Heart, which Realizes the Ultimate Condition, which is even intimate with the Divine Condition from its beginning, and which is only purposed toward that Realization, only intimate with That Divine Reality. The knowledge of death, however it may come to you through life's experience, should become the wisdom of such self-transcending practice.

When you take up the Divinely Self-Realizing Way of the Heart, you are not concerned any longer about "facing death", because you understand that death is not any different from all the other limited conditions of existence. It is a vision of egoity to the ego, perhaps. And to practice the Way of the Heart Happily, you must be free of egoic vision, in the form of death or in any other form.

It is useful, even necessary, to be made serious by the observation of the death of others and the observation of the potential of death in yourself. This is the seed of a good lesson. But you should not thereafter be concerned about death, always facing it, holding it before your mind, struggling with it as if you must perform some heroic gesture in the face of it or do something about it.

DEVOTEE: Yes. Yes. Frantically try to become Illumined or do something.

SRI DA AVABHASA: You can stand free of death right now by getting the wisdom of it. You can stand free of it right now. You must! To stand free of death is essential to the Way of the Heart. You must take the fact of death seriously. You must get the Lesson of life,[1] which includes the Lesson of death, then. You must be disposed differently and oriented differently. You must become free in your heart through self-understanding. You must use the conditional self, or the body-mind, differently, on the basis of that wisdom.

DEVOTEE: I feel I am beginning to let things go. I feel not dissociated from things but detached from them.

SRI DA AVABHASA: It is not even a matter of letting them go. The effort of letting anything go is an act, a strategy, a defense. "Not-grabbing", "grabbing", "letting go"—these are all descriptions of actions you might perform when concerned about death. I gather you are, at the moment, rather concerned about death. You have a somewhat different hormonal message cycling around in your poor little body than some of these others, who are somewhat more youthful than you, have cycling around in their poor little bodies. The hormonal messages are different, but the Truth is the same.

DEVOTEE: The writing is on everybody's wall.

---

1. "The Lesson of life" is Da Avabhasa's term for the necessary ordeal in each individual's practice whereby all un-Happiness and all seeking are fundamentally, and most deeply, understood. It is the understanding that no conditional seeking can achieve Happiness but that Happiness is inherent in Existence Itself. As Da Avabhasa has succinctly summarized it: "You cannot become happy. You can only be happy."

119

SRI DA AVABHASA: Yes. The body is mortal. So what? It always was, and it is. You exist in the context of mortality. You must practice the Way of the Heart in that context. Only by exercising yourself in wisdom, in practice, in the context of the Way of the Heart, are death and all the other limitations of life, here and hereafter, transcended. You must be free in your feeling presently and not be concerned. You must take the Lesson of life and death seriously. In the Way of the Heart, you take it seriously by gaining wisdom from it and becoming differently purposed as a result. You have always been mortal. Whether or not you have thought about that fact or believed it, it has always been so.

So—you are being impressed at a certain age. One could be impressed at a much earlier age. What is the import of the fact of death? Wisdom, and to be re-purposed to Divine Self-Realization. By that unique purpose and practice, death is transcended, as life is, as the body-mind is. You are only sixty-seven. In the context of life as it is these days, you could live for another thirty or forty years, even longer.

DEVOTEE: Tied up with tubes and things.

SRI DA AVABHASA: Not even that. You could be a very healthy, vigorous man. You still are. You could continue to be healthy and vigorous for another ten, twenty, thirty, forty years, even longer. Who knows how long? But you are already thinking about the end. The end is just as obvious to anyone who is serious at any age. Perhaps it took you until sixty-seven to become serious. That does not mean your life is coming to an end. If you start thinking that way, you will bring your life to an end.

Get wisdom from the vision of death. Get the Lesson from it. Be differently purposed. Actually practice the Way of the Heart. Stop thinking, thinking, thinking, reading, reading, reading, talking, talking, talking. Demonstrate a unique sensitivity, a unique force of participation. Observe yourself. Discipline yourself. Be calmed. Release your energy and attention from this knot of thought and concern. Gesture toward the Ultimate Purpose of Divine Self-Realization. Do it now. You must also do so after death. As a practitioner of the Way of the Heart, you should be doing it in every moment of life, at every age of life. It is no different for you than it is for anyone.

You could have ten, twenty, thirty, forty, fifty more years. Some may just have another two weeks. Who knows?

DEVOTEE: Better to do it before death than after.

SRI DA AVABHASA: You must do it after in any case. Death is just another category of conditional existence, just another instant, another part of the process. The same Law pertains always. What will you do now? What will you be purposed toward? What discipline will you assume? What will be your practice?

DEVOTEE: Right now.

SRI DA AVABHASA: Now. Yes. It must be now. And if now, it will be then also. And if now while alive, so also in the context of the process of dying, and if then, then after death, whatever may appear. You must equip yourself with wisdom, and death always was the possibility, always was and always is the possibility in the context of the body-mind. This is what must be understood, and this is what must also be transcended.

The great force of wisdom begins with such understanding and the capability to observe oneself, the intelligent application of self-discipline, the work of listening,[2] and then the realization of hearing, or most fundamental self-understanding. In principle you have plenty of time to do all of that.

DEVOTEE: Hallelujah!

SRI DA AVABHASA: Just as everyone else does. Your age does not make a bit of difference. What difference does age make? It is already true that everyone here is bodily going to die. It does not make any difference how old you are.

---

2. "Listening" is Da Avabhasa's term for the orientation, disposition, and practice of the beginner's developmental stages of preparation and practice in the Way of the Heart. To listen is, in the context of a life of devotion, service, self-discipline, and meditation, to give one's attention to Sri Da Avabhasa's Teaching Argument, to His Leelas (or inspirational Stories of His Life and Work), and to feeling-Contemplation of Him (primarily of His bodily human Form) for the sake of awakening most fundamental self-understanding of the self-contraction, or hearing, on the basis of which practice may begin to develop in the Spiritual stages of life and beyond.

CHAPTER 15

Are You Sure
That You Survive Death?

a Talk by Da Avabhasa
July 3, 1987

D EVOTEE: Heart-Master Da, I do not know whether we survive death or not. I am not even really sure what it means to survive death. But I remember that in a Talk You Gave years ago You Said something like, "After death, your deck is reshuffled." I understood You to mean that after I die, there is nothing left of myself as I now know myself to be.

SRI DA AVABHASA: How much of yourself, as you are, do you know yourself to be anyway?

DEVOTEE: That is a good question!

SRI DA AVABHASA: I do not remember that Talk in particular, but you could say that, most fundamentally, I was suggesting that you cannot predict what will happen to you after death. Rather, you must be submitted to the Divine, or That Which Is, Ultimately. The events after death can be just as confusing and just as limited as the events during bodily life.

Knowing that you survive after death is not a matter of faith. It is ordinary knowledge, just another understanding that contributes to your capability to surrender to the Divine Self-Condition in every present moment while you are alive.

The knowledge that you survive after death is not even consoling. After death, the conditions of your existence will be just as limited as the conditions of this physical body. In some fundamental sense, your deck is shuffled. You cannot depend on persisting in any state. Then, as now, you cannot depend on what may appear to be, nor can you depend on your limited view of what is arising. Therefore, instead of depending on the conditions of existence, which are always only changing, you must become associated with That Which Is Ultimately, the Divine Reality, Which is Unconditional and Changeless.

The Divine Reality cannot be shuffled because That never changes. What changes is always shuffled, and reshuffled. Conditional existence is always a kind of incomprehensible illusion, what is traditionally called "maya",[1] unless you understand its most fundamental Principle, which is the Divine, or Ultimate, Reality, or Happiness Itself.

What else about that?

DEVOTEE: I guess the confusion I have about it is that it does not make any difference to me right now whether or not I survive after death.

SRI DA AVABHASA: I am sure it would make some difference to you if you could know absolutely that "when you die, you're dead", as opposed to "when you die, you continue". Isn't there a difference between those two propositions?

DEVOTEE: Would I continue as something that I am familiar with?

SRI DA AVABHASA: Not necessarily. Those two propositions represent two entirely different realities, and neither proposition offers you, as this present body-mind, any certainty to hold on to. However, the two propositions affect your relationship to conditional reality entirely differently. The proposition "When you're dead, you're dead" says one thing about the universe, and the proposition "When you die, you continue", whatever the possibilities may be, suggests a totally different reality.

To know that you survive after death does make a difference, although it does not change the fact that you cannot rely on the continuation of anything. The fact that you continue after death is not something you believe in. It is not a faith, nor is it merely positive in and of itself. It is just patently true, just as the physical dimension of your conditional existence is clearly true to you now.

1. "Maya" is a classical Hindu term that literally means "she who measures". Traditionally this term is used to indicate the "deluding" or "veiling" force of the Universe, which is presumed to distract all beings from direct Realization of the Divine Condition.

"Dead, you're dead", "Dead, you continue"—which of those two propositions you choose makes a great deal of difference because they suggest two completely different conceptions of reality. The difference between those two conceptions of reality has a great deal to do with your present life. Doesn't it? Doesn't which one you choose make a difference?

DEVOTEE: It does.

SRI DA AVABHASA: But it does not make a difference of faith, or create something for you to hold on to. You will continue after death, but there is still nothing to hold on to in the fact itself that you continue. After death, all kinds of changes are possible, and they can be equally as bewildering as the present one—I presume that is what you are also suggesting. Only the Divine makes a difference in the process of your continuing.

And the Divine must be discovered. If you are to discover the Divine, yes, you must accept certain inevitabilities, like survival of death, which is just part of your comprehension of reality and your understanding of the purpose of conditional existence. The Divine is the import of ordinary facts like the survival of death. Such facts, in and of themselves, are not consoling, even the fact of your survival of death.

So—what you are saying is right. There is nothing consoling about the fact that you survive after death, but, nonetheless, the fact itself is important. If you understand what it means, it tells you something about your existence even now, and it tells you what you should be doing right now, which is not merely indulging your separate and separative self and trying to be ultimately consoled as a human being, but rather transcending your egoic self by giving your egoic self up to That Which Is, Ultimately, surrendering to the Very Divine, Reality Itself, That Which Is All Bliss, Happiness Itself, the Very Divine Self.

That is the import of your life—right now. And it will be so after death likewise. The conditions that arise after death are just as potentially deluding or overwhelming or uncomfortable or temporarily pleasurable as your present experience. To know that is not consoling. But to know that is important, because it tells you how to live now.

CHAPTER 16

Get Up from Bed
and Drop Dead!

a Talk by Da Avabhasa
April 6, 1979

SRI DA AVABHASA: In this life you must become devoted to absolute, heart-felt surrender to God so that (ultimately), through practice of the Way of the Heart in My Company, you Outshine Earth, humanity, the material universe, and all persuasions of body and mind and pass into the presently unexperienced Realm of God. The true purpose of your life has nothing to do with the realm of appearances, which has its own cycle of past and present and future. All that arises to attract you in this great universe in which you are appearing is not your business. All that arises is dying anyway, being transformed out of the realm of appearances.

DEVOTEE: Including ourselves! This is a chilling realization!

SRI DA AVABHASA: It is not chilling if you will Realize your True Condition and the True Condition of everything arising.

The death of everything is simply the transition of everything into the next dimension. Many people associated with your past have already experienced it. They may not know very much about it, any more than they knew very much about the process of life. Perhaps they all have comprehended something about it, but they have been transformed. And they are so mysterious to you that whatever they might have been during their lifetime, they are now heroes for having died!

Those who have died are mysterious to you because while alive they were exactly like you. It is amusing to look at photographs of relatives and others from your childhood who are now dead. You knew them all

125

very well. They were basically ordinary people, like you. In their moment, grinning at the camera, they knew nothing more nor less than you, fundamentally. Yet now they have been zapped out of this experience, whereas you have not.

You are all like astronauts—your whole lifetime is associated with preparation for the launch! This life is just a transition to another place. All those people you knew once have continued in the process of existence. They have been initiated into something you have yet to confront.

Do you not think death is a weird initiation? Yes. That is why you must learn wisdom while alive. You must die while living. You must surrender during the waking state, while perfectly healthy, in the natural course of your existence—profoundly, and then frequently, commonly, regularly, constantly. Dying is self-transcendence, sacrifice, surrender. If you practice such self-transcendence while alive, through practice of the Way of the Heart that I have Revealed to you, then the physical event of death is just another moment of a process that has engaged you all the while. Thus, it is not a threat. And from the point of view of right sympathy and right surrender, you can realize the tacit meaning, significance, and direction of this whole affair in which, out of nowhere, you and everyone are existing in these bodily forms. Look at all of you sitting around in this room here, completely unable to account for anything! Your situation is weird!

You should begin to enjoy losing bodily consciousness and going on to another state, but you resist it. There is pleasure associated with dying, but, like excrement, death is virtually taboo in the common world. You are not supposed to enjoy it. The Sages, however, know this pleasure. They know they must enjoy death, and they become pleasurably associated with it. Such individuals transcend fear while alive, just as you must do. You must be able to enter into the condition of death as a matter of course in your waking life, every morning. Get up from bed and drop dead. Realize Ecstasy to the point of transcending death!

To lose bodily consciousness is a natural expression of religious ecstasy. All the Yogas strive for it, not as a form of suicide or a negative act—after all, one does return to bodily consciousness. But to surrender to the point of transcending your fixed association with the body and to enter more profoundly into the Domain of Transcendental (and Inherently Spiritual) Divine Consciousness, or your True Condition, is one of the possibilities of bodily existence. When, through practice of the Way of the Heart, you become able to enter that state of bodily surrender at will, you lose your fear, which you have acquired through being confined by repetitive experience to the limited self-sense. You feel negative about existence because of this sense of limitation. Therefore, understand all experience and enter into another disposition, bodily, literally, physiologically, and relationally. Be truly a servant in the world, and be nothing else. Enjoy no other disposition than ecstasy and ecstatic service.

DEVOTEE: Heart-Master Da, I feel that one of the reasons we do not willingly lose bodily consciousness is that we are not sure we will return.

SRI DA AVABHASA: Yes, but when you are giving yourself up to the Divine Reality, why should you be concerned about such a thing? To withhold is not to serve. Any state other than direct, heart-felt surrender is an unending torment, leading more and more to profound despair. Therefore, as My devotee, simply practice surrendering this contraction, become ecstatic, enter into the domain of love, surrender to Me, and, thus and thereby, to the Divine Person Revealed in My Company.

If you will do this, even bodily surrender becomes your business. As a natural expression of its ecstasy, the body yields the sense of its independence, its fixed attention and sensation. In ecstatic practice, the loss of bodily consciousness is quite natural. Yogis describe it all the time. After a period of deep meditation, sensations arise indicating the loss of bodily consciousness, and the Yogis enter into higher states of mind, such as fifth stage conditional Nirvikalpa Samadhi, or some other ascended condition to which they devote their attention. The loss of bodily consciousness is the root of such expressions as the one attributed to Paul in the *New Testament:* "I die daily." It is to give yourself up simply, to give yourself up to God to the point of death, without negative connotations but in the most positive sense.

The loss of bodily consciousness, among other events that may arise quite naturally, is one of the signs of ecstasy. Presuming this experience may occur from time to time, you allow for it in the Meditation Hall or while you are lying quietly. Other bodily, vocal, emotional, and mental phenomena may also arise as part of your ecstatic practice.

In your practice of the Way of the Heart, you will notice changes in your bodily state, and at some point you will notice that you abandon bodily consciousness altogether. Eventually, in Divine Enlightenment, you will Realize that you are never in any sense whatsoever in a body anyway, and, therefore, you no longer need to go into a state of meditative absorption in order to lose bodily consciousness. You might do so at times, but it is no longer necessary.

Whether you are conscious of the body or not, your essential disposition is always the transcendence of this realm, through religious and Spiritual practice, not clinging to it, living in it Happily, in love, and always in ecstatic Divine Communion in My Revealing Company. Ultimately, when you Realize the Divine Self-Condition, at death, you naturally pass out of this realm into another Dimension of existence—not Yogically conceived but beyond conception, not a specific subtle or astral place but beyond the mind, not any planet in this universe, not a higher place, not an advanced moment in human evolution, nothing like that at all, but ecstasy, total surrender to God of everything associated with so-called "you".

You will notice that you yourself, like all the other phenomena associated with you, are a contraction in the Infinite Field of Self-Existing and Self-Radiant Consciousness. When the knot that is you is undone, you will need no more conversation about reincarnation, or anything else for that matter.

Give yourself up completely, ecstatically, in feeling-Contemplation of Me. This is My Recommendation. Instead of making great plans for this world, accommodate it in the natural way and give yourself up to ecstasy, or self-transcendence. Just how much of this human adventure will you try to fulfill, satisfy, maintain, sustain by effort, accommodate? You could give yourself up to an ecstatic life altogether.

But before you get involved with anything on any day, get up from bed and drop dead! First, before you become involved in anything you are likely to be attached to that day, practice surrender, through the most basic practice of the Way of the Heart, which is feeling-Contemplation of Me. Such surrender may involve loss of bodily consciousness and whatever else happens when you release your self-contraction to the Divine Person through feeling-Contemplation of Me, which is your true business anyway. Give yourself up, through meditative and devotional activities of feeling-Contemplation of Me, and then begin your associations of the day. Then throughout the day maintain sacred occasions, such as study of My Heart-Word and your personal and constant surrender to Me directly, and, thus and thereby, to the Divine Person, in the form of all your actions.

If, when you awake, you give yourself up to the point beyond death, then anything you might become associated with that day will be met with freshness only. It will have no binding power. Only something done twice binds you. Therefore, give yourself up to the point of death, and then do whatever one who is My devotee does that day, ecstatically. Then go to bed that night surrendered to Me, and, thus and thereby, to the Divine Person, and awaken in the morning and, with a great will, give yourself up again to the point of death. Nothing that was, even the day before, will remain to bind you. Then, as is your daily rule, do everything Happily and in love that same day. What you do you will not be doing twice. What you do will always be fresh and thus not binding, because you are only surrendered from the heart in Love-Communion with Me.

All your actions now are determined to fulfill or reinforce your present state of body-mind. The ecstatic practice of the Way of the Heart that I am Describing, however, involves the total transcendence of your present state of body-mind and any past or future state. Such transcendence is a different existence altogether than you have reinforced in your behavior and associations throughout your life.

When you begin to integrate yourself for significant periods each day with this process of the body-mind, you will begin to adapt to the Dimension with Which you become associated by this practice. Your practice will verify itself with many changes, if you engage it profoundly. To begin, you must practice this surrender in formal meditative feeling-Contemplation of Me for a significant period of time each day, and also in random, and more and more constant, feeling-Contemplation of Me throughout each day. Over time, the effect of your practice and its significance will increase.

Yes, you must die every day. You must enter into each day as a person newly born, free, not at all bound to your egoic self. My recommendation that you drop dead every day is an amusement, but I am Talking about ecstasy. The one thing you fear is death, because you are holding on to your egoic self. If you give up your egoic self with the full force of emotion, you also die. You transcend the physical and mental limitations of the egoic self. You must feel death as ecstasy and be free of your fear of it. The business of your life must become ecstatic surrender through the most life-positive association with Me, as the Adept Heart-Teacher and True Heart-Master. Do not live a dreadful, fearful, mysterious association with death.

It is not that physical death is itself so profoundly important. What is important is the transforming process of which it is a manifestation. That process must go on while you are alive, and, when it occurs, it is equally as profound as any physical death. Therefore, honor and be enthusiastic about the Spiritual Process of which death is a part.

CHAPTER 17

The Choice of Happiness

a Talk by Da Avabhasa
July 5, 1987

DEVOTEE: Heart-Master Da, I have always feared that experiences after death can be more bewildering and more profoundly disturbing.

SRI DA AVABHASA: More bewildering and disturbing than what?

DEVOTEE: Than the waking state. Will I lose whatever Realization I have while I am alive by being distracted by experience after I am dead?

SRI DA AVABHASA: Why should you persist in any attitude in life or after death that would require you to lose Realization, since Realization is not something that happens to you to begin with? Realization is a direct expression of your own consciousness. Knowing that, why should you participate in either life or death in such a way that Realization would be lost?

DEVOTEE: Well, seeing how distracting life is . . .

SRI DA AVABHASA: If you allow the events of life to confound your Realization in life, you are likely to do the same thing after death, aren't you?

DEVOTEE: Yes.

SRI DA AVABHASA: Why should you want to do that? You are asking about death as if it is something that happens <u>to</u> you, as if things just happen <u>to</u> you after death. They do not just happen to you any more than things just happen to you while you live. I Call you to awaken to the Way of the Heart while alive, whereby conditions, or apparent un-Happiness, are transcended, and to persist in it. Such persistence is the means of your cooperation with that process while you are alive and after your death as well. Why would we continue to discuss the possibilities after death merely in the framework of things that just happen to you?

Your question comes from bewilderment. It comes from a personality that is rather weak in the responsibility of such practice, and you are projecting that weakness onto future possibilities even while you are alive. You might as well just have asked, "Could something happen to me this evening, could something happen to me next week, could something happen to me in ten years, that would be so distracting that I would be even more bewildered than I am now? Could I lose everything that I am gaining now or have gained?" It is the same question. And it is a reflection of your disposition. It is not a reflection of conditions themselves. Conditional existence is only as bewildering as you are bewilderable. And there is no limit to your possible bewilderment, while you are alive or after you are dead.

What is the Great Matter to be "considered", then? Your participation in conditional existence—which obviously must be transformed or, yes, there only is bewilderment. And that bewilderment will not be cancelled merely by your death. Things can appear to happen to you after death just as they can appear to happen to you before death.

Bewilderment is what makes conditions seem to be merely happening to you, seem to be controlling your state, seem to be determining your condition, seem to be determining your state of Realization or non-Realization. All this that seems to be happening to you is an illusion, a self-created form of bondage, which requires that you observe your separate and separative self and understand your separate and separative self and come to a point of new responsibility in the midst of conditions.

That is what we are "considering". That is what must be understood. Otherwise, bewilderment will continue. There is nothing inherently more bewildering now than anything that is happening after death. It is all a modification of the same Divine Condition that Is, presently.

Therefore, what is your relationship to conditions? That is the real question. Your ability to be bewildered depends entirely on your orientation to conditions and not on whether you are alive or whether you are dead or what effects seem to be happening. The conditions of existence do not determine your bewilderment. Conditions are not inherently distracting. They are only distracting to you if you are disposed to be distracted. Conditions can be difficult after death. They can be difficult before death. Presently you have the same kind of psychic capability, the same ability to be disturbed, if you like, that you could potentially have after death. It is all a play upon the same Divine Condition. It requires for its transcendence, then, exactly the same capability that is a possibility for you presently.

If you like, you can think of it this way: You create mind. By your reaction, your disposition, your degree of responsibility, you determine the tendency of mind and your disposition altogether. And, if you like, you can think of after death as a time when mind makes you, when your tendencies persist and determine further experience. On the other hand, the same option is given to you, the same capability to understand, to transcend, and to Awaken to the Real Condition is also persistent after death. It is not lost by dying.

You have already created much mind, much tendency, much bewilderment, and those things are tending to reinforce themselves and to persist. You are being apparently played upon by them. But while you are alive, you do have the option to observe yourself and to transcend all of that which has already accumulated and which you are tending to reinforce. The same is true after death as before death.

And after death, there is not merely a continuation of the waking state. All the varieties of states potential in the condition of life continue after death. While alive in the body, you are not only awake, but you also dream and sleep and experience the variations on these—unconsciousness, revery, hallucination. The waking state is not just one thing, either. It is a variety of tendencies, reactions, states of mind, states of feeling, states of body. A very wide range of possibilities is associated with the born condition in the body. Likewise after death. All the states and all the variations on them persist by tendency in the context of certain conditions, which in their time and place will seem given or normal to you, just as conditions now seem to be.

Nonetheless, there is still the fundamental Call of Divine Reality Itself to observe, to understand, to transcend, to assume responsibilities, to outgrow, to Awaken altogether. Will you or won't you after death is not the question now. The question now is, Will you or won't you now? What will you enforce, or reinforce, while continuing in this body? That is the real question that comes to you presently, because what you do about it in the present moment and in all future moments will of course determine what comes after death.

If you really understand this, then you become serious. Life and death and what happens after death will stop seeming to be some mechanical event that is just happening to you, a given form that you get from conversations with others. Instead of letting it all happen, instead of doing it by rote, you must become seriously involved with what is going on, observe yourself, understand yourself, realize the capability to grow beyond, to be Awakened, to Stand Free. You become devoted to the Truth, then, not merely mechanically involved in destiny, or karma.

The after-death states are really karmic conditions, just as the states of the body or the states experienced in the context of bodily life. All conditional states are karmic, or, in other words, the product of the universal display, or of the fields of energy associated with the cosmic design. The possibilities are not only numerous but in some sense you could say they are infinite. In any case, they are all built upon two basic trends of energy, one that you might call "positive", and the other that you might call "negative". Just as much potential positive and negative is potential after death as during bodily life.

The fundamental Law is the Law of self-transcendence, Awakening to That Which Is, Ultimately.

As I have pointed out to you, whether or not there is survival after death is not important in the sense that, if you could find out that, yes, indeed, there is survival after death and that it is also inevitable, that certainty would become a reason to feel consoled or feel good or relax your fear of death. It is not that at all. To feel good about death is not the reason to come to some basic certainty about it. Rather, as I pointed out to you, the reason for coming to some basic certainty about death is so that you will come to an understanding about the nature of conditional existence.

Whichever of the two decisions you might make—yes, there is survival after death, or, no, there is not—each of those two propositions determines a view of reality, a view of life, a view of conditional existence, and each enforces a habit. There is nothing fundamentally consoling about the reality of the survival of death if you understand what the entire process entails. It is not consoling. And in any case, the events that happen to you after death are not knowable in advance. They will be determined altogether by your habit while alive. That is certainly true, if you understand all of this.

The question about survival after death is very important to practice of the Way of the Heart. To come to a certainty about it in the affirmative suggests something about the nature of existence that makes real practice, serious practice, a necessity, and it will make you serious rather than just a gleeful believer. When some Spiritual Teachers are asked, "What will happen to me after death? Will I survive death?" they say, "Why are you concerned about the future? Why aren't you dealing with what is happening right now?"

That response is true enough. You must ultimately deal with existence in the present. All of your "considerations" must include the capability for real life. But, on the other hand, it is not frivolous to "consider" survival of death. Whether or not you survive death is worthy of serious "consideration", because an understanding of death indicates to you the nature of conditional existence. If rightly understood, the certainty of survival after death will lead you to serious practice of the Way of the Heart. It is one among many factors that can do this. Therefore, I do not see any reason to dismiss such a discussion.

The question of survival after death is not some oblique question that cannot be answered. One can come to an understanding about all of this, come to a point of view about it even, by studying the information that exists about it. The report of mankind is full of information about death. That report can be examined with seriousness and with discrimination, just as your present life and experience must be examined with seriousness and discrimination, and on that basis you can come to a serious and right understanding about it.

What is conditional existence all about? What is it for? How are you purposed—really? If the question of conditional existence is not serious enough to you and you never answer it, and you continue to live as doubt about it, amused by the possibilities of both propositions, you will never realize a point of view about it and, therefore, you will never come to a point of view about life itself, about existence altogether. Without understanding, you will never become serious, then, you will never become purposed, you will never transcend yourself, you will never become involved in the process that is most fundamental to Existence Itself. It is right and appropriate and basically necessary to come to a real and "considered" position about the survival of death for the sake of your practice of the Way of the Heart, not for the sake of consolation or for the sake of mere believing.

Practice of the Way of the Heart is not merely about improving your state while alive and then who knows what happens after that. Practice of the Way of the Heart is about participation in Existence Itself, That Which is most Fundamental and, therefore, That Which Ultimately Transcends your present lifetime, Which Transcends your apparent individuality, Which Transcends this appearance and all other possibilities as well. Therefore, even while alive, you must participate in That Which Is Ultimate. This means you must come to a real understanding about That Which Is the case altogether and about that which is true about conditional existence altogether.

You do know that you can suffer greatly while bodily alive and that really there is no limit to how profoundly you can suffer. Just so, there is nothing about dying that is going to eliminate the possibility for suffering. This is true. Mere death is projection into a scheme of things that is full of both positives and negatives. The knowledge of some basic factors of the death process and the after-death process can be presumed on the basis of serious "consideration". On the other hand, much of it remains a mystery, because it is not entirely pre-determined. It is something you are creating, in some basic sense, by the form of your participation in existence even presently.

If you have a serious appreciation of the nature of possibility even while alive in the body, you will no longer frivolously or mechanically indulge in life. You will, rather, submit that process to the Law, to the Greater Purpose, the Ultimate Purpose, the process of submission to Happiness. To submit to Happiness one cannot merely choose positive possibilities, because the negatives are all part and parcel of anything that may be positive in some moment or another. To submit to Happiness one must submit to That Which Transcends positive and negative. Therefore, to submit to Happiness, one must submit to the process of self-transcendence and of transcendence altogether. Submission to Happiness requires profound seriousness and freedom from frivolousness, mechanical tendency, and mere conventionality. You must become involved in a profound investigation of yourself, the results of your activities—the immediate results, the longterm results, even the results that pass beyond the death of the body.

Why should you organize yourself relative to conditional existence, presently and potentially in the future, in order to realize un-Happiness and bewilderment and non-Enlightenment and non-Realization? Why should anyone make such a choice? Can you justify making such a choice? Make the choice of Happiness Itself and Realize It, and do That Which is Realization. Be Realization. Realize the Power of Divine Self-Realization, and you will also lose the fear of losing that Power and that

Capability under some circumstance that you cannot account for presently, such as something that might occur after death. The more you Realize the inherent power of self-transcendence, the more you lose that fear.

You have an idea that somehow time is going to take care of everything. You must understand that the mechanics of conditional existence do not lead you to Happiness. They do not do anything of the kind. Happiness is a matter of understanding and transcending all of it. This is something, of course, that you must come to understand and realize by making a serious investigation of conditional existence.

If you become serious, then you will also not devote any great amount of time to being a beginner in the Way of the Heart. You can move with great intensity in every moment. You can accomplish the foundation of practice of the Way of the Heart directly and, therefore, as quickly as possible. Likewise, your participation in all the developmental stages of the Way of the Heart will be profound, most intense, serious, and for real. What is to be transcended in the context of any developmental stage will be transcended in your case directly and, therefore, as quickly as possible.

Just as the choice of anything but Happiness is unreasonable, so the choice of anything but that serious and most intense and quickening disposition is unreasonable. Yet you see that, by tendency, you seem to propose an alternative to what is only reasonable. Therefore, you are just oinking into your karmas, submitting to changes, and consoling yourself by imagining that identifying with the body-mind has something to do with religion.

True religion does not have anything to do with unconsciousness. True religion has everything, and, most fundamentally, only, to do with responsibility for participation and transcendence. And nothing else is true religion. This also is something you must come to understand and realize. This understanding belongs to the foundation of the Way of the Heart. It belongs to the beginnings of the Way of the Heart. The more you mature, even in the beginning developmental stages of the Way of the Heart, the more you will demonstrate this intensity, this seriousness, this reasonableness, this intelligence. It is not intelligent merely to submit to time, merely to submit to changes, or only to submit to possibility and conventional hopes.

A real and intelligent investigation of the things of conditional existence ought to dissuade you from such casualness. Human beings seem to be always creating a fantasy version of reality, and they seem also to be enclosing themselves in it through all kinds of social and cultural instruments, so that they do not have to come in touch with reality or real cosmic Nature. But how does cosmic Nature work? How does conditional existence work? Take a look at it. It is not leading any conditional being toward immortality or real Happiness. Even by stealth or strategy you cannot realize immortality or real Happiness by manipulating conditional possibilities. All your manipulation is ultimately confounded by events in conditional Nature, including death.

While alive, you may constantly enforce certain kinds of experiences that you find pleasurable and try to enclose yourself in those things—friendships, sex, food, entertainments—as if pleasure were a kind of immortality that would continue forever. But death comes anyway. Suffering happens anyway. Frustration happens anyway. Loss happens anyway.

Last week several well-known entertainers died, some of them known even worldwide as what we might call "archetypes of civilization". They represent to everyone signs of evident self-fulfillment, being artful in entertainment, being famous, being wealthy, being amused and amusing. Basically, all you know of those people are their ceremonies of entertaining you in the movies and on television.

How much else did you know about them? Did you know anything about their lives? Did you know anything about their lives in their later years? Anything about their experiences of dying? Their experiences in the process of death? No. Like Mickey Mouse, they remain archetypes of Happiness that suggest that human life is ultimately an entertainment, or that civilization wins, or that the pleasures of life are sufficient.

What these people are otherwise is not projected to you. Such entertainers are shown to you through the ceremonies of their entertaining of you, but you are not simultaneously shown their real lives. You do not see a movie and then see another film recounting the real life experiences of the stars in between the making of their fantasy movies. You see someone on television, but you are not also shown his or her real personal life and sufferings and doubts and disturbances.

So who died? The character in the TV series did not die. The elegant dancer did not die. The TV programs and the movies still exist. You can still watch them. But the stars were real human beings. These were real people who died, and they really suffered, and they were really bewildered, and they were very likely un-Realized.

Just as these professional entertainers are projected to you only through their archetypes, only through their ceremony of entertainment, likewise you are tending to try to do the same thing for everyone else. You are playing a civilized role, an archetype, a ceremony, a self-presentation that is supposed to continue the daily lie, to make life into a ceremony that opposes reality, real cosmic Nature, real Happiness, the underworld of real processes, so that you can keep amused. In some sense, you exist as a kind of vaudeville entertainer.

Everybody presents himself or herself as an entertainer in a civilized game of giving certain signals that say, "Yes, life is fulfilling. It is supposed to be purposed for its own sake." The other aspects of yourself are supposed to be kept hidden, kept very personal, kept in a certain sphere of some people whom you engage in a more personal way while the ceremony goes on, while you continue to play your part.

One of the major obligations human beings feel is to be a kind of archetypal participant in the human ceremony and not to digress from it, not to renounce it, not to step aside, not to step back, not to examine it as a totality, not to transcend it, not to fail to be an archetype of one kind or another, not to fail to support the conventional illusion that everything is getting better and better merely by going on.

This intention to be a civilized archetype is a very basic motive in your life that you must examine. You falsify yourself. You make yourself into a persona constantly. You make yourself into a mask constantly for this purpose. Yet, nonetheless, you are going to die. You suffer. You grow old. You have your doubts. You are going to suffer. You can lose. You are wondering about it all. When will that other part of you be taken seriously? When will you deal with it? Where will you deal with it? Under what circumstances?

CHAPTER 18

The Significance
of Renunciation

a Talk by Da Avabhasa
July 13, 1982

SRI DA AVABHASA: Everybody goes to the same place after death, but very few stay there. Because there is a certain amount of recorded data about the process of death, some people have suggested, "Why don't we just commit suicide, then? It sounds like there is much more that is desirable in the after-death realms than there is in this world."

The truth of it is that everybody does go into a sublime condition after death. It is simply that people do not have the capability to remain in that condition. Everybody has the potential for higher, subtler, more pleasurable worlds after death, but most people do not have the capability to stay in those worlds, even to fully perceive them and enter into them.

By virtue of the tendency of attention, and as a consequence of lingering ego-contraction and lingering association with the gross orientations of attention, human beings are associated with a condition that is less than what they desire. Because of this, some people choose a renunciate path in this life. Even though they are born into this life as a consequence of the movement of attention, they give no energy to the reinforcement of this consequence, and they devote their entire lives, at least from the moment of renunciation, to an alternative to this consequence.

They do this by various means, among them simply purifying the motions of attention, releasing attention from this orientation, and devoting attention to the Transcendental Condition, either actually, through the submission of attention to its Source, or metaphorically, through gestures toward God-ideas. By various Yogic means, they move attention out of its association with the nervous system and the downward-outward motions of the energies of the brain, so that they can concentrate in actual, concrete conditions above and beyond the gross plane.

This is the significance of renunciation, which, in its traditional form, is typically ascetical. Traditional renunciation is based on an original acknowledgement, coming out of either experience or belief, that what we are experiencing presently is a mental phenomenon. It is not mental as distinct from physical. The traditional presumption is that what we call "physical" is mental, and that it is a product not merely of personal mind, but of a universal, cosmic process, and that what we call "physical" is not merely objective, elemental stuff, but it is also a psychic process. If all objective events are psychic processes, then what we call "objective events" are mental events, or forms of mind. And this is precisely what is traditionally realized. This is the unique realization that makes greater human endeavors possible.

There can be secondary and inauspicious and unillumined motives for renunciation, but the fundamental reasoning behind the motive to renunciation is the realization that this gross existence into which we are born is brief, generally painful—at best an alternation between pleasure and pain—never completely fulfilled, mortal, and profoundly limited. But what makes that reasoning into renunciation rather than mere despair is the presumption that all arising conditions are mental phenomena occurring in cosmic mind, that all of the cosmos is mind, all phenomena are possibilities in mind, and, therefore, it is possible, as an alternative to merely devoting your life to fulfillment in this plane, which is a consequence of a certain kind of mind or attention, to devote your life to letting go of the tendency that produces this orientation, this consequence, attention to this particular possibility. Instead, you can devote your life to releasing attention from this orientation and liberating it to move either into a higher possibility or into the Divine Self-Domain Itself.

Renunciation is typically associated with a kind of monastic practice, strictly limited and celibate, but it need not be.[1] Whatever form it takes,

---

1. Da Avabhasa has indicated throughout His Wisdom-Teaching that it is not necessary to live a monastic style of life in order to be a true renunciate. True renunciation in the Way of the Heart is not strategic. It is founded in a progressive process of self-understanding, whereby all forms of the self-contraction are transcended. Through this process, and through an intelligently conservative discipline of the body-mind, an individual's attachments, motivations, and desires are naturally, not strategically, renounced.

renunciation is the basis of the Spiritual Process. It is the basis of the Way of the Heart as of any other God-Realizing Way. It is based ultimately on a clear vision of the limitations of this life, a clear Realization of the Status of existence altogether. And when that Realization becomes most profound, then the practice becomes one of transcending this realm and all limiting realms. That truly creative or Liberating process occurs in the seventh stage of life. In a certain phase of the seventh stage of life, a habit of life arises, which I call "Divine Indifference", that may appear to be like traditional renunciation, monastic or extremely conservative in its appearance.

Even so, renunciation is the basis of the Way of the Heart in all its developmental stages, even the preparatory stages, and it need not, as a style, be monastic. But such renunciation must essentially bear authentic characteristics. In other words, it must be about the liberation of attention from confinement to and obsession with and limitation by this present appearance. And, finally, when attention is free, it must be about the devotion of attention to its Source. When that Source is Realized to be the Source-Condition of all phenomena, then, in the seventh stage of life, the process is the Divine Recognition of conditions, so that the motives of attention dissolve in the Divine Self-Condition.

So—as I began to Say—everyone goes to the same place after death, but few stay in that place. If, instead of preparing yourself through a life-long practice of renunciation, or devotion to higher possibilities, or even to the Divine Condition, so that you can stay in at least a superior position, if not remain in the Ultimate Position—if, instead, you have devoted yourself to mere fulfillment in this plane without understanding why you have arisen in it and where it is arising altogether, then at death, even though you may have a momentary glimpse of the Great Condition and of higher realms, you will gravitate, through the force of the habit-energies of attention, back into more and more gross and limited conditions simply because you are habituated to them, not because some sneering Deity wants you to go back and suffer in a realm like this. There is no such attitude in the Divine.

Therefore, since the destiny of the body-mind is merely habit, it is appropriate to devote yourself principally, while alive in such conditions as this, to the liberating of attention from its habit so that it is free to Realize its Source, free to Divinely Recognize all phenomena and, therefore, to transcend the tendencies toward limiting phenomena. This is the point of view of renunciation. Renunciation is the right point of view toward life altogether, because life is a mental phenomenon, a vision that is the consequence of a certain habit of attention. Life in this form is not demanded of us by the Divine, nor by any Ultimate Law. It is here to be understood and transcended.

To understand and transcend this life requires intelligence and discipline. If you do not apply such intelligence and discipline during your lifetime, then at death you will at most have a temporary release, a glimpse of high things, and a gradual return to an order of phenomenal limitation very similar to the one that applies in this moment here.

The ordinary life that does not transcend itself is based upon the principle of egoity, or things as they are appearing to be. It is devoted to the fulfillment of that ego, or separate and separative self, in the midst of things that are now appearing. It does not take anything else into account. That egoic point of view generally does not realize that this apparently manifested existence is simply a phenomenon of mind, a psychic event. The ego makes a stark distinction between conscious awareness and objective appearances.

Therefore, even in the moment when you are aware that you are clearly participating in a phenomenon of mind, you divorce that conscious awareness from all that you perceive. You do not see that all of this is mind. You see it as a starkly gross, hard limitation over against conscious awareness. Consciousness becomes smaller and smaller in the midst of that presumption. You do not see that you are having a vision.

Therefore, you are, in effect, in this moment even, falling back from the Great Vision that has been Granted to you. The presumption of egoity is itself a way of falling back, a way of despairing, of not acknowledging Consciousness Itself to be the Principle in which cosmic Nature is arising, not acknowledging that cosmic Nature is a psycho-physical, rather than a merely physical, phenomenon. It is a great matter to simply realize that all of cosmic Nature is a psycho-physical phenomenon, and that psyche, or mind, is as much a part of what you are seeing as the "thingness" of it.

We are in an infinite expanse of mind. Mind is energy. And the principle of mind, or energy, is Self-Existing and Self-Radiant Being, Consciousness, Love-Bliss Itself. The world of objective Nature is arising in That. But the degraded consciousness in this world perceives Consciousness Itself to be present only as personal mind, and it conceives of personal mind as somehow only a secondary effect of material existence. It acknowledges the body to be in the plane of reality, and it thinks of mind and conscious awareness as spurious secondary illusions.

Of course, from that point of view there is no option but to live for the sake of personal fulfillment in the midst of the limitations as they seem. The principle of self-fulfillment is the basis for all common society. The search for self-fulfillment has driven everyone mad. That is why very few people understand the Truth of things, or what conditional reality is really composed of, and, therefore, very few people can apply themselves to a life-practice of any great significance.

Typically, everybody is just being mechanically determined, and people are so degraded by false notions that they cannot even "consider" Spiritual practice, a renunciate way of life, a deliberate life-discipline that transcends the motives to this experience, and deliberately prepares attention for gradual movement into a much broader plane of existence during this life or after death.

Of those who can take up a way of life based on such an orientation, even very few of them conceive of what the ultimate goal of such renunciation should be. Therefore, of those who die, all of them go to the Great Place, but few stay There. Of those who are born into this world, almost all of them return here. Very few conscious entities are able to pass out of this realm completely at death and go on to a higher realm, and of those who can separate from this condition of limitation, even fewer enter into the Divine Self-Domain.

You think that you are having your present experience at the level of the body. But you are not present as the body. Your awareness of the body is very subtle, at a level of electronic wizardry. And just how your present perception is developed is very mysterious. It is not by being out here at the periphery of this flesh-body, just being this meat. You are conscious, perceiving this appearance in a very mysterious fashion at the electronic level, at the matrix of mind and body. That is where you exist presently. This arising world is a vision, an appearance, a plastic of sensations made into what seems to be a concrete force, image, limit. But it is a psychic phenomenon.

Mind is not separate from cosmic Nature, either. Mind is part of the condition of cosmic Nature. Cosmic Nature is a psycho-physical phenomenon. It is a plastic. Mind is present as attention in all of that, moving mysteriously in an electronic field. That you are here is simply a fact of the moment. It is not necessary. Even in the moment it is only an appearance.

If you can truly understand this, see what this moment is composed of, how it is arising, what the process is that is determining it, then you can devote your life to a different kind of work than people typically do. Although some might, for good reasons, take on the style of the monastic renunciate, there is no absolute need to do so, because that is simply a style—for many, another form of seeking. It is not necessarily any more fruitful than a much more middle kind of path, a path of equanimity rather than asceticism.

Therefore, rather than Calling all My devotees to the ascetical style, I simply Call you to self-understanding and responsibility. If that responsibility is applied to the point of basic equanimity, it is not necessary to superimpose on it any more ascetical a style than is characteristic of you personally, because the import of renunciation is not to suffer or to negate yourself. The import of it is to free attention from bondage to this bodily-based orientation. Equanimity is sufficient. In the condition of equanimity, attention is free. Then you devote attention to its Source until it Realizes its Real Condition and the Condition of everything that arises, and then the process of Divine Recognition replaces the process of the devotion of attention to its Source.

In the seventh stage of life, at some point, the characteristics of the more ascetical appearance of renunciation may begin to appear. In any case, life falls away, and death comes to all. But in the case of those who prepare for an alternative to this limit, death is a greater event than it is for others.

It is not that everyone does not survive death. Everyone does, in fact, survive death. And even everyone has a glimpse of the Great Condition at death. In fact, even during life everyone has glimpses of It, in certain circumstances, in certain moments even, in deep sleep and in uncommon moments of the breakthrough of attention beyond its current, grosser limits. But those who live their lives relieving attention of the burden of the bodily-based orientation, of the habits that lead to this orientation—those people move on and stay in a condition that is at least higher than the present one.

DEVOTEE: You have Said that people think renunciates do not have anything. But actually they "have" something else.

SRI DA AVABHASA: Yes. To the outside viewer, renunciation looks like the denial of everything, the negation of happiness, the negation of pleasure, the negation of possessions. But the secret of renunciation is the devotion of attention to a Condition that is other than the one that is apparent, particularly to the outsider's view. One who is a Realizer as well as a renunciate may appear to others to have nothing and to be enjoying nothing, but he or she is actually having something else and enjoying something else.

Of course, false renunciation is another matter. There are those who think that by negating themselves they will somehow be gifted with something great, whereas they are really just making nothing out of themselves. This is just another one of the temptations of the un-Enlightened. Therefore, I remind you again and again that the ascetical appearance is a style. The style may be natural to some at an early stage, and it may even appear quite naturally at some point in the seventh stage of life. But it is, in the general case, not obligatory. By applying the ascetical style to yourself, you may simply be negating yourself, making nothing out of yourself, hoping that self-punishment will lead to Divine Self-Realization, whereas it does not. It leads to depression. No being needs nothing!

The real principle of renunciation is the transference of attention, not the suppression of the living being. Attention should first be transferred to its Source. Otherwise it will not be able to break through the limits of its objects. All its objects will always bind it, always act as an illusion, an obstruction to Divine Enlightenment. Therefore, rather than recommending the Way of the stages, I recommend the direct approach of equanimity based on self-understanding, the approach of developing equanimity and freeing attention, then using free attention to Locate its Source, and then Realizing the Condition of its Source. Then, when that is done, the process of Divine Recognition, the Way of the seventh stage of life in the Way of the Heart, begins.

This approach fulfills the purpose of renunciation. The Way of the Heart is, therefore, a renunciate Way, because the principle of its practice is to transfer attention from the binding effects of its present associations, the habit-energy associated with its present associations, the humorless devotion to its present associations, and to transfer it into the Domain of Divine Reality, to Realize its Ultimate Condition, and, therefore, to Realize the Siddhi,[2] or Capability, for the Divine Recognition of whatever conditions arise, so that even during life in the moments of subtle vision and ascent, or after death in the same process, the alternatives to Divine Translation will be Recognizable.

---

2. In Sanskrit, "siddhi" means "power", or "accomplishment". When capitalized in Da Avabhasa's Wisdom-Teaching, "Siddhi" is the Spiritual, Transcendental, and Divine Awakening-Power of the Heart that He spontaneously and effortlessly exercises as Sat-Guru.

This world is simply one of the alternatives to Divine Self-Realization. There are many other such alternatives, represented by all possibilities. If you do not Divinely Recognize possibility, if you do not Divinely Recognize phenomena, whatever their status in the scale of high and low in the pattern of energy or the pattern of phenomenal possibility, then you will tend to locate as attention, and conditional being, and existence in a realm that is less than the Divine Self-Domain.

CHAPTER 19

This Liberating Impulse

a Talk by Da Avabhasa
February 1, 1985

SRI DA AVABHASA: Spiritual life is about Realizing utter Love-Bliss, greater Bliss than is realized through sex or any other conditional experience. Such Love-Bliss is available before, during, and after any conditional experience. If you Realize It, if you devote your life to the Realization of That, then That is what you get—a life devoted to the Realization of That, a life of Communion with That. Then you will link your present life with What is Prior to this life, whereas if you devote yourself to the human conditions of existence for their own sake, you do not link yourself to What is Prior to this life. You link yourself to the same thing again. You perpetuate it, through reincarnation or simply through repetition in one form or another after death.

I have pointed out to you on a number of occasions that while you live in conditional form, you make mind, you create the psyche, through associations, repetitions, reinforcement. When you die and the body drops off, mind makes you. After death, you live in the world of mind as you have created it while alive. The after-death states have been called "bardos",[1] or "planes". Really, all such concepts are simply descriptions of how the mind operates dissociated from physical embodiment. You will spontaneously, through no will of your own, enter into realms of mind after death that correspond to your state of mind—not just your thinking mind but your subconscious and unconscious mind, the whole force of your tendency toward objects and conditional states. The realms with

---

1. The Tibetan term "bardo" means "gap". It denotes any interval of suspension, but particularly the "intermediate" state after death and previous to rebirth. The *Bardo Thodol* or "Book of the Dead" distinguishes six types of bardo: waking, dreaming, meditation, the death process, the after-death state, and the search for rebirth. These represent different states of consciousness as well as different realms of experience.

which you will be associated will be changing. There is a possibility of spending experiential time in such places. They are much like the realms you visit in dreams, but you will feel you are really there and not merely dreaming.

Mind makes association with realms that seem pleasurable, and after death you may pass in and out of these realms. But if you observe how desperate, egoically "self-possessed", depressed, craving, and dissatisfied you are generally, you will appreciate more profoundly what is likely after death and into what kinds of mind-realms you will be drawn. They are hells, purgatories, dark passages. They seem to go on for vast periods of time, even until they exhaust themselves and you pass out of them as you pass from one dream to the next.

It is said traditionally that a human birth is extraordinary, auspicious if it is rightly used, and should not be wasted. This is because the human form has the potential to be associated with the full range of conditional experience—gross, subtle, and causal—and is also not merely a mind-realm as the after-death states are, although it is such a realm ultimately. But, experientially, as a human being you are not merely living in the mind condition. You are living in the bodily condition. To be able to exercise yourself bodily, functionally, relationally, puts you in a position to indulge mind, but also to change it, to transcend it. To be embodied is to have a unique relationship to mind, which will then affect the after-death states when the body is thrown off.

If you merely use up your life, indulging mind as it already is, as you accumulated it while alive, then the after-death states will be conventional, mediocre, relatively unpleasant, perhaps dreadfully unpleasant, until another embodiment. If you use your life for the sake of transcendence and change mind, purify mind, release yourself from its limits, move into a higher consciousness, a higher mind, move even beyond mind to the point of complete Divine Enlightenment and relinquishment of conditional existence, Divine Translation is the Destiny you will Realize. But even if you do not fulfill the course of self-transcending practice to that ultimate degree, after death you will at least be associated with the ascended realms, the higher frame of mind, rather than the hells, the purgatories, the lesser states, where people rattle against one another like they do here.

Time in those hellish realms is even longer, but it does exhaust itself eventually, so that there is new embodiment in a form such as this or something that fulfills its characteristics in a similar fashion, thus giving you the opportunity to transcend the mind but in a more profoundly purified condition. Re-embodiment is then associated with a capability to link up with the Spiritual Process in its advanced stages.

What you are doing in this lifetime links up with all future time. If it is not utterly real to you yet that there is such time after death, then practice self-transcendence in the context of the realities that are obvious to you, and that practice is sufficient. Whether you know about what passes after death or not, you still can observe what is going on with you now, observe the self-contraction and its consequences, and come to the point of being moved to transcend it. You need not believe in the afterlife to do all of that. You can still receive My tangible Spiritual Heart-Transmission and enter into the life of Spiritual devotion to Me, whether or not you have any real sense of the afterlife. You can still enter the entire Spiritual Process in My Blessing Company. And all the same reasons for entering into it still exist, whether you know there is an afterlife or not.

I have just Described to you the process that works after death, and at some point you will have real experience of it. You will very likely in the course of your practice of the Way of the Heart come into contact with subtle experiences that confirm the survival of death and the existence of subtle realms, or mind-realms, and that show you something about how it all works. Even if you do not have much experience of it, if you enter truly into Divine Communion with Me, the Spiritual Process will self-authenticate Eternity and prove to the heart that this embodiment is not the end of existence, or even its purpose. Existence is purposed toward Love-Blissfulness, Freedom, and Divine Happiness.

While you live in bodily form, therefore, it is good for you to become dis-eased. It is good to feel dissatisfied and to seek beyond the conditional, ordinary, conventional apparatus of life, until you come into contact with Wisdom. Through that contact, the search itself will be transcended. Until then, the search is useful. It is the motive of dissatisfaction. Although it is the pursuit of satisfaction, it also contains the element of dissatisfaction. Seeking thus leads toward many things, including all kinds of self-fulfillment. It also leads to contact with religion and Spiritual life. But when you enter into My Sphere, into the Sphere of this Divine possibility, then you enter into the Sphere of "consideration" that will undo the search and its root, which is self-contraction, or egoity.

You can enter into this process without any beliefs or presumptions about an afterlife. But I must simply, among other things, Tell you what that is all about, since it is real and it is My experience. What happens after death is directly associated with what happens while you are alive. It is not that you merely live and then the body falls off and you drift into the eternal sublimity. And it is not that you merely live an ordinary life, struggling however you choose to live, and then go to heaven.

Death is simply the falling off of the physical vehicle. That is all that it is. Everything else continues, unless all the vehicles, all the aspects of the conditional self, are released through Divine Self-Realization. In the typical case, the ordinary human case, death is simply the abandonment of the physical. Everything else that you are as mind, psyche, personality, and desires continues, but without the anchor of embodiment. You do not wake up in your physical bed and your physical room, with your physical associations. The anchor drops off, and you drift into the bardos, the realms of mind. Where you drift is determined, therefore, by your mind, your state of mind altogether, what you have reinforced through your life-action.

The conditional cosmos is structured in such a way that, in spite of all errors and egoity, all beings will ultimately be purified. But if you know that even though this is so, you still might have to go through billions upon billions of lifetimes under all kinds of dreadful conditions, including spending uncountable spaces of time in hells of suffering, then there is no consolation in the knowledge that everyone will ultimately be Liberated. Therefore, you must know how you can cooperate with the Liberating Divine Principle so that you are not reinforcing egoically "self-possessed", disturbed, painful conditions of existence, but are rather advancing toward and entering into more and more of the profundity of Perfectly self-transcending God-Realization and the Ultimate Destiny of life in the Divine Self-Domain. This is what you must devote yourself to, what you will devote yourself to if you understand, if you hear Me and see Me and Awaken Spiritually through My tangible Spiritual Baptism.[2] Then your life must become cooperation with that Liberating Force.

That Divine Force will not only involve you in changing your action while you are alive so that you live a better life and are happier in your relations. All such changes are temporary. Fundamentally, what that Divine Force does is to Liberate you from mind. And all of this is mind, even this [touching His Body]. Physical embodiment is mind. It simply

---

2. Sri Da Avabhasa's Spirit-Baptism is often felt as a Spiritual Current of Life descending in the front of the body and ascending in the spinal line. Nevertheless, Sri Da Avabhasa's Spirit-Baptism is fundamentally and primarily the moveless Transmission of the Heart Itself, whereby He Rests the devotee in the Heart-Source of His Baptizing Spiritual Current and Awakens the intuition of Consciousness. As a secondary effect, the Spirit-Current Transmitted through His Great Baptism serves to purify, balance, and energize the entire body-mind of the devotee who is prepared to receive it.

carries with it the illusion that you are mind interiorly, but, in fact, you are physically present, physically active, and can therefore change mind, release mind, purify mind, transcend mind. This is true. This is how the Liberating Principle works within the realm of cosmic Nature. It gives you the opportunity to transcend that which is cosmic Nature, which is mind.

All of conditional existence is nothing but mind, constantly being modified, affected, changed, caused by apparently discrete entities. It is a vast, unfathomable complex of planes and beings, tendencies, experiences, realms within realms, imaginary realms that are just as real as real realms—there is nothing that is unreal, because it is all mind.

You are in bondage to mind. You are in bondage to objects. Not understanding your egoic self and the Great Reality, you are tending to presume this quality of mind you are experiencing by virtue of human birth, and you are trying to fulfill the ego, release it, or bring it into a state of total enjoyment. This search is a false principle. It is something you can struggle to fulfill, and you cannot even fulfill it completely. At any rate, in such pursuit you do not involve yourself in the principle of self-transcendence.

Because of how things are, you must transcend these conditions, not merely struggle to fulfill yourself within them. You yourself are a condition among these conditions. Conditioning, mind, all limitation of Divine Love-Bliss, must be transcended. This understanding and the encounter with the Living Divine Adept make the Spiritual Process possible. Therefore, when you come to hear Me and see Me, then you must become involved in the process of self-transcendence, or, in other words, the process of mind-transcendence. Ultimately, to go beyond mind altogether is to be Divinely Translated.

What you build up subjectively while you are bodily existing becomes your experience after death. What you purify and transcend while physically existing will not be your experience after death. What you make your object while alive will continue to be your object after death. Desires not fulfilled or transcended are your mind after death. Complexes, fears, obsessions are your mind after death. Thus, the Spiritual Process really is the purification and transcendence of mind, which is the same thing as the purification and transcendence of conditional self, or conditional existence altogether.

The very best situation to be in at the point of death is utter mindlessness. I do not mean you should have an empty head at the moment of death. I mean you should be utterly purified of the self-contraction, the mental tendency, such that you are only involved in the Free Condition of

Divine Love-Bliss. The best situation, the best condition to be in at the point of death, is the Divinely Self-Realized Condition of the seventh stage of life. Generally, that Condition points toward Divine Translation at death.

To be literally living in earlier stages than the Divinely Enlightened Condition at the point of death in general indicates what your destiny will be after death. Your stage of life is a very basic indicator. Most people do not go beyond a complicated, stressful, un-Happy involvement in the conditions associated with the first three stages of life. Such individuals do not go to heaven. They pass into experiential realms immediately associated with this material frame, as in dreams, now without the anchor of the body, appearing to spend all kinds of time in lesser conditional realms, often very unpleasant, literally what could be called "hells". Those who pass into the ascended stages of life—the "advanced" fourth stage and the fifth stage—will pass into the subtler realms of the Cosmic Mandala,[3] temporarily enjoying a somewhat more blissful experience until mind exhausts itself.

Mind, you see, is a kind of generative force. When forms are established in it, it produces experience until it wears down. All experiences within the Cosmic Mandala are, therefore, temporary, but some are much more difficult than others. Those in the outer range of the Cosmic Mandala are the more difficult. Beings there live a short time. There is more struggle, more threat there. The realms closer to the center of the Cosmic Mandala are associated with more glamorized conditions, beautiful spaces, and so forth, but the urge of conditionally manifested beings is likewise not ultimately fulfilled there. The urge to Complete Freedom, or Divine Self-Realization, is not fulfilled in those realms, and they also are temporary experiences.

Beings do sadhana in those realms. They practice the disposition of God-Communion, and they are not merely there to fulfill the pleasurable possibilities associated with their realm. At least this is so in the higher realms. In the lesser realms, where ordinary people living in this world might pass after death, conditional beings are not any more occupied with the motive to Perfectly Self-Transcending God-Realization than they are here. The lesser subtle realms are the same kind of place as this realm basically, although individuals are somewhat more tenuously associated

3. The Sanskrit word "mandala" (literally, "circle") is commonly used in the esoteric Spiritual traditions to describe the hierarchical levels of cosmic existence. Heart-Master Da Avabhasa uses the phrase "Cosmic Mandala" to describe the totality of the conditional cosmos. For a full description of the Cosmic Mandala, including an artist's rendering of the visual image of the Mandala, see chapters 24-26 in Part III of this book.

with experience there. Experience is more plastic in some way, and individuals there experience something like the dreamer's involvement.

Conditional beings are aware of having rather unusual abilities even in these lesser realms. They can pass in and out of places and circumstances and move about by an act of will, but all the time they still move within the lesser frame. The more profoundly aggrieved, gross, negative characters do not even wander in the middle-class streets of the afterworld. They settle into dark places and sinister scenes. They struggle, unable to get out for long periods of time, as you would in a nightmare—but they do not have the body in bed to wake up to. The mind freewheels on its own, as if they were stuck in a room watching a television program and did not have the ability to turn off the television set—but in this case they are actually in the program.

DEVOTEE: Heart-Master Da, do they stay there until the experience runs out?

SRI DA AVABHASA: Yes. And it runs out eventually. Such realms are usually described as hells where individuals are caught for thousands of years. Imagine yourself sitting in a box for ten thousand years! Such descriptions are in some sense metaphoric, but nonetheless they contain some truth, because time does appear to be real in these places.

Often religion is preached in this world through representations of the afterlife, threatening you with fire and brimstone on the one hand if you do not get straight, and offering you the pie-à-la-mode heaven on the other hand if you believe and behave. But, as I indicated to you, if it is not real to you that the afterlife exists or what it is all about, to try to threaten or attract you with these stories has no significant effect on you. I am simply Telling you about the afterlife because it is My experience and I want to account for it all. It will also be your experience at one time or another. It already is the experience of many people. There is, therefore, no reason why I should not Speak of it.

But I am not giving you a heaven-and-hell speech here. You need no belief system to involve yourself in the Spiritual Way of life. Therefore, I confront you about what is real to you, what is your experience. I point to the search, the self-contraction. I Call you into relationship with Me to receive My Spirit-Baptism. The Spiritual Process does not depend on systems of belief. It is true that at death you do not just disappear into unconsciousness, fall asleep, and forget everything. Mind goes on, and

153

mind controls you, and you no longer have the anchor of the body. If it is not real to you that the process of mind continues after death, still the separate and separative self and how it works is real to you now, and the Spiritual Process is real to you if you have experienced My Spiritual Heart-Transmission in My Company. In any case, the Spiritual Process is about self-transcendence, or transcendence of mind, transcendence of the psychology of attention. Whatever the structure of reality is in your view, the process of your existence is controlled by the mechanism of attention, the psychology of the self-contraction, and the degree to which you have transcended attention. Life is mind. Life makes mind. Life suffers mind. And life can be the transcendence of mind. Life as a process of the transcendence of mind, or of the psychology of attention, is Spiritual practice. A life devoted to self-indulgence without God-Communion, without self-understanding, without self-transcendence, is suffering.

Even those devoted to Perfectly self-transcending God-Realization suffer, but they suffer in the peripheral vehicles of the conditional self. In Communion with Me, you contact the inherent Love-Blissfulness of existence, and those aspects of your existence that are conditional, in which you are suffering, or even experiencing pleasure, become literally peripheral. You can enjoy that Fullness, then, even prior to Divine Enlightenment. It is simply that in the passage between the sixth stage of life and the seventh stage of life, the Fullness of Divine Self-Realization is permanent, no longer conditionally Realized.

Even so, the conditional periphery remains, but one's involvement with it changes. In the context of phenonemal conditions, one can be effective in Liberating or Blessing others. Even in the seventh stage of life, however, there is a struggle, as you see in My case. There is no end to the struggle with conditional existence. I could have bypassed some of it by simply not Teaching. But I had no choice in this matter, fortunately or unfortunately—fortunately for you perhaps—because Divine Re-Awakening in My case was not associated merely with Divine Self-Realization in the sense that I could have dropped out and disappeared. It was associated with the spontaneous appearance of the Siddhis of My Teaching Work.[4]

4. Da Avabhasa has indicated that, following His Divine Re-Awakening in 1970 and until His Divine Emergence in 1986, certain Siddhis manifested in Him that enabled Him to do His Teaching Work, the primary one being the capability to Perfectly identify with others, assume their karmas and their conditions, reflect them to themselves, and meditate them. Describing the Siddhis of His Teaching Work in 1982 He said:

I Submit My Self to devotees to the degree of becoming them, to the degree of taking on the condition

I have no attachment to this world for its own sake. My involvement with this world is simply for the sake of Liberating others. I am the Manifestation of that Principle in cosmic Nature Which is Liberating. I do not otherwise have any impulse to be associated with conditional existence, but I am bound to it nonetheless, because of this Liberating Impulse.

My devotees who enter into the seventh stage of life will participate in that Liberating Impulse in various ways, but their struggle will not be like My own, because they will not have the Siddhis that are uniquely associated with My Birth. Even so, they must carry on their Blessed existence under the real circumstances of conditional life with other people.

This Effort that Works through Me will not go on forever. It has its logic, its course, its structure. Its results depend on its reception. My Impulse is Complete for the Divine Self-Realization of others and the establishment of the Way of the Heart. But whether the Way of the Heart will be established or not depends on its reception. It could be rejected. It could be made into garbage. All the time there exists a tendency to reject it and make it into garbage, as with everything else that appears in the conditional realms, where everything is tending to be destroyed.

You may live relatively long. Already many of you have lived long lives compared to how long most people have lived in this world. Even so, in every moment of your existence there is the possibility of dying, the possibility of becoming diseased, the possibility of loss, the possibility of disconnection from others, the possibility of suffering. Your conditional existence has been threatened from the moment you were born. Threats are always arising, in you and outside you.

Everything that appears in the conditional world is tending to be destroyed, tending to come to an end, because it does not just appear on its own. It appears in conjunction with many other entities, motions, tendencies, programs, plans, disturbances. Every life, every impulse is associated with a creative effort to accomplish and to survive. That effort characterizes Me and My Work. You have seen what a difficult struggle it has been for Me to keep My Work going during all these years. It is not just difficult at this moment. It has always been difficult. The tendency has

---

in which they exist, and I Teach in that circumstance. . . .

I enter into this body . . . in order to be *just like you and to "consider" this body-mind with you, to animate it with you, to be exactly that and to transcend exactly that. This is My unique way of Working. There are some precedents for it traditionally, but it is basically a unique way of Working necessitated by this particular time and place. (September 15, 1982)*

always existed to destroy it and bring it to an end, as well as to simply not use it.

I can Work to bring the Process of real life into being and to establish it, but it still can be made into garbage, if you will not receive it and assume the responsibility of continuing with that Impulse to make it survive. I have, therefore, had to magnify My Impulse to keep it going. Well—you must do likewise. If this Impulse is going to have effect, if it is to survive through and beyond My Time of human existence, you must make it survive. You must use it. You must practice it. You must become rightly aligned to Me. You must fulfill it. You must advocate it. You must make your gathering strong—not just you in this room but all those associated with Me, all those who will read or listen to this Talk someday.

CHAPTER 20

Your Destiny after Death

Da Avabhasa's Oral Communications
April 9 and 17, 1991

SRI DA AVABHASA: The "death games" recommended in popular literature these days are, in general, procedures that can be relaxing and consoling, but they do not have the ability to change your destiny after death. A pretense exists today that an individual can be "enlightened" or "go to heaven" on the basis of what he or she does during the death process. This is not true. A wide range of destinies are possible after death. A superior destiny, even to the degree of Divine Self-Realization, requires profound sadhana throughout one's lifetime, and even throughout many lifetimes. "Death games" will not change your destiny, although they may relax and console you.

Therefore, My Instruction to My devotees is to do real sadhana throughout life and to continue that sadhana in the process of death.

If you are interested in going beyond your ordinary and lesser destiny, you should respond to Me and to the Way of the Heart by doing the sadhana I have Given for the sake of your Liberation. You should not expect some technique you might do on your deathbed to Liberate you.

To achieve a superior destiny after death, even the Ultimate Destiny, you must have the ability to transcend mind and the limiting tendency of attention. After death, your destiny will be determined by the tendency of mind and attention. That is the way it is. The kind of destiny you experience is determined by the sadhana you have done during your lifetime and by your Realization at the time of death.

Ultimate Liberation is Most Perfect transcendence of the mechanism of attention and of mind altogether. Therefore, Ultimate Liberation requires Most Perfect transcendence of desire, or the motives of attention. You may have glimpses of sublime things and attractive light in the process of death, but such phenomena are not in themselves Divine Enlightenment. Even if such phenomena arise, the ordinary individual has no capability to keep attention in that sublime Condition after death, and he or she generally drifts into the lesser conditional states via the lesser conditional tendencies of the mind.

There is no unique technique to use in the death process. You cannot go any further after death than your karma dictates or than your lifetime of sadhana makes possible. If you are My devotee, just because you are dying, you should not do anything different at death than you have done in a lifetime of sadhana in My Company. At death, you should engage the same practice and process in relationship to Me as you have done in meditation according to your form and developmental stage of the Way of the Heart.

The popular death and dying movement is supported by people without ultimate Wisdom who represent themselves as guides in the process of death. One of the popular techniques of the death and dying movement is the instruction to "go into the Light". "Looking into the Light" does not really have anything to do with what happens after death. All the instructions to "look into the Light" are a technique to relax people into the process of death and to help them to feel better while alive. There is already a psycho-physical tendency in the body-mind to have such an experience. Therefore, you need not guide yourself into it. Even though this tendency exists, however, people do not remain in the Light. Their attention goes to conditional states.

Basically, the popular exercises are tidbits people take here and there from the reports of near-death experiences. On the basis of these reports, people create programs for death and techniques to help them feel more relaxed about dying. What occurs after death, however, they do not know, because the after-death experience is created by one's karmic tendencies, and it is only affected by real sadhana. Mind, or its absence, determines where you will go.

There is a tendency in the popular literature about death to think of the Light as an ultimate, heavenly realm. It is not that at all. It is more like a window in the midst of the field of perception. "Going into the Light" is a process of ascent corresponding to the fifth stage of life. It is not the ultimate process of sadhana. The ultimate process is not about ascent, descent, or merging into some Super-Object, such as the Light. The ultimate process is about Realizing the Perfectly Subjective Divine Self-Condition.

CHAPTER 21

After Death, Mind Makes You

a Talk by Da Avabhasa
December 11, 1988

S RI DA AVABHASA: People tend to think that at death maybe you are just dead, or else you will go to heaven. For most people, death is in the future. It is not connected with the present. However, what occurs after death is actually determined by how you live and by your state of consciousness.

During life, the individual consciousness is limited by the physical vehicle, defined by the brain, the nervous system, the mechanism of the body. You are kept from access to most of mind by this barrier of brain and nervous system. Therefore, most of mind is in the so-called unconscious. Because this is so, it is possible to just live your life on the basis of the stimulation of this bodily entity, and to take from life the pleasure that you can. Such is the choice that many make, because they do not understand what is on the other side of the barrier that is the body. But the barrier is lifted at death, and you fall into the domain of the so-called unconscious.

Before death, you make mind, and after death, mind makes you. Mind is your circumstance after death, and not just the thinking mind of your limited conscious awareness. The unconscious is your circumstance after death. You know the potential in your life for dreams. If you stay healthy and keep your mind focused on positive thoughts, perhaps you will not have a bad dream, but still the nightmare is there all the time. And after death, you no longer have the physical means to prevent the unconscious from becoming conscious.

If you use the circumstance of the present body-mind as a means to purify the unconscious, or the mind that is outside the realm of the brain and that is presently cut off by the brain, then the mechanisms of the unconscious will not control your destiny after death. On the other hand, if you use your lifetime simply as an opportunity to indulge in bodily-based existence, you do nothing but add to the sum total of karma in the unconscious, which then becomes your destiny. Therefore, you must get wisdom, you must understand, you must do sadhana and be purified of karma.

People think that perhaps the brain is everything, perhaps mind is the brain, perhaps when you are dead, you are dead. It is not true. Nevertheless, the brain is a limiting mechanism that keeps you from having certain kinds of experiences. The brain exists not to evolve so you can have all experiences, but to limit and define the kinds of experiences you can have. Most of what is potential as experience is outside the brain-mind and, as a general rule, not accessible. Sometimes openings may occur beyond the brain-mind, and you may have unusual experiences, some positive, some negative. But for the most part, you remain in a state controlled by the brain-mind. Your thoughts and experiences relate to your present physicality.

Therefore, for the most part, people think that life is about the experiences of the present body-mind. They do not understand the purpose of the limit on experience, which is to purify the karmic mind that preceded the present birth. You must devote your life, not to the fulfillment of the bodily personality, but to the purification of karma through transcendence of the bodily personality, so that in death, when you lose the vehicle that presently shuts off experience, and when all experience is available to you, your experience will be auspicious, because mind has been purified and attention has been given to its Divine Source-Condition.

The degree to which you have done all of this—in other words, the stage of life you represent in manifestation—will determine the quality of your experience after death. The body is a limit. People are always wondering, "How come, if I perform good and right action, I do not always get good results? How come all these really bad guys are having an apparently good life? Everything good seems to happen for them. How come all these virtuous people are suffering so terribly?"

In the context of bodily existence, results do not necessarily immediately follow. The place where results occur is outside the brain-mind. You are either getting the results of purifying the unconscious, or you are getting the results of adding to it and complicating it. In the context of the body, you can be performing actions that are building up karmic destiny, but, because of the present destiny and tendencies of the body, what we might call "good results", apparently, are taking place. Yet some other person who is actually purifying the sum total of karmic bondage through right action may be having a difficult life.

The more you mature in your practice of the Way of the Heart, the more you come to appreciate what is really going on and what kind of mechanism you are associated with here. People generally, especially Westerners, and "Westernized" individuals, tend to make the casual choice of bodily self-fulfillment. This is a tendency of the ego in general, no matter what the person's place of origin, East or West.

Westerners, or "Westernized" people in general, have a certain Omega-like orientation.[1] I have observed in My Work in the West that people struggle intensely against the demand for self-discipline. They are always struggling: Should they discipline themselves? Or should they go for the good life? You are always thinking about this nonsense, because you have so little experience and so little understanding of what is really taking place. You will not resort to Wisdom. People generally do not resort to Wisdom or to Realizers. Therefore, they just go along with the programs of the body and the mind.

You are not going to experience a collective destiny after death. You are going to experience a personal destiny, a destiny that ultimately goes beyond individuality. You are not going to realize after death what every-body thinks life is about. You are going to realize the sum total of your karmic tendencies. Therefore, you should use this lifetime of practice in My Company to be purified of these tendencies.

One could say that sadhana altogether is basically self-purification, that it is not that the Divine must be found, but, rather, the things with

1. Sri Da Avabhasa uses the term "Omega" to characterize the materialistic anti-Spiritual culture that today dominates both West and East. The Omega, or Occidental, or Western, strategy is motivated to the attainment of a future-time, perfected ordering and fulfillment of the conditionally appearing worlds through the intense application of human invention, political will, and even appeal to God conceived as Creator or Power apart. It is associated with the left hemisphere and the analytical functions of the brain.

In contrast, Da Avabhasa calls the characteristically Oriental, or Eastern, strategy the "Alpha strategy". Just as Omega cultures seek to perfect and fulfill the world, Alpha cultures pursue an original or non-temporal and undisturbed peace, in which the world is absent (and thus unimposing). The Alpha strategy is associated with the right hemisphere and the synthetic or holistic functions of the brain. Although the cultures that were originally founded on the Alpha approach to life and Truth are fast disappearing, the Alpha strategy remains the archetype of Spiritual life, even in the Omega culture.

Neither the Omega strategy nor the Alpha strategy Realizes Truth, as each is rooted in the yet-to-be-inspected, observed, and understood action of egoity itself, which motivates all human interests short of Divine Self-Realization. Both the Omega and the Alpha strategies only dramatize the ego's desire for escape and fulfillment, and thus each tends to perpetuate the ego itself.

which you are deluding yourself must be released. The Divine is the very Context of existence, yes, but self-contraction has also taken on all kinds of forms, the summary of which is non-awareness of the Divine Self-Condition.

Therefore, sadhana is basically purification of these forms of self-contraction. Sadhana is not about what people commonly call the "good life", which is a "Westernized" view of self-fulfillment. Sadhana is not that at all. However, a person who does sadhana can, and rightly should, in general, maintain positive life-signs, helpful signs, positive relational signs. All such signs are simply expressions of the disposition of sadhana, which is not about pursuing self-fulfillment or glorification of the egoic self, clinging to qualities of life, relationships, experiences, and limitations for their own sake. The daily qualities of life may be generally whole and positive by your standards, but still you must do the sadhana of self-transcendence. Likewise, if the qualities of your life at the moment are not particularly positive, you must do the same sadhana.

From the point of view of sadhana, then, it does not make any difference whether the qualities of any given day are positive or negative, because you must do the same thing in any case. Sadhana in the Way of the Heart is important not only to destiny after death but to this lifetime also. But the truths that are to be valued are not merely those of physical design. Rather, the great virtue of sadhana is advancement in the stages of life. As one's practice matures and becomes most profound, the state of one's consciousness is transformed. The general life-signs become more and more characteristic of renunciation, and the quality of individual consciousness exhibits the characteristic of Realization, progressively, in the advanced and the ultimate stages of life.

In general, then, the destiny after death corresponds to the Realization while alive. That being the case, it is also clear that, except in the case of Divine Enlightenment, you are given the opportunity for further growth after death. Even so, all that takes place in the Context of a Paradox and a Mystery of unfathomable proportions. The signs of time and space in that Mystery are not comprehensible from the present worldly point of view.

Fundamentally, you can say that sadhana is a process of self-purification. It is about the Outshining of all forms of limitations by the Force of Divine Consciousness Itself. It is about magnifying the Force of Consciousness Itself, the Force of Love-Bliss Itself. This Force purifies and releases.

In Satsang[2] with Me you are coming into contact with that Virtue. As you mature, you become a more and more responsible participant in the process of self-purification, or, ultimately, Outshining. The Bliss of Divine Reality is simply the Absolute Objectless Expansiveness of Mere Being, without a trace of limitation. It is Self-Radiant, Love-Blissful, Absolute.

Between this apparition that is the body-mind and such Realization, there is much, much more than merely living and much, much more than "talking"-school[3] attitudes and gestures. Real sadhana is necessary. Resort to Grace is necessary. Grace must Work. This is necessary.

2. The Sanskrit word "Satsang" literally means "true or right relationship", "the company of Truth, or of Being". In the Way of the Heart, it is the eternal relationship of mutual sacred commitment between Sri Da Avabhasa as Sat-Guru (and as the Divine Person) and each true and formally acknowledged practitioner of the Way of the Heart. Once it is consciously assumed by any practitioner, Satsang with Heart-Master Da is an all-inclusive Condition, bringing Divine Grace and Blessings and sacred obligations, responsibilities, and tests into every dimension of the practitioner's life and consciousness.

3. "Talking"-school is a phrase coined by Sri Da Avabhasa to characterize those whose approach to sacred life is dominated by talking, thinking, reading and philosophical analysis and debate, or even meditative enquiry or reflection without a concomitant and foundation discipline of every aspect of body, emotion, and mind.

He contrasts this ineffectual—and often presumptuous—"talking"-school approach with what He terms the "practicing" school. Those who belong to the "practicing" school in any tradition are committed to the ordeal of self-transcending discipline in every area of life, under the guidance and challenging Mastery of a Sat-Guru.

CHAPTER 22

The Scale of Limitations and the Glorious Domain of God

by Da Avabhasa
July 2, 1980

Death can occur at any moment in human development, or evolution. Death can occur at any stage of Spiritual practice or Realization. Whenever it occurs, if you will surrender into God in love, through the process, or Yoga, of death, you may, in the event of death, transcend many or even all of the human limitations that would require future embodiment, adaptation, growth, learning, and evolution in the scale of limitations. The death process is so profound and inclusive of all that is Man that right participation in the event can even bring about self-transcending growth into the advanced stages of Spiritual Realization, and even the ultimate stages of Transcendental and Divine Self-Realization.

It is true that growth, evolution, and Divine Self-Realization through self-sacrifice (or self-transcendence) are the proper and necessary "business" or art of one's lifetime—and if you are not sufficiently prepared by Spiritual surrender in life, you cannot expect to be magically evolved merely by the intrusion of death. But death is a transforming event that can provide opportunities for surrender, self-transcendence, and growth that may not otherwise or often appear within the limits of your lifetime. Therefore, if you are prepared through right, self-transcending, loving, and surrendering activity while alive, those same qualities or activities can be magnified in their effect in the event of death.

My devotee should participate in the death process as I have Instructed.[1] But he or she should also practice the Way of the Heart in the same manner that he or she was accustomed to practice it under the daily circumstances of living. In whatever moment death begins, practice surrender of egoic self via the same form of the Way of the Heart that you were exercising up to that moment in life.

In the full maturity of the seventh stage of life, the death process is essentially free of the limiting implications it may seem to have at any other or previous stage of life. Then death, like any other experiential event, appears as nothing more than a temporary and superficial modification of the Self-Existing and Self-Radiant Divine Being, or Divine Self, or Consciousness Itself. Therefore, ultimately, death is easy, without terrible significance or binding power.

In the future, for mankind or some other race, on Earth or elsewhere, death may no longer exist as an arbitrary intrusion or accident that interferes with the completion of the total work or necessary sacrifice of a lifetime. Then life and death will be a truly conscious exercise in manifestation. And all beings and things will exist simply as patterns in Light, or Self-Existing and Self-Radiant Divine Being, growing and changing through ecstatic self-sacrifice in the unthreatened Environment of Love-Bliss. In that time, death will only be the final stage in a history of transformation, from first appearance (or birth) into the phenomenal realm of sacrifice until Ultimate Divine Translation into the Glorious Self-Domain of Eternal Union, Unity, and Happiness. So be it.

---

1. A summary of Sri Da Avabhasa's Instructions on how to practice in the midst of the death process may be found in chapter 43 of this book.

PART III

"After Death,
Mind Makes You"

Sri Da Avabhasa (The "Bright")
Sri Love-Anandashram, November 1991

"After Death,
Mind Makes You"

INTRODUCTION

I s there anyone who does not want to know what happens after death, really, authoritatively? The mystery of what it is to be "dead", what part of us survives, whether reincarnation is true and how it works are huge questions that human beings have always puzzled over. There have been some indications of real answers to these questions in the Spiritual traditions, especially in esoteric texts such as the *Tibetan Book of the Dead*. And now there is a growing body of "scientifically" documented knowledge about out-of-body experiences and near-death phenomena. But what you are about to read in Part Three of *Easy Death* you will find nowhere else. Nor will you discover such Wisdom through any ordinary near-death experience. Sri Da Avabhasa's description of the total structure of the cosmos and its laws of operation is completely unprecedented. Only a Being Who has Transcended birth and death completely could Give such a Revelation.

In Part Three, Sri Da Avabhasa makes plain that the physical dimension of the cosmos is only a very narrow band in the total spectrum of what exists. We are already alive in far greater dimensions than we are normally aware of—although in dreams and visions, out-of-body experiences, and more profound moments of meditation we may have glimpses of what lies beyond the physical body and its world.

The cosmos is only Light. This truth is acknowledged by all the great Realizers, and now also in the discoveries of modern physicists delving into the mysteries of matter and energy. But until Sri Da Avabhasa, no one has ever unveiled the total picture made by this immense spectrum of light. In His monumental Talk "The Cosmic Mandala" and in "The Divine 'Brightness'" (the excerpt from *The Dawn Horse Testament* reprinted in this Part), Sri Da Avabhasa sets forth in comprehensive detail the grand design within which we exist. The Revelation is overpowering—the answer to aeons of speculation, mythology, and partial visions of the nature of existence.

Understanding this greater depth of existence is essential preparation for the revolution in our awareness that comes about when we die. Otherwise, the death transition can be very confusing and disorienting. What we encounter at death can be compared with the dream state— except that we have no body to wake up to! Suddenly we are set loose in a vast plastic of lights and forms and events that are simply "mind-stuff". These are the infinite realms of mind, for, as Sri Da Avabhasa Explains:

Mind is not merely in the brain and less than the brain. Mind is the circumstance of limited consciousness in its association with objects of all kinds. Mind is universal, infinite in extent. And if you put yourself into a position to explore the roots of experiencing, you are going to enter into a realm of mind in which you realize mind to be greater than mere daily thinking and social consciousness. (p. 178)

Most of the realms of mind are filtered out of our ordinary waking experience in this life by the mechanism of the human brain (see "The Gross Personality, the Deeper Personality, and the Ultimate Identity", pp. 226-32). That the brain screens out so many layers and forms of experience is actually very helpful to us. After death we have no protection against the chaos of unlimited mind-forms—because we no longer have a physical body to anchor and control our experience. Attention moves at random to whatever attracts it, and destinies are created on the spot. This is what Sri Da Avabhasa means when He Says, "Before death, you make mind, and after death, mind makes you."

Becoming aware of the unlimited possibilities within the cosmos naturally leads to the issue of reincarnation. Does human embodiment recur, and if it does, does it happen to everyone? As with everything else, Sri Da Avabhasa does not approach the subject conventionally. He is not asking us to "believe" in reincarnation—He is merely Offering His own observations on the process. One of the questions He "considers" is why we tend not to remember past lives. Are we, in fact, the same one who existed in past lifetimes, and, if so, in what sense? Who or what is it that persists from lifetime to lifetime? These are important questions, and a thorough discussion of them and many other aspects of reincarnation is to be found in "The Paradox of Reincarnation" (pp. 217-25), and "There Is No Entity That Passes from Lifetime to Lifetime" (pp. 233-39).

Even if these Essays prove reincarnation—and they certainly do present a compelling Enlightened logic for it—is reincarnation a consoling prospect anyway? Is the Cosmic Mandala as a whole, or any of the myriad realms within it, a comfortable or consoling place to be? Sri Da Avabhasa does not suggest this. He is moved to Reveal the total picture of existence, but not so that we will be encouraged to look for some glorious or exotic experience, now or after death. The cosmos is a ceaseless play of changes, and any experience inevitably passes away. Rather, Sri Da Avabhasa is inviting us to understand the fleeting and unsatisfactory nature of all experience, and become wise. Our ultimate destiny is nowhere in the Cosmic Mandala. Our ultimate destiny infinitely transcends the Cosmic Mandala. This is the real secret contained in the Talks and Essays of Part Three.

CHAPTER 23

Death Is an Entirely Different Event Than You Think It to Be

a Talk by Da Avabhasa
August 11, 1979

SRI DA AVABHASA: Many energies and psychic processes are associated with a person's death, and if you are around a dying person, you can become sensitive to these energies and processes. If you are professionally serving someone who is dying, for instance, and if you allow yourself to be sensitive, as well as professional, then you are in a position to observe the transition of death, as one might in a more natural society. Although you may not be an intimate of the person, you may temporarily be an intimate of a kind, and, as such, you have a kind of psychic entrance into the person's domain. In some sense, therefore, you must endure the person's transition, even though you may not know the person well. You must psychically participate in the process of releasing. You must transcend the awesome effects of witnessing the death, and you must then return to a state of equanimity. In doing so, even though you may only be casually associated with the person, you represent one of the helpers in the person's transition.

DEVOTEE (a physician): There are physical signs as well. The pupils dilate, and certain things occur even before you can sense that the person is actually gone.

SRI DA AVABHASA: There is a sense of energy, a psychic sense of the death.

DEVOTEE: Yes. It is the opposite of a birth. At the time of a birth, all of a sudden there is a great, expansive energy or space, and an entity has become present. But deaths seem to be the opposite. There seems to be a kind of vortex, or a void.

SRI DA AVABHASA: Have you all experienced that sense of a burst at the moment of a birth? You may have discounted it because you thought it was just your enthusiasm for the birth that suddenly made you happy. But if you will be sensitive to it, you can sense a presence entering the room, a bursting in that is somehow different from the moment when the being was still in the womb.

DEVOTEE: It is a very blissful feeling.

SRI DA AVABHASA: Yes, there is a great deal of energy associated with it, and also light. I remember the sudden light in the room at the time of a birth. I did not ask if anybody noticed it at the time, but I can remember having that impression. There was a literal light, a life-color, a redness. There was a great deal of energy associated with the sudden beginning of an independent life, or a life that is now at least relatively independent as compared to its existence in the womb.

People have many fears about death because they think of death in the cold terms of the physical snuffing. They do not think of death at all in terms of the energies and psychic changes associated with it and the actual transition, all of which are noticed even by doctors, and which are documented in reports of the extraordinary phenomena experienced by people who seem to have died and are resuscitated. Such witnesses report that the tangible life-presence that is the human being does leave at some moment in death. That process must be accounted for in any speculation about what happens after death. Some sort of destiny is obviously implied by it, whatever we may want to say it is altogether. It is a noticeable transition, and it is not about the physical body in itself. Such understanding is very helpful in integrating one's emotion with the possibility of death.

When you witness the birth or the death of another, and, ultimately, if not before, when you experience the process of your own death, you feel naturally aligned to the laws that govern conditional existence. You are immediately awakened to the energy dimension, or the psychic dimension, of the process of life and death. Only when you limit yourself to the external view, cold and bereft of experience, do you fall prey to the rigid, anxious vision of death. Even life seems dead and threatening if you do not see it from the enlivened, life-positive, and Divinely Enlightened "Point of View".

Death is one of the great events that you tend to view coldly, because you are bereft of experience and bereft of an intimacy with death whereby you can immediately account for the energy and the psychic dimension of the process. When you only think about death and do not have much experience of it, you think of it in terms of the "meat body" only, and it looks terrible.

Actually, when you associate with the event of death in the same way you associate with the event of birth, many more things are accounted for in your feeling, in your psyche, in your energies altogether than you can now, in your anxiety, bring to the thought of death. When you are confronted with death, those things are instantly there, just as there is something instantly present in a woman at the moment of the labor whereby birth is accomplished. All kinds of force and chemistry and bodily capability and mental capability appear that a woman in labor could not have drummed up before the event came upon her. Many women have told Me, "You cannot ever be prepared for it." When it actually comes, it is greater than you ever presumed, and yet it is all there to happen. Suddenly you have the capability for it.

Just so, you must have a capability for death. You must participate in death. And it is best to become congenial with it while alive. Begin to become involved in death as a psychic and energy event and be ultimately relieved of your fear through the Spiritual Process. Your conventional fears are relieved when you become intimate with processes that must necessarily involve you at death, and, therefore, you do right to be intimate with them while you are alive, so that you do not live a life generated by cold fear. Live a life that is life-positive, sympathetic with the things and conditions of life, understanding their processes, always enhancing life through the fulfillment of life-positive laws. You do not become life-negative by witnessing death. See it. Witness it. It is something entirely different than in your fear you presume it to be. Any experience that you actually endure bodily includes suddenly the whole psychic and energy dimension.

But when you think of death, you think of it only as a physical thing, and you cannot associate psyche and energy with it. Because you think the being is just snuffed out by death, you are in fear of it. Yet the actual event is a psychic and energy phenomenon as well as a physical one.

Therefore, death is an entirely different event than you think it to be in your fear, in your intellectual analysis of it, generally bereft of experience, bereft of intimate witnessing of the process in others, and bereft of witnessing similar processes in your own body-mind that ultimately become death.

CHAPTER 24

The Cosmic Mandala

a Talk by Da Avabhasa
July 11, 1982

I

SRI DA AVABHASA: It is more or less common knowledge, at the present time, that you are not merely seeing what is external in this room. Your seeing is, in fact, an electronic apparition, developed in the nervous system of the brain. You have no direct connection to the gross object, or objects, that you are seeming to view at the present time. In other words, you are having a vision. You are not merely seeing a gross environment, but you are having a vision of a gross environment.

Likewise, your sense of being physically embodied is communicated to you through the electronics of the nervous system. You are experiencing an apparition, an electronic sense of being identified with a gross physical body. The position in which you are experiencing perceptions is an extremely subtle position. You seem to be possessed of very gross, tangible objects of attention, but none of the objects with which you are associated are actually gross and tangible to you. They are all electronic apparitions.

Because of the tendency to be identified with the body, and also because of all the taboos associated with conventional consciousness in this world, people do not investigate, or thoroughly explore and "consider", the status of their own experience in any moment. Therefore, when they have uncommon experiences, such as near-death experiences or even mystical experiences, they interpret and modify those experiences, or only move into certain kinds of experiences, because of limiting tendencies or presumptions of mind.

Mind is not merely in the brain and less than the brain. Mind is the circumstance of limited consciousness in its association with objects of all kinds. Mind is universal, infinite in extent. And if you put yourself into a position to explore the roots of experiencing, you are going to enter into a realm of mind in which you realize mind to be greater than mere daily thinking and social consciousness.

Those who take up the discipline of Yogic mysticism learn in the process to become responsible for the tendencies of mind and attention that cause certain experiences to arise, or cause attention to gravitate toward one or another kind of phenomenon, or cause limiting interpretations to be superimposed on experience. Through the science of Yogic mysticism, living beings can enter into a pure perception of the mechanism of human existence.

By contrast, the spontaneous experiences of people in the near-death condition are really impure perceptions of the mechanism wherein experience is arising, because those who experience them are not completely responsible for attention, and, therefore, for mind. Likewise, in the ordinary waking state, because of the conditional limits of attention, people are engaged in an impure perception of the present phenomena of ordinary waking consciousness. They do not directly enter into an awareness of things. They are living out a conventional destiny based on un-Enlightened presumptions of born existence in this world. People do not typically enter into subtler phenomena, or the mechanisms that are the source of gross experience, and, even if they do, whether intentionally or unintentionally, they tend to enter into them via irresponsible attention— or attention that is habituated to a limited state of self-identification, limited associations, and mind-forms that are developed in the un-Enlightened drive of the individual for consolation and survival.

But in the near-death experience, and in the death experience, which will come to everyone, attention moves directly into, through, and beyond the subtler mechanism of the brain and nervous system, and then, ultimately, into the Source of phenomena, mind, and the mechanics of attention. The Source of phenomenal appearances is a great Power. It is Love-Blissful Energy. It is called "Shakti" in the Hindu tradition. It is Maya, or the binding power of creation. It is a dimension of the Transcendental (and Inherently Spiritual) Divine Being, in Which you inhere, and with Which you are, ultimately and Perfectly, Identical. But because you are related to That with Which you are ultimately Identified, and in Which you inhere, on the basis of an already presumed limitation of being, you do not live on the basis of Identification with the Divine Self-Condition.

The situation of conditionally manifested beings in this world is typical of conditional beings in all worlds. You are presuming a limited condition of being, based on identification with attention in your current state of embodiment. The embodied attention is surrounded by a massive psychic form or individuated state of energy. And each of you is living out that condition in the gross plane of embodiment. You have the opportunity, in the subtler range of your existence, to explore more subtle conditions of existence and even the Ultimate Divine Self-Condition of all existence. That opportunity is directly available to you in the present moment, but you are dissociated from it through the habit mechanism of attention. Likewise, in sleep, in dreams, in reveries, in near death, in death, in your life of aspiration and creativity, in all kinds of moments, you are thrown out of the circumstance to which you are tending to bind yourself habitually, and you have the opportunity to perceive, or intuit, That Which is Ultimate or Divine.

But the state of your attention, which is a mechanical gesture of individuated consciousness within the frame of conditional possibilities, determines your experience. If an individual enters into the near-death state or the actual death state in a moment of Spiritual maturity, having (through real self-transcending Spiritual practice) become responsible for the mechanism of attention, so that the body-mind is in a state of equanimity and attention is inherently free, then whatever secondary phenomena may occur, the Primary "Phenomenon" will be directly obvious.

What people are seeing in the near-death state are mind-forms, or tendencies of mind. The tendencies of their attention are causing them to gravitate toward apparitions in the universal realm of appearances. Thus, people do not generally report a direct awareness of the mechanism whereby phenomena are arising. Rather, they describe secondary visions.

II

SRI DA AVABHASA: If attention were free to simply see the universal mechanism in which the phenomena of near-death experiences are arising, however, what would be seen is a Mandala of light, or light-energy, made of concentric circles.

In the *Tibetan Book of the Dead*, it is said that after death a person will immediately enter into the Clear White Light. This is the White Brilliance, the primary Light from which all colored light comes prismatically. The curve is the sign of the crystalline prism that is conditional existence, which breaks up the Whiteness into colors. Just as a rainbow is red and yellowish at its outer edge, then blue toward the center, the outer field of the Mandala is golden-yellow with reddish or pinkish colors at its periphery and blue toward the center. But at the most distant central point is the White Brilliance.

In death, attention moves directly into the White Brilliance. If people talk about seeing down a tunnel when they are entering into the near-death state or the after-death state, generally the tunnel is the indigo field that surrounds the blue. As they enter into the blue, they seem to pass down a long tunnel made of the indigo field. Then they see into the blue field itself, and if they do not become involved in the blue field, they will see beyond its possible visionary phenomena or apparitions. The blue field itself will seem like a tunnel that moves into the distance and may even curve slightly to the right, so that the White Brilliance seems to be directly ahead of them, but just slightly around a curve. The light even looks as if it is shining against the left wall. That White Brilliance is not merely objective to attention. If It is Divinely Recognized, It is Realized to be the Native Self-Radiance of Self-Existing Divine Being, or the Transcendental (and Inherently Spiritual) Divine Self. Only if it is Realized as such will attention enter into the Domain of Whiteness and stay there. That is Divine Translation, or entrance into the Divine Self-Domain.

But human beings are controlled by the mechanics of attention. They are already identified with lesser states by virtue of the habit of attention. Thus, as it is said in the *Tibetan Book of the Dead,* if there is no ability to remain in the White Brilliance, or the Clear White Light, other apparitions will immediately appear. The *Tibetan Book of the Dead* describes a developing sequence of apparitions, at the end of which occurs re-embodiment in the gross plane. The book is in fact a record of the real investigations and real experiences of highly Spiritualized individuals who had the capability to enter fully into the process of death and life. The process they describe as the return from the White Brilliance, or the Clear White Light, to embodiment is in fact inevitable in nearly all cases.

Each of the levels of this Great Mandala of the Cosmos represents a quality of energy, or light. In each of the rings or portions of this Mandala that move out from the central Whiteness are infinite numbers of possible worlds and kinds of embodiment. In this gross plane in which you now exist, you are at the outskirts of the Great Mandala of the Cosmos at this present moment. There are grosser conditions of awareness, grosser possibilities, than the present one, which may be called "hells", or degraded states, or states of embodiment less than human. They may appear as forms of worlds other than the present one, as well as states in the plane of this gross world that are not necessarily apparent to vision.

You are presently existing in the outer frame of the Great Field of the Cosmic Mandala. Unless there is responsibility for attention, there will be no movement closer to the Center. Unless there is Divine Enlightenment, there will be no permanent residence in the Center, or the Source, of the Cosmic Mandala, and there is no permanence anywhere but in the Source. All possibilities, all forms of embodiment and experience in the planes of manifested light, or the rainbow of the Cosmic Mandala, are temporary.

It is possible to live a long time in any plane. It is even possible to live a long time in this gross world under certain conditions of Yogic transformation. It is possible to appear as an ordinary human being in this world for hundreds or thousands of years. Typically, people live for just a few years, but they could live longer. To live longer is not to Realize Divine Enlightenment—it is simply to live longer. It is possible to realize a state of relative equanimity, in this world or in any other world, and to live more peacefully, more happily, more pleasurably, more sensibly, more sanely. Even so, so to live is not itself to be Divinely Enlightened, nor is it a permanent condition. Sooner or later life comes to an end.

Subtler worlds exist closer to the Center of the Cosmic Mandala. Even in the golden-yellow ring there are subtler worlds closer to the Center. In the blue field, there are all kinds of worlds. In general, to live in any of the worlds closer to the Center is to live in a condition that is more benign, with greater powers and with a greater range of phenomenal possibilities, than the usual life in this gross world. But to live in these worlds is not to be inherently and Divinely Enlightened, Free, or immortal. Nor would immortality be desirable in those planes, because there is no Ultimate Happiness there, even in the state of equanimity.

Equanimity is simply the sattvic, or balanced, condition in any realm of possibility. Equanimity is not an end in itself but simply a ground on the basis of which attention is relatively free. What you do with attention on the basis of equanimity is the means for the transcendence and transformation of destiny.

DEVOTEE: Heart-Master Da, you have mentioned that there are worlds for each color in the rainbow. People have said, for instance, that they have gone to green worlds.

SRI DA AVABHASA: Yes, every kind of possibility exists. Everything that mind can be can also be objectified as a world. And in each realm, each stage in the Cosmic Mandala, all the colors are potential.

When you enter into the subtler energies or mechanics of the visual system of the brain, you may visualize this Mandala. That visualization is not the same as the viewing of the Cosmic Mandala Itself. Under certain conditions of relaxation and dissociation of attention from the body, it is possible to see this Mandala by pressing the eyeballs and concentrating toward the Center of the brain. What you see then is the Cosmic Mandala, but it is the Cosmic Mandala represented at the level of the structure of light associated with the brain and the nervous system. It is a kind of personal version of it, therefore. Because the Cosmic Mandala is duplicated in every fraction of all appearances, it can be visualized in the structures of your own brain. But after you pass through that limiting structure, you see the same representation of light beyond the brain, through other media of phenomenal appearance.

People who are near death and people who are having a low-grade mystical experience will see the Cosmic Mandala in, and limited by, the plane of the brain. The vision of the Mandala would not appear if the brain were not still active, or if the conscious being were not still attached to the body. But if, when you see that representation (as you may in certain mystical states and in the transition to death), you concentrate upon it and hold to the Center, then you will also pass beyond the brain into the cosmic dimension of light outside the brain. By concentrating on this representation of the Cosmic Mandala in the brain, you can move beyond the brain, even while alive, to see structures beyond the brain, in the realm of mind, or psyche, that is cosmic in scope.

If you do not hold to the Center as you concentrate on this Mandala, you will not see the complete Mandala. At first you may not see it at all. You may just see a dark field, with flashes of light, or lightning, or geometries. Then you begin to see the Cosmic Mandala appear by degrees. You may at first see a golden, sunlike light, or you may see a silvery-bluish, moonlike light. Or you may see a reddish light, or lights of any color. They may appear as a relatively diffuse or generalized field, rather than a spot at the center. The degree of concentration and freedom of attention from the body and the diffusing mechanisms of its brain determines the degree to which you will clearly see the Cosmic Mandala in total. Whether the entire Cosmic Mandala or only a portion or a representation of it appears, if you do not continue to hold to the Center, you will not see the rest of it, or you will not see it clearly, or you will stay in the periphery and not go to the Center. To the degree you do not hold to the Center, and to the degree you do not visualize the Cosmic Mandala completely, you will tend to gravitate as attention, or as mind, into representations that develop in the different fields of the Mandala.

Thus, if attention is held in the golden-yellow field, visions will begin to appear in a golden-yellow field. Or you may pass through the tunnel of the indigo into the blue field. But then the blue field itself, instead of appearing with the White Light at the Center, will appear to be a room or a place at the end of the tunnel. Originally what is seen in the blue field, apart from the White Light that appears in the midst of it, is a place of churning forms, a kind of bluish plastic. But other, very strong, clearly defined, primary colors and shapes also appear in it. It almost seems like a clearly defined room when you first see it, but then, when you clearly visualize it, you will see that this blue field contains something like distinct forms, but that they are not really separate from one another, and they are moving around. As soon as you dwell upon the blue field, the mind will cause it to turn into particularized forms. Attention will move via mind, in that particular plane of the Cosmic Mandala, into places, visions, and environments. Environments may thus be entered into in the blue, or the golden-yellow, or any range or representation of this Mandala.

This is why I have recommended to My devotees that the best discipline at the point of death, or in the midst of the death process, no matter what they have done all their lives, is to relax and to release all hold on the body and the mind and states of attention through feeling-Contemplation of Me. Transcend fear through such surrender, and ultimately a visual representation of the Cosmic Mandala may appear. If it does, keep your attention to the Center of it. Do not be satisfied with lesser representations of the Cosmic Mandala, such as a golden light, or a bluish light, or any other light. Keep holding to the Center until the entire Cosmic Mandala appears, and keep holding to the Center until you move into the White Field. Even though this exercise will not be sufficient for moving permanently into the White Field, it will be a purifying gesture that generally will serve your transition and that is, therefore, positive.

In any case, attention will tend to gravitate from the White Field back into lesser planes and visions. You will see other individuals. Helpful people will appear, and you will move into another condition quite naturally and easily. It happens in every case.

These transitions after death are not all pleasurable, however. All kinds of uncomfortable apparitions and apparently hellish circumstances may appear. Circumstances may arise that apparently will justify fear and sorrow and anger and desires of all kinds, and you will tend to locate there for a time. The secret is to keep surrendering these reactive emotions and their desires and keep holding to the Center, not fixing on these visions but understanding them as mind, as possibilities determined by your own habit of attention. Relax that habit of attention. The more you do this, the more you will release the quality that is tending to arise, and you will minimize the stresses that may be associated with the transition.

In any case, sooner or later a relatively fixed condition will arise based on the limits of your ability to release and transcend the mechanism of attention. In that condition, whatever you may or may not remember about your practice of surrender, or self-transcendence, you will be embodied, fixed, related. That is precisely what has happened to you here.

If you can achieve a state of Spiritual maturity and responsibility in life, then you will not experience the utter lapse from responsibility and general intuition of the Awakened Condition at death and after death. You will possess the arms to transcend attention in whatever condition arises after death. Likewise, you will have those arms during this lifetime if you will "consider" the Way of the Heart and take up its practice. Your experience will more and more authenticate, verify, and justify the Way of the Heart.

However, the experiences associated with Spiritual practice are not significant in and of themselves. They are, in general, just objectified states of attention, or mind-forms, states of energy. You must understand them, release them, and move beyond them.

Until attention is Free in its Source, it cannot remain in the Divine Self-Condition. You are brought into that Condition at death, but you do not and cannot remain There, in spite of your belief in It and your desire to stay There, unless you have done the sadhana, or real Spiritual practice, whereby you become responsible for the habit-energy of attention and Realize its Source-Condition. That Realization requires profound clarity, devotion, commitment, and practice.

Thus, it is very unusual for any living being to pass from this world, or any other world, into the Divine Self-Domain and to remain in that Source-Condition. People can have temporary experiences of It, however. For example, in near death and death, experiences of this Mandala of

Origination can be generated, or a temporary perception of this Origin may be experienced. It is always there to be glimpsed.

At death there is a movement into the Clear Light, and there may be temporary experiences of the Clear Light while you are alive as well. But you will not have the ability to remain in that Condition, or even to Realize What that Condition Is, except to perceive a Clear Brilliance and feel a sense of temporary freedom, unless you are responsible for the movement of attention. In spite of any secondary desires to remain there, you will automatically drop back from the position of the Clear White Light into the planes of existence, through the blue and the yellow into the gross condition again. This is absolutely inevitable. There are no two ways about it.

No vicarious means exist for escaping that inevitability. No mere belief in Jesus, or God, or any superior power is sufficient to move you into the Divine Self-Condition. No amount of knowing about the mechanisms of that transition, no amount of knowing about the mechanisms of the arising of experience, is sufficient to enable you to move beyond these limitations into the Divine Self-Condition. Only the actual practice of the transcendence of attention, wherein its limiting tendencies are overcome and it achieves the freedom to "Locate" itself in the Divine Self-Domain, is sufficient. There is absolutely no other way to be Liberated from the binding conditions of the cosmos.

To casually presume you will begin with a little improvement of life and a positive aspiration and belief and hopefully awaken to the capability for Liberation is a weak proposition. It is an excuse not to practice. If you truly understand the process, you will realize that you have no option but to deal directly with the mechanism of attention. The Way of the Heart is not the piecemeal path of the progressive stages of life. It is not the path of the devotion of attention to phenomena, high or low in the scale of conditional Nature. As soon as attention is devoted to objective manifestation, either in the form of this apparent gross realm or in the form of any subtle apparition, it is subject to the binding power of the objectified force. The objectified force of conditional Nature, even the objective White Light, has the effect of binding you until you are free of the egoic significance of attention.

Therefore, the Way of the Heart is most direct. It is not the path of the stages, fulfilled by moving attention into subtler and subtler dimensions of objective existence. It is the direct Way of returning attention to its Source. If the Way of the Heart is taken up, then the path of the stages is bypassed. In order to take up the Way of the Heart, however, it is necessary to be prepared for such direct practice. You do not become prepared for it by taking up the practice of the stages of life. You prepare yourself by restoring equanimity to the body-mind and freeing attention from the binding concerns of the body-mind, through self-surrendering, self-forgetting, and self-transcending feeling-Contemplation of Me.

This is a much simpler proposition, and it forms the basis of the culture of practice in the Way of the Heart. This culture of practice is a culture of preparation relative to the first five stages of life, wherein the body-mind is restored to equanimity, and attention is freed of its binding association with the body-mind. Then, when the body-mind is thus balanced and attention is thus freed, you can actually take up the practice of the direct submission of attention to its Source.

III

SRI DA AVABHASA: Divine Enlightenment, in the seventh stage of life, is the Great Way of the Heart. It is the Way that I have come to Reveal. It is the Great Condition of existence. It is the spontaneous Way of life that is lived by those who have Awakened to the Divine Self-Condition. Previous to such Divine Awakening, human beings have the capability to move as attention into the Mandala of the Cosmos, and into subtler states, but they do not have the capability to enter permanently into the Divine Self-Domain, Which is the Perfectly Subjective Source of all conditions. But once Divine Enlightenment is the case, then there is the capability to move into the Divine Self-Domain. It is possible to be Divinely Enlightened in any domain. In the seventh stage of life, a Divinely Enlightened being can appear in any domain whatsoever, in any one of the levels of the Cosmic Mandala. But until there is Divine Enlightenment, it is not possible to transcend all domains.

The Great Siddhi of Divine Enlightenment is the capability for free attention. It is the most useful ability, and the ability that human beings develop on the basis of their primal motive toward release. The unpleasant mood that is un-Happy, fearful, wanting to be released, is your best advantage in the embodied condition. That desire to be released becomes the capability of free attention when you really exploit it and devote yourself to it. In that case, the motive to release ceases to be merely an unpleasant disease. When you acknowledge the motive toward release and make it the mover of your life, you transcend your seeking and your bewilderment. You become associated with real practice, real responsibility. Then that motive toward release becomes the simple movement, or capability, of free attention.

That is why the unpleasant mood, or primal motive, toward release is so valuable to you—not for its own sake as a mood, which is relatively unpleasant, but because, once you really use it and reclaim it from its dis-eased and un-Happy condition, it simply becomes free attention, or that which is inherently free, inherently released, and, therefore, that which inherently satisfies the motive toward release.

IV

SRI DA AVABHASA: Attention moves in a great electronic field, a three-dimensional realm of little electronic dots. Attention in itself is one dot, in one position in this moment and in the next moment in another position, not just on a two-dimensional screen, like a TV, but in a three-dimensional realm of an infinite number of electronic dots. Attention can move to any one of those spaces instantly, without moving through everything in between. Attention is just the point of awareness, keyed into a great electronic medium that has the capability to represent itself as solid appearances, or just light, or appearances of energy, or darkness, or nothingness.

Truly, the entire affair is absolutely terrible. It is a horror to contemplate. The only thing that makes it not seem horrible to you is your capability to achieve a state of relative equanimity in your present condition. You can balance yourself, feel relatively relaxed, and enjoy something like a pleasurable feeling, but you are still not immortal, Divinely Enlightened, Free, Happy. You are just intoxicated with equanimity. That is why equanimity is not an end in itself in the Way of the Heart. It is simply the base for free attention. You must do something with your attention, having realized equanimity. You must not just hang around in a sattvic state, righteously enjoying your balanced condition. That condition will last only as long as conditions permit it to last in this world, and it will cease at death. Because all kinds of influences can interfere with it, your equanimity is not an end in itself.

To bring the body-mind into a state of equanimity is useful. In equanimity, the body-mind has secondary associations that are pleasurable. But basically equanimity is only useful. In equanimity, your attention is free from bondage to those conditions that are now in a state of balance.

Thus, you must use equanimity as a disposition on the base of which you can Realize the Source of attention.

Your conditional, or apparently individuated, consciousness is just like a point moving in an infinite, three-dimensional crystal, or plane, or sphere, of dots. It feels individuated, separate, and trapped. Wherever it is, it sees everything around it. Wherever you look, everything surrounds that center of looking. In the next moment, you are in this spot, or that spot. There are always the surrounding forms, motions, and energies. You are trapped as this little point in the midst of them.

You must take attention away from its preoccupation with, or bondage to, this infinite medium of dots and let it fall back into the Contemplation of its own Source. When that is done most profoundly, then there is the inherent, or tacit, spontaneous Divine Recognition of the Infinite Field in Which this mechanical act of attention is being moved. Then, whenever attention does move, and wherever it moves, its condition and its objects are inherently, instantly Divinely Recognizable. They are still what they are as an appearance, but they are Divinely Recognizable as unnecessary and non-binding modifications of their Source-Condition. They do not have the capability to destroy Divine Enlightenment, or the Realization of the Truth. Even so, you must persist in this Power of Divine Recognition. It is a kind of Yoga of Divine Enlightenment. Unless you persist in it, attention will simply continue to arise mechanically in this great crystal, or Mandala. And, Divinely Enlightened or not, the environment of limitation still exists.

Thus, in the Divinely Enlightened Disposition, you must exist moment to moment as the Siddhi, or Power, or Disposition, of Divine Recognition. This Power will Divinely Transfigure, Divinely Transform, and Divinely Translate attention and its field into the Divine Self-Domain. Therefore, ultimately, all of that will be replaced, or Outshined, by the Divine Self-Radiance, the White Force in Which it is appearing. The environment of appearances is only an apparition based on the mechanism of attention. If attention is transcended in its Source, the environment of appearances is Divinely Recognizable. If the Power of Divine Recognition is magnified, then all these conditions will be Outshined by the Divine Self-Radiance That is the Source of cosmic Nature.

That is Liberation. That is Divine Enlightenment in Its ultimate sense. The Siddhi of Divine Enlightenment guarantees that Liberation. Divine Enlightenment Itself is certainly Liberation, but It is not an end phenomenon. It is the Native Condition. That Native Condition is a Siddhi, a

Great Power, Which permits you to transcend the limiting force of the Cosmic Mandala. That is the esotericism of the seventh stage of life. That is the Process to which all those who respond to Me are being Drawn. It is That to Which you are invited. But you can only participate in That if you actually live the Way of the Heart, achieve equanimity and free attention, resolve attention in its Source, and then persist in the spontaneous Siddhi, or Process, of Divine Recognition, until there is the Outshining of conditional existence.

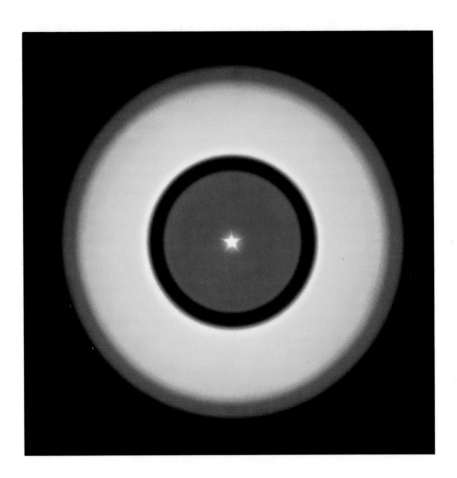

The Cosmic Mandala

CHAPTER 25

The Penetration of the Cosmic Mandala

by Da Avabhasa
July 20, 1982

I

This is the progression of lights seen in the Cosmic Mandala (or the Great Wheel of Objective or Cosmic Appearances) as attention and the Spiritual Current of Divine Life ascend through and above the body-mind:

1. red: In this grosser light, the internal workings of the entire physical body may be seen, without the mediation of the gross physical or bodily senses.

2. golden yellow (like a sun): In this etheric[1] and lower mental light, the phenomena of exteriorization (or "out-of-body experiences", called "OOBEs"[2]) are experienced and seen (i.e., the room, other physical places,

1. In Sri Da Avabhasa's book *Conscious Exercise and the Transcendental Sun* (p. 27), the etheric dimension of life is described as follows:

The etheric dimension of force or manifest light pervades and surrounds our universe and every physical body. It is the field of energy, magnetism, and space in which the lower or grosser elements function. Thus, your "etheric body" is the specific concentration of force associated with and surrounding-permeating your physical body. It serves as a conduit for the forces of universal light and energy to the physical body.

2. Out-of-body experiences (OOBEs), sometimes called "astral projection" or "astral travel", are a universal human phenomenon. They have been experienced in every time and culture, though they have tended to remain an esoteric or hidden subject in many societies, especially the post-industrial West. Typically, during an OOBE, the individual continues to experience his or her ordinary state of awareness, but from a point or points outside the physical body. A common feature of the initial moments of an OOBE is that the person notices he or she is floating near the ceiling, or above his or her physical body, and looking down on it. Many people experience the sensation of inhabiting a second, non-physical body (commonly known as the "astral body", which is the energic duplicate of the physical body, and which may also be the double seen in phenomena of bodily bilocation). The second body is usually garbed in familiar clothing and is generally unable to exert any influence on the physical world. That body is, in general, even unable to be physically seen, heard, or felt by physically incarnate others. Events witnessed during OOBEs have in some cases been documented as accurate perceptions in scientific experiments.

etc.), and this is also the light in which the etheric and lower mental worlds (which are only slightly subtler than the gross worlds) and etheric and lower mental beings (including discarnate entities, or ordinary individuals who are in the after-death state) are seen.

3. silvery white (like a moon): In this somewhat higher or subtler mental light, association and identification with the gross physical body and gross physical world are no longer operative, and, via this light, transition is made from the etheric and lower mental to the somewhat subtler mental, or dream-like, realms of appearance.

4. dark blue or black (like a void): This is the empty or apparently light-less space between the grosser and the truly subtle states of phenomenal appearance—and in that "light" there is a suspension of the appearance of objects (as in deep sleep).

5. brilliant blue: This is the light of the higher subtle, or higher mental, worlds, beyond the gross and etheric and lower mental planes—and in it subtle visions of higher beings and higher worlds are seen. (In this brilliant blue light or space, which may appear like a tiny object or spot, or else like a great space, all the colors revolve in a ceaseless flux, and concentration in this light causes that flux to take on the forms of subtler beings and subtler worlds and Super-Cosmic Apparitions of the Divine Being.)

6. Brilliant Clear White Light: This is the Radiant Core of lights, beyond all the gross, etheric, and mental lights, appearing at first as a five-pointed Star in the center of the brilliant blue light, or as a White Source-Light at the end of a blue tunnel, or as a Radiant White Apparition of the Adept Realizer, and leading into an Infinite Space or Realm of absolutely Clear White Brilliance, beyond the planes of mind. (It may be entered temporarily via ego-based attention, in death or in meditation, but it is finally entered in Divine Translation, the culmination of the seventh stage of life, wherein the Source-Condition of attention has been Realized and all conditional forms of the objective cosmos have become Divinely Recognizable.)

II

The Cosmic Mandala may be seen (in part, as a whole, or in the form of the Ultimate White Brilliance), in meditation or in death, by individuals in the first six stages of life, but in such cases the ego-contraction causes attention to drop back or withdraw from the Clear

White Radiance and into the brilliant blue and golden-yellow fields (which are, in terms of size, the two primary divisions of the colored spectrum of the Cosmic Mandala), thus, in most cases, producing return to or reincarnation in the subtle and, finally, the gross planes of phenomenal appearance. It is only in the seventh stage of life, by the Power of Divine Self-Realization and tacit or inherent Divine Recognition of conditional phenomenal existence, that Divine Translation into the "Bright" Divine Self-Domain is possible. Therefore, it is only in the seventh, or egoless, stage of life that visions of the Cosmic Mandala are non-deluding, non-binding, and of ultimate significance.

Even so, such visions are probable previous to the seventh stage of life, especially in the case of those who practice meditation in the Radiant Company of an Adept, and also in the event of death in the case of all human beings. Therefore, I have felt it useful to Communicate and "consider" the "esoteric secrets" of the Cosmic Mandala here.

The various lights of the Cosmic Mandala appear whenever the Spiritual Life-Current and attention in the physical body ascend into and above the brain core. The lights ultimately appear in the form of concentric circles (with the red light or the golden-yellow light at the outer circumference and the White Brilliance at the center).

III

The Cosmic Mandala is not in you (the egoic body-mind). You are in the Cosmic Mandala. The ego is not Perfect. The ego must be transcended in That Which Is Inherently Perfect. If you seek the Cosmic Mandala in yourself—or even if you seem to find It in yourself—you are deluded, limited, and bound by yourself. Therefore, do not seek within yourself and high in yourself for the Great Form. Such is only the path of "Narcissus", or self-worship.

The ego cannot Penetrate or Transcend the Great Mandala of Apparitions. The ego is not the Way. Transcendence of the egoic self-contraction is preparation for the Way, but the Transcendental (and Inherently Spiritual) Divine Self is the Way. In and by the Transcendental (and Inherently Spiritual) Divine Self, all the realms of conditional appearance are ultimately Outshined by the Self-Existing and Self-Radiant Condition and Domain that is both the Perfectly Subjective Source and the Objective Core of the cosmos.

CHAPTER 26

The Divine "Brightness"

an Excerpt from
The Dawn Horse Testament
by Da Avabhasa

The Great Mandala Of The conditional or Cosmic Domain May Appear In (Total) Vision (or In many fractions and forms of vision), Both during life and after death. The various Cosmic planes or worlds May (Therefore) Be perceived, As In a dream, or More Concretely, With Varying Degrees Of Clarity, Detail, and Completeness, With all their kinds of beings, forms, and events, and With Varying Degrees Of Your Participation.

Just So, The Great Cosmic Mandala Itself May Be Perceived In Vision. It Appears As A Circle (Self-Generated In Its Own Space). The Circle Is Itself A Gathering Of Circles, Each Set Within The Other, Concentric, Formed As A Radiant Wheel or A Well or A Tunnel (and Thus A Mandala) Of Great Formative Lights. The Outer Ring Is Narrow and Red In Color (and Generally Set Against An Ambiguous Outer Field That Is Rather Dark, or Perhaps Somewhat Luminous, but Not Tending To Distract attention). The Next Ring Is Yellow, and It Is Wide. Then There Is Another Narrow Ring, Of A Moonlike Whiteness. Then Another Narrow Ring, Apparently Black, or The Color Of Indigo. And The Last Ring, At The Center, Is A Radiant Blue, Wide As The Yellow. In The Center Of The Radiant Blue Is The (Apparently Objective) Brilliant Clear White Five-Pointed Star.

Each Ring Of Color Is An Energy-Field Of A Certain Range Of Vibration (Made By Apparent Modification Of The Self-Radiant Spirit-Energy Of Divine Being). Within Each Ring, There Are Countless worlds and beings, each Characterized and limited By The Vibratory Field In Which they appear. The Outer Rings Are Grosser, or Of A Lower

Vibration, and Existence In Them Is Brief and Difficult. Those Closest To The Center Are Subtler, or Of A Higher Vibration, and Existence In Them Is More Pleasurable, More Prolonged, Less Threatened, but Nonetheless conditional, Changing, Temporary, Made Of many limits, and Moved By A Necessary Struggle. The Radiant Blue Is The Most Subtle, and Existence There Is limited By Great Powers and Great Longing For Divine Love-Bliss, Which Is Finally Realized Only In The Exceedingly "Bright" (and Perfectly Subjective) Feeling-Domain Of Self-Existing and Self-Radiant Divine Love-Bliss. And the human world Is Also Within This Cosmic Mandala Of Lights, In The Outer or Grosser Fields Of Red and Yellow.

The Vision Of The Cosmic Mandala May Be Perceived As A Whole, or In Part, Either Enlarged Or Reduced To A Point. Therefore, A Point or A Spot or A Circle May Be Perceived, Made Of Any Color, or A Group Of Any Of The Rings Of Associated Color. In any moment, A Sudden Spot Of light May Be Perceived To Fly Out Of the eyes, or one of the eyes, or Else Flash Before the internal vision, Attractively.

Any kind of pattern or scene May appear In Meditation or Random vision. Any kind of adventure may be experienced, before or after death, in this or any other conditional world.

All worlds Are A (Merely Apparent) psycho-physical Display, Made Of Divine Self-Radiance, By Spontaneous and conditional and Merely Apparent Modification Of That Radiance. All conditionally Manifested beings (Even in and as their present bodily or otherwise Apparent forms) Are spirits, or conditional Modifications Of Transcendental (and Inherently Spiritual) Divine Conscious Light. All visions Are Made Of The Same Mandala Of (Apparently) Modified Clear White Light, The Light or Self-Radiance or Inherent Spiritual Radiance Of Transcendental Divine Being.

Therefore, In The Process Of Divine Translation (Realized In The Way Of The Heart), all conditional worlds, all conditional beings and events, all conditional forms of the psycho-physical self, and All The Cosmic Colors Yield To The Divine Star (Itself), and, Therefrom, To The Most Prior (and Perfectly Subjective) Source-Condition Of Even The Divine Star, and, Thus and So, Enter (and Dissolve) Into The Divine "Brightness" (or The Inherent Spiritual Radiance, or Transcendental Love-Bliss) Of Self-Existing (and Perfectly Subjective, and Necessarily Divine) Being (Itself), Which all-Outshining (and Utterly All-Outshining) "Brightness" Is Itself The Divine Self-Domain.

In That Process Of Divine Translation, The Divine Star Ceases To Be (and To Appear As) An Object. Indeed, Divine Translation (Realized In

The Way Of The Heart) Occurs Only If My Devotee Is (By Grace) Fully Awake To All The Forms Of My Revelation Of The Divine Person[1], and, Therefore, Only If My Devotee Is Established In The Transcendental, Inherently Spiritual, and Divine Self-Condition, Divinely Recognizing The Apparently Objective Star (If It Appears), and all objects, and Even The Feeling Of Relatedness[2] Itself As The Only One (and Not Other, but Only Self-Radiant Oneness, Without Division or Separation). Therefore, In The Event Of Divine Translation, The Apparently Objective Divine Star, Divinely Recognized, Becomes A Transparent Doorway At The Heart, The Same As The Self-Existing and Self-Radiant Field That Is Consciousness Itself, The "Bright" Itself, Glorious Beyond Conception, Full, Without The Slightest Absence or Threat, More Than Wonderful, All Delight, Heart-Feeling Without limit, The Unspeakable "Embodiment" Of Joy, God-Great!

How Will This Divine Translation Be Accomplished? By Love! Only Submit To Me In Love's Embrace, Attracted Beyond the Separate and Separative self. Therefore, Hear The One Who <u>Is</u> Love. See The One Who <u>Is</u> Love. And Practice In The Heart-Manner I Am Revealing To You.

---

1. As Adept Realizer, Da Avabhasa Reveals the four Great Forms of the Divine Person, which are: the bodily (human) Form of the Realized Adept; the Spiritual and All-Pervading Heart-Presence of Love-Bliss; the Transcendental (and Inherently Spiritual) Self; and the "Bright" Divine Self-Condition.

2. The "feeling of relatedness" is Sri Da Avabhasa's technical term for the root-feeling of separation, separateness, and separativeness, the feeling of "difference", the essence of self-contraction, or the avoidance of relationship. It is the essence of attention itself, the root structure or activity that is ego. It is Most Perfectly transcended in Divine Self-Realization.

Heart-Master Da discusses the feeling of relatedness in detail in the final sections of His Essay "The ego-'I' is the Illusion of Relatedness", which is published in the book by the same title.

CHAPTER 27

Death Is a "Radical" Fast

by Da Avabhasa
January 1979

Death is a purifying crisis of the lower or elemental or gross dimension of the body-mind. It is a "radical"[1] fast. When the cooperative process of the play of the gross or elemental dimension of the body-mind with the etheric is no longer sufficient to purify, balance, and intensify the gross appearance of the whole body (gross, subtle, and causal—or physical, emotional, lower mental, higher mental, and egoic), the grosser part is eliminated temporarily. Then the conscious being withdraws into the etheric dimension of the subtle realm to be refreshed, after which a new elemental form is acquired or expressed through the process of gross birth.

Those who are attuned while alive to the ascent of attention to the higher dimensions of the conditional being may be projected there at death—bypassing the etheric dimension. They may dwell there, in the higher dimensions, indefinitely, and they may never again be obliged to descend into the grosser forms. However, they are not thus Liberated, or Divinely Self-Realized, but they are simply organized by birth into the subtle planes.

Others may be obsessively oriented to the vulgar elemental plane, or suddenly brought to death in a manner that leaves them in shock, so that they remain focused in the subjectivity of gross elemental desires and reflections, and either invade the elemental plane in ghostly fashion, are quickly reborn, or merely sleep for a time between death and rebirth.

---

1. The term "radical" derives from the Latin "radix", meaning "root", and thus it principally means "irreducible", "fundamental", or "relating to the origin". Because Sri Da Avabhasa uses "radical" in this literal sense, it appears in quotation marks in His Wisdom-Teaching to distinguish His use of it from the popular reference to an extreme (often political) position or view.

But those who are My devotees to the degree of Most Perfect Sacrifice while alive are, ultimately, Divinely Translated from the gross and subtle frames. Ultimately, they are released from the causal seed of their own transmigration, and they are directly Divinely Translated into the "Bright" Divine Self-Domain, Infinitely Expanded from the contracted views of conditional existence, high or low.

CHAPTER 28

The Two Ways of Death

a Talk by Da Avabhasa
February 1, 1980

SRI DA AVABHASA: Much of the world's great Wisdom-Literature proclaims that, without God-Realization, life is chaos and a torment, and you should therefore drop all your worldly entanglements, reduce everything to nothing, and become fixed in God-Communion. That Teaching having been realized, however, you are further instructed by the great Teachings that the world is the Play of God, and that the right and orderly functions of life are God-Realizing when they are lived as God-Communion in every moment. Thus, you are led from reductionism into the realization that the actions and cause-and-effect processes of ordinary life bring blessings into experience. Therefore, the ultimate Message of Spiritual Teaching is not reductionism but the elaboration of life as a complex and beautiful form of association with the Divine that constantly changes and that comes to an end at death.

In a certain sense death is a reductive sacrifice, or a yielding of the conditions of this life. Meditation is also frequently described as a duplicate of the sacrifice that is complete only in death. But life is not meant to be death. Life is meant to be self-transcending sacrifice in God. At some point, the ceremony of death is appropriate, but one should not look for death in the meantime. One should live in the Present God, not the God who waits on the "other side". If you will live Ecstatically, the circumstances of your life will develop harmoniously, and you will enjoy the meditative capability for complete surrender without bringing your lifetime to an end. Then, when the ceremony of death obliges you, you must surrender all the qualities of body and mind in the Divine Being, without demands, utterly purified of motions, having been released, or surrendered, to Divinity.

Is there an Eternal Divine Domain? Yes, there is. Likewise, there are all the worlds apparently in between, all the lesser domains, the lower and temporary heavens. These lesser heavens are actually experienced— not merely hallucinated or created in revery—by living people while they are alive. The visions experienced by remarkable individuals in profound Ecstasy are actual descriptions of worlds into which one could be born. Even the Self-Domain of God—Which is not conceivable but Which is only Realized, through utter surrender of all phenomenal possibilities— may be intuited to exist. This Divine Self-Domain is Realized in Its Fullness by the Divinely Enlightened beings, and It is glimpsed in moments by those who are Awakening.

To intuit the Divine Self-Domain is possible for all beings, but to Realize and be "born" into It is another matter. No one knows how great the Divine Self-Domain is, because It is Inherently Perfect. Its Quality, Its Environment, is Love-Bliss. It is a world of Inherently Perfect Happiness. In other words, It is only Given by God. It is nothing you can conceive or create. It is beyond your present mind. You cannot even reflect It as an image, although perhaps you may perceive a likeness or symbol or dream of It. But however great the domains you may envision, where beings with great Spiritual powers live in Ecstasy, these are still the domains of cause and effect and temporary experience.

One of the two ways of death described in the *Bhagavata Purana*[1] duplicates the process of conventional Spirituality, the goal of which is the ultimate abandonment of the body. Attention, no longer bound by the physical body, remains in the higher mind and moves to subtler worlds, which are as beautiful and attractive as this world is to you now.

However, that Scripture cautions that all worlds are temporary, arising in Kali's devouring mouth.[2] All worlds come and go. You can be bewildered by them, and attached to them, and ultimately confounded by the fact that they come to an end. You may remain in them for a time and then drift back into lesser states. It is true that, yes, there is a way after death whereby one can temporarily, through the mind or through the

1. "Puranas" are traditional Hindu devotional Scriptures in which the life stories of Great Realizers are chronicled, along with the stories of the Hindu Gods such as Siva, Krishna, and the Goddess. *The Bhagavata Purana*, or *Shrimad Bhagavatam*, is rightly esteemed as the most complete and authoritative exposition of ancient knowledge in the literature of the Hindu tradition of Spirituality. Its roots are in ancient oral traditions, but it was put into writing between the fifth and tenth centuries C.E.

2. Kali is the Hindu Goddess who embodies the transforming or destructive aspect of the Divine Being.

process of the ascent of attention, enjoy subtler, happier, longer-lasting conditions of existence, but they are also temporary, and they ultimately end in the Great Dissolution, or the Divine Translation of all cosmic appearances.

The second way, and the better way, of death, is to surrender the mind as well as the body, not only at death but also while you live. Body and mind should become a sacrifice at the moment of death. One should not follow the mind at death and abandon the body. One should abandon body and mind and enter into the Domain of the Heart, the Domain of Ecstatic Love-Bliss, Wherein one neither craves nor pursues the experiences that the mind can know, and Wherein one's destiny is determined by God.

The best way to die, as well as the best way to live, is to surrender body and mind through the self-transcending Ecstasy of God-Communion. The Purusha,[3] the Divine Person, the embodied Power, Influence, and Help of God, symbolized by Krishna in the *Bhagavad Gita* and the *Bhagavata Purana*, says, "Those who do this will come to Me. All others will go to various places at death, and all human beings will have various experiences while alive, but those who take up the true Way of life—which is to surrender to Me, surrender to the Purusha, the Divine—will come to the Purusha at death."[4] One who surrenders body and mind to the Divine Being, Truth, and Reality does not linger in the cosmic realms with which the mind can become associated, and which even the body expresses in this realm. He or she passes beyond all worlds and is drawn to the Divine Self-Domain.

The Divine Self-Domain is not nothing. You do not surrender to nothing. You surrender everything simply, but surrender also fulfills the Law. That is, if you will surrender everything—all the associations that you egoically choose, conceive, and cling to—you will inevitably Realize God.

Thus, Krishna instructs in the *Bhagavad Gita,* "Abandon all 'dharmas'[5] except the Dharma of surrender to Me."[6] In the ritual of death, for instance, do not take up the dharma of association with the higher mind

---

3. The Sanskrit word "purusha" means literally "man". Here, as in some Yogic traditions, it refers to the Divine Person, or Transcendental (and Inherently Spiritual) Divine Being.

4. This is a paraphrase of the *Bhagavad Gita* 9:25.

5. The Sanskrit word "dharma" stands here for "rule" or "custom". In this context it refers to the many paths or esoteric ways by which Man endeavors to seek the Truth. Krishna exhorts his devotee Arjuna to turn from all lesser or conventional dharmas and to follow the great Dharma or Way of devotional surrender to the Divine Person. In its capitalized form, the term "Dharma" denotes the Divine Law.

6. Quoted from the *Bhagavad Gita* 18:66.

so that you will go to a happier realm or planet. It is possible to move with the higher mind and, at least temporarily, experience good results. But the principal recommendation is to abandon all dharmas, all rituals of cause and effect that yield results, good or bad, and simply surrender to God. The Divine Person Teaches, "Those who surrender to Me inevitably come to Me."

One does not Commune with God in order to realize good results in the realms of embodiment, although to realize good results in life is traditionally regarded as a Divinely ordained ritual that one can perform. God Gives us ways to live and act that will produce pleasurable results in this realm and in other realms after death. But the best Way, the true Way, the only ultimately Happy Way, is simply to surrender body and mind and all possibility and Commune with God through Ecstasy. Those who surrender will go to the Realm of the Purusha, Which Realm, although suggestively described in books like the *Bhagavata Purana,* fundamentally cannot be described but only offered. What is offered to you is not the result. What is offered to you is God. Therefore, choose God. Know that every choice developed through action has its result. The result of surrendering everything in God is to be drawn into the Realm of God, simply, Prior to all manifestation, Prior to all possibilities that come to you.

The devotee who yearns toward God, therefore, is drawn, progressively, into the Divine Self-Domain of God, drawn out of the human lifetime or a lifetime in some super-planet out in the galaxies—not into the subtler worlds, not into any embodiment, but into the true "Heaven", which is Only God, God Realized directly, Prior to the possibilities and the media of independent existence. Only God is promised. God and Godly life are Given as a result of surrender.

This present world is also the Loka, or Realm, of God. The Purusha is the Master of this world also. Therefore, this world can be lived and need not be abandoned strategically. Your Ecstasy transcends it. Furthermore, your egoic strategies are not the appropriate position from which to determine whether you should continue to be a human being or not. It is given to you now to be a human being, and that is fine. If it is given to you in the future to be a human being again, then that is fine, too. You live in the Love of God.

The ultimate import of the total process that is called "life" is the transcendence of all embodiment in the conditional realms, high and low. The Purusha Calls you to the Eternal Domain, Prior to the reflected realms of the mind. All the displays of the universe—the realm of the Goddess, the realm of the moon, the realm of reflected existence, high and low—all the realms lie in the tooth of Kali and not in the Domain that is God, God Only, God Prior to the manifestation wherein you can become deluded.

This is the Message of the great Scriptures: The Domain That is Very God is the Offering of God to all beings who will surrender. That Domain is your destiny, whatever you experience in space-time, now or in another lifetime. As My devotee, your devotion to Me must, therefore, be so mighty that you always in every moment tend to the Divine Self-Domain, and you must live so Ecstatically in Divine Communion with Me that, although you are a human being, you are as if dwelling in the Realm of God.

Everyone should see God while alive. Everyone's life should become play with God, not with possibility. Do not live as the independent ego who is suffering under the tooth of Kali. Be God-born, now, in this circumstance, and also ultimately. View your death not as some terrible happening but as a ceremony of worship. How you live, how you enter into that ceremony, determines the future, because you are bound by mind to the machine of cosmic Nature. But if your surrender is complete, then your destiny is Only God.

The Ecstasy of such complete surrender Divinely Transfigures and Divinely Transforms a human life, but its purpose is Divine Translation into the Divine Self-Domain. The "practice" of God-Realization[7] is surrender to the point of Divine Translation, not surrender to the point of benign change.

Your impulse, however, is toward change. Emerging from the chaos of egoic "self-possession", you are greatly relieved to be made Happy, even in this embodiment, by association with God, which will lead you more and more profoundly toward Divine Translation into the Divine Self-Domain. By "Divine Translation" I mean not merely the body's disappearance in a blast of light. The phenomenon of light may be an effect of Divine Translation, but not its import. I mean by Divine Translation that the apparently individuated consciousness, the apparently independent being, has entered into the Self-Domain of the Divine, Prior to all cosmic possibilities.

---

7. Sri Da Avabhasa's use of quotation marks around the term "practice" indicates the paradoxical meaning of this word when applied to His Divine Self-Realization and to the Divine Self-Realization of all practitioners of the Way of the Heart. In the seventh, or Divinely Self-Realized, stage of life in the Way of the Heart, the psycho-physical expression of that Realization is, so to speak, a "practice" only in the sense of simple action. It is not, in contrast to the stages previous to the seventh stage, a discipline intended to counter egoic tendencies that would otherwise dominate body and mind.

There is no Happiness except in utter surrender. When you cannot surrender, when you cannot go beyond the feeling that you are confined to your egoic self and its limited cycle, then you feel tormented. Not to be surrendered is suffering. Only Ecstasy, the actual capability to surrender effectively, to feel the freedom that you feel only when you have actually surrendered—only that is the real process, real life, Spiritual life.

The Way of the Heart is founded neither on the ideal merely to improve human life nor on the strategy to escape human embodiment with its cycle of birth and death. The Way of the Heart is founded on Ecstatic Communion with Me, and, thus and thereby, with the Divine Person, and, although it inevitably leads toward improved conditions in this world and improved embodiments after death, ultimately it becomes so profound that you are Divinely Translated out of the realm of the body-mind, out of the realm of mind and reflected existence. Divine Translation is the end of the Spiritual Process. There is no Spiritual Process beyond that Realization. Until then, existence is a creative act of surrender in which you transcend the limits appearing to the body-mind.

CHAPTER 29

Your Whole Life Determines the Process of Your Death

a Talk by Da Avabhasa
July 14, 1987

SRI DA AVABHASA: As long as the life-force connection, or the energy connection, or the light connection, to the physical body remains, any dimension of the body can continue to inform the consciousness of the living entity during the process of death. But when the energy connection is broken, then no dimensions of the physical can continue to influence the entity. When the energy connection is broken, the entity—I am referring to the dead person or the person who has relinquished the physical dimension in the death process—may perceive the gross physical but is no longer connected to it by a thread of energy.

Until that disconnection has occurred, however, a variety of phenomena, not necessarily gross ones, may be experienced in the body. A person could be in a coma, or at least in a deep state of physical unawareness, but still be informed by subtler aspects of gross physical activity, including brain changes.

But if the thread of life-energy is broken, the body no longer has any influence on the entity. If the thread of life-energy is not broken, and depending on the kind of association that continues with the body, certain kinds of grossly determined phenomena, even subtler aspects of the gross body, may continue to demonstrate themselves to the consciousness of the apparent entity.

Obviously, as long as there is brain activity and an energy connection, the entity can continue to be informed by the body and feel in association with it. Many people have out-of-body experiences while alive.

They view the body as if they are outside it, and yet the energy connection remains. Their experience is not necessarily generated by the brain or by other physical activity. They are dissociated from the body, but they are not disconnected from it. They are not conscious as the body. They are not open to receiving bodily impulses.

They could begin to receive messages from the body, however, as soon as familiarization, or re-identification, with the physical returns. Then the connection, which had not been broken, which existed by virtue of the energy association, is restimulated by input from the body and its brain. This is how the entity becomes reassociated with the physical.

Even while alive, you may be sufficiently dissociated from the physical body and its brain that you are no longer receiving their input, not only in out-of-body experiences, if you happen to have them, but in sleep. If your brain were monitored while you are in a state of deep sleep, it would appear to be variously active in cycles, but you are not necessarily monitoring its activities while you sleep.

So also in the death process. Although you may not be monitoring input from the brain or the rest of the body, the energy connection may not have been severed so that you still have the potential for association with the physical. On the other hand, association with the physical may not occur. In the final process of death, it definitely does not occur. The energy link, what is called the "silver cord", is broken. The energy connections associated with the heart, the brain, and the viscera are severed, and from that point there is no input from the body any longer.

The individual who is exteriorized, or disconnected from the physical body and in the etheric body, may be aware of the body, knowing it is there in some sense, wondering about the situation, but, no matter how familiar he or she feels with that body and with those in the room, he or she cannot reassociate with the physical. Mind activity goes on, but it is not brain-determined.

Brain is not mind. Brain is a vehicle of mind. Brain is a limit on mind as well as a servant of it. Like many other organs of the body, the brain is a mechanism that limits energy. It is associated with fields that transcend the body but are yet associated with it. The body is one with these fields, and it is apparently a part of them, but the physical body can be relinquished while other "bodies", if you will, may remain active. Then these bodies must also, in their turn, be transcended in the pattern of growth. But until they are transcended, there is still apparent individuation and still an apparent psycho-physical entity.

This is why, you see, you are not all of a sudden projected on Infinity when you die. You are still identified with bodies, or fields, that apparently individuate Consciousness Itself. You are not projected to Infinity at death, at least not in the typical case, because there is still identification with limits, limited fields, limited organs, limited bodies, if you like, or "sheaths", as they are called in the Hindu tradition. These limits persist. They do not disappear just because you have died physically. And they continue to determine the form of your awareness. They determine perception. They determine your capability to experience in the planes of the cosmos, and their force, when it is not transcended, limits your capability to transcend the cosmos.

Basically all that happens at the point of death is a relinquishment of the physical body. That within Which the physical body appears is not lost, and everything subtler than the gross physical entity remains as a force of individuality. Therefore, you do not go any further than you have outgrown your egoic and limited self.

Ultimately, you do not go anywhere anyway. The Heart, the Position of Divine Being, just experiences Itself through apparitions within the fields of cosmic Nature, which project themselves spatially in a great space and in time.

DEVOTEE: Heart-Master Da, Chögyam Trungpa and others in the Tibetan Buddhist tradition talk about heat around the heart region at the time of death. Is that heat a sign of a connection to the body?

SRI DA AVABHASA: There may or may not be heat. There is the tendency in the Tibetan tradition to affirm that there is heat because that tradition interprets experiences to suggest that an entity, a "soul", or a continuous self, suffers as the body-mind in the gross context and separates from the physical at death. In any case, there could be a feeling of heat or some perception of energy around the heart region, because the heart region is the primary Seat of Divine Being.

Even though death has occurred to the point of severance from the influence of the physical, the continued existence of the entity, or the individual being, or the persona, may continue to show itself, particularly to others, as signs on the physical body, as heat or energy around the heart, or a glow of energy around the body, or a tendency of the body not to decay as readily as one might expect, and so forth. These signs do not mean that the entity is in the body, but its continued existence, and the ultimate import of its existence, is somehow registered in the physical.

Such things are possibilities. But the individual, the entity, exists in the Greater Context, or the Totality of existence, the fundamental Context that is the Heart, or Divine Being, including, therefore, even Its conditional possibilities—gross, subtle, and causal—in the great space-time domain that is the Cosmic Mandala. You must exist in that entire fold.

Certain signs may or may not appear relative to the physical. The Tibetan tradition particularly emphasizes that such signs may appear because of that tradition's doctrinal position. In some sense, adherents of the Tibetan Buddhist tradition expect such signs to be there. Because of their point of view, they comprehend the death process through such signs and they may also, at least sometimes, observe some of these signs.

It is a possibility that there may be signs associated with the physical body even after death has clearly occurred, particularly in the case of individuals who are highly advanced in the Great Process, or, otherwise, in individuals who, by virtue of their presumptions while they lived, continue to show similar signs in the physical after they die. The appearance of these signs could also be culturally determined. But their significance is still the same, and they can be understood in terms of the totality of this reality that we "consider" completely apart from the doctrinal presumptions of a culture.

DEVOTEE: Heart-Master Da, might these signs be just a reflection of the Yogic capabilities of the dying person, even though the subtle cord had actually been severed?

SRI DA AVABHASA: It could be, but not necessarily.

DEVOTEE: So it is not necessary to conceive of the conscious being as still connected to the body.

SRI DA AVABHASA: Such signs are a demonstration through the body. There could still be a connection with the body, not animating the body in its gross form but animating it at the subtle and central dimension of the heart, yet still showing itself physically, therefore, by some energy and heat, even for a time, over the heart region, even though the body is a corpse and there are no other signs whatsoever of any animation of the body.

In some sense you could say that there still is a connection with the body. What is called the "silver cord" may be broken, but the silver cord is itself a metaphor, a kind of doctrine. There actually could be a visual perception of something that looks like a silver cord of energy coming off the top of the head, but, simultaneously or independently, rays of energy coming out of the heart may also be perceived. There is still a cord, if you will, to the heart, branched off in three places—right, middle, and left.[1] Similarly, a thread of energy may be seen entering into the solar plexus or the visceral region. And all three of these may be seen simultaneously—a thread of force going into the visceral region, a thread of force going to the heart, and a thread of energy going to the top of the head or even down into the depth of the brain or to the third eye?[2] All or any of these may be perceived.

To talk about the threads of energy as a cord is to simplify the matter. Typically, if there is full relinquishment of identification with embodiment, there will be a tendency to move out of the body and to dissociate from it through a subtle energy connection through the top of the head. But it is quite possible to not make that complete dissociation.

Some traditions look to see whether or not the person dies with the eyes closed. If the eyes are open, this suggests that he or she departed the body through the eyes, they say, and thus went into the lesser subtle worlds rather than merging with the Divine Star, or the central Light of the cosmos. Or the eyes may be closed but looking down rather than turned up, suggesting that the conscious being passed out of the body through the lower organs, through the viscera, or through the left side of the heart, rather than through the right side of the heart or the central region of the heart, suggesting, therefore, that the conscious being associated itself not with the subtler planes in the cosmos but with this grosser dimension. These are the kinds of suggestions that are traditionally read through such signs.

1. Sri Da Avabhasa describes three stations of the psycho-physical heart of the body-mind as follows: The physical organ, whose epitome is on the left side of the chest and which corresponds to the gross dimension of the conditionally manifested being as well as the waking state; the psychic, feeling center in the middle of the chest, which corresponds to the subtle dimension of the conditionally manifested being and the dreaming state; and, finally, the Heart-Root or functional seat of the essential self on the right side of the chest, which corresponds to the causal dimension of the conditionally manifested being and the sleeping state.

2. The "third eye", also known as the "single eye", the "mystic eye", or the "Ajna Door", is the subtle psychic center, or chakra, located between and behind the eyebrows and associated with the brain core. The awakening of the ajna chakra may give rise to mystical visions and intuitive reflections of other realms of experience within and outside the individual. The ajna chakra governs the higher mind, will, vision, and conception. It is sometimes also referred to as the "Guru's Seat", because the Spiritual Master's Spirit-Baptism, or Blessing, contacts the devotee at this center.

The possibilities are rather complex. If you can, within your own experience, you must come to some understanding of the possibilities. Most fundamentally you must look at your own tendencies of attention and your own experience, see them in the context of the "Great Picture", yes, but practice the Way of the Heart, understand the possibilities your practice is allowing you, and do not tolerate those limits, but always be moving beyond them. Continue to relinquish while you live, in the death process, and after death. Always move beyond, relinquish.

In the precise moments of dying, and shortly after death, certain specific signs in every individual case may be read in a variety of ways, depending on the tradition or the cultural point of view, the design within the fields of the cosmos that the individual shows, and so forth. In other words, you will not see a demonstration of every aspect of these possibilities in every individual in death. You will see one or the other basic configuration.

The totality of the process must be understood through a total experience, even while you live, that accounts for all possibilities. Such a total experience is generally registered in Enlightened beings, who see it all while alive and who Demonstrate the ultimate possibilities in their death. In the case of all other conditionally manifested beings, a somewhat lesser demonstration will occur at death, just as there is a lesser experience of all possibilities while they live. The limits are shown in everyone except those unique individuals in whom all limits are transcended.

The death process in the case of any of you will correspond basically to your realization while alive, and much of it occurs as an inevitability. It will just happen a certain way, depending on your development altogether. It is not that now you are dying and you have the option to do something completely different. Your whole life determines the process of your death, not merely what you do on the spot in the event of death, although there are also obviously some options then, depending on the force of your participation in the process of death and the force of your relinquishment.

DEVOTEE: The *Tibetan Book of the Dead* emphasizes that there is help at the moment of death, although one must be sufficiently prepared to receive it.

SRI DA AVABHASA: Yes. It is generally assumed in all traditions that because death is such a profound transition, help can change things—the help of others, the help of your tradition, but also the help of your own intention or exercise during that time. Because death is so unusual, so profound, it is assumed that a new option has somehow been given to you because you are dying. It is true that changes can occur because you are dying. But, most basically, what you have realized through the total exercise of your life will determine the event, will certainly be enforced there, even though you have something of an option through help of all kinds and through your own endeavor. In the process, there is also, of course, the option of further growth in the death process and afterward.

DEVOTEE: You Said the other evening that a Tibetan Buddhist may actually not go through the process of dying described in the Tibetan doctrine.

SRI DA AVABHASA: He or she may have the prescribed Tibetan visions. Who knows? You could have any kind of vision. Nonetheless, your psyche is predetermined by how you have lived altogether. Because I was brought up as a Westerner in this Lifetime, when I was having all kinds of subtle visions, particularly in the earlier period of My Sadhana, I had many very powerful Christian visions that required My response. But then I understood them to be just the local psyche of this Life's adaptation. I responded to them with some humor, and they passed. But I did not have only Christian visions. I had visions that belong to all traditions, even visions that did not seem to relate to any tradition at all.

The psyche has many layers, and the local psyche—in other words, the psyche you have developed by adaptation in your present lifetime, the psyche of the basic tradition in which you were brought up—is the first layer. Therefore, if any of you should begin to develop a visionary life, if you should enter into the ascending practice of the Way of the Heart, you will at first tend to have visions that are associated with the traditional adaptation of your childhood. They will pass, and other visions will also very likely appear. But this first level of the psyche will manifest itself. This is why you must have a humorous, if you will, or truly serious, understanding of the nature of vision itself. Vision does not appear for its own sake. It is really a kind of washing, a phenomenon of purification.

The phenomena associated with the ascending process are most basically signs of purification of the psyche, the relinquishment of psychic limitations. You will tend, therefore, to have visions associated with your early-life adaptation, the psychic expectations of the most gross and most ordinary level of your adaptation while alive. Then, if you have become familiar with other traditions or visionary or mystical possibilities, they will also appear. If you take them seriously, hold on to them, seek them out, stay with them, look for them each time you meditate, look for them in dreams, they will persist. But if you practice the Way of the Heart and if your orientation toward such phenomena is the correct one, the Liberating one, then these traditional mystical phenomena will be allowed to arise and pass away. They have their term, and, after they have arisen and passed away [He snaps His Fingers], that is it—a dead corpse there, terminal, the end of that. When this washing occurs, therefore, to some basic degree that is the end of such visions and their implications.

CHAPTER 30

Stay on the Zero

a Talk by Da Avabhasa
October 17, 1977

S RI DA AVABHASA: There are all kinds of ways to exist after physical
death. The typical report of people who have clinically died and
then been resuscitated or who have visited others through psychic
means after death is that they pass out of the physical, usually via a
sudden rise above the physical body so that they see the body from
above. Then they are aware of other people who lead them away from
the scene. Initially they experience a feeling of release, and they are
happy that they are not trapped and that they have survived. They look at
the body and even feel somewhat detached in viewing it. They might
have some sort of a recounting of memories of their life.

Then, shortly after the moment of physical death, they are met by
other people, either relatives or just helpful people. Sometimes they might
have a visionary experience of some individual or archetypal being with
whom they have some religious connection who draws them sympathetically out of the realm of the earth, or just friends or dead relatives or
helpers—very often reported to be in white—who lead them into a clinical
setting, a kind of sleepy, convalescent environment, where they are treated
rather like patients for a while and allowed to become accustomed to the
new situation and to the fact that they have left the physical realm and the
individuals they were associated with there.

When they have completed that period, in general they move into the
etheric plane, going right outside the "hospital" and into a world very
similar to the gross world they have left. There they carry on in a sort of
leisure world that is a duplication of what they were doing while alive. It
is not a place designed for growth or self-transcendence. It is more for

rest, relaxation, recuperation, having friendly relations, doing ordinary things without any changes, in an environment of restfulness.

Following that, there are experiences of transformation in more dreamlike states, seeing the evidence of their past life and their old inclinations, seeing visions, being drawn up into other possible realms of experience.

If they immediately go into that kind of convalescent situation, it is a sign that they are not going to go beyond it into subtle realms, that they are going to rest there for a while, in periods of sleeping and dreaming, become more closely associated with a new birth, and eventually "fall asleep" to the after-death realm and awaken in a new physical condition, a new birth.

DEVOTEE: How long is the period between death and rebirth?

SRI DA AVABHASA: It is futile to talk about it in terms of how long a time it is, because you are out of the sequence of the time-space of the ordinary world. You exist in the chaos of time and space in which the only sense it may make is created by your own tendencies of association and experience. It is not a fixed realm any more than your own mind is. What do you dream at night? You have the possibility to dream anything. Just so, the after-death states are psychic states that create appearances that are based on your own tendencies and that generally lead you back to another physical incarnation.

How long does it take? People say it is thirty years, centuries, a moment, three days—it is futile to try to describe it in terms of time, because you are out of the sequence of time. In the logic of things, really, it is not necessary to be born again in the future of the world you left. You could just as well be born in the past of that world, or in another world altogether. It is all in imagination anyway, all merely in mind, in other words. You cannot comprehend it any more than you can really comprehend this world.

Human beings tend to become established here in a presumed logic of sequences because of the apparently fixed imposition of physical reality, but that physical reality is arbitrary and chaotic. Because it is repetitive, you tend to think it makes sense, but it makes sense only in terms of the experience itself. Once you are driven out of the time-space sequence, you realize that your experience does not make any sense at all. Two arms, two legs, and a head have no necessity. You could just as well have a thousand arms, a thousand heads, and five bodies! Even the configuration of your own body is arbitrary.

DEVOTEE: Heart-Master Da, in a dream I experienced this place of recuperation You are describing, and I had the feeling that everyone there was basically rather dumb and satisfied with their condition.

SRI DA AVABHASA: Just as they were when they were alive.

DEVOTEE: Yes, and that is what was disturbing to me. I saw the relationship between the way people were living there and the way people, including myself, live in the place I remembered. I could see that way of living as a passive relationship to You and to the whole possibility of Spiritual life, and I could see what that passivity leads to. It was not a consoling state at all. It really bothered me quite a bit.

SRI DA AVABHASA: The purpose of such dreams is to show you just that, to give you a little distance from what you are tending to realize, from what your destiny is tending to become, just like moments of insight while you are alive in the gross plane, when you suddenly get a feeling for the destiny you realize by acting by desire and habit.

Most people live by tendency, and they do not enjoy the capability of free feeling-attention whereby they can cut through conditions that arise. If they do not enjoy that capability while they are alive, they will not enjoy it at the moment of death.

Death is not liberating. Death is a cycle in the realm of conditional Nature. If you are living by tendency while alive, you live by tendency after death and move into the standard transition and back again. You repeat that cycle again and again and again without any insight, essentially repeating the same life over and over again and the same basic destiny determined by your tendencies, becoming associated with the same kinds of qualities, the same kinds of people, the same kind of drama, the same kind of script with your intimates, the same kinds of interests in the pleasures of the world, everything basically the same, experiencing a certain level of agony that comes naturally when you are trapped in a fixed condition but never experiencing that agony or dilemma to the point of a crisis in consciousness that breaks out of the pattern.

Spiritual life is not in itself about being able to experience many different levels of possibility, either in this world or beyond it. It is about

Realizing the right position in the midst of experience so that you can pass beyond the fixed impositions of experience that are determined by the focus of attention in certain functional levels. You can pass through the Spiritual Process in this world and not necessarily have dramatic psychic experiences of other planes. You may perhaps have occasional glimpses of other planes, but the import of Spiritual life is not how many psychic visions you can experience. The disposition you Realize in the gross plane enables you to transcend not only the lower imposition of the gross plane, but the subtler, or what is above the heart.

Having Realized that capability, then, in meditation, at the moment of death, in that great moment of change, you can pass through the limitations in that moment, experience them for the first time, at least insofar as you can recall, but pass through them, pass right through that "convalescent home", just keep right on going, stay on the zero, go right down the thread of experience, the center line of experience, and pass through the phenomena that are tending to arise, without fixing on any of them.

You must enjoy that capability while you are alive, though, if it is going to be true of you also in death.

CHAPTER 31

The Paradox
of Reincarnation

a Talk by Da Avabhasa
December 8, 1980

I

SRI DA AVABHASA: In order to "consider" the possibility that you may remember past lives, if indeed you have lived before, you must first "consider" the process of memory. How do you know that any memory is real? You call some mind-forms "memories". When you say, "I remember that I went to the beach yesterday," you feel that you are not hallucinating or indulging in a fantasy, but that this memory is a concrete reflection of reality. Even so, how can you be certain of the reality of any thought that appears as memory? And how do you differentiate such memories from unreality, fantasy, archetypes, or images and ideas that have no reference to what you would commonly call "reality"? How do you know that your so-called memories of yesterday are not hallucinations? Such memories must be self-authenticating so that you can distinguish them from fantasy.

DEVOTEE: Heart-Master Da, I have memories that seem stronger than dreams, but I cannot tell whether my mind is fantasizing very strongly or if they are real memories.

SRI DA AVABHASA: This is a terrible fate, to be unable to know whether the contents of your own mind are merely mind-forms or reflections of real situations in life!

When you describe a memory of something you did yesterday, you determine it to be real not only by reflecting in your awareness a scene that apparently happened yesterday but also by identifying with an apparently individuated self that was present there. When you remember your very early childhood, and even your infancy in this life, you can be certain these are real memories because you identify with an apparently individuated self that has continuity through the sequence of time that is this present life. However, when you are fantasizing about the past and speculating about the possibility of a past life, you do not consciously identify with an independent self that was present in that past event.

DEVOTEE: Is it not possible to be so psychically awakened that we could tap the memory of past identification and re-identify with a past life?

SRI DA AVABHASA: Yes, but such a memory would be authentic only if you were as certain of it as you are of your memories of yesterday. You must have a fundamental feeling that you existed then and that the same continuity exists between yourself now and yourself in a past life as exists between yesterday and today in this present life. If you cannot identify yourself in those presumed memories, you may not claim them to be real. Without the continuity of the individual self, they are just suggestive mind-forms. They could be total fantasy. They could even be images of someone else's lifetime!

What if you felt today that you are a completely different being than you were yesterday? What if there were no continuity of the individual self since yesterday? Even if you had memories, vague impressions about existence yesterday, you would not feel such mind-forms to be real memories, because you would have no sense of identification with the person in yesterday's setting.

You must remember the individual self as well as its experiences and relations. The egoic self in daily life is a convention of psycho-physical birth. The sense of a separate "me" arises from and depends upon self-limiting identification with a body-mind. Perhaps between lifetimes the individual self identifies with a psychic structure that then assumes a physical dimension in each lifetime. However, that psychic identity would have to be acknowledged as continuous from lifetime to lifetime if you are to call your remembrance of past life a "memory". Otherwise such a memory is just a mind-form.

DEVOTEE: This remembered sense of separate self is not dependent on the body, then.

SRI DA AVABHASA: Obviously it is not dependent on this body, because this body was not present in the past lifetime. But possibly a more subtle aspect of the body-mind, also tacitly identified as the individual self, survives death and becomes reassociated with phenomenal conditions of bodily existence upon rebirth.

DEVOTEE: The possibility of continuity from lifetime to lifetime seems strange to me because what we call the "individual self" seems to be always changing.

SRI DA AVABHASA: The individual self of your present lifetime, the one you refer to as "me", does change. You look much different now, for example, than you did thirty years ago. Still, a sense of identification with all the events of that changing self continues from birth until death.

Is death just another one of the changes superimposed upon the continuous sense of separate and separative self? If so, then you should be able to remember past lifetimes by reflecting on the past associations of the very same individual self that you now animate. If not, then perhaps other models for the process of death can make sense to you without meaning necessarily that death is an ending only. In any case, you should be able to determine once and for all whether you are a reincarnated being or another kind of being that is nonetheless inhering in an eternal Process or Condition of existence.

DEVOTEE: Heart-Master Da, the evidence reported in studies of reincarnation and near-death experiences indicates that there is the probability of reincarnation.

SRI DA AVABHASA: But we are having this discussion because they point only to a probability! Reading those studies, you might conclude that reincarnation is a probability, but you cannot presume reincarnation to be true until you have remembered your own past lives with the certainty that your memories are real. You must prove or demonstrate reincarnation to yourself through the exercise of your own conscious awareness. If there is some continuity of presumed individual self-existence between your present life and a past life, then you should be able to remember a past life with the same fundamental certainty with which you remember yesterday. Now, you may not be able to remember a past life as casually as you remember yesterday. You most probably must enter into deeper levels of physical and psychic reflection, just as you must do perhaps to remember traumatic events of the present life. Through such reflection, however, you should be able to reconnect with the experiences of past lives.

DEVOTEE: Heart-Master Da, as I lay in bed last night before going to sleep, I tried to get in touch with my past lives. But I was afraid to experience fully the mind-forms that appeared, and I felt obstructed by my fear.

SRI DA AVABHASA: Obviously fear is a fundamental obstruction to memory, even memory of the present lifetime. You do not feel comfortable with reliving a moment of great pain and suffering. A superficial level of memory is available to you to help you remember difficult times, but to remember them fully requires a different commitment. Often, in order to recall traumatic events or infantile experiences, people must be hypnotized or led into a deep revery. Likewise, in order to recapture memories of past lifetimes, you must first go beyond the limitation of your superficial consciousness and then transcend your fear.

Everything that occurs between your present lifetime and what may be past lifetimes is profoundly traumatic. Just as you may feel afraid to see a ghost or some disembodied spirit, similarly you may feel afraid to recall past lives and the states that may arise in the interim between lives. In order to establish continuity between the present lifetime and a past lifetime, you must be comfortable with feeling disembodied! You cannot merely leap into a memory of a past lifetime and remember it as your own experience. You must also recover the continuity between the lifetimes, or you will not have the certainty that your present self experienced that past event. In order to reestablish the feeling of continuity between this lifetime and any past lifetime, therefore, you must become comfortable with the state you may have realized during the intervals between lifetimes.

You have a tacit fear of such a possibility, as you also now fear the future events of your present lifetime, especially your death. Just as it is very difficult in this moment to feel comfortable about dying and encountering what comes after death, so you would find it equally uncomfortable to relive such experiences from the past. Until you are altogether comfortable with the changing process of existence, you will not be able to recover, with a feeling of continuity, events that are previous to this life. You might become comfortable enough to recall somewhat modified or random versions of events that relate to the past, but in order actually to feel them, as they were, as authentic memory, you must reestablish the continuity of individual self.

II

SRI DA AVABHASA: Since the time of Sigmund Freud, it has been conventionally presumed that traumatic events early in people's lives can enforce emotional characteristics, neuroses, tendencies, and rituals of behavior. Psychiatrists and psychologists commonly presume an unconscious mind—dissociated from the memory and the ordinary consciousness of the waking state—that constantly affects one's feelings and behavior. Those who study the mind from the point of view of this presumption do not acknowledge the phenomenon of reincarnation. However, it may be reasonable to presume that past lives may affect the formation of patterns of behavior and neuroses, just as events hidden from memory in the present life are presumed to do.

In the setting of psychoanalysis, the psychiatrist controls the process of the recollection of traumas. He or she uses techniques of deep revery, hypnosis, and dreams, all states wherein the defensiveness of the waking state is temporarily weakened. Similar processes are used in the traditional religious and Spiritual setting for the investigation of reincarnation, although typically the techniques are not applied by another individual. Rather, through meditative exercises engaged over a long period of time, the individual enters into the same domain of conscious awareness that is also made available through revery and hypnosis.

In both meditation and hypnosis, one must become more and more capable of association with the unconscious and transcend the ordinary waking state in which one tends to be fixed and limited in one's attention. Therefore, until you can comfortably enter into the domain of the unconscious, you will not be able to move with the mind into a broader field of space and time than the one experienced in your present self-confinement.

In general you do not read other people's minds, you do not see the future, you are not expanded in the mind. Rather, your attention is confined to the fixed, gross self. As soon as the mind begins to become comfortably awake at those levels that are presently unconscious, you begin to live in a broader mental field, associated more fluidly with other beings and with the total circumstance of your present life. Likewise, you associate more freely with future time and with past time, and you regain many psychic abilities.

You do not presently possess these psychic abilities only because of the traumatic suggestiveness of human existence itself. Your attention and mind and being are fixed into rigid self-contraction. The egoic self feels identified with the physical body, and the mind follows suit. The so-called conscious mind typically is a superficial mass of language and perceptions that are timed with and fixed upon "me", the separated, fearful, physical personality. As soon as the self-contraction begins to loosen, much of the mind that is now called the "unconscious" becomes the natural domain of conscious awareness.

In current psychological thought, it is presumed that certain areas of conscious awareness are supposed to be unconscious, as if the unconscious were a functional necessity. It is true that certain levels of being now unconscious are associated with your instinctual, animal-like, vital-physical nature. But it is also true that another aspect of the unconscious, or what is not immediately available to the waking mind, is superconscious, and represents an expansion of conscious awareness into greater states of possibility.

This superconscious is not commonly acknowledged or understood by psychologists. Even the so-called conscious mind, about which scientism claims knowledge, is not an absolutely fixed or knowable state. Every conscious being represents a different quality of conscious awareness, a different possibility of attention. As many variations in individual consciousness exist among human beings as there are differences between human beings and other creatures.

Therefore, although the force of Illumined Divinity and the greater influences of the Living Divine Spirit are effective in your life, in general you are not aware of them. You cannot participate in the superconscious because your attention is frozen in the waking state in the limitations of self-contraction. You are locked into a single aspect of the brain so that attention may not spread into other areas of the brain and the body altogether. You cannot radiate or expand into the full field of mind. Thus, you fail to participate in the larger field of conscious existence because you are locked into this self-knot, a midrange, a "braindom" of limited consciousness, that does not extend your control over either the lower or the higher features of the brain.

Consequently, you not only lack profound memory of past lives, but you also have no intuition of your future in this lifetime. Neither do you enjoy conscious psychic association with other beings and the universe. You do not see the dead and you do not see subtle phenomena. Most importantly, you do not enjoy unobstructed association with the Self-Existing Self-Radiance of Divine Life Itself.

You are not literally un-Enlightened—the body-mind is a structure that rests in all of the possible features of existence, and that is always a present extension or direct modification of the Divine Self, which is Self-Existing and Self-Radiant Divine Being. But because of the ego-contraction, attention is limited, and your presumptions, mind, emotion, body, and relations are all negatively controlled. Your destiny remains this fixed and limited affair that apparently is not Illumined even though it is structured in Illumination.

You must overcome this tendency of recoil that confines your attention. You must transcend the limiting power of attention itself and simultaneously Identify with What the conditional being Is fundamentally. As soon as that process of transcendence begins, you awaken to features of conscious awareness that are otherwise elusive, such as memories of past lives, and you also begin to transcend the very mechanism that creates reincarnation as a negative phenomenon. You transcend the presumption of the limited self sense by Awakening to Transcendental (and Inherently Spiritual) Divine Consciousness. Thus, through the process that restores you to the memories of past lives, you begin to transcend the context in which past lives make sense. You transcend the self-knot that is the root and cause of limiting reincarnation. To become so Awakened does not necessarily mean that reincarnations cease, but, rather, that the principle that determines reincarnation as a negative event has been overcome. You may still be able to recollect past lives, but ultimately the presumption that creates such lives is dissolved. After such Awakening, any future lifetimes will be determined by a greater Principle than the unconsciousness of conventional being.

Thus Awakened, one can "consider" reincarnation not merely as a curious cultural belief or something to hold on to because one is afraid of death. Once you are Awakened, reincarnation is observable, even perhaps at that point insignificant, a presumption just as logical and tenable as your ordinary presumptions about the world from the conventional scientific point of view.

Reincarnation, then, describes the connectedness between lifetimes that establishes conscious existence as continuous rather than episodic, or appearing only when a body arises and disappearing when a body dies. Reincarnation is a subject of very sophisticated knowledge, something you are capable of understanding only in an expanded state of consciousness. Thus, there is no reason for ordinary people to walk around with beliefs about reincarnation. You cannot really verify such ideas anyway until you enjoy a state of consciousness in which they are obviously true. Religious people in general feel obliged to believe all kinds of nonsense to which they have no real connection. Most such ideas are just traditional lore, stories and conceptions created to console fearful people with superficial beliefs.

As you achieve greater levels of maturity in the Spiritual Process, perhaps extraordinary knowledge will verify itself in your own case, and you will be able to discuss it intelligently with other people. Perhaps, at some time in the natural course of evolution, human beings in general will achieve such a state of conscious awareness that reincarnation will again be a subject of ordinary presumption based on self-verifying experience in the lives of most people. Then it will again be maintained as a cultural presumption, not just a curious artifact from ancient days when people were involved in the processes by which reincarnation became obvious to them.

From the "Point of View" of Divine Enlightenment, however, the process of reincarnation changes "radically". In the Divinely Awakened State, the convention of self-identity is still presumed on the basis of continuous bodily existence, but at the level of Consciousness Itself there is no sense of identity with a personality that is limited by a body. Rather, the individual consciousness, or apparently separate being, is Realized to be Identical to What is Transcendental and Infinite. In such a Liberated State, That is What one Is. The body does not define a separate and separative self except as an ordinary convention in the theatre of relations.

At the level of mind in the Divinely Enlightened one, there is no constant chatter reflecting and reinforcing the limited self sense. For such a one, the mind's content could even belong to other people and other dimensions of time and space. To "consider" past lifetimes from the "Point of View" of Divinely Enlightened mind, one would have to presume that one was incarnate as every other being that had ever existed! If one's Very State of Being and Consciousness is Realized to be the Very State of Being and Consciousness of all other beings, then how can one presume a model of reincarnation based on a single body and its past relations? That process would be at most a kind of superficial dimension of one's existence, but not the Truth of one's existence. The real fact of one's existence is not that one is a reincarnated individual, but that one is identical to everything and everyone altogether and is actually existing as all beings. One is Identical to the Divine Reality. That is the Truth. The conventional model of reincarnation serves egoic self-consciousness and limitation, and it does not acknowledge the much more paradoxical nature of our Real Existence.

Thus, to talk about reincarnation before such Divine Awakening tends to be deluding. It tends to reinforce the conventional, limited model of existence. You can understand reincarnation only when you have Awakened to the Infinite Paradox of your Real Existence. In one sense there is reincarnation, and in another sense there is no such process. Likewise, there are individual beings, all the relations of those beings, and the infinity of the phenomena of the world, but, on the other hand, there is nothing but an Unqualified Fullness. There is multiplicity, and there is a Oneness of Fullness that is No-Thingness.

If all these descriptions are literally true, then what is the real description of existence? It must be that all are simultaneously true. Therefore, the final descriptions of your existence are full of paradoxes. Ultimately, you must become speechless.

CHAPTER 32

The Gross Personality, the Deeper Personality, and the Ultimate Identity

a Talk by Da Avabhasa
August 15, 1988

SRI DA AVABHASA: The "deeper personality" is a term I use over and over and over again. It includes everything that is called the "subtle dimension" of the conditional being and also what is called the "causal dimension" of the conditional being. It is not really "high". It is not really the subtle, you see. It is the <u>deeper</u> personality. It exists prior to the physical. It is not unconscious. It is functioning, conscious, but the body and its brain have no awareness of it. You do not think its thoughts. You do not have its memories. You do not remember previous incarnations, usually. But even so, this deeper personality is appearing. Its destiny is being manifested through the present incarnation. Its tendencies are being shown there. Just as the physical body shows its lineage by looking like its parents, so this deeper aspect of the personality demonstrates its qualities, its lineage, its past, through a wide range of tendencies—not in the verbal or conceptual mind, you see, but in the dimension of mind that is commonly called the "unconscious" from the point of view of body-based psychology. It is outside the brain.

Instead of appearing as thoughts, therefore, the deeper personality appears as tendencies and qualities. Physically any individual looks like his or her parents, grandparents, great-grandparents, back through time. But that individual does not know his or her ancestors unless he or she is informed about them. If at birth you were separated from your mother and father, you would never know who your mother and father were, or your grandparents, or your great-grandparents. You would have to be informed about them.

The physical personality is not inherently aware of its lineage. Why, then, do you expect the deeper personality to be inherently aware of its lineage? And why do you as a gross personality presume you are a reincarnate? You are not a reincarnate. The personality of which the typical human being is aware is simply the gross personality, the physical vehicle itself, the brain-based mind, even the etheric energy. This is what most people call "I". That one is not a reincarnate. "I" has no memories of past lives because "I" has not had any past lives but only parents and grandparents and great-grandparents and great-great-grandparents. But the deeper personality has previous incarnations.

The physical personality is not ordinarily aware of the dimension of the personality that has past lives, but that dimension nonetheless appears through the physical in the form of tendencies. And it can come about that there is a transcendence of grosser limitations and an opening to subtler, or deeper, aspects of the conditional being, in which case various aspects of deeper experience may appear, including perhaps the memory of previous incarnations—not the previous incarnations of the bodily personality but the previous incarnations of the deeper personality.

Even this deeper personality is not the Ultimate Identity of the conditionally manifested being. The Very Self, or Divine Consciousness, is the Ultimate Identity, and this Consciousness is aware of both the grosser personality and the deeper personality. Whatever is arising, the same Divine Self is aware of it. But, in the mechanics of manifestation, the grosser and deeper aspects of the conditionally manifested being are in fact two different beings, so to speak, two different mechanisms in the cosmic domain that coincide in any present lifetime, but the deeper part is outside the brain-mind. Its mind is not what you call "I" but a form of mind outside the range of your experience except in the form of urges, tendencies, destiny, operations at the level of what is commonly called the "unconscious".

Becoming sensitive to the deeper personality is generally associated with the "advanced" context of the fourth stage of life and the fifth stage of life. There may be some signs even earlier. As soon as you begin to become sensitive to the deeper personality, or you start incorporating the mind of the deeper personality into the play of your life, then you start identifying with that, becoming limited by that, urged by that.

You get more mind, in other words. That is why I Call you to the "Perfect Practice".[1] I do not even recommend that you fulfill the practice of the "advanced" fourth stage of life and the fifth stage of life in the Way of the Heart. If you must, of course, I have indicated to you what the process is about and what it requires. But I am Calling you to enter directly into a relationship to Me such that those stages may become unnecessary. Among other aspects of sadhana that are uniquely Given to you if you enter into right relationship to Me, it is likely that you will be able to move to the "Perfect Practice" at the point of maturity in the "basic" context of the fourth stage of life in the Way of the Heart and not have to enter into the glamor of the deeper personality.

In the conventional traditions of esotericism, the realm of the deeper personality is regarded to be the realm of Enlightenment, or the realm to be attained. It is the domain within which you discover the higher realms of existence within the cosmic domain. In the conventions of religious esotericism, to enter into that domain and then ascend higher and higher within it, or perhaps to Realize fifth stage conditional Nirvikalpa Samadhi, is regarded to be a goal of practice, or the goal of practice.

But, as I just indicated to you, all you gain by developing this subtler sensitivity to the range of mind outside the brain is more mind, whereas the process of sadhana in the Way of the Heart is a process of the transcendence of mind, or conditionality. There is no advantage in getting more mind. There is no advantage in going through the process of purification, or release of mind, if you only go on to get more mind. It is just that some people have such strong inclinations, such karma, in the deeper personality, that as soon as it begins to become uncovered, all those urges appear, and they must do the sadhana in that context.

Even such individuals who by birth are karmically disposed at the level of the deeper personality to this more ascended experience, or subtler dimension of life, may be relieved of that destiny without having to practice in the "advanced" context of the fourth stage of life and the fifth stage of life in the Way of the Heart if they will enter into this relationship with Me rightly and fully, and truly do the sadhana of the Way of the Heart as I have Given it. Then the process works to purify them without their having

1. The "Perfect Practice" is Sri Da Avabhasa's technical term for the discipline of those practicing in the sixth stage of life and the seventh stage of life in the Way of the Heart.

Devotees who have mastered (and thus transcended the point of view of) the body-mind by fulfilling the preparatory processes of the Way of the Heart, may, by Grace, be Awakened to practice in the Domain of Consciousness Itself.

The three parts of the "Perfect Practice" are summarized by Sri Da Avabhasa in chapter 43 of *The Dawn Horse Testament* and Described by Him in detail in *The Liberator (Eleutherios)* and *The Lion Sutra.*

to go outside the brain-mind and become attached to the deeper aspects of mind.

The gross physical dimension of your appearance now is the context of your most effective sadhana—not the subtle, but the gross. You are naturally concentrated in it by your immediate association with the physical. The deeper personality is the background of all of that, so whatever sadhana you do in the body, you are doing it effectively in the realm of the deeper personality as well. You are effectively purifying the deeper personality in your sadhana. You need not necessarily enter into the sphere of mind outside the brain and start wandering in it, you see. You can do sadhana in My Company in the context of the body until maturity in the "basic" context of the fourth stage of life in the Way of the Heart, and that will be sufficient basis for taking up the "Perfect Practice". You need not unlock the "Ajna Door", or the door to the subtle planes. However, if there is a strong inclination in that direction and exceptional signs of the ascending type, then that sadhana becomes necessary and appropriate.

If it is necessary for you to have subtle experiences, then you had better be prepared to relinquish them. If your Guru Stands Prior to the fifth stage of life, then you submit the fifth stage of life to That One. Your acknowledgement of the Realizer, your acknowledgement of the Guru, indicates to you what you must surrender, what you must transcend. If your Guru has transcended everything, all the stages of life, all the egoic stages, then that is what you must surrender to relate to That One. You cannot just say, "I will surrender this and that ordinary stuff in my life," and yet inwardly maintain the glamor of your egoic "self-possession".

If your Guru has transcended all of that, then that is what you surrender, and in fact that is how you transcend it. Don't you understand? You do not transcend these deeper parts by entering into them. You transcend them by surrendering them. You surrender them at the Feet of your Guru, and then you do not have to enter into them. You follow the course your Guru gives you. This is one of the functions of the Guru, to be there to tell you when you are doing it wrong!

Therefore, if you decide to visit subtle worlds, I am here to direct you properly beyond all of that, to Touch you on the head, if necessary, to wake you up, to divert you perhaps, to Instruct you somehow or other, or just to Stand there Firm, Prior to your diversions, expecting you to come and make your submission as you are supposed to do every day as My devotee. And then you will not be bothered by these things.

Likewise, relative to the gross personality and the earlier stages of life, you transcend them, not by entering into them and indulging yourself, but by surrendering them. And you surrender them, not by struggling with yourself and trying to get rid of them, but by finding your Guru, surrendering to your Guru, Contemplating your Guru instead. What is the best cure for any moment of tendency? Remember Me. See how simple it is. That is the sadhana of the Way of the Heart, then. If you find Me out, if you truly Contemplate My bodily (human) Form, My Spiritual (and Always Blessing) Presence, and My Very (and Inherently Perfect) State, then you Realize that My Sign is not fifth stage states, it is not psychic states, it is not Yogic states. It is the Very Self.

By your Contemplation of Me, you are surrendering everything less. Therefore, if you truly Find Me and enter into this Contemplation of Me, you immediately, directly, transcend all the egoic stages of life, all the limitations, and you very directly, then, move through the course. How do you think these two ladies [pointing to two devotees practicing in the ultimate stages of the Way of the Heart] got to do that? Because of some superhuman effort on their part? No! Because of some superhuman effort on My part! It is by their association with Me, their feeling-Contemplation of Me, their Remembrance of Me, their acceptance of their relationship to Me as the Principle of their lives—that is how they were able to make that transition. That is the secret of sadhana for everyone. That is what makes sadhana a Gift.

This sadhana of the Way of the Heart is a relationship to Me, as I have been telling you over and over again since the first day you came into My Company. Since the first day I began to Teach, I have made this clear. This sadhana of the Way of the Heart is a relationship to Me, not merely techniques for you to come to take away and do on your own. The sadhana of the Way of the Heart is always this relationship to Me, whether you are in My immediate physical Company or not. It is this relationship to Me, this feeling-Contemplation of Me, and this feeling-Contemplation of Me is always surrender of your egoic self. It is surrender of what you would otherwise be up to in that moment. It is redirection of attention.

In some moment, in this moment, your attention is going toward something or other you would do with the gross personality or the subtle personality. Instead, via the same mechanism of attention, submit to feeling-Contemplation of Me. Do this over and over again, more and more consistently and profoundly, and you see how purifying it is. And by it you make room for My Spiritual Heart-Transmission. The process is multiplied profoundly by that Transmission. Then it becomes a truly Spiritual process. It gets magnified profoundly. The purification, in other words, becomes more profound, but your submission to Me must be great first. You must be heart-related to Me first.

Sadhana is not some fantasy or some option that maybe is true or maybe not, or maybe you should do it and maybe some people like doing it and other people do not. It is a much more profound matter than that. It is the profound matter. It is what existence is about. The world propagandizes itself, diverts everyone through the mechanism of attention, guides everyone in the direction of self-fulfillment, as if the purpose of existence were to become attached to the conditions that are appearing. The purpose of existence is not in its action. The purpose of existence is inherent. Its purpose is to be submitted to What Is Inherently.

The purpose of existence, then, is to transcend conditions, or modifications of What Is Inherently. If you do not live this surrender, this process of self-transcendence, you are binding yourself in this lifetime and beyond it. And being limited basically to the consciousness of a gross personality, you do not understand what you are doing. You do not understand the consequences of your own actions. You have lost the thread of tradition and the ancient experience. You do not know what you are creating for yourself as a result of your actions in this lifetime. You are frittering your lives away with Western and "Westernized" karmas, and you do not understand the results of doing that, in this life and after it. You spend your life puzzling away whether or not there is God or whether or not there is any survival of death. And all the while there is God and there is survival of death.

But there is more than God and survival of death. There are laws that govern the survival of death. There are many different ways to get up in the morning, too, many different experiences that follow getting up in the morning. So with death. What determines the experience? What determines the experience is what you have inherited in the deeper unconscious being as a result of your action when you had the capability of bodily action. I remember Saying to you many years ago that while you are alive, you make mind, and when you die, mind makes you.

By your action all the while, even now, you are putting things, so to speak, into this unconscious, this deeper personality, which is outside the brain. You are enforcing and reinforcing patterns. You are patterning it. You are in some sense indulging in what is there in the unconscious, but

231

you are also adding to it. And all your life, in most cases, the unconscious is just that—unconscious. That is why you wonder whether you survive death, because you are not aware of the greater part.

Then, when you die, the waking consciousness falls off, the physical falls off, and what was unconscious before, which is outside the brain, is now who you are—and where you are. It is a place, you see. It is the mind-realm. This is what follows life. Death is by no means simply a doorway to heaven. What is on your mind now when you lose physical attention? What kinds of thoughts do you have, what kinds of dreams do you have, what kinds of fears do you have? Whatever they are, they make your experience after death. While you are alive, you have physical concentration and a brain that locks you away from the so-called unconscious. You have an opportunity while alive to purify yourself, but what is to be purified is outside the brain. You think it does not even exist, so you just indulge yourself in physical life as if the physical exists for its own sake.

The physical is not there for its own sake. It is there to help you purify the deeper being, the deeper personality, to the point where you can Realize What Transcends even the deeper personality. Conditional existence is an opportunity for Realization. But most people do not understand that this is so. The body-based mind, the gross personality, is ruling the world, creating world-culture, creating everyone's destiny. What I have fully Realized and am Offering as an opportunity to you, and to everyone in general, may not make sense to most people. They have lost the tradition, lost the experience.

Nonetheless, many people might be somehow attracted to this Offering because ordinary existence does not go all that well. Because devotion to one's gross existence does not produce Happiness, people become dissatisfied with the whole range of "things" and become heart-sensitized to some degree. Many may, therefore, be capable of responding to this Offering, and, through "consideration", may develop an appreciation for the opportunity.

CHAPTER 33

There Is No <u>Entity</u> That Passes from Lifetime to Lifetime

an Excerpt from
The Dawn Horse Testament,
by Da Avabhasa

After bodily death, The conditionally Modified Spirit-Energy Of individual personality Becomes Progressively Re-Associated With The Vibratory Zone Of The Cosmic Mandala That Corresponds To The conditional Tendencies That Remained effective At the end of the previous lifetime (or After The Completion Of The death-Process, or Release-Process, That Ended and Followed the previous lifetime). Thus, After bodily death, conditional self-Consciousness Is Progressively Re-Collected Via The Spontaneous (but Habit-caused) Motions Of attention. After the gross body Is Relinquished (In The death-Process), Many Patterns Of psyche (or mind) and form (or body) arise and pass away, in a sequence of various planes of experience, until the re-attainment of a more or less fixed embodiment (or "reincarnation", or re-birth, as a conditionally Manifested psycho-physical personality) in one of the planes Of The Cosmic Mandala (<u>Possibly</u> Even in the same plane and general locale as in the previous lifetime).

People Often Wonder Why, If All Of This Is So, they Do Not Remember previous lifetimes (or previous circumstances Of conditional Existence). Of Course, some people Do In Fact Remember previous lifetimes (or previous circumstances Of conditional Existence). Very Often Such Remembering Occurs Spontaneously, In dreams, or In reveries, or In

Meditation. Even So, most people Claim Never To Have So Remembered. The Reason For This Is That There Is No entity that Passes From lifetime To lifetime. What Proceeds From lifetime To lifetime Is The conditional Process Itself, Not a Fixed (or Eternal) "personal" entity (or An Independent and Separate individual Consciousness).

The present lifetime (or the Apparent present personal entity, which is Only the Apparent and conditional body-mind) is the effect of what came before it. The past lifetimes (or All The Cycles Of conditional embodiment) are effective as causes for what Follows them. It Is Not That a Conscious and Remembering entity lives, dies, and is re-born. The True and Only Conscious Self Is Inherently and Inherently Perfectly and Perfectly Subjectively and Always Transcendentally Existing, or Existing Always Already Most Prior To conditional events and The Memory Of them. Re-birth Is Simply The (Apparent) Continuation Of The Process Of causes and effects That Produces mind and body. The Transcendental, Inherently Spiritual, and (Ultimately) Divine Self Never Changes, but It Is That Which Becomes Aware Of the present body-mind that has been caused By (and is Continuous With) The Residual (or Effective) Tendencies Of the past body-mind. Therefore, The (Ultimately) Divine Self Will Tend (In the form Of Processes In the body-mind) To Continue To Presume That It Is a conditional self, Until The Divine Self Awakens To Its Real Condition (In The Event Of Transcendental, and Inherently Spiritual, Divine Enlightenment).

The Transcendental (and Inherently Spiritual) Divine Self Is Always Already Existing Transcendentally (or Most Priorly). It Is (Itself) Never an entity (or a conditional, Separate, Independent, and Migrating self, or individual Consciousness). The Transcendental (and Inherently Spiritual) Divine Self Does Not Move From lifetime To lifetime. Lifetimes Reproduce themselves (As effects Follow causes). The Transcendental (and Inherently Spiritual) Divine Self Merely (and Only Apparently) Observes The Chain Of events As they arise. Therefore, The Divine Self Does Not, In Itself, Remember the past, For It Does Not (and Did Not Ever) Really Become a psycho-physical entity in the present.

The Transcendental, Inherently Spiritual, and (Ultimately) Divine Self Does Not, In Itself, Have A Memory Of past lives. As Soon As the present lifetime (or Even the present moment) passes, The (Ultimately) Divine Self Ceases To Identify With it (Unless A Memory arises In mind To Suggest Such Identification). Therefore, The Chain Of lifetimes (or The Progression Of experiences of conditional mind and embodiment) Is Itself

The Memory (or The Mechanism Of Memory). If past moments in the present lifetime Are To Be Remembered, The Only Requirement Is That attention Pass Through The Relatively Superficial or Surface Strata Of The Chain Of Recent Memory. However, If past lifetimes Are To Be Remembered, attention Must Migrate Through The deep psychic Core Of The Memory Chain. And This Does Not Tend To Occur (or To Be Noticed), Unless an individual Is Disposed (and, Perhaps, Even Intentionally Oriented) Toward Such psychic Exploration.

You Are Not the Same entity or personality that lived in many past lifetimes. You Are The Transcendental, Inherently Spiritual, and (Ultimately) Divine Self, Presently (but Only Apparently) Aware Of a body-mind that is itself a direct effect of many past lifetimes. Therefore, Memory Of past lifetimes Will Not Necessarily Characterize Your experience in the present lifetime, but Your experience in the present lifetime Will Necessarily Reflect or Express The Remaining (or effective) Tendencies Of all past lifetimes and causes that directly preceded or caused the present lifetime.

Every birth (or re-birth) Is A Plunge Into material (or Otherwise conditional) ignorance (With Coincident Loss, or Forgetting, Of Divine Ignorance Itself).

Every lifetime Is Begun With (and By Means Of) The Loss (or Forgetting) Of Every Previous (and Otherwise Eternal) Wisdom-Advantage.

At birth (or, Otherwise, whenever Identification With the present-time born-condition Is Presumed), All That Was Realized Previously (or, Otherwise, Priorly) Recedes Into The Unconscious and Subconscious "Background" (Of the deeper personality), and all that Was Previously (or, Otherwise, Priorly) Released Returns (In One or Another Manner, and To One or Another Degree) To The Immediate "Surface" Of Direct (perceptual and conceptual) Awareness (or the Conscious mind, or body-mind, of the gross personality).

In Order To Serve In Bodily (Human) Form, Even I Was Required, By My Own Choice, To Relinquish My Own Eternally Free Condition, and, Thus, By Submission To Identification With My Own conditional Body-Mind and Circumstance, To Forget My <u>Self</u> (Until, By Means Of My Own Unique Ordeal Of Self-Remembering, I Should Re-Awaken To My Self, and Even, At Last, "Emerge" Most Perfectly, <u>As</u> My Self).

Therefore, Even Though My Own Motive Toward Even This (Now and Hereafter and Inherently and Inherently Perfectly Me-Revealing) Bodily (Human) Birth Was Great Love-Sympathy For all conditionally

Manifested beings, and Even Though This Bodily (Human) Birth Was (Thus and Altogether) Intended Toward A Divinely Great and Divinely Enlightened and Divinely Enlightening Purpose here and everywhere, My Intentional Assumption Of This Bodily (Human) Form Required The Self-Sacrifice Of My Own Eternally Free Love-Bliss-Condition (Just As even all ordinary-born beings, born Without Such Divinely Self-Aware Intention, Sacrifice Eternal Freedom and Perfect Love-Bliss By their Natural Submission To The Cycles Of conditional birth and desiring and death).

Each and every born lifetime Requires many (even "ordinary") helping associations (Even "Carried Over" From lifetimes past), and Every Kind Of Greater or Great Growth and Greater or Great Realization Requires Great Good Company and Great (Divine) Help, or Else The "Background" Strengths (or All The Virtues and Realizations Hidden or Forgotten In The Subconscious and Unconscious Deep) Will Not Re-Surface, or Otherwise Come Forward, To Consciousness. And, Ultimately (In Due Course), It Becomes Clear That Not Even Any Kind Of Growth Is The Purpose Toward Which conditional Existence Should Be Devoted, but, Rather, Ultimately, conditional Existence Should Be Devoted Only To Perfect Transcendence (or The Perfect "Out-Growing" Of conditional Existence Itself, By Means Of The Realization Of The Un-conditional Condition That Was, and Is, Always Already The Case). Therefore, Ultimately (and By Means Of Perfect Submission To The Inherently Perfect, and Necessarily Divine, Self-Condition Itself), conditional Existence Should Be Devoted To Perfectly "Out-Growing" (and, Thereby, To No Longer Making or Perpetuating) The Otherwise Repetitive Cycles Of births and lifetimes and deaths.

Even Though All That I Have Done By My Own Ordeal Of Submission To Bodily (Human) Form and Purpose Has, As A Result Of My Eventual (and Inherently Perfect) Re-Awakening, My Subsequent Teaching Work, My (Eventually) Perfect "Emergence", and All My Blessing Work, Become Good Company (or Satsang) and Great (and Necessarily Divine) Help, Forever, and For all, It Also (In Due Course, In My Spontaneous Play Of Divine Recognition) Became Necessary (and Inevitable) For Me, As A Fundamental Part Of That Good Service, To Become Spontaneously and Divinely Indifferent To Even All Intentions and All Sympathetic Attachments (Even While Yet Appearing, In A Simple and Spontaneous Manner, To Be Actively Animating Intentions and Actively Maintaining Sympathetic Relations). By Thus Standing Free, Abiding Merely In My "Bright" and Very (and Inherently Perfect) State,

Prior To (and Inherently Free From) All Gestures Of Work (or Active Purposiveness), and All Gestures Of Sympathetic Attachment (or Active Relatedness), I Also Allow Even My Bodily (Human) Form and My Spiritual (and Always, or Inherently, Blessing) Presence To Merely Be, and Only Thus To "Work". Therefore, By This "Bright" Indifference, I Affirm, and Confirm, and Demonstrate To all That, Ultimately, and At Last, Every conditional Sympathy, Every conditional Purpose and Intention, and Even conditional Existence Itself Must Be Perfectly Transcended, and (Thus) Perfectly Relinquished, In Only That Which Is Only and Itself and Inherently and Divinely Perfect, or Else conditional Existence (Perpetuated By another conditional birth, and lifetime, and death) Will Inevitably Continue After the present-time lifetime and death.

Therefore, In The Context Of the present lifetime, You Will experience The Motions and The Results Of All effective Tendencies That Continue From the past. If You Do Not Transcend Those Tendencies, You Will Duplicate or Repeat or Regenerate the past, In A Mechanical, Automatic, and egoic Manner, and You Will (By Virtue Of A Mechanical, Automatic, and egoic Involvement In conditional Processes) Generate Similar or Even New conditional Tendencies, Which Must Be Fulfilled (or Made effective) In the future (Even In future lifetimes). If Devotion, Service, self-Discipline, and (Most Fundamental) self-Understanding Characterize the present lifetime, To The Degree That There Is Some Real Advance Beyond the limits Associated With The First Three Stages Of Life, Then presently effective Tendencies Inherited From the past Will Gradually Dissipate, and future experience (during or after the present lifetime) Will Be Associated With Positively Improved Attitudes (or Increased psycho-physical Equanimity) and Even (Perhaps) With higher (or subtler) possibilities (of experience and knowledge) Within The Cosmic Mandala. And those who Listen To Me, and Hear Me, and See Me, and Practice The Total Way Of The Heart Most Profoundly Will Really Transcend The Entire Process That Generates conditional Tendencies, So That Divine Translation Is Realized, Either At the end of the present lifetime, Or, In Due Course, Through The Ordeal and At the end of any number of future lifetimes.

Therefore, It Is Profoundly Useful For You To Realize (Whether Through Memory, Or Through Intelligent Observation Of The Always psycho-physical Laws and Mechanics Of Cosmic Nature, Or, Most Simply and Directly, Through The Illuminated Certainty or Inherent Faith That Must Awaken Via The Heart-Effective Grace Of True Satsang With Me, and Through The Subsequent Heart-Effective Grace Of My Given and Giving Spirit-Baptism) That conditional embodiment (or Apparently conditional Existence, Manifested As a body-mind) Tends To Reproduce itself Inevitably. Once a body-mind Is Assumed, another body-mind Will Certainly Follow, Unless Divine Self-Realization and Inherently Most Perfect Renunciation (Of conditional self-Existence) Intervene To Break The Spell. It Is Simply A Matter Of The (Apparent) Laws or Habits Of Cosmic Light, or Of conditionally Modified Spirit-Energy. Spirit-Energy Cannot Be Destroyed, and Once Spirit-Energy Is (Apparently) Modified conditionally (or Once A conditional Motion Is Established), The Process Of Modification Will Tend To Continue, Indefinitely, Until The Tendency Toward conditional Modification Is Itself Transcended and Outshined In The Native Condition (Self-Energy, or Self-Radiant and Inherently Spiritual Being) Of Transcendental Divine Existence.

Spirit-Energy Is Eternal and Constant. Spirit-Energy Cannot Be Destroyed, but Spirit-Energy Can Be Apparently Modified (or Apparently Converted and Changed Into conditional forms). And Once Spirit-Energy (or The Inherent Radiance or Spirit-Force Of Transcendental Divine Being) Is Apparently Modified, Its conditional forms Can Change, or Else Dissolve Into other forms, or Even (If Grace and Practice Coincide) Be Resolved Into The Original or Un-Modified State Of Self-Radiant "Bright" Spirit-Energy and Transcendental Divine Being Itself. Indeed, One Of The Apparent Laws or Habits Of Spirit-Energy In The Context Of The Cosmic Mandala Is Not Merely That conditional forms Can Change and Dissolve, but That they Always Tend To Change and Dissolve. Therefore, Once The Self-Radiant Energy or Spirit-Force Of Divine Being Becomes (or, Really, Appears To Become) a conditionally Manifested form, being, or process, that conditionally Manifested form, being, or process Tends Immediately and Constantly To Change or Dissolve. So It Is (everywhere) Within The Cosmic Domain, and So It Is With (and Within) Your Own body-mind. Because All Of This Is So, conditional Existence Obliges You To Observe, Endure, Most Fundamentally Understand, and Really Transcend Every Kind Of Change and Dissolution (Including The Blows Of Apparent loss and death).

After the death of an individual, his or her Destiny Is Generally Determined By The Stage Of Life (and The Degree Of self-Transcendence) In Which he or she Was Really Active At the time of death. Those who die young, or who Otherwise Fail To Demonstrate Superior Tendencies (or Great Spiritual, Transcendental, or Divine Signs)

That Are Otherwise Latent and Even Somewhat Active At The Subconscious Level, May Possibly Pass Into higher (or subtler) planes (or Even Be Divinely Translated) In death. Even So, In General, Clear Signs That Correspond To One or The Other Of The Seven Stages Of Life Will Characterize living individuals During the (Generally Extensive) period of ordinary or typical living that Immediately Precedes the time of their death, and their Destiny After death Will Tend To Correspond To The Tendencies Associated With Those Signs.

CHAPTER 34

There Is Nothing Left but the Ash

a Talk by Da Avabhasa
August 15, 1988

DEVOTEE: Heart-Master Da, I do not altogether understand Your Description of the Great Event of the Vedanta Temple[1] as Your Submission of the gross body, and the culminating Event of Your Divine Emergence[2] as Your Submission of the deeper personality.

SRI DA AVABHASA: In the Great Event at the Vedanta Temple, both the gross and the deeper aspects of the personality became submitted in Divine Self-Realization. There was nothing that was not transcended in the Great Event in the Vedanta Temple. But Realization was Prior to this Birth. From birth, as I have Said to you many times, My Work was with this Vehicle, to make it an Agent of further Work. The first Work was dealing with the body-mind itself, that Vehicle itself, until it ceased to be an obstruction to What is Prior to it and it could confess That.

All of that Work occupied the first thirty years. The Great Event at the Vedanta Temple is the completion of that, Sahaj Samadhi, full Awakening. It is not that something was left over that still needed to be done for the

---

1. Sri Da Avabhasa spontaneously Re-Awakened as the Divine Self while sitting in a small temple on the grounds of the Vedanta Society in Hollywood, California, on September 10, 1970. This State of Divine Enlightenment that He then Realized was the same as the Divine Self-Condition that He had Known at and prior to His Birth. This Great Event and its significance are discussed in His Spiritual Autobiography, *The Knee of Listening*.

2. On January 11, 1986, at Sri Love-Anandashram, His Hermitage Ashram in Fiji, Sri Da Avabhasa passed through a profound Yogic Swoon, which He Described as the initial Event of His Divine Emergence. That great Crisis dramatically transformed the character of His Spiritual and Transcendental Work with His devotees and the world.

For a complete description of the Event of Sri Da Avabhasa's Divine Emergence, see pp. 37-39 in the introduction to this book. Also see *The Divine Emergence of The World-Teacher*, by Saniel Bonder.

sake of Divine Enlightenment. That is not the proper understanding. But the gross vehicle and even the deeper personality are themselves karmic mechanisms. This body looks something like My parents, you see. It has certain physical tendencies, organ tendencies and whatnot, that are a combination of My mother and father and tendencies inherited from generations before them. The tendencies of this gross personality are not limited to physical signs. Characteristic personality signs, emotional signs, habits, gestures, a mass of things, pervade the entire gross personality, and they are simply an inheritance from the line of this body's parents.

That gross body still existed, with all its past and so forth, after the Great Event at the Vedanta Temple. Likewise, the deeper personality. The deeper personality was not something of which I was unconscious. I was not locked in the brain. Even before the Great Event at the Vedanta Temple there was a Great Awakening and Awareness of the deeper personality, experientially, Yogically. The deeper personality is what you call the "reincarnate", or the "reincarnating personality". It is also, like the gross being, a karmic entity, a product of cosmic exchanges. It has a karmic destiny. Just as the body has a karmic destiny by virtue of its lineage, the deeper personality has a karmic destiny by virtue of its lineage.

In a birth of any individual, the deeper personality becomes conjoined with a gross personality. But the deeper personality functions outside the brain, appears in the form of tendencies and destinies added to the gross personality. This is why, in addition to the many qualities this body has inherited from its parents, many other qualities have been Demonstrated in the Lifetime of this apparent bodily personality that are nothing like My mother and father. My sister, for instance—this body's sister—I'll use the conventional reference—My sister is much more like My mother and father than I am. Her destiny, her lifetime, has been very much more a duplication of their particular qualities.

I should have been living the life of a simple householder on Long Island. I should have gone into the window business. That would have been a duplication of My mother and father. I did not do anything of the kind, though, and you cannot account for the difference by looking at My mother and father or grandparents. In the lineage of this body, you cannot find the reason for that difference. The reason for that difference is on two levels: one, the Very One Born in this vehicle, and the other, the deeper personality, the karmic vehicle that is operating prior to the brain. That one also has its own destiny, its own signs that it has been showing all throughout this Life.

Sometimes some of you like to "consider" the possible previous Lifetimes of This One. It obviously has all kinds of qualities of a high Yogi. Some of its unique personality characteristics can be seen, because they are quite different from the characteristics of My mother and father, quite different from the lineage of this gross personality, which you have observed.

Likewise, after the Great Event at the Vedanta Temple, that entity, so to speak, or mechanism, still existed. It was not cancelled. If it had been cancelled in that Samadhi, death would have come shortly thereafter. Instead, these vehicles persisted as they were the day before the Great Event at the Vedanta Temple. They did not suddenly disappear or become utterly different because of the Great Event at the Vedanta Temple.

The full Awakening to the One Appearing through these forms took place there. And this released the Siddhi of Who I Am into the context of this body-mind, and it spontaneously initiated the Siddhi of My Teaching Work, which was the Siddhi of Submitting these gross and deeper mechanisms to others in the play of My Teaching. This was a Purpose inherent in Who I Am, and also a Purpose rather characteristic of this deeper personality. This is a part of its Sign, too, then—that motive to Teach, to be so Submitted.

You can see, then, how those mechanisms influenced, or were the materials of, My Teaching Work. It was Enlightened Play, "Crazy"[3] Play, yes, but it used these mechanisms just as they were. Because they were

---

3. The term "Crazy" characterizes aspects of Sri Da Avabhasa's intentional Teaching Work (1970-1986), as well as the Divinely "Mad" or mind-transcending Quality of His eternal Realization.

In many esoteric sacred traditions, certain practitioners and Masters have been called "crazy", "mad", or "foolish". Tibetan Buddhist Saints of this type are given the title "lama nyonpa" ("saintly madman") or simply "nyonpa" ("madman"). In whatever tradition and time they appear, these individuals violate prevailing taboos (personal, social, religious, or even Spiritual) either to instruct others or simply to express their own inspired freedom.

Heart-Master Da Himself Taught in a unique "Crazy-Wise" manner. For sixteen years He not only reflected but also Submitted completely to the egoic limits of His early devotees. He Submitted His body-mind to live with them, and to live like them, and in Consciousness He lived as them. By thus theatrically dramatizing their habits, predilections, and destinies, He continued always to Teach them the Liberating Truth, to Radiate Divine Blessing through His own Person, and to Attract them beyond themselves to embrace the God-Realizing Way that He Offers. This daring assumption of the lifestyles and the lives of ordinary people, to plant in them the seeds of self-knowledge and Divine aspiration, characterized much (though not all) of His Teaching Work.

Now, since His Divine Emergence in 1986, Sri Da Avabhasa no longer Teaches in the "Crazy-Wise" manner. Nor does He continue to identify with egoic aspirants or the egoic world. Instead, in His Blessing Work, He "Stands Firm" in His own Freedom, spontaneously Revealing the Divine Self-Reality to all and Calling all to conform themselves to Him (and, thus and thereby, to the Divine Person) through practice of the Way of the Heart. His non-dualistic Freedom in itself, from the point of view of the illusory rationality of the separate, egoic mentality, is a Divinely "Crazy" State and Manner of life. Thus, Heart-Master Da's Service to others in His Divine Emergence Work, in which He is spontaneously Moved to Bless all beings, can likewise be called "Crazy-Wise".

like people are generally, these mechanisms were allowed to be that way, to function with others in the ordinary way, to Combine with them in an extraordinary way also, in this Revealing Teaching Play. The vehicles were Re-Awakened to Who I Am, within the context of Great Realization. Nonetheless, these mechanisms were still themselves what they were, and they became readily available for a unique Work.

That was My Teaching Work. And the Teaching Work was done completely, to death. In that death, the vehicles became changed. The vehicles were not different the day after the Great Event at the Vedanta Temple, or the moment after, but they were different the moment after the Event of My Divine Emergence. Those who were there observed this in one way or another, immediately after that Event and in the months since then. It is there to be observed, at any rate, and some have observed it. The vehicles themselves became Divinely Transformed.

This of course is part of what I Talk about in terms of the seventh stage Demonstration, this Divinely Transfiguring and Divinely Transforming Work, to the point of Divine Indifference. The Sign of Divine Indifference, and also an advanced form of the Sign of Divine Transformation, has been more and more magnified since My Divine Emergence such that the vehicles are no longer in play. They are no longer becoming the likeness of others in Submission to others. They are Submitted entirely to Who I Am. The circumstance of relationship to Me can therefore no longer be one of this form of interplay, this form of exchange, with My devotees.

Therefore, the circumstance of the relationship to Me necessarily becomes one in which the practitioner of the Way of the Heart must submit to Me. You see what the significance of My Divine Emergence is, then. There is nothing left of the gross and deeper personalities of this apparent One. There is nothing left but the ash. This is why Samadhi Sites,[4] so-called, are created for Realizers in various traditions. Since ancient times it has been understood that the process of Realization is itself a kind of fire that burns out impurities, releases karmas, removes the obstacles to Realizing What Is Inherently So, or always already the case.

---

4. Traditionally, the death of a Realizer is called his or her "Mahasamadhi" or "great Samadhi", as such a being does not "die" in the ordinary sense of being helplessly subject to the body's death process. One who already Stands Prior to the body-mind merely releases it at death and continues to Abide in his or her Samadhi, which transcends the realm of visible appearances.

The Samadhi Site of the Realizer is the burial place of such a one. Such a Site is highly valued by devotees, as it is understood that the body of the Realizer continues to Transmit great Siddhi even after death.

In the case of the Realizer, it is presumed that the fire has been allowed to burn everything. When an ordinary individual dies, his or her friends honor what the lifetime was supposed to be about by burning the body and offering prayers of release to continue that fire. But the Realizer's body is, in effect, already ash, vibhuti, Prasad,[5] even while alive. Therefore, the bodies of such individuals are often, not always, but in many traditions, preserved and made the center not only of people's practice but also of a temple or what becomes a temple. So in this case, then. In some sense it has always been the case with This One. In Reality it is so, even all during this Lifetime. But, on the other hand, you also see the sequences of the unique Demonstration of intentional Birth for the sake of Liberating others.

In This One's case the movement is from the Divine Self, acquiring the deeper and grosser aspects of personality for the sake of others. In the case of conditional beings ordinarily, it is the reverse. A gross personality reaches toward the deeper personality, and the deeper personality reaches toward the Divine Self. Two different intentions, coming from two different directions. The meeting of these two is the Great Secret, valued since ancient times. The Incarnate Realizer, the Divine Self Incarnate, Submitting vehicles to the point of naked, most direct association with living beings, and the devotee, surrendering all these vehicles to the One Prior to all karma, and yet paradoxically Incarnate, or Present. It is the meeting of these two that is the Great Secret.

The Great Secret of sadhana is not that a karmic entity, an ego identified with the gross or the deeper personality, does things to itself to get free. This never becomes freedom. This is simply manipulation of conditional energies, manipulation of mind and body. There may be some potential for what you might call "evolutionary changes" in such manipulation, but such changes are still karmic in nature. In true sadhana, such an apparent individual becomes devoted to surrendering to, submitting to, a Realizer who has done the Work of turning the body-mind into ash, the Very Self becoming Prasad, so that you can take It and Contemplate It, be moved by It, Lived by It, Awakened by It. This is the great and ancient Secret.

This is exactly what I have Demonstrated to you. Now it is up to you to respond to Me or not. The only right response to Me is the sadhana of

5. In Sanskrit, "Prasad" is equivalent to "Grace" and means "the return of the gift to the giver". "Prasad" signifies all the kinds of offerings given to the Realizer by his (or her) devotee and then returned by him, such as sacred ash (or vibhuti), sweets, Blessed water, and the like, as the tangible Blessing of the Giver of Divine Grace. The ultimate Prasad is the Realizer's constant Gift of Himself to His every devotee.

the Way of the Heart. Anything other than that is continued identification with the karmic vehicle, the karmic mechanism, the ego, the body-mind, gross or subtle or causal. And for the most part, except for occasional experiences, most human beings are only aware of the gross personality. But, as I Said, the deeper personality is operative, full of tendency, destiny, unique characteristics that cannot be accounted for strictly through the parent-line. In terms of awareness, however, it is the gross personality that the individual is aware of.

The brain is regarded by most people to be a great mechanism, a large part of which is not used yet, and such people think that we are going to grow more and more into extraordinary abilities by using more and more brain. Only within the realm of the cosmos itself is that true. In other words, there is room for development of more mechanical capabilities in this brain mechanism, but the most fundamental function of the brain is to act as a barrier to what is outside the gross mechanism. The brain is there so you will not think the deeper being. The brain is there to lock you out from the deeper personality. Now, why? Not because some evil has overcome you, but because it is not good for you to become involved as an ego in the great range of all possibilities. To do so would be binding.

You are born in physical form for a unique purpose, which is to be purified. You are not born as a human being merely to be a human being, merely to be this physical person and get fulfilled. You are born to a circumstance of conscious awareness in which the karmic is beyond your awareness, prior to your awareness, so that you can be purified, so that you can be concentrated in the physical and do sadhana there, which in effect will release you from the unconscious and the tendencies hidden there. Fundamentally, you are already in a circumstance that is the appropriate one for sadhana. You need not first enlarge your mind and your sphere of experience into the subtle play.

A traditional indication of this is in the *Old Testament*. What do you think the story about the forbidden fruit is about? It is about unlocking the key of the brain and getting out of the brain, which is a barrier to the esoteric knowledge proposed there in that garden. Now, on the one hand, that story is part of what you might call an esoteric tradition that hides things from the common people, so to speak. On the other hand, there is also a fundamental principle there that has to do with Liberation.

Physical incarnation specifically bars you from what you, while alive, usually might call the "unconscious", the deeper part. It focuses you in the physical. That very phenomenon, being focused in the physical while the brain bars you from subtler aspects of existence, is what is valued in the traditions when they say such grand things about the unique opportunity that is human birth. It is precisely that circumstance that is the unique opportunity, being barred from the unconscious, or what then becomes the unconscious, being given the opportunity to transcend yourself by being concentrated in physical life and limited in experience by the brain. This enables you to be purified of your karmas if you will use your lifetime for that purpose. If you simply indulge yourself in that circumstance, you will imprint more into the unconscious, and then after death the unconscious becomes your circumstance in a variety of different ways, some of them possibly amusing and many of them not. In any case, it is bondage.

The purpose of physical existence is, therefore, not merely karmic in some negative sense, as if you have done something and now you have to be physical, as if you have "fallen". No. Physical embodiment has the purpose of Divine Enlightenment, the purpose of purification. But you must find this out. This principle was traditionally communicated. Yet it is getting lost in the shuffle of materialistic culture. The link to the Great Tradition is being cut off. Just as the brain cuts you off from much of experience, culture cuts you off from the rest of it, and you are left with nothing but the automaticities of physical existence, with no apparent purpose other than to survive.

If you will receive My Teaching Revelation, if you will "consider" it, if you will become responsive, then you become capable of making use of this lifetime for the purpose that it inherently can serve. The brain is a limit, yes. It is a limit on a limit. It is there to relieve you of certain kinds of experiences, certain kinds of destiny, temporarily, so that you have the opportunity to break the spell, so to speak, of that karma. Therefore, it is possible in the human lifetime not merely to evolve so that you have subtle experiences. It is possible in the context of a human lifetime to move out of the domain of the first five stages of life into the domain of Transcendental, and, ultimately, Divine, Self-Realization. That is the uniqueness of human birth—not that you evolve subtly, but that you can transcend gross and subtle, all aspects of the conditional personality, in Ultimate, truly Divine Self-Realization. This is the Great Secret of the significance of human birth.

If you accept this as so, then you must not allow yourself to be controlled by the apparent purposes of the body-mind. They are karmic tendencies. Rather, you must submit the body-mind to the Great Purpose. And the Great and ancient Secret of how to do that is to submit the body-mind within the Great Relationship, the Sat-Guru-devotee relationship, in which you constantly engage in Contemplation that relieves you of the karmic tendencies of attention. By these means you are purified and brought to the point where the "Perfect Practice" and Divine Self-Realization, to use My own language to describe the process, become possible.

That is what I am Calling you to do, then. Accept the Dharma, the Law, the purpose that is inherent in your birth. Take up the sadhana of the Way of the Heart in My Company, and prepare yourself by right sadhana for the "Perfect Practice". Do not blithely, through all your fantasizing, look forward to some inward Yogic destiny. Rather, understand what the process of sadhana is about. It is not about psychism and subtle experiences. It is fundamentally about purification to the point where the psycho-physical mechanism is no longer an obstacle to your assumption of the Native Witness-Position.[6] It is simply a matter of purification, until the Witness-Position is obvious and you can take up the "Perfect Practice".

Your life, then, is for the purpose of purification—not self-indulgence, not the fulfillment of a destiny or tendency, but the submission of that destiny or tendency, that mechanism itself, to the point of transcendence, such that you can stably Stand in the Position that is always already the case, that is inherently Free and does not wander. Therefore, at death you will not be reincarnated. At death, in other words, you will not drift into the unconscious, the realm of the deeper personality, the migrating entity. Instead, at death, the conditional personality itself and all its signs will be released.

Fundamentally that process takes place in the Divine Awakening that is the transition to the seventh stage of life. That is the purpose and the process to which I Call you in My Company. That is what I Serve by My Mere Presence here.

---

6. When Consciousness is free from identification with the body-mind, it takes up its natural "Position" as the Witness of the body-mind. The stable Realization of the Witness-Consciousness is associated with, or demonstrated via, the effortless surrender or relaxation of all seeking (and release of all motives of attention) relative to the conditional phenomena associated with the first five stages of life.

Identification with the Witness-Position, however, is not final (or most Perfect) Realization of the Divine Self. Rather, in the Way of the Heart, it is the first stage of the "Perfect Practice", which practice Realizes, by Heart-Master Da's Liberating Grace, complete and irreversible Identification with Consciousness Itself.

For a complete description of the Witness-Consciousness, see chapter forty-three of *The Dawn Horse Testament.*

CHAPTER 35

I Am the Divine Agent

a Talk by Da Avabhasa
May 31, 1980

DEVOTEE: Heart-Master Da, what would be the process if <u>You</u> died? In my case, no doubt, some subtle part of me will continue because I perhaps will not have surrendered so fully in this life, whereas You have Surrendered completely in Your Life. When I try to imagine what that Surrender is for You, I want to know more about it, although You have Said there is nothing for me to know about it, and I do not have a feeling-connection to it, either.

SRI DA AVABHASA: That is appropriate—you are not Me. You have a feeling-connection to <u>your</u> life. What will occur in My case at the point of death has no more significance for you than I may suggest it has. It is simply the Process that I will be required to endure. If I indicate to you that there is something about My own Passage from this world that is useful for you or that represents Help in your case, then that aspect of My Transition is an appropriate concern of yours, because I have Given you a link to it. But otherwise there is nothing inappropriate about the fact that you do not know much about what is going to happen in My case, because I am the only one involved in it, just as probably no one else here in this room knows very much about what will happen in your case.

But anyway, was that the end of your question? Were you actually going to ask Me what will happen in My case?

DEVOTEE: Yes, I was.

SRI DA AVABHASA: Nothing ultimately is going to happen in My case that has not already happened. What I will be doing in the future beyond this Lifetime is another matter, but what may be Realized through death I have already Realized.

On various occasions, I have passed through the death experience as it relates to Spiritual life. There have been major events of this kind in My Lifetime, such as the first time I went to India, when I met Rang Avadhoot while I was at Swami (Baba) Muktananda's Ashram.[1] That event was not like other events of that kind in My Life. It was not simply the experience of losing bodily consciousness and having an astral experience of some sort, although I have had innumerable such astral experiences, as many people have. In that event in particular, for instance, all the structures of the body-mind were penetrated.

The average human being loses bodily consciousness at death and then passes into psychic and mental states and states of experience that seem relatively concrete, loses consciousness at times, and eventually, without any recollection of previous existence, passes into a completely new embodiment to manifest the same tendencies, which are like seeds deep in the psychic being, but without the memory of past lifetimes, at least at the level of superficial mind.

However, there is a mechanism present in the mind, the brain, the psyche, that may be penetrated, and, once penetrated, that permits the Realization of the Divine directly without intervening media, without mental or psychic forms. Once that mechanism is penetrated, Consciousness penetrates all egoic limitations, all limitations of mind and body, all the planes of subtle existence. That mechanism is simply, directly Awakened to the Divine.

This is what occurred in My case at Baba Muktananda's Ashram, except that there was a sudden return of most of the usual aspects of My ordinary physical life. The Re-Awakening of God-Realization without limitation by any factors of experience of mind or body had occurred, and yet there was this body-mind with all its ordinary qualities and all its ordinary associations.

1. Here Sri Da Avabhasa is referring to an event that occurred during the course of His own Spiritual Sadhana, while He was a devotee of Swami Muktananda, on His first visit to Swami Muktananda's Ashram in Ganeshpuri, India, in 1968. During this visit, Heart-Master Da received a brief glance from the Adept Rang Avadhoot, who was visiting Swami Muktananda's Ashram at that time. A short time later, as a result of the combined initiatory Transmission received from Rang Avadhoot, Swami Muktananda, and Swami Nityananda (via his burial shrine, or Samadhi Site) during this visit, Heart-Master Da was spontaneously drawn beyond the body-mind and the world into fifth stage conditional Nirvikalpa Samadhi.

It was something like existing in two dimensions at the same time.

The dynamics of this Re-Awakening produced the events of the approximately two years between that event at Baba Muktananda's Ashram and the Great Event in the Vedanta Temple, when equanimity was restored in the body-mind and the difference between the exalted state of God-Realization and the ordinary phenomena of the body-mind ceased to exist.

Therefore, it is not that I am looking forward to death as a way of returning to God. There has not been any loss or separation. The implications of the usual passage from life no longer exist in My case. There is no progress of passing through levels of existence, astral planes, and all the rest, through many lifetimes, ultimately to break through to the Divine Absolute. For Me, the passage of death is simply an ordinary passage, a change in the environment of My Work, something like moving from here to New Zealand and establishing My Work there. However, for people in the stages of life previous to God-Realization in the seventh stage of life, death has evolutionary implications. For them, death is about experiences that arise previous to complete Release in God.

The Awakened Spiritual Master remains in the human plane while he (or she) lives, Functioning with Divine Siddhi, Divine Power, the Powers of God. The activities of such an individual generate an Influence in every plane of experience. Therefore, such an individual represents a unique, living Opportunity—even, I might Say, a Machine of Divine Liberation, except that it is not mechanical. It is useful for people to come into contact with such a Mechanism, not only to engage in the Play of Divine Wisdom and the life of Spiritual sacrifice in the Company of that individual, but to surrender to the Divine Being by surrendering to and through that individual. The relationship of surrender to that Divinely Self-Realized individual creates a unique Mechanism for the transformation of those who will make that gesture of surrender.

My own Spiritual Life, My own Biography, although it may represent all kinds of lessons, Demonstrates that I am a unique Advantage of Divine Service for the sake of My devotees in the world. It is not simply that I remain behind to tell you and write down for you how you can do it. I Invite you to a relationship with Me in which to live it. If you will live this relationship with Me, then the Service of God becomes available to you in a fashion that does not otherwise appear to be available to humanity.

The human Spiritual Master is the fulfillment of Man in God. And once the Divine achieves Agency through such an individual, all humanity gains an Advantage that Serves their fulfillment of the same Process. What is of ultimate significance to you is not what will happen to Me at death but how your relationship to Me all your life and all My Life, beyond My Lifetime, beyond your lifetime, serves your Realization of God.

Apart from the Service to your Divine Self-Realization that is this relationship between us, there is not much significance in any of the Personal details of My Life. They are only interesting or uninteresting. They are just whatever they are. The real significance of My Personal Life is not any of those details, but it is how the relationship with Me Serves the Process of your Divine Self-Realization.

What difference does it make that someone has been permitted to Realize God through this Process? The difference it makes is that humanity acquires a Mechanism for Divine Association, for the Transmission of Divine Wisdom, for the Transmission of Spiritual Influence, for the establishment of a culture of Wisdom that it does not have otherwise.

Therefore, if you can enter into devotional relationship with Me, the Divine Power, or Siddhi, or Mechanism, that is Awakened in Man, when Man achieves Perfect Intimacy with God, is Incarnate and has Agency in the world, for the sake of everyone else. It is not merely the kind of Agency that involves My Talking to you about Spiritual things—that is only an aspect of It. Fundamentally, I am the Divine Agent of the Self-Existing and Self-Radiant Divine Being, Truth, and Reality.

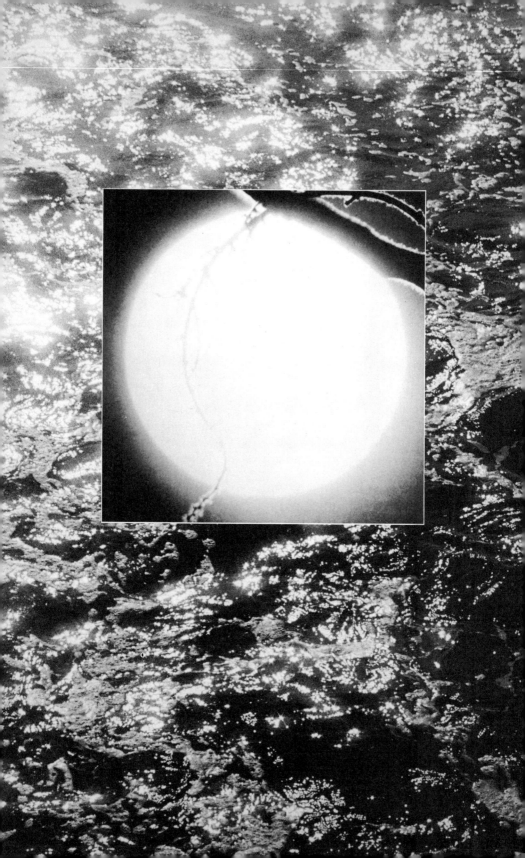

PART IV

"You Will Treat One Another Differently in Death"

On Serving the Death Process

Sri Da Avabhasa (The "Bright")
Sri Love-Anandashram, September 1991

"You Will Treat One Another Differently in Death"

On Serving the Death Process

INTRODUCTION

This section of *Easy Death* Teaches us about transcendence relative to the humble process of dying itself, and it offers practical advice about how death should be served.

Once the breath and heartbeat cease, most of us relate to a dying person—whether as friends, relatives, or medical professionals—as if he or she were merely the physical body, the pile of elements before us. But how could the energy and life of the person we have known just evaporate in an instant? We should not simply submit to what Da Avabhasa has referred to as a "vulgar model of existence". Death is a complex psycho-physical process that takes time to accomplish—because we are more than just the physical part that dies. After the vital signs disappear at the moment of clinical death, the etheric body (an energy correlate of our physical bodies) begins to detach from the physical. When the etheric energy of the living being detaches from the physical and then dissolves, the deeper aspect of the being is allowed to move on to the next cycle of growth and experience. And that entire transition may take three or three and a half days to complete.

Sri Da Avabhasa Calls us in this section to "remain sensitive to your present relationship with that one who has been irrevocably transformed before your eyes" and to serve the death transition of another with this understanding. Stay feelingly connected to the one who has died. Encourage the one who has died (who may still be sensitive to verbal communication) to surrender all hold on this life and to cooperate with the ongoing process of change that death involves.

255

This is a very different picture of death than the one we have been accustomed to! It calls into question much of what we tend to do with the dying and newly dead. What, for example, is the effect of using life-support machines to artificially prolong life? Are we preventing the natural process of bodily release and thus creating difficulty for the departing individual with this well-intentioned gesture? Do autopsies, embalming, hasty burial, or cremation interfere with the death transition? Here Sri Da Avabhasa addresses these matters, making it very clear that it is best to minimize disturbance to the dead person and to create around the body an atmosphere that is quiet, calm, and meditative. In this protected setting, the most benign transition can be supported.

Serving the dying calls us to exercise faculties of feeling-awareness that are only possible through real self-transcending practice. If we are sensitive to what is Real beyond the limits of the many experiences that may arise in death, we will be able to participate ecstatically in the relinquishment that death involves, and we will also be equipped to freely serve the process of death in others.

For many people, bereft of the understanding of death that Sri Da Avabhasa offers throughout this book, grief at the death of a loved one is a terrible ordeal that is never fully overcome. But this need not be so. Mourning is natural, a healthy release, but prolonged and crippling grief is unnecessary. Sorrow, like all other reactions to life, relaxes when we gain a greater perspective on death itself. In Sri Da Avabhasa's Words:

When you penetrate the apparent identification of the living being with the body-mind, you realize the Divine Nature of your intimates, the Divine Nature of the world, and you become free of identification with change. Then changes can take place, and you participate freely in that process. (p. 268)

Individuals of great Spiritual advancement are thus the best servants of the dying (and of the living). They are also, in the event of their own death, a sign to others of the greater meaning of death. For a Realizer, death is not the involuntary departure from the physical realm that an ordinary individual experiences, as Sri Da Avabhasa makes clear in this section. For the Realizer, death is a supremely conscious affair, a matter of abiding in a state of ecstasy utterly beyond the body.

Thus, Part Four focuses all that has been Revealed in *Easy Death* into a practical course of action that we can take as death approaches—a course founded in awakening to the Great Reality in Which we presently appear and in Which we will also one day disappear.

CHAPTER 36

Death Is a Perfect Insult

by Da Avabhasa
June 22, 1977

H uman beings live like knowers, striving toward absolute information, but death is a perfect insult that frustrates all knowing. The
death of an other convicts you of your own death, and makes
you wonder. But no ultimate knowledge comes from this wondering.
Death is the frustration of knowledge. The knowledge that an other has
died is itself the frustration of all knowledge. You are not knowing in
your wondering about death. You are contemplating Mystery, the answer-
less Paradox of your living existence. The death of an other and the death
of "I" confound the whole spectacle and consolation of knowledge. Death
is not the attainment of any state you can know. Death is sacrifice. The
only way to come to terms with death is to come into a harmony with its
Process, its Way. And death is sacrifice, not knowledge or a Way of ultimate knowledge. Death is the sacrifice of knowledge, of independence,
of experience, and of presumed individual self.

The observation of the death of an other and the conviction of one's
own necessary death are not a means to knowledge but a means to sacrifice. Sacrifice is the Law. Knowledge or secure independence is that
which is sacrificed. If you truly observe and feel the death of an other,
you are moved to live by Wisdom rather than by knowledge. Wisdom is
the presumption of alignment with the Way, or process, of existence,
which is Sacrifice. But knowledge is only a reflection of or about the way
things work. The knower is independent, not a participant in the process
that is observed. But Wisdom is always already confounded, relieved of
independence, so that there is no option but to submit to the process of
existence itself.

257

"I" is the whole body. But "I" does not know what a single thing <u>is</u>. "I" cannot inspect the existence of any thing and know what it <u>is</u>. "I" is, therefore, not a point of view toward or other than the <u>existence</u> of any thing or condition that arises. At the level of Very Existence and Very Consciousness, "I" is identical to every thing or condition that arises. The "whole body", then, simultaneously includes all that arises (past, present, and future, or forever), since, at the level of Very Existence and Very Consciousness, "I" is unable to differentiate itself from any arising in order to know what it <u>is</u>.

At the level of the experiential body-mind, "I" can know <u>about</u> things arising. The body-mind, or "me", appears and functions relative to all other arising conditions. Therefore, born existence is the play of knowing <u>about</u>, but it simultaneously exists as the Consciousness than Which there is no other, for "I" does not know what a single thing <u>is</u>, and, therefore, "I" is every thing. "I" includes the <u>existence</u> of all that arises. The Condition of "I" is That of Which all arising is only a modification or variation—but Which is not Itself ever in any sense changed.

Such is the Paradox that is "I" in the case of every one. All arising and all beings are described by this Paradox. And the ultimate destiny of "I" is likewise necessarily contained in this same Paradox. It is Mystery. "I" is eternal sacrifice, without ultimate knowledge. Realization of the Paradox of your existence is not knowledge (a position independent of the Paradox), but it is Wisdom, or the tacit presumption of the Way of the Paradox itself. If "I" presumes the Way of Divine Ignorance, the Law is fulfilled, and "I" is free to live and exist prior to fear, even though "I" constantly moves in Mystery and is given no ultimate knowledge. If the one who is "I" does not presume the Way of Divine Ignorance, the Way of the Process of existence, but seeks knowledge instead, then fear is the motive of that one's life, and existence itself always appears to be at stake.

The recent death of an other and the death of "I", which is yet to come, are a perfect insult to all knowledge. If you rest in this insult, then you are moved to the life of Wisdom, wherein no answer and no experience can ever possess or define you. Wisdom presumes the Paradox and the Mystery of existence. Wisdom is moved to the Way of sacrifice, to Love, to present Happiness, and not to the Way of ultimate knowledge. Knowledge is never more than knowledge about—and knowledge about is confounded by death. There is no knowledge about things that is senior to death. Death is the transformation of the knower. It is fundamentally a process of the knower rather than a process of his or her knowledge. Death is a process in which the knower is transformed, and all previous or conditional knowing is scrambled or confounded in the process of death. Therefore, to "consider" death is fruitless, since the knower is what is changed by death.

To confront death in Truth you must be humbled and confounded. The death of an other reminds you that in every moment you are principally confronted not by defined objects that are independent of you but by an indefinable process that includes you. The death of an other reminds you that sacrifice is the Way of Life. When you confront the death of an other, you are confronted by Mystery, or Paradox, and you are confronted by the demand for participation, or sacrifice, founded in the acceptance of the necessary Paradox, or Mystery, of existence. Wisdom is such acceptance, and the participatory sacrifice is Love, or present Happiness. It is unobstructed feeling-attention in all relations. It is to dwell in the profundity that confounds all knowing. It is to resort to the presumption of absolute Ignorance as the Truth of your unknowable existence.

Therefore, in the face of the death of an other, be confounded and moved to God. Remain sensitive to your present relationship with that one who has been irrevocably transformed before your eyes. Let the grosser part return to the disunion of original elements. But remain free and Happy, allowing that one to be a blissful sacrifice in the Mystery that also obliges you. Hold on to no thing and no one, not even your apparently individual self. Be certain of no knowledge. Be the sacrifice of all conditions in every moment, and thus abide in Communion with the eternal Truth, wherein the root of your independence is eternally hidden and your common Identity is always already Revealed.

In this way you will affirm and participate in the necessarily eternal Existence in which you all appear: Surrender into Infinity with all your friends and hold on to no thing or condition that ever appears. Forget all things in present Happiness, and so forgive the universe for all its playful changes. Always love one another, and so forgive one another for appearing, for changing, and for passing out of present sight. So be it.

CHAPTER 37

How to Serve
the Dying Person

a Talk by Da Avabhasa
May 31, 1980

DEVOTEE: Heart-Master Da, my mother is dying, and tomorrow I am flying to be with her. I would like to know how to serve her best. She has lost the use of speech and movement, but she responds with feeling to some things around her.

SRI DA AVABHASA: Has she outer awareness?

DEVOTEE: Yes, but she has no mind.

SRI DA AVABHASA: Does she have memory? That is, does she know who people are?

DEVOTEE: No, not really, though she smiles when she hears I am coming to see her.

SRI DA AVABHASA: There is really nothing unusual about her state. She has physical sensation and outer awareness. She responds emotionally. She notices events at some level. Although dying, she is basically there. You can therefore relate to her through all the means whereby you would ordinarily relate to her.

Over the years, I have told many stories of the summer I spent as a chaplain in a mental hospital during My training in a Christian seminary. Among My obligations was to comfort people who were dying or close to death. I remember on one occasion going to see a woman who had no outer awareness whatsoever. To talk to her or to try to elicit her acknowledgement of Me as a human being was futile. Still, I was capable of all My bodily and emotional and mental activities, even though she was not, and, therefore, I could approach her and serve her Spiritually.

Just so, you also have all your faculties and abilities, and you are fully alive as My devotee and conscious in this world. Therefore, you should do for your mother all the things that I recommend and that you know to do in the company of someone who is dying.

You are not yet, at least, limited by your mother's absence of awareness. She still has the basic faculties that make a relationship with her possible. You should speak to her, even if she does not speak to you, and give her the feeling that there is nothing negative between you. If there has been anything negative between you in the past, you should, through your conversation, make it clear to her that you forgive her and that you feel forgiven by her. Make completely clear to her that you no longer feel any limitations in your relationship.

If you like, you can read to her what I have Communicated about the death process and about simply surrendering—that she should have no fear that death will destroy her, that death is simply a transition into other experiences that also pass, that eventually she may resume a human existence, or at least perhaps a personal existence in an environment, and that as she passes through these stages of experience after she leaves this world, she will be given help. It is true that after your death people come to help you, telling you where you are and what is happening to you, just as people do in this realm. Try to bring to her a sense of the reality of her situation, not the dismal downtown expectation that "when you're dead, you're dead", because that view is completely untrue and worldly and a terrible vision.

When the present body becomes too weak to go on, it is quite naturally abandoned, but the process of abandoning the body is not the destruction of the individual being. Light cannot be destroyed. Light is always conserved. Because human beings are essentially forms of Light, they continue to exist after death, but they also continue to undergo transformations. The purpose of your existence is to surrender to Light Itself, until, instead of realizing only the changes and the transformations, you have Realized Light.

Your mother, then, should surrender to God, or the One Who is Living her, knowing that God is Light and Love and Fullness and Happiness and Purpose and Creative Will, and she should let herself be carried without fear from this world by that great Influence. Make sure she knows that you love her and that there is nothing unfinished between you and her that demands her attention. Let her feel completely free to relax into the death process when it finally occurs. In the meantime, she should simply surrender, know she is loved, and know that you, as well as the others who are intimate with her and who may also be with her, feel that she loves you. Such heart-felt communications, because they are natural and human, serve the transition at death.

When the event of the death of another finally occurs, although the emotion of sorrow will naturally arise, you should remain My devotee in that moment, and, instead of merely feeling sorrowful, surrender through feeling-Contemplation of Me in that moment, giving the one who has left your company your full permission to release all hold on this present existence. You should release the dying one. You should cooperate with the person's release from this life and not, in effect, try to trap and keep the person here. The process into which he or she is entering is God-made and inevitable. By trusting that process and by continuing to surrender with full feeling and love of Me, and, thus and thereby, with full feeling and love of the Divine Being, you, too, can be adjusted to it.

Thus, you must be active in the event of your mother's death as you are also while she continues to live. You must realize equanimity through your own love and trust of the Divine Process. Then, in the actual event of her death, you must continue to love and trust this Process and give her permission to pass out of her present relationship with you, even to pass completely out of your sight.

In the days following her death, you should allow yourself to be sensitive to any unusual sign of her presence. It is quite typical that after the death of an intimate, people have dreams or unusual experiences that are synchronistic with that person's passage. Such phenomena do not necessarily mean that the person is trying to communicate with you, but simultaneous or associated events typically arise. Therefore, allow yourself to be sensitive, and such events may be part of your own experiential evidence of the realities of this transition that we call death.

Death is not an ending. Thus, most likely, after a few days those experiences will stop, because the psychic part of the conditional being has separated not only from the physical body but in general from the environment. It has gone on to its further destiny. You may have other experiences from time to time, particularly if you, the person still living, maintain an emotional attachment to the one who has passed.

Generally, however, you should release all of that. Release the person fully as he or she is dying and during the few days after his or her death, until you are yourself completely content and surrendered in Divine Communion with Me and can continue your practice of the Way of the Heart here without lingering in this event.

CHAPTER 38

Death Is a Living Process

a Talk by Da Avabhasa
June 20, 1977

SRI DA AVABHASA: When someone dies with whom you have a relationship, the conditions of your relationship have changed, because one of you no longer has the medium of the gross body through which to live the relationship. You still live through your own gross body, but the gross body of the other person has ceased. It is just a lump of elements. It is returned very quickly to elemental states. The body is decomposing. It is not that person anymore. The person who communicated through that gross body-mind is no longer present in a familiar form.

Maintain feeling-attention. Do not recoil. That one is dead, and you tend to feel only separation and your recoil into sorrow, anger, and fear. Simply permit the relationship to exist. If you do not recoil, you will remain sensitive to the present condition of the relationship. You will be able to feel and consciously participate in that relationship, however it may be communicated to you.

Death is a moment of change. If you cannot deal with change in the ordinary round of days, you will have great difficulty dealing with somebody's death, as well as with your own. A moment of change such as the death of another propels you into Mystery. You must confront a wall of ending that you cannot cross. Whatever may be available psychically to your experience, you still cannot cross the barrier. No form of conditional knowledge enables you to cross it. You are projected into the Mystery, the fundamental Divine Ignorance, that is altogether true of you, even in the present moment. No one can anticipate, let alone predict, when he or she is likely to die or when relationships are going to change dramatically, or when somebody else is going to die.

Thus, you are profoundly obliged to Realize the Truth in this moment, to fulfill the Law, to live the Way of real life, because when the change does come, either as your own death or the death of an intimate, your preparation is tested at that moment. After death, you will be neither more nor less than your condition of Realization at the moment of death. At death you cannot take anything with you except your relative freedom. You cannot take with you all the mental strategies with which you hide from your mortality from day to day.

When someone dies, you tend to identify the body as the person. When you see that it is dead, you grieve. Actually, the dead body only looks like the person, but it is no longer animated. It is no longer a personality. If you could look at it in a few weeks, it would hardly be familiar. It very quickly returns to elements. It is just chemistry, turning into elements, disintegrating. The body is not the person at all.

To whatever degree you have a connection with the individual, maintain the connection and see what the relationship amounts to at this point. Basically, live to him or her now in the Spiritual sense as you should have been doing when he or she was alive, so that he or she can realize the necessary changes. Do not hold the person to the body, to the personality. Do not hold the person to anything. Allow the person to return to the great Infinite Absolute that is available to him or her. Remain sensitive to that relationship as love in the present, and do not become obsessed with artifacts like the corpse that is lying there, because that corpse is not that one. Nor was the person limited to that gross body while he or she was alive. The body is just a lump of elements.

It is a general but not an absolute rule to keep the body for three days before burial or cremation. To keep it for three days allows the process of separating the subtler aspect of the individual being from the gross fleshy form, returning the gross being to its elements, and making the transition to the subtle dimension. It is not so much that the individual being is consciously hanging around during the three days, although it is possible. On the subtlest level, the separation of the subtle being from the gross being is taking place.

One of the reasons to keep the body for three days is that, in most cases, only the elemental dimension of the individual being is dead. In the usual individual, the etheric dimension, the energy "double", continues to exist. The etheric body of the usual person is absolutely identical to the physical body during life and very closely integrated with it. During the process of death, the etheric separates from the elemental. It is generally held that three days are needed for that process of separation.

It is best not to disturb the body during those three days and not to disturb the psyche, not to try to hold the person with your reactivity. Live the relationship, be sensitive to the relationship, and let the relationship change. After three days, return the body to the elemental realm. Some religious traditions, such as Christianity, continue to identify the body with the person. Christians regard the body to be a something that will arise from death when Jesus comes again. But such is false mythology.

The body should not be cut apart. It should be left intact. Of course, in death, bodies are sometimes mutilated and must contend with the routine interference of autopsy and embalmment. But this is not optimal. It is best that the body be left alone. Since most of the time in our society it is likely that there will be some interference, it is wise to leave the body undisturbed for at least a half hour or an hour immediately after the death. If you conduct a vigil of three days, treat the body during the three-day period as respectfully as possible, and then literally return it to the elements.

The best way to return the gross being to the elements is to burn it. When the body is buried in the earth, the process of decomposition, though still a fire, takes a longer period of time. At death the gross is submitted to the etheric. In the case of some Realized individuals, in the advanced and the ultimate stages of life, the etheric body dies also. It separates from the rest of the subtle body, and it dies. It pervades the environment and does not travel with the conscious being.

Death is a living process. It is not an ending. It is a very profound transformation. Therefore, it is something to which you must be sensitive, and you can only be sensitive to it if you do not recoil and turn in on yourself. You must stay turned to the relationship. Then you may see signs preceding the death.

Death is a living process, a form of continuation, a transformation of the person's state. Everybody who has a relationship to that one is experiencing a transformation of that relationship. If you have a basically incidental relationship to the person, if he or she is not someone with whom you are constantly, daily intimate, as people are who live with one another, you may not notice any more about the passing, perhaps, than you did about the person's life.

Yet everybody who knew the person at all experiences a kind of philosophical or Spiritual awakening to the mystery of death, and you must confront that mystery, not necessarily as psychic awareness, although some people, when they hear of a person's death, may be able to recall signs of the coming death. I have had many such experiences during the days previous to the death of people I have known. Such experiences are not signs that death must follow. They are symbolic. They only signify death after the fact of death. It does not happen that when you see signs suddenly you know that someone is going to die, unless of course you have a premonition of someone's death. Such premonitions may arise sometimes, but most of the time the signs that appear are simply the signs of the process of separation in advance of the physical death.

What is important in your own case, though, is not your belief that various things occur after death. It must become obvious to you what takes place after death. But this certainty comes only when you permit yourself to feel and experience and live fully the Spiritual Process. Then you will be certain of your present condition, and the phenomena around you will begin to become transparent. Their true Condition will begin to become obvious to you, and the reality of death will begin to become obvious. But if you remain reactive and egoically "self-possessed", you will never have any certainty about the death process. You will be full of doubt, and you will suspect that death is final. You will not have a living relationship to everything. Then if you see someone dead, you are not alive to the person, you are not still in the feeling relationship to him or her, and, thus, you are not aware of his or her present existence. You are dead yourself.

Therefore, the sight of a dead person is a kind of death to you. It is a test, a trial. And there is a certain Grace in being able to see the death of others before your own, because you can become conscious of the Mystery of things and perhaps be moved to penetrate the whole affair of death. Thus, you are projected into that Mystery when you see another die, and you are forced to be reconciled with that person's death.

Most people settle for a little reactive grief or even the inability to feel grief, until the memory of the person starts to fade and then eventually goes away. This is how most people deal with another's death. But if you remain in the feeling relationship, open, and sensitive, if you live a life of God-Communion, then, when you witness the death of another, you can be projected into that Mystery very fully. You will simply continue in relationship with whatever the individual is altogether. You will simply go through a change in your relationship, not an ending of it. And the change may be very remarkable. You may no longer be able to differentiate that intimate from the Infinite.

Therefore, unobstructed feeling is God-Communion. That feeling, though, is not realized when you focus on the apparent individuality of someone and identify that person with the body-mind. Thus, when you realize unobstructed feeling, or a love relationship to anyone, you are identical to what everyone really is, and you identify the person with that same Condition of Love.

When someone dies, it is that unobstructed feeling that continues. It is the unspeakable Divine. In the midst of that Divine Condition, various phenomena, appearances, illusions, and hallucinations constantly arise. Mind and body seem to modify this core of Love, but It essentially remains undifferentiated. You only are in touch with It, however, through feeling, through love. Your individuality, the "me" that loves, becomes associated with It. But when you penetrate the apparent identification of the living being with the body-mind, you realize the Divine Nature of your intimates, the Divine Nature of the world, and you become free of identification with change. Then changes can take place, and you participate freely in that process.

Death is really a very simple matter. You see how casual it is—somebody just goes. Death is casual, like a tree falling in the yard, since there is no respect in this place for your continued existence. There is a respect for your constant change, perhaps, but not your continuation in any state. Changes are constantly forced on you, and you see how little tolerance you have for them. You demand consolation and repetition. Therefore, you do not gain anything by dying. You do not go to heaven or to some place wonderful just for dying. The condition of this realm is lost to you, and you simply return to it because this realm is what you are equipped to experience.

The Mystery is not really found in death and life, which are to be realized as a lesson. The great Mystery is to persist in Truth as a discipline to the point of the dissolution of all the necessity for the repetition of any limitation. To be born in such a place is not evil, but to be born Divinely Enlightened in this place is a very different matter altogether than just being born in it. It is a matter of being completely Free of the un-Enlightened presumption that produces experiences in the future.

If you are Free of the illusion and the presumptions of independent consciousness, the separate experiential ego, all changes are manifested by Divine Will. You need not be concerned about them anymore. Then you are not creating future experience nor prohibiting it. The future will be whatever it is, and you are already Free of it altogether. If you appear in a world like this, then fine, that is where you will serve. If you are in another kind of world, that is where you will serve.

But merely to die is not to accomplish anything. In fact, you have lost something if you have wasted opportunities to grow during your lifetime. It is better to use up your life in the fire of Spiritual practice, to use whatever Grace is Given to you. Do not waste your life rehearsing your limitations or your concerns, because you do not know whether or not you will survive to be ninety years old as you may imagine. You may only have four or five years to fulfill your practice.

If, as My devotee, you only practice the Way of the Heart nominally, you do not gain liberation from the earth-realm as a result. At best you may change your circumstance somewhat, or change your desires so that you are born into a somewhat better circumstance, but it will still be one without Wisdom. There is no point in entering into death, or another rebirth, without Wisdom. You must practice the Way of the Heart to the point of Wisdom, so that you no longer exist in the unillumined state. It is not necessary to be able to move to higher realms at will. What is necessary is to Realize the Truth, absolutely.

You must be My devotee in the fullest sense, not just mentally and emotionally. For My devotee, death is a transition into a different condition altogether, even if it entails a future rebirth into the same realm as this. If you do sadhana to the point of Divine Wisdom while you are alive, you will not be reborn less than Wise.

CHAPTER 39

You Will Treat One Another Differently in Death

excerpts from three Spiritual Discourses
by Da Avabhasa

SRI DA AVABHASA: I watched a bit of a dreadful documentary the other night that made much of corpses. There is something you must understand about corpses. Corpses are the remnant of human beings, but as soon as a human being becomes a corpse, it is no longer a human being. It is just the bodily remnant returning to the elements. Therefore, to the living, corpses tend to look rather grotesque.

We have an initial responsibility to the dead to serve their transition, and to do so requires a time of being aware of the face and the appearance of death. But only those fitted with wisdom should serve the dead. Others necessarily must observe the dead sometimes, but images of death, images of corpses, films of corpses, photographs of corpses are sometimes a rather evil message to the living. They suggest to the living that the living should identify with the mask of the corpse as if that were the destiny of Man. But it is not.

A human being never looks like a corpse. A human being never is a corpse. Only corpses are corpses, and they are already part of the earth. A human being always looks alive. When a human being is dead, the body is not the human being anymore, although the corpse may need to be addressed for the sake of the one who has just died, briefly, in order to serve the transition at death.

You may be shocked by viewing corpses because, in your egoity, in your self-contraction, already with despair in mind, you get a message that suggests this is where you are going, this is the meaning of life, this is what a human being becomes. It is a false message. That is not what a human being becomes. As soon as the conscious being leaves, the body becomes a corpse. That which is the human being is transferred and continues in another process.

You must sensitize yourself to that possibility in yourself so that you will not make much of corpses. Yes, there is something to be understood about death, and something in reality to be confronted about it. But visions of corpses suggest an even ultimately destructive philosophy, a strictly materialistic and vulgar state of mind.

Perhaps it is appropriate and useful for you sometimes to view the dead, but you must do so with wisdom and not make much of that image. Participate with the human being while it lives in the body and then after death. And to participate with the human being after death is to participate with a being who is no longer in the body. (August 13, 1987)

◆ ◆ ◆

SRI DA AVABHASA: Ordinary people have such a gross point of view of what life is that they regard death to have taken place as soon as they notice the grossest signs have stopped. They are not aware of any subtler evidence. Therefore, as soon as the grossest signs have stopped—generally heartbeat, breathing, perhaps even certain brainwave patterns that can be measured in hospitals—as soon as those things cease, that is death. Because people generally do not have any subtler awareness, because they do not think any subtler process might be continuing, they think that at that point you can do anything you want to the body—put it in a refrigerator, shoot it up with fluids, remove its blood, do autopsies, remove body parts and use them in the body-part bank, bury it, burn it, treat it like an object.

The point at which separation occurs is variable, you see, because it depends on the state of the individual altogether. In general, when the gross signs cease, death has not taken place except at the grossest level. There is still a subtle connection, and the individual should be regarded to be in a kind of samadhi, without bodily awareness, but nonetheless with some sort of connection to the body still existing, a state in which there is perhaps some gross visualization of the room and people or some subtler awareness, but yet some connection, some subtle thread of energy and association, still continuing with the body. It should be presumed in general that this connection continues to exist. Allowing three days to pass, rightly relating to the individual during those three days, and even afterwards during whatever you do with the body at the end of three days—all of that is a useful service to be performed by the intimates of a person who has died.

Basically, what is to be presumed about someone who dies is that the person has entered into a kind of samadhi. That is all. When you go to sleep at night, you are not aware of the body, but people do not burn your body up, nor do they go into grief because you are not moving around the room. You need a subtler awareness to deal with the fact of death. Having developed that, you understand that it is simply the case that death is samadhi, either as continuing experience of a conditional kind, with subject/object phenomena of one or another kind, or without such phenomena. But there is only change after death, not cessation merely.

In their agitated state, people are clinging to existence in this conditional form, and therefore they are not sympathetic with the possibility of samadhi. They do not have a feeling for the Gracefulness of "formless" samadhi—if nothing else, as a release from the binding torment of conditional existence. In this state, there is no mind, no body, no memory, no disturbance, but it is not negation. It is no-thingness, but, even so, it is blissful. It is a state of release. It may only be temporary in most cases, because subtle motions of mind are still there in seed form, which evolve and eventually create mind-forms, rebirth, conditional experience of one or another kind, so that the cycle happens again.

Phenomenal states can arise between gross births. There is a between-lifetimes period that is like sleep and dreams and that is mind made. But it is not just interior to the conditional self. It is a participation in cosmic time and space and place and experience and relations in a subtler form. You must have a subtler understanding when it comes to death. Otherwise, you will only be staring at the corpse, with your attention embedded in your own gross existence, and you will collapse into despair. Without understanding the process of death, your grief, or sorrow, becomes the means of destroying the egoic self, rather than transcending it, and reduces existence to a gross form in which nothing but despair is appropriate.

Therefore, to rightly encounter death in others as well as in yourself, you must understand, and practice Spiritually, and develop a more profound level of experiential awareness. What should you do with someone who dies? You can bury or cremate the person. Whatever you do, you should relate to the individual rightly after the period of death. Burial or cremation should be delayed for at least a few days, and three days is a good rule of thumb. Perhaps cremation is at least symbolically the best expression of what should be done for someone who has died, the fire being the ultimate sign of your release of that person, rather than clinging and holding on.

People in Western and "Westernized" cultures like to bury people because they are very basically involved in ancestor worship, and they have a sort of golem-like attachment to the dead. They like to have the bodies planted out there so they can use them as murtis, or sacred images, fret over them, and feel they still have a connection to them. They do not want to let them go. Therefore, cremation is a better sign of the right way to relate to the dead. Do not be involved in ancestor worship. Let the dead go, let them be transformed into something other than your ancestors, and let them be free. You should not bind them, or yourself.

Spiritual Masters are not always buried. Ramakrishna, for instance, was cremated. Rang Avadhoot was cremated. Nityananda was buried. Maharshi was buried. There is no absolute tradition. People in different parts of India do different things. Different cultures do different things.

DEVOTEE: Heart-Master Da, You once gave a beautiful Talk about the need of Americans to know where the bodies of the dead are. You said this is why drownings are so traumatic for families, because they lose the body.

SRI DA AVABHASA: Because you know that the connection exists between the entity and the body, at least temporarily, you can care for the body properly for a few days. But if the body is not there, you still have the basic form of association, which is the psychic ceremony of release. And, in any case, that is the principal aspect of your responsibility for someone's death, the principal form of service to be performed to those who are dying. Basically, grief, or the period immediately after somebody's death, is a purgation, a release of the dead and the living. It is a psychic ceremony. There are various objective references in that ceremony, usually the body of the individual, and ceremonies to perform, things to say, but it is essentially a psychic ceremony of release, in which you release the one who has passed on to go on and be transformed, not to be the same and stay. Likewise, you must be released yourself from the binding power of memory, because remembering will only create the artifact of sorrow. You must be released of the binding power of memory associated with anyone who has died, so that your consciousness can rest in its Native Condition, in the Divine Being. Therefore, death is a ceremony for all. (April 29, 1982)

◆ ◆ ◆

SRI DA AVABHASA: The vulgarization of human life is something that must be changed, and among the things that must be changed is the kind of treatment the dead generally receive, even the kind of treatment the sick receive from medical people whose sole purpose is to keep the individual alive. Only on some level is that purpose laudable and right. As long as life can be maintained, as long as the individual can exist fruitfully and consciously, it is appropriate enough to take life-saving measures. But much of what is being done has the purpose not to provide a vehicle of embodiment for someone's Spiritual practice but rather to fulfill the vulgar idealism of keeping someone alive, which is based on fear and non-sensitivity to the state of someone who is dying.

Therefore, people take bizarre measures to keep someone alive even if only in a vegetable-like form, as machine-made life, and some even attempt such things as freezing people when they are dead, so that they can be re-animated two hundred years from now when there exists the medical ability to treat them.

All these points of view are based on a vulgar model of existence and do not take into account the real significance of death and the process the entity must endure when it dies. You must start treating one another while you live and after you die according to real wisdom, real understanding, and sensitivity. Then you will live with one another differently, and you will also treat one another differently in death, which is a very profound affair that you, the living, affect by the various things you do to the body and the various ways you relate to someone who has died.

Particularly in the case of Adepts and greatly advanced practitioners, what follows the cessation of breath, what follows obvious physical death, is actually a period of samadhi in which there is no animation of the physical body or the physical brain of any kind that can be detected in general by medical or scientific means. Yet in someone who is in a highly evolved state, an "inner breath" still goes on, even a kind of meditative state. A kind of samadhi still associated with the body is possible, particularly in the case of Adepts or greatly advanced Spiritual practitioners. Those who are attuned to this process know when the entity is still there, not just hovering but still associated with the body in samadhi or, in the case of a less evolved practitioner, in a kind of sleep.

Particularly in the case of an individual who has literally entered into one of the great Samadhis of Realization at the point of physical death, the Samadhi remains the context of that individual for some period of days. He or she is still alive, still associated with the physical—the physical body is still part of the conscious being—but he or she is in Samadhi during that time.

In any case, to separate from the physical takes a certain period of days for all entities generally—sometimes the separation is quick, but, in the Way of the Heart, My devotees take the possibility of a gradual separation into account by allowing a few days for the separation. The minimal time that should be allowed, as a general rule, is three or three and one-half days or so. This is the most common traditional period of time, but frequently more time than this is allowed. Particularly in the case of an Adept or a highly evolved Spiritual practitioner, it might be found appropriate to allow more time.

What must be done, then, is to observe the state of the body after death and, in the case of Adepts and advanced Spiritual practitioners, generally keep the body in a seated position, a meditative posture. In any case, keep the body undisturbed, surrounded by people who know what they are doing there. Generally, for most individuals, perhaps three or three and one-half days is sufficient, and then, generally, cremation should follow. Even after cremation, a period of time should be set aside when some people consciously regard the individual, and work on his or her release, meditating while regarding the person with the disposition of release, even for days or weeks, until there is a general feeling that the entity has passed out of the gross plane altogether.

In the case of an Adept or an advanced Spiritual practitioner, perhaps the best rule is not to set any limit on time. Keep the body in a place undisturbed, and when you begin to see that the body is breaking up, or starting to decay, that is the sign that the "inner breath" has gone, because, even if the body of the Adept or advanced Spiritual practitioner has had a disease, a certain degree of preservation will be obvious in the body, certainly for hours afterward, very often for days, even weeks. Perhaps the best rule, therefore, is to allow time to pass until you begin to see the signs that the body is decaying.

[Da Avabhasa reads from a traditional text] "In Tibet some great Lamas and Yogis who have experienced the state of Dharmakaya[1] may sit up two or three days in meditation posture after death."

They allow them to stay in that state, you see.

---

1. Mahayana Buddhism distinguishes three aspects of the Total Reality—the three "bodies" of the Buddha—which are the Dharmakaya, the Sambhogakaya, and the Nirmanakaya. The senior aspect is the Dharmakaya, or "Body of the Law", which is the Formless, or Uncreated, Transcendental Reality.

"When very highly-realized Lamas die, they will often stay in that posture after death, meditating for from three to seven days—perhaps even longer. When the meditation is over, they have realized enlightenment, and the body will collapse."[2]

In the case of Realizers and advanced practitioners, when the body shows signs of collapsing, or when the body will not sit up naturally, when it starts falling over or when there are signs of decay, or when there is a sensitivity on the part of those who have some real feeling for this process that the "inner breath" or the "inner life" of the body-mind has separated out, then it is appropriate to take the next step, which is burial or cremation—generally cremation, except in the case of an Adept.

There is a tradition for preserving the body of the Adept. Sometimes the body is not merely not cremated, but it is embalmed in various ways. Devotees of the Adept sometimes lacquer the body, or do all kinds of things to keep the body physically preserved. Sometimes the bodies of Teachers in the Orient are kept in various monasteries. The Sixth Patriarch, for instance, and others in his tradition were lacquered, and their bodies are still sitting in monasteries—at least they were until recently. In Tibet there also exists the tradition of embalming individuals and keeping their bodies. There is also a tradition for cremating even Adepts, but you can see the usefulness, not necessarily in embalming or trying to keep the body from decaying, but of not cremating the body of the Adept. The body of the Adept is kept as a focus of Grace, a Samadhi Site is constructed, properly made, properly served and so on, and the body is buried, generally placed directly in the earth or perhaps kept in a chamber without embalming. And then the place is used as a temple, a point of contact.

In the case of some rare Yogis, the "inner life", or "inner breath", does not leave the body. Jnaneshwar, who is known for his commentary on the *Bhagavad Gita* called *Jnaneshwari,* is presumably one of those individuals who at the point of death went directly into Samadhi and has kept his "inner breath", or the "inner life" associated with the physical body, ever since, for hundreds of years. His body is still in the place he prepared underground, beneath a temple that was built over it, and it has been left that way ever since. It is said that a few hundred years later another individual, I believe it was Eknath, went down into the chamber where Jnaneshwar's body is, touched the body, and reported that it still

2. Venerable Lama Lodö, *Bardo Teachings: The Way of Death and Rebirth,* revised edition (Ithaca, New York: Snow Lion Publications, 1982), p. 8.

felt warm and that it was still preserved and supple. It is not physically animated, but the "inner breath", or Yogic life, is still associated with that body. The place is, therefore, a useful place of meditation.

Presumably, even though the "inner breath" in the particular form that preserves the body may pass at some point, the body of every Adept, having been the vehicle of the Nirmanakaya,[3] or Enlightened body-mind, during that physical lifetime, remains a useful seat of Spiritual Transmission, and the place where it is buried will remain a useful seat of Spiritual Transmission. Somehow the Life or Light of Spiritual Transmission will remain. (October 15, 1982)

3. The Nirmanakaya, or "body of manifestation", as described in Mahayana Buddhism, is the human physical body of the Enlightened Adept.

CHAPTER 40

The Celebration of Passing

excerpts from three Spiritual Discourses
by Da Avabhasa

SRI DA AVABHASA: The natural life-current is not dependent on the body. Its continued association with the body at death is just a sign of the state of the individual, and its withdrawal from the body is a natural event. It is possible that the natural life-current remains associated with the body of any dead person, even individuals who did not show any evidence of a Spiritual life while alive. The critical period is the early days following death, when it is important to keep from disturbing the body. To disturb the body then is just like disturbing somebody in meditation, although the dead person will not wake up and say, "You're bugging me!" It is useful to think of disturbing the dead body as the same as disturbing someone who is meditating, or disturbing someone in Samadhi.

This is one of the reasons why you must leave the body alone, let it remain in a natural state, create an environment that acknowledges the Spiritual Process, an environment of release and calm and acceptance, an environment of Spiritual sanity. All this helps the individual to participate in the transition. Those who serve the individual's transition likewise go through various changes of purification and release, and the experience of such people can be quite profound.

There are two stages to physical death. One is the stage we generally acknowledge to be death—cessation of physical activities, including the flow of blood, patterns of brain activity, and so on. But there is a second stage, particularly evident in some people, of a current, or a kind of "inner life", that remains associated with the physical for a time after clinical death. When that current goes, the second stage of death is complete.

Now, in the general case, the second stage occurs in the instant of physical death, or shortly afterwards. In other cases, the second stage can take longer to complete itself.

Then there are stages of dissociation beyond the physical death. The next stage takes place out of the body, the transition from looking at the body, being in the environment somehow, and observing people while outside the body. For this reason, when people are attending someone who has died, they must release the person from this life and psychically affirm his or her transition by feeling the dead person and helping him or her to transcend astral fascination with the body and reluctance to leave it. Do not give the dead person reasons to hold on to this life.

DEVOTEE: Heart-Master Da, I noticed something interesting about that process of release in the case of my aunt, who was like a mother to me for many years. She died in 1950. Her mother, my grandmother, who had never allowed her to marry, had a profoundly suppressive attachment to her and kept her very close. At the time my aunt was enduring her terminal illness, my grandmother called in every healer on the planet, convinced that this lady was saintly and that she had to live. In spite of all that, she did die, and my grandmother refused to accept the reality of her death.

A few months after my aunt died, my cousin visited the family house for the first time in years. He was a political scientist at Princeton University, and he did not believe in ghosts at all. But Aunt Adelle appeared in his bedroom there one night. She was completely terrified, and she said, "You've got to tell Aunt George to let me go. I'm trapped." He ran screaming out into the streets in his underwear and left very shortly afterward. But he did tell my grandmother that perhaps she should pay attention to the message.

At about the same time, I had been studying spiritualistic psychic phenomena with a well-known psychic in California. I attended a seance with her at which St. Teresa of Avila manifested for someone and left a rose in the middle of the room. The psychic asked me if I would like to see anybody, and I said that the only person I knew who had died was my Aunt Adelle. Within a minute the ectoplasm filled up, and there appeared a form that looked and spoke just like my aunt for about a minute. She showed a great reluctance to be there. She said, "Who are these people? Why have you brought me here?" As soon as I saw that my calling to her was inappropriate, she went back into the spirit realm.

SRI DA AVABHASA: You can see how this kind of spiritualistic game is a kind of net to trap beings who exist in subtle form and draw them from their dreamlike state into a weird revisitation of this gross plane.

You can also see how very important it is that the intimates of someone who has died release the person in the event of death. It is not only the attachment of the now dead person to this world that keeps the person here. The attachments of others to the person are a kind of net that prevents the person from release.

Therefore, it is very important that everyone have a Spiritual understanding of the death process and acknowledge it, accept it when it does occur, and participate in the process of release to let the person go on to another destiny. (December 8, 1982)

◆ ◆ ◆

SRI DA AVABHASA: Just as the recently dead can be helped by their friends' reminding them of what is going on when the physical body is dead, so also those recently dead who are locked into the etheric and who are what might be called "ghosts" can be helped. Those individuals may not be present in the physical plane all the time. They may pass into unconsciousness and then return again. They may go into some field of subjective revery, and it is in that plane that they experience what could be called "hells" and difficulties and strange frustrations, like strange dreams. Then they may again return to association with the physical plane while they are yet in the etheric body, invisible to most others but perhaps even experienced there.

Some of you may have had experiences with such individuals, perhaps people you knew and whom you experienced in this way shortly after their death. I have had contact with many such individuals. They can be released by associating with them very much as you would associate with someone who is alive right now. You must help them be aware of their actual situation, because they think they are still physically alive. They have not quite figured out their situation. It is a problem to them. They are not in a normal state. They are emotionally shocked and agitated, strangely attached to people and places.

The one major thing that is going on with them is that they are not aware they have died. They think they are alive, and yet something about their situation does not quite make sense to them. They cannot get people to respond to them, and the people who are in the rooms that used to belong to them act as if they are not there. Yet they move around and they do things like everybody else. They could sit and watch TV with you at night. They could hang out in your rooms, watch you have sex, even try to have sex with you.

The one thing you can do to help them is to make them aware that they are dead, explain what has actually happened to them, and describe the next step of their relinquishing, relaxing, letting go, moving on. Such direct address to these individuals, if you have some perception of them, can be useful to them. (July 3, 1987)

◆ ◆ ◆

SRI DA AVABHASA: Ordinary people live to fulfill the physical dimension of existence. Therefore, they are shocked and disturbed by death. They want to forget death. They want nothing to do with it. They are only totally threatened by the death of another, and they typically experience extraordinary grief.

In itself, the grief of being separated from the company of another is natural. But debilitating grief, grief that prevents you from associating with the one who has died, that prevents you from releasing that person and serving his or her continued process of relinquishment—such grief is not good.

You must be prepared for your own death, and you must be prepared for the death of others. You must serve others once they have died, because they have not disappeared nor ceased to exist. You do not want them to become ghosts, trapped in the etheric body, so that they roam in this world for decades and more before they are able to pass on. You must serve their ability to notice their condition, relinquish it, and move on from the physical.

Mourning (perhaps that is not even the best word for it—the celebration of passing is perhaps a better way to describe it) should be a process whereby the person who has died, or given up the physical, is given the opportunity to notice that fact and to see that all his or her friends and relations also notice it and know that he or she has passed.

In the Way of the Heart, all those participating during the vigil should remind the individual, through prayers, affirmations, and reading My Wisdom-Teaching, that he or she is undergoing a process of letting go. They should point out the next step and encourage the person to relinquish the physical and move on. (July 3, 1987)

CHAPTER 41

The Best Form of Grief

excerpts from three Spiritual Discourses
by Da Avabhasa

In the following excerpt, Da Avabhasa begins by talking about a letter He received from Jon Rottman, a devotee whose six-year-old daughter, named Leela, was in the hospital about to undergo a potentially life-threatening heart operation. This excerpt is taken from the book Love of the God-Man, *by James Steinberg (published by the Dawn Horse Press), in which the remarkable story of this event is told in its entirety.*

SRI DA AVABHASA: I received a note from Leela's father, Jon Rottman, who was very emotional about her ordeal. He wrote that he was brokenhearted when he said goodbye to Leela in the hospital in the last moment of seeing her before the operation. He had heard My Admonition about thinking happy thoughts about children, and it had helped him, but he was still profoundly sorrowful about her. His emotion became exhaustion, and he went to sleep. While he was sleeping, he dreamed she was calling to him for help, and he gave her some helpful advice in his dream. When he woke up, he felt much better. All his sorrow was gone.

His story is interesting for what it reveals in general about our sorrow for others. Very often we must go through a crisis of grief, or sorrow, in our relationships for one reason or another. You may notice that your sorrow has a great deal to do with a tendency to identify with another, to be the other. You are sorrowful for yourself as the other, as one who could be in his or her position. You think your sorrow is about your losing that one or being separated from that one or suffering some threat to that one, and those realities are a part of your sorrow, certainly, but another major dimension of sorrow is your identifying with that other, being that one, and thus being sorrowful for yourself.

This dream crisis was therefore important for Leela's father. His game of sorrow was broken when he was able to experience her as an other. Because he had to make the gesture of helping her, he could see her just as herself needing something from him. That perception changed his gesture toward her, and he stopped collapsing into egoically "self-possessed" sorrow as if he were Leela. He saw that she was just herself. His sympathy for her changed into a more compassionate, loving, and helping gesture. He realized he had a responsibility toward this person. He stopped the game of identification and broke the sorrow.

I would say this story describes a universal event in the breaking of sorrow in anyone's case. The other evening another devotee told us of her sorrow when her grandfather died, including her identification with her grandfather, her being somebody dying, her being "poor me". Most of you have likewise had the experience of grief when someone has died. You can therefore understand that a major dimension of your grief is that you are identifying with that someone as if you are that one. At the same time, you are thinking that your grief is about losing that someone, but it is principally about being a "poor me".

Grief is broken when you achieve the objectivity that Leela's father achieved, when that one becomes an other to be served, to be acknowledged. Yes, you must deal with your own life-difficulty, but your grief is broken when you are restored to relationship with another, when you break the bond of identification with another.

To identify with another and feel sorrowful about the other person is to identify with another in a rather childish way. It is to become a child and to feel sorrowful about yourself childishly. Childishness is a primary content of grief. When you understand that, and when the other becomes objectified, someone to whom you must relate and whom you must even serve, then a great mass of grief is relieved. The objectification of another, or the re-achievement of relatedness, is a primary factor in the transcendence of grief. It does not make the ordeal of loss easy, but it is an interesting process. (May 20, 1987)

◆ ◆ ◆

SRI DA AVABHASA: If you have any leftover business with someone, you should resolve it with the person before he or she dies, and not even as he or she is dying. You really should not leave that leftover business unfinished. If there is anything left over, and the person is dying, you can in a quiet way do the work of forgiveness, but dramatizations of heavy grief and exaggerated emotion do not generally serve dying people. Such dramatizations trap their attention and tend to confuse them and make them feel they are not free to leave. Generally, such dramatizations are not appropriate.

The circumstance of dying should be calm and straightforward and sensitive to the dying person. The signs the living give should be the signs of self-transcendence. Your manner should correspond to the instruction you are giving the dying person. This is important.

Of course there is grief, but grief should not become a dramatization that could disturb the dying individual. If some people become a little overwhelmed with grief, it is best that they leave the room for a time and handle their grief with their friends. Therefore, you should prepare not only the dying person but also the people who surround the body of the dead person during the vigil.

Much of what passes for service to the dead in the common world is a ceremony of grief. Because people do not quite believe that there is any continuation after death, they take the opportunity of a social occasion for indulging in grief, talking about the old times, weeping, getting together and crying on one another's shoulders, and saying a few things to the effect of "Maybe so-and-so is still up there in heaven watching us", but otherwise clinging to that individual, even rehearsing clinging for several days. This is generally not useful to anyone, either those who are grieving or those who are dead or dying.

It is not that grief should be cancelled, but the best form grief can take is continuous feeling-association with the dying or dead person—and release, not only release of one's grief but release of the other. Adaptation to the new situation should be the work of the observers of the dying and death of another as well as the work of the individual who is dying or who has passed on. (July 12, 1987)

◆ ◆ ◆

SRI DA AVABHASA: Expressive grieving is traditionally conceived to be a useful process that releases not only the living person who has suffered loss through the death of another, but also the one who has died. This principle is acknowledged in some traditions by the practice of hiring professional mourners to grieve and weep and serve the process of release.

Those close to the dying individual will naturally, and should, demon-strate signs of grief. Grief is part of the process of release, not only for the person who is dying, but also for the person who is grieving. Therefore, you must account for anyone's expression of grief, but in such a way that grieving does not interfere with the vigil conducted for the sake of the dying person. People who do not know what to do with their grief and whose activities have nothing to do with letting go, or with the process of release, may interfere with the dying person.

People who are serving the dying person must also avoid excessive busy-ness, such as the endless agitating of the body and talking to the body that is typical of fascinated people who fall into a manipulative mode around a dying or dead person. Be mindful not to make the vigil into an elaborate ritual. During the vigil, you need not read or chant constantly but only occasionally. Most of the time the vigil should be conducted quietly, through the meditative releasing of the people who are participat-ing. Those who are grieving should enter into meditative release and the process of letting go. Therefore, do not overdo the activities of the vigil. Make sure everything is done in an appropriate way and measured by people who are rightly trained.

It is good for those who know the dead person to be together. This is why traditionally a funeral is a social gathering, very often at the house of the person who has died or the house of his or her family. Such a social event gives all those who have known the person the opportunity to express their grief, to inspire one another with right understanding, to strengthen one another, and, in the case of My devotees, to inspire one another to the practice of devotion to Me.

Funeral homes at times provide for such an occasion, although often there is a dreadful atmosphere in such a place, where all the pews or chairs face the casket and the entire room is pervaded by the feeling and even the smell of the corpse. Of course, sometimes a funeral home may allow for appropriate interaction between people. But generally the room where people gather should be in a different place—either a different room or, preferably, a different building—from the place where the person has died or where the vigil is being done.

One of the purposes of the vigil is to educate, inspire, and guide everyone who is bereaved and who is also participating in the vigil. Therefore, inspirational guidance should be communicated to everyone who attends the vigil about how to deal with the death of another, in general not in the same room with the body but in an adjoining room. (April 13, 1991)

CHAPTER 42

Transcending the Ritual of Sorrow

a Talk by Da Avabhasa
February 9, 1983

SRI DA AVABHASA: The sorrow you feel when someone you know dies is, at least to some significant degree, a learned response. Perhaps it could be accounted for totally as a learned response. In any case, it is a response you must ultimately overcome. It seems to you to be a natural response, but it is in fact rather automatic, learned, and conventional. It is the response you feel you are obliged to make, whereas the only real response to which you are called has nothing to do with sorrow.

You tend not to be equipped to demonstrate freedom from sorrow when somebody dies. Rather, you become involved with the vision of death in front of you, the leftovers, the grotesque meat-form that is breaking up and returning to the elemental state. Under such circumstances, you forget the point of view of Truth and basically indulge in the presumption that death is a problem.

Death is a living event, and sorrow is a basic component of your reaction to somebody's dying. Sorrow is ego-based. It is your way of dwelling on what you have lost. The feeling of sorrow does not really take into account the one who has died except as something from which you are separated. Thus, most of the emotions you indulge when somebody dies are your own problems, reactions you must deal with or overcome.

Even so, it is not altogether inappropriate to be sorrowful when someone dies. But you must find another resource, a greater capability, through which to be free of the vision of death that is pushed in front of you at such a time. The sorrow you feel at someone's death is not just the result of memory. It is ritual, like so much of the rest of what everybody does repetitively, compulsively, constantly, hour after hour, day after day, from birth until death. People generate very few truly appropriate actions in the whole period between birth and death.

Most of the sorrow associated with death, therefore, is totally unnecessary, a self-destructive and other-destructive ritual. Passing through the ritual sorrow and complication relative to the sickness or death of someone with whom you had a very strong emotional connection and daily dependency is perhaps inevitable. You must still overcome your sorrow, but sorrow is at least temporarily appropriate. If you have a rather distant relationship to someone who dies, however, then hearing of his or her death is almost like reading the obituary column in the newspaper.

Reactivity is basically a ritual you engage all day long, week after week, month after month, year after year, as you cycle through the ritualized demonstrations of mind, emotion, and body. There is no ultimate necessity for it. Your emotional reactivity is an organized form of behavior for which you are not responsible, and your irresponsibility is the problem of life, the "Dreaded Gom-Boo".[1]

This imaginary disease is not merely a little bit of philosophy. It is a ritual life, a prerehearsed, prefigured automaticity you crank out every day of your life in relation to standard events. You are always doing it. You live as if you are diseased. The Dreaded Gom-Boo is a real disease in the sense that you experience it and are animated in it every day of your life, but it is imaginary, or unreal, in the sense that it is not necessary, not based in reality. It is just an automaticity. It has no necessity.

Since the Dreaded Gom-Boo is unnecessary, there is therefore no necessity to devote your life to overcoming it! You should understand it and transcend it directly. But people are so full of their rituals, so bound up by forces of habit and states of reactivity, that they are not free to practice Spiritually, because they must attend to all their rituals and serve their egoic priesthood. It is almost as if they were paid employees of cosmic Nature! Because people have all these obligations, they are, therefore, not free to practice Freedom and Truth. They are devotees of the sect of cosmic Nature, death, and egoity, just cranking out this life of reaction.

1. "The Dreaded Gom-Boo" is Sri Da Avabhasa's term for our presumed separation from the Divine Condition, which traditional religion treats as a form of disease to be cured by conventional means such as prayer, fasting, meditation, and various belief systems.

Well, either there is Truth or there is not. If there is no Truth, then you might as well continue to do what you are doing. But if there is Truth, then you must make room for It. You must give up your commitment to conditional Nature and become involved in a totally different kind of existence. To do so is your business, and only you can do it. Only you can renounce the cult of your false suffering.

DEVOTEE: Heart-Master Da, I remember when I received the telephone call from my brother notifying me that my father had died in London. He was fairly young, about sixty-two, when he died of throat cancer. I had not had any relationship with him for fifteen years except for one meeting, because I was a member of a monastery of Yogis whose discipline included separating from, or abandoning, karmic influences.

SRI DA AVABHASA: Transcend nothing, leave everything—was that it?

DEVOTEE: Yes. But I remember being very surprised by the fact that for about an hour I passed through quite an emotional catharsis about his death. I saw that I had never really made a connection of mutual understanding with him during his lifetime. He had never understood why I went to the monastery, and I had never really understood him, perhaps. I remember feeling, "If only we had had one last conversation and really straightened out our relationship."

SRI DA AVABHASA: The more dependent you are on some personality who is dead or dying, the more fully you enter into the ritual and the more exaggerated you become in its expression. But it is really yourself that you are dealing with. Your primary activity in relation to the death of another is self-meditation, a "Narcissistic" ritual in which you feel confounded, frustrated, reactive, and basically disconnected. The feeling of disconnection is an essential part of your reaction. You are rehearsing a rather infantile condition, a gesture with which you have been involved since birth and the acknowledgement of your independent existence.

To hear of somebody else's death is just an opportunity to rehearse the fearful un-Happiness you feel in relation to your own death. When you hear of another's dying, you indulge in that pattern either slightly, but nonetheless really, or very dramatically. Yet it is really your own wound, your own disease, that you are ritualizing. Very little that you do in relation to someone who has died has anything to do with him or her. Most of what you do has to do with yourself. It is a ritualized expression of your own difficulty.

You are going to die. There is no doubt about that. And everybody you know is going to die. Thus, it is your business while alive to really deal with the great fact of death and be free of egoic ritualization relative to it. Part of the essential matter associated with Spiritual life is to deal with that very disease, that very ritual response to death, so that you are free to die and change altogether in every way, and also free to have others do the same thing in your lifetime.

You really have no right to defend yourself against death, either your own or someone else's. Every moment of your living should take the inevitability of death totally into account. If you are living consciously, therefore, when you are obliged to encounter the death of someone else, you are equipped to be as free as possible of the ego-based ritualization. You do not then defend yourself against the mere fact of the death, but rather you participate in the whole affair, even continue to engage in that relationship, in free, Spiritual terms, with the least impediment created by your own reaction, your own un-Happiness relative to death, your own apparent independence.

To the degree you feel you are just an independent, mortal being, you will be ritualized in your response to everyone else's death. There really is only one death—anybody's death. The same ritual is always enacted. And what are you dramatizing? Your own decomposition, your own derangement.

Death is the ultimate fact of life, not merely the end of it. This world is just a bardo, a place of transition. There is whatever there was before, there is whatever there is after, and there is Whatever there Is Ultimately. And Whatever there Is Ultimately is the Ultimate Fact before and during and after whatever is going on now or then, past, present, or future. To deal with that Ultimate Reality, you must be free of your ego-based ritualization of existence and be always encountering the reality of the life-process, not divorced from it through ritual. All this social face, these bodily attitudes, the tendencies toward emotional reaction, dependence and independence, all the character games you play all day long, all the ways you deal with primary events in life, are all a ritual, a defense, an expression of "Narcissus", the self-contracted personality that is fundamentally devoted to defending itself against the realities of the Living Process and, in the process of that defense, divorcing itself further from the Ultimate Condition in which these changes are occurring.

289

In your clinging to your relations, you are rather sorrowful and dependent. You feel that certain relations are necessary for your sense of Happiness. Particularly in certain moments you feel this, and you feel this in some ultimate sense about everyone on whom you depend and whom you want to keep around you all your life.

Actually, however, you are completely free of dependency. True Happiness is not dependent on anything. It may seem to be dependent on something now, but It could just as well seem to be dependent on something else in the next moment. You seem to be dependent on someone now, but you could just as well transfer your dependence to someone else. You can make a whole series of connections and engage in the ritual feeling of dependence, feeling Happy, more or less, in those relations, but actually you are always playing on a reservoir of Happiness that lies in the Divine Self-Position.

You feel so dependent on someone in the present that you would be sorrowful if he or she left you, but you can transfer the same interest to someone or something else and feel just as Happy, so that the previous one could leave you. This ordinary fact tells you that you are not really dependent on anyone or anything, but that you are engaging in a ritual of dependence, and locating your Happiness in various relations. Actually, however, you are playing on Something Inherent in your own Place, and in your own Condition.

Happiness is not dependent on the objects and relations of life. It is Inherent in the Divine Self-Position, or in the Real Condition of your life. Your noticing of this is the beginning of renunciation, the beginning of the expression of true understanding, which does not dissociate you from relations but simply associates you with a greater Principle, the Great Principle. Instead of making Happiness depend on your relations, therefore, you should magnify Happiness in your relations. You should magnify That Which is Inherent in your own Place, rather than depend on relations for the feeling of Happiness.

If you depend on relations for the feeling of Happiness, that feeling will always be corrupted and threatened and will always be associated with the mechanism of dependence. Likewise, you will always be moved to become independent, because you do not like the feeling that Happiness is dependent on someone else, some condition, some object, some circumstance. You do not really settle into even these dependencies. You rebel against them and become dissociative in relations on which you depend. You corrupt your Happiness even in circumstances wherein you do have the option to be Happy.

You must discover the Fullness of Happiness that is Inherent in the Divine Self-Position. Discovering Inherent Happiness, you do not thereby dissociate from relations. Rather, you have the capability for relationship. If you are already established in That Which Is Happiness, in other words, then you are capable of relationship.

The summary of the Hebrew Law as attributed to Jesus is "Love God absolutely, and <u>then</u> love your neighbor fully." However, you do not tend to live according to this Law. You live its opposite. You make your Happiness depend on relations, and, therefore, you are always suffering in the context of relationship—suffering dependence, manufacturing independence, corrupting your relationships, going from object to object, relationship to relationship, struggling all your lives in a circumstance wherein you ritually make Happiness depend on relationships and struggling with that very fact, resisting that very ritual.

You live the Law backwards. Instead of living from the point of view of Happiness, love of God, and submission to the Divine Reality, you live in submission to others, objects, and relations. In moments you find a certain kind of Happiness in those relations and circumstances, but It is always being corrupted and threatened, so that you eventually forget Where the Happiness Is. You forget where you put It. You forget Where It comes from. You forget Its Source, you forget Its Origin, you forget Its Divine Nature, you forget your actual Divine Condition.

You must remember that Divine Condition. You must find Happiness in your own Place. You must find It in God, not the God outside or the Parent-God of the childish ego. Transcending the ego in the Divine Self-Position, you must directly find the Source That Is Happiness, Freedom, Love-Bliss, Free Consciousness, the Fullness of Divine Being.

Having fulfilled the first and fundamental aspect of the traditional Law to love God, and economized by that Realization, you should enter into the sphere of relationships. Thus, you should enter into relationships not on the basis of the psychology of dependence, wherein you lose Happiness or feel It to be threatened or allow It to be disturbed by the mechanisms of relationship, but magnifying that Happiness Which Is in your own Place or in the Divine Self-Position. Then you are free to play your relations, and they are no longer the expressions of dependence on relations or objects for Happiness.

To Realize Happiness, however, you must be profoundly devoted to That Which Is in the Divine Self-Place. You must be constantly and consistently established in that Well of Being, to the point of dissolving the rituals of the Law played backwards and the ritual reactions of ego-based living. Instead of being established in the ego, therefore, which is already separate from Happiness and finds It only simulated through the mechanics of relationship, you must be established, prior to the ego-base, in the Divine Self-Position, Which is All-Love-Blissful. Then you may enter into relations as the play or the expression or modification of that Reality.

In doing so, you will be free in relationship, not free of relations in the sense that you are detached and do not care about them, but already Happy, magnifying Happiness by blessing others, and thereby always allowing change and inevitable separations to occur in the framework of this born existence. If you fulfill the Law in its right arrangement, then, ultimately, your immersion in this great Well of Happiness will Outshine the noticing of relations and objects and the separate "I", or the functional ego. All that is arising is nothing but a play on the Divine Reality, a modification of That. Therefore, if you Realize That Most Perfectly, the play of modification will first be Divinely Transfigured and Divinely Transformed by this Love-Blissful "Brightness". Then you will become Divinely Indifferent to the play of modification. Eventually, the play of modification will cease to be noticed, and, ultimately, in Divine Translation, it will disappear and dissolve in the "Bright" Love-Bliss of Divine Being.

This is a summary of the true Wisdom-Teaching, and it must apply to every aspect of your living. Therefore, it must apply to all your troubled wondering about death and separations of all kinds.

CHAPTER 43

Surrender beyond Everything and Everyone

*Three excerpts from Da Avabhasa's Instructions
on how to participate in the death process,
for those who have formally chosen
to practice the Way of the Heart*

S ri Da Avabhasa's Instructions for those who are dying (as well as for those who are living) depend on one simple but very profound principle: "You become what you meditate on." Throughout this book, Sri Da Avabhasa points out how we create our destiny in every moment—by what we do with our attention. He makes very clear that what happens to us after death obeys the same law—our habits of attention determine what our experience will be when we die and after we die.

Sri Da Avabhasa's Purpose in this world is to Attract our attention, to lift it from what is limited and mortal to what is Enduring. He does this not for His sake but for our sake. Because He is One with the Very Divine, when our attention is caught by Him, by His Mysterious Attractiveness, we are spontaneously relieved of our preoccupation with separate and separative self. In such moments we are free to feel the Divine Condition That Eternally transcends change and death.

As Sri Da Avabhasa Explains:

> *There is one law: You become what you meditate on.
> This is the process through which I become your unique
> Advantage. When your attention is concentrated in Me,
> you are Contemplating That Which is Full—a
> complete Revelation. Simply by granting Me attention in
> all the moments of conditional existence, the total
> Spiritual Process can be activated in you by Grace. There
> is no possibility that it will not work in your case, whoever
> you are—no possibility. No one is damned. No one is
> inherently or essentially limited. In relation to the Divine
> Person there are no limits. All are Given Grace fully,
> openly, and without limitation. (October 11, 1985)*

Sri Da Avabhasa has Given His devotees the practice of feeling-Contemplation of Him, which is the process of beholding Him with full feeling-devotion, directly or through a photograph or simply by remembering Him. Through such feeling-Contemplation, Sri Da Avabhasa's Attractiveness Draws His devotees more and more beyond the limits of egoic self into the Feeling of His Being That transcends body, mind, and egoic self. Whatever His devotee's emotional state or life-circumstance may be at any time, the practice is always the same, and it is the means by which the Native Happiness of existence can always be contacted. (Sri Da Avabhasa has fully elaborated the practice of feeling-Contemplation in The Love-Ananda Gita.*)*

Even in death, feeling-Contemplation of Sri Da Avabhasa remains the principal practice for His devotees, because Sri Da Avabhasa may always be located on what He calls "the grand scale of My Being", which knows no limit in time and space. As He Says to His devotees, "I will always be with you, even in death."

Despite the fact that the practice of feeling-Contemplation is extremely simple, to allow this practice to mature and become true Realization requires that every aspect of the body and mind be conformed to that Contemplation and what it Reveals. Thus, Sri Da Avabhasa has provided various forms of what He calls the "conscious process", or specific means by which attention can be surrendered in feeling-Contemplation of Him. Secondarily, He has Given supportive practices for the control of bodily energy that He calls "conductivity", which balance the body and free attention for feeling-Contemplation. In these Instructions, He refers to the basic forms of the "conscious process" and "conductivity" as they are to be practiced in daily life and during the death process.

The following is a composite of Sri Da Avabhasa's summary practical Instructions on how to practice while dying for all those who choose to practice the Way of the Heart:

SRI DA AVABHASA: As My devotee in the Way of the Heart, your practice, in life and in death, is Ishta-Guru-Bhakti Yoga,[1] or the fullest self-surrendering, self-forgetting, and self-transcending devotional resort to Me. In addition (or on that Foundation), you should also practice the various by Me Given forms of the "conscious process" and "conductivity" that are appropriate to your present form and developmental stage of the Way of the Heart.

I have Given a range of practices for My devotees to engage at death, depending on their present form and developmental stage of the Way of the Heart. The basic practice for all is that of self-surrendering, self-forgetting, and self-transcending feeling-Contemplation of My bodily (human) Form, My Spiritual (and Always Blessing) Presence, and My Very (and Inherently Perfect) State. That practice of feeling-Contemplation of Me should be facilitated by the use of My Murti.[2] And My devotee should extend the practice of feeling-Contemplation of Me by means of the by Me Given "conscious process" of either Name-Invocation, or Sat-Guru-Naama Japa, or self-Enquiry, or Re-cognition, or the "Easy Prayer", or the Prayer of Remembrance, or Mahamantra Meditation, or Feeling-Enquiry, or (in the seventh stage of life) Self-Abiding Divine Recognition—whichever of these practices My devotee has already been engaging in meditation (or, in the seventh stage of life, in Sahaj Samadhi), in either

---

1. Ishta-Guru-Bhakti Yoga is a compound of traditional Sanskrit terms that denotes the principal Gift, Calling, and Discipline Sat-Guru Da Avabhasa Offers to all who would practice the Way of the Heart.

"Ishta" literally means "chosen", or "most beloved". "Guru", in the reference "Ishta-Guru", means specifically the Sat-Guru, the Revealer of Truth Itself (or of Being Itself). "Bhakti" means, literally, "devotion".

Ishta-Guru-Bhakti, then, is devotion to the Supreme Divine Being in the Form and through the Means of the human Sat-Guru.

"Yoga", from a Sanskrit root meaning "to yoke", "to bind together", is a path, or way, of achieving Unity with the Divine.

2. "Murti", in Sanskrit, means "form". Traditionally, as well as in Sri Da Avabhasa's usage, the primary meaning of "murti" is "representational image". Murtis (Forms or Representations of the Divine) of all kinds, such as statues, paintings, and photographic likenesses, are used by traditional practitioners of religion and Spirituality as a focus of worship and meditation. In the Way of the Heart, a Murti is a photographic or artistic Representational Image of Sri Da Avabhasa.

the Devotional Way of Faith or the Devotional Way of Insight, according to his or her present form and developmental stage of the Way of the Heart.[3]

Additionally (and likewise according to his or her present form and developmental stage of the Way of the Heart), My devotee should, in the death process (as also in life), engage the by Me Given three-part process of "conductivity": First, feel, from the heart, in all directions, boundlessly (or to infinity); second, relax the body and conduct the energy of the body-mind (and, as Grace will have it, the Spirit-Current) from base to crown; and third, conduct the energy of the body-mind (and, as Grace will have it, the Spirit-Current) in the pattern of the Circle,[4] via the cycles of the breath.

Because the process of death naturally involves a process of release via the spinal line, intentional upward spinal release is an appropriate exercise in the death process. Therefore, for most practitioners of the Way of the Heart, the exercise of feeling-release of the body-mind toward the crown of the head, via the spine and above, is the principal "conductivity" practice at death. (April 9 and 13, and December 8, 1991)

---

3. The Devotional Way of Insight and the Devotional Way of Faith are the two forms of practice in the Way of the Heart that characterize meditative feeling-Contemplation of Heart-Master Da Avabhasa through every developmental stage.

The Devotional Way of Insight is a technical process of (primarily) feeling and insight, whereby the practitioner, while engaged in feeling-Contemplation of Sri Da Avabhasa's bodily (human) Form, His Spiritual (and Always Blessing) Presence, and His Very (and Inherently Perfect) State, observes, understands, and feels beyond the self-contraction in Divine Communion.

The Devotional Way of Faith is a technical process of (primarily) feeling and faith, whereby the practitioner is heart-Attracted by Sri Da Avabhasa's bodily (human) Form, His Spiritual (and Always Blessing) Presence, and His Very (and Inherently Perfect) State to feel beyond the self-contraction and is thereby spontaneously awakened to self-understanding and self-transcendence.

The varieties of the "conscious process" enumerated in this passage are engaged by formally acknowledged practitioners of the Way of the Heart, according to their present form and developmental stage of practice. For a fully detailed description of each of these practices, the form and developmental stage of the Way of the Heart in which each are practiced, and how they relate to practice in the Way of the Heart as a whole, see Sri Da Avabhasa's Masterwork, *The Dawn Horse Testament*.

4. The Circle is a primary circuit or passageway of the Living Spirit-Current and the natural bodily energy as they flow through the body-mind. The Circle is composed of two arcs: the descending Current associated with the frontal line, or the more physically oriented dimension, of the body-mind; and the ascending Current associated with the spinal line, or the more mentally and subtly oriented dimension, of the body-mind.

◆ ◆ ◆

In the following Instructions, Sri Da Avabhasa Tells practitioners of the Way of the Heart exactly how to participate in the process of death and how to practically apply the practice of conductivity as death approaches:

As you approach and enter into the death process:
Settle your affairs in this world.
Forgive and be forgiven.
Relax clinging and attention relative to all the relations of body and mind.

Accept the naturalness, orderliness, and purposiveness of the death process, and relax or surrender into each of its stages as it appears.

Release and relax all fear and simply surrender into cooperation with the death process like a woman in labor—and, like a woman in labor, consciously and bodily accept and "feel through" even the more painful, embarrassing, unpleasant, or chaotic aspects of the total event.

Outer and bodily awareness will gradually disappear in the death process, but it is not necessary to "lose consciousness". Simply keep attention on whatever replaces your present bodily and outer awareness.

As outer awareness begins to subside, begin to practice the "dead pose"—that is, systematically relax the body, beginning at the feet. Relax from the feet progressively toward the crown, withdrawing attention from each lower part to the next.

Surrender thought by keeping attention on the actual and progressive process of death and ultimate emergence from the present body-mind.

Breathe as evenly and easily as possible, but progressively surrender the entire process of sensation, breath, and heartbeat.

Release the body, emotion, and attention into the Divine Life-Current via the spinal line of the body and toward the crown, until there is emergence from the body-mind via the crown, if Grace will have it, into the next or new dimension of experience.

Whatever experiences arise after awareness of the dying body passes, continue to feel through and beyond all recoil of egoic self or toward egoic self—but surrender beyond everything and everyone into the Divine Current of Love-Bliss that is within and above egoic self and all beings and phenomena. (May 21, 1980)

◆　◆　◆

In the following passage, Sri Da Avabhasa provides Instruction for practitioners in the ultimate stages of the Way of the Heart, or those who practice the "Perfect Practice":

SRI DA AVABHASA: The practice at death is different for those practicing the "Perfect Practice" of the Way of the Heart. In general, My devotees who are practicing the "Perfect Practice" go beyond breathing-"conductivity", although there may be moments at death, just as there may be moments in life, when it is appropriate for them to engage in such breathing-"conductivity".

My devotees who practice the "Perfect Practice" in the sixth stage of life and the seventh stage of life in the Way of the Heart should participate in the process of death as follows:

Simply Identify with Consciousness Itself Prior to the body-mind and all movements and changes.

If you have Awakened to the seventh stage of life in the Way of the Heart, "practice" Divine Self-Abiding, Divinely Recognizing all that arises and utterly transcending all that arises to the degree of Most Perfect Divine Indifference and, finally, Outshining, or Divine Translation.

Upward "conductivity" via the spinal line is appropriate in the death process for all other practitioners of the Way of the Heart, and it is also generally appropriate for those practicing the "Perfect Practice". But practitioners of the "Perfect Practice" should also engage in the more profound practice of Identifying with Consciousness Itself Prior to the body-mind and all movements and changes. (April 9, 1991)

PART V

"I Will Always Be with You, Even in Death"

Leelas by Devotees of
the Divine World-Teacher
and True Heart-Master,
Da Avabhasa (The "Bright")

Sri Da Avabhasa (The "Bright")
Sri Love-Anandashram, November 1991

"I Will Always Be with You, Even in Death"

Leelas by Devotees of
the Divine World-Teacher and True Heart-Master,
Da Avabhasa (The "Bright")

INTRODUCTION

Many years ago, during Sri Da Avabhasa's Teaching Work, one of His devotees confessed to Him in a letter her fear of dying in the midst of an operation she was scheduled to have that week. In Heart-Master Da's response to her, He Said, "I will always be with you, even in death."

Years later, in recounting this story, Margaret Linde describes how loved and relieved she felt by these words from her beloved Sat-Guru. Only a Being Who has already transcended the boundaries of life and death can make such a statement and be believable. And only such a Being can truly guide us in life as well as in death.

The Truth of what Sri Da Avabhasa Says in Part Four about how to die and how to help others die has been proven time and again in the experience of His devotees. Devotees approaching death themselves or serving the death of another have given the same testimony again and again—each one has experienced the tangible Grace of Sri Da Avabhasa transforming pain and fear into the peaceful surrender and release of an "easy death". Part Five is devoted to Stories by His devotees telling of Sri Da Avabhasa's Blessing in the face of death.

Sri Da Avabhasa did not come into this world just to talk about death! Every single day He shows His devotees by Word and Touch and Glance what it is to be ecstatic in God-Love, what it means to transcend our small selves and the painful limits of this world. What kind of Being is it who could deal with a terrified man rapidly bleeding to death on a tiny, remote island in the middle of the night—Who in such a situation could humorously relieve the man's fear and guilt, requiring him to stay present in the body and feel the Bliss that transcends pain and death? Who could it be Who would suddenly go to the bedside of an aged, dying Fijian, draw him out of his coma and caress his fear away?

Sri Da Avabhasa does not even have to be physically present to Work such tranformations. The Blessing Force of His Being transcends time and space, as the Stories told in this section bear out. Thus, each of these stories, or Leelas, is in its own way a Miracle Story.

The word "leela" in the Indian tradition means "sport", the Play that occurs when the Divine Assumes a human form. In the life of Sri Da Avabhasa a Divine Play is taking place that can relieve the burden of separation and death for countless numbers of people. We are all living in a time of unprecedented Grace, because we are able to witness this Divine Leela of Sri Da Avabhasa, witness it unfolding before our very eyes. Ultimately, all Sri Da Avabhasa's Words in this book can only be understood in the light of His Leela, the incomprehensible Blessing implicit in everything that He does and Is.

There is nothing glamorous about death—or about life. Ordinary existence in and of itself is a horror—Sri Da Avabhasa has never minced His Words on this reality. But in the sphere of His Love something begins to change. When His Grace is active in any situation, frantic attachment to others and things starts to relax, to become humorous, Happy, and free of bondage. Then we become capable of love and real service to others. The Leelas told in this section are like flashes from the facets of a diamond—brilliant moments of the one enduring Story of Sri Da Avabhasa's Transparent God-Play, made Manifest in this world to relieve our bewilderment, to regenerate our true Happiness, and to Vanquish all illusions of limitation and death.

CHAPTER 44

The Only Way Out

PART ONE

The Great Giver

by Frans Bakker, M.D.

Frans Bakker

The consulting editor for Easy Death, *Frans Bakker, was born in Djakarta, Indonesia in 1939. From the ages of three to six years, he was interned there, with his family, in a Japanese concentration camp. The intense suffering he witnessed at that time made him acutely aware of death and gave him the urge to become a healer.*

Returning to Holland after the war, he went on to qualify as a doctor. Dr. Bakker later became co-founder of a Health Center in Rotterdam that attracted international interest for its innovative approaches to health and healing.

After meeting Sri Da Avabhasa while on a visit to California in 1975, Dr. Bakker moved there to be with his Spiritual Teacher.

In California, Dr. Bakker became one of the co-founders of the Radiant Life Clinic and Research Center, which was inspired by, and founded on, Sri Da Avabhasa's Wisdom-Teaching. For many years now, Dr. Bakker has traveled worldwide, lecturing and giving seminars on all aspects of the Way of the Heart, including many seminars on "Easy Death".

I t was December 24, 1983, at Sri Love-Anandashram, in the Fijian Islands, and Sri Da Avabhasa was celebrating the Feast of God in Every Body[1] with His devotees. Sri Da Avabhasa is, as His Name "Da" indicates, the Great Giver. Often at the celebratory time of "God in Every Body" during His Teaching years, He would literally overwhelm all those around Him with gifts He had Lovingly gathered over the course of the year.

On this night, I was among a group of about thirty devotees sitting on the floor in Heart-Master Da's room. A Giving Tree (Sri Da Avabhasa's name for the celebratory tree we decorate with lights and ornaments) sat in the corner, its colored lights blinking in endless rhythm.

Heart-Master Da started to give gifts to all who were in the room. His first gift was meditation pillows for everyone, made from stuffing from a Japanese-style mattress that He had slept on for a long time. He had specifically requested that these pillows be crafted for His devotees, and each pillow had colors selected specifically for the recipient. They were all very beautiful.

Then He Gave all the other presents—one by one, person by person. It took Him hours and hours. He beamed almost the whole time. He would Say, offering a special gift to someone, "This is for you. It is eight hundred years old. It has only been worn by one other person." Or: "I have had this in my room for years—wait, let me unwrap it for you." They were not ordinary gifts. At times He looked like an excited child— so happy to Give.

I cannot describe how deeply all this affected my friends and me. It was so wonderful to give and receive without any holding back. Everything seemed so simple, free, and unobstructed that night in the Company of our Heart-Friend and Lover. The room seemed full of light

---

1. Heart-Master Da's devotees now call this celebration "The Feast of the Love-Ananda Leela" ("Love-Ananda", one of Heart-Master Da's Names, means "the Divine Love-Bliss") or "Danavira Mela" ("Festival of the Hero of Giving"). This Feast is an extended celebration of giving, particularly the Giving that is Sri Da Avabhasa's constant Sacrifice.

and love. The lights on the Giving Tree were twinkling happily. There was much laughter all around. I sat there watching it all—the surprised exclamations of my friends, my great shaven-headed Heart-Teacher— beaming with joy. At one point, unable to contain myself any longer, I cried my heart out for sheer Happiness.

I was seated at the back of the room near a door with glass windows. One of my friends, Tom Closser, was sitting a few feet away from me. He was a big muscular fellow, his head shaven like Heart-Master Da's was at the time. To be living as a Spiritual renunciate was quite remarkable for this man—he had a checkered past about which he sometimes felt deeply guilty. Perhaps as a result of this guilt, Tom was also known to be accident-prone. On this wonderful night, he had just received his presents from the Hands and Heart of Sri Da Avabhasa. He had resumed his place near me when, all of a sudden, he stood up and began walking toward the door. Tom was intending to look for his wife, who was caring for the Ashram children, even though Sri Da Avabhasa had Said that she would receive her gifts later and it was unnecessary to look for her. Tom had hardly turned toward the door when he tripped over one of his presents and started falling towards me.

Again, Tom was a big, bulky, broad-shouldered man, and I became instantly frightened for my physical safety as his body crashed towards me. I lost the mood of God-love and curled up in self-defense. I saved myself from harm, but did not do anything to cushion Tom's fall. He came down on top of me, and his outstretched arm crashed through a window behind me. The glass ripped the upper part of his arm, instantly causing profuse arterial bleeding. Warm blood spurted all over me, soaking, within moments, the new meditation pillow I just received from my Heart-Master. Instantly the place was in consternation. We rushed Tom out of the room, put a tourniquet around his arm, and transported him to a building we used as a small medical clinic. Tom had lost a lot of blood—he was in serious danger.

While Daniel Bouwmeester, the physician in charge, ministered to Tom, Sri Da Avabhasa asked me to step outside the clinic and tell Him in full detail what was going on from a medical point of view, and what we were planning to do. I was struck by His composure. It was absolutely clear to me at that moment that <u>circumstances do not affect His Realization</u>. Everybody was panicking and had lost the mood of Happiness and God-love except for Heart-Master Da Avabhasa. He was simply present, even matter-of-fact. In His Freedom, Sri Da Avabhasa showed complete clarity in dealing with the situation before us. He was helping me tremendously, getting me to focus my own attention and become effective in the situation. I told Him that our friend Tom had arterial bleeding.

"What does that mean exactly?" He asked.

"It means that we have to stop the bleeding for now and that he has to be operated on as soon as possible."

"Can you do that here?"

"No, it is a question of vascular surgery—we couldn't do that here."

My friend Daniel had since telephoned the nearest major hospital, which was on a distant island, and he joined our conversation at this point. He was very concerned. He had just found out that there was no way to get a helicopter to Sri Love-Anandashram in the middle of the night. I looked at my watch. It was 1:05 A.M.

After we had explained to Sri Da Avabhasa that we just had to stop the artery from bleeding in the meantime, we accompanied Him inside to attend to our friend. The place looked like a war zone. Tom was lying on a table, his eyes closed, softly moaning. Tom's wife, Lynne, was holding his good hand, crying. Others were milling around, trying to help out in various ways. Heart-Master Da stood next to Tom, leaning on His Staff. He was Happy and relaxed.

Dan and I reinspected the wound. It was quite big and gaping. Dan located the bleeding artery deep in Tom's upper arm and discovered that he was simply able to apply direct finger pressure in such a way that the bleeding would stop while circulation to the arm below the cut could continue. This was very good news, because we knew that if we had to use a tourniquet for the fifteen hours it would take us to get Tom to the hospital, he would be in danger of losing his arm.

I looked at Tom and sensed that my friend was already out of his body. I knew this was not good for his physical well-being. His past history of mishaps and being accident-prone flashed through my mind.

Heart-Master Da obviously knew what was going on, and He pointed out Tom's state to all of us. He dealt with the situation forthrightly. In a loud, powerful Voice, He summoned Tom, Saying, "Look at Me! Look at Me! Look at Me!!!" His demands brought Tom back to his body, and Tom feebly opened his eyes. Heart-Master Da then Said, "Good, keep looking at Me! Do you dig Me? Do you? Do you love your Master? Come on, tell Me!"

My friend said, "Yes," still faintly.

Sri Da Avabhasa: "Then Love Me! . . . Feel Me! . . . Breathe Me! Come on, do it!" He whacked Tom's chest in the heart area with His Hand, and vigorously moved it down toward his navel. "Feel Me . . . Do you feel this? . . . Then breathe it down. . . . Breathe Me!" He was saying all this over and over again, His Hands passing down Tom's body multiple times, showing graphically that, in this life-threatening situation, he should affirm life and support it by breathing the life-force down in the frontal line of the body.

I could literally see Tom coming alive again. For a while, even the bleeding stopped totally. Once more fully conscious and alive, Tom started to feel the incredible pain caused by the cut in his arm and the tourniquet around it. The pain was only visible on his face—he did not say very much.

Then Sri Da Avabhasa Said, "Look at Me. Keep on looking at Me. Keep your attention on Me!! Is the pain really bad?"

"Yes."

Heart-Master Da's questioning changed direction: "Can you feel how bad the pain is?"

"Yes."

"But you do observe the pain, don't you? You observe the pain . . . you are observing the pain, are you not?"

"Yes, I am, Master."

"So 'you' are in the Witness-Position relative to the pain. You are the Witnessing Consciousness Itself, painless, timeless, and unqualified. Can you understand that . . . are you with Me?"

"Yes, I am, Master."

"Good, now, can you find the Bliss in Consciousness? Can you find the Bliss in Consciousness that is prior to pain? Can you find that Bliss? It does exist. I promise you! It does exist. There is Bliss in Consciousness prior to all pain, prior to all experience!"

I watched in amazement as Heart-Master Da, through His Words and His Spiritual Transmission, drew this man into the entirely different position of simply Witnessing and observing the pain rather than identifying with it. All of us in the room were drawn into the same freedom, to some extent, while this was going on. It was remarkable to be drawn into this freedom in the face of death. My friend was steadily regaining his humor and liveliness as Heart-Master Da Avabhasa kept talking to him.

Suddenly Sri Da Avabhasa started joking around with Tom. "You ruined My God in Every Body Day! People will be talking about this for many years, even many centuries to come." He threw back His Head and laughed loudly.

I could hardly believe what was going on. First Sri Gurudev brought Tom back to life, literally from the edge of death. Then He brought him in touch with That Which transcends day-to-day life and bodily existence altogether. And now He started dealing with his chronic feelings of guilt, which had somehow provoked this whole incident! Heart-Master Da was addressing my friend's guilt, without holding back. He said, "Now listen Tom, you don't have to be guilty anymore. What is guilt? Who cares about guilt? Do you really believe God cares about your guilt? Do you think I do? Do you think you have to pay to be free of it? No, God is Forgiveness. I don't give a damn for what happened in the past. Just give it all up. Give it all to Me."

Tears were welling up in my eyes. I realized that our Heart-Guru never gives up! Tom had been with Him for years and years, and was now dramatically playing out his emotional disturbance—to the point of death—but Sri Da Avabhasa was right with him once more. There was healing going on here far beyond that of a mere laceration of the arm!

With Tom now already alive and relaxed, Heart-Master Da continued to joke around. He took some surgical scissors from our tray and started cutting the hairs on Tom's chest, cracking jokes about his hairiness— meanwhile taking an opportunity to lay His healing Hands again all over Tom's chest.

After He finished, Heart-Master Da asked where the opera singers were. Two of our friends, Crane and Bill, had rehearsed an operatic aria for that evening, a duet from *The Pearl Fishers* by Bizet. They had not performed it because of the accident. "Somebody should go and get them. We need some singing here," Sri Da Avabhasa Said.

After a few moments, Crane and Bill came in—confused, frightened, and concerned about the accident. Heart-Master Da asked them to sing. They opened their mouths and tried, but all they could get out were a few squeaky notes. How could they sing while their friend was dying? Heart-Master Da immediately criticized them for not putting out energy. "Your friend may be dying! He needs a lot of life-juice, not just some squeaks," He suggested. They tried again. It sounded better, but Sri Da Avabhasa commanded them to sing it over and over again until they had completely transcended themselves and put their whole hearts into it. He also asked Tom to critique the singers and tell them how he felt about their performance, and Tom did!

Finally Bill and Crane did belt out the duet from *The Pearl Fishers* wholeheartedly. While Daniel and I were still working on Tom's arm, Heart-Master Da Avabhasa looked over my shoulder and asked me if I had ever been in a situation like this before. I said, "Not for a long time. I had to breathe really deeply in the beginning to avoid fainting!"

He laughed and remarked: "I'll bet you thought you came for a vacation on beautiful Naitauba [the Fijian name for the island]. Well, this is it, Frans! Spiritual life is nothing like a vacation. One moment you are in God-love, the next moment you are tested. Life is about change and death. Can you still be Happy under these circumstances?" I took this as a rhetorical question, and felt it did not need a direct answer. It made me realize however, that I had had a gloriously Happy day until the moment of the accident. Then I had lost it in the panic of the life-threatening moment, and then, slowly but surely, Heart-Master Da Avabhasa had Shown me, through His Great Example, that you could still be Happy even under dire circumstances. His Happiness had proven, through the extraordinary events of the evening, to be more effective in keeping Tom alive than our attitude of concern.

Whatever Heart-Master Da had done with Tom had its direct effect on me. He had been like an impassioned coach, walking His players through a complicated, difficult exercise. He had the vision, He showed how it was done, and we did it slowly, hesitantly. Nevertheless, we trusted Him, because He was right there with us, with everything He had to Give. We could do anything, even if it was very difficult. That is how I felt.

Finally, when daybreak came, a helicopter arrived. We could hear the sound of its propeller blades from afar. It landed and we quickly lifted our friend inside. Daniel and I were going to accompany him to Suva, where Fiji's main hospital is located.

It felt very strange to leave this enchanted island, hovering over it for a few moments and seeing all our friends waving goodbye. Then there was only the dark ocean and the sound of the helicopter for an hour and a half. Now and then we talked softly to Tom. Dan and I took turns holding our finger on Tom's brachial artery. Finally we arrived at the hospital, which, in contrast to Naitauba, was a place of edgy emotions, disease, limitations, and death. We spent three days there after the arterial surgery operation, which was successful.

Several weeks later, when Tom came back to the island, his arm was in a cast. Heart-Master Da wrote "Asshole" on it and laughed loudly. He then looked at my friend affectionately and Said, "I had better give you a

'Da' too. You need it." While everyone watched in wonderment—for Sri Da Avabhasa only very rarely consented to sign His Sacred Name, for any reason—He signed His Name "Da" on Tom's cast.

PART TWO

Remembrance of My Sat-Guru Was My Anchor

by Tom Closser

Tom Closser

As I was carried out of Sri Da Avabhasa's House immediately after the accident, I became especially sensitive to noise, and could hear the voices of everyone around me. Inside the clinic, I heard the lady who was holding my head, a registered nurse, whisper to someone that I was going into shock. Just then, I realized that I was moving up and back, and that I was outside my body.

Sri Da Avabhasa had gone outside, and I could hear Him talking, but I was still in the room watching everyone from above. Sri Da Avabhasa came back in the room. When He was talking outside, I could tell He had been talking about how serious the situation was. But when He came inside, He was joking and making light of it.

Spontaneously, I began to move back and forth between two vantage points: I would hear Heart-Master Da addressing me from the point of view of the body, and then I would observe everything from the higher,

312

detached position again. Because this switching back and forth was so uncontrollable, I started to get anxious. The more anxious I became, the more I seemed to fix in the out-of-body state.

I could tell that Heart-Master Da was trying to keep me associated with Him in the physical body, but the pain and fear kept driving me out of it. When I was out of my body, there was no pain—it was very calm and dissociated—even euphoric. Sri Da Avabhasa was moving His Hand up and down my chest, and He started kidding me about my tendency to be a macho man. He humorously said that maybe one of the ways He could deal with this self-image of mine was to trim the hairs off my chest. He began to run His Hand down my chest, and snip a little bit of the hair above His Fingers, and then move His Hand further down and snip there. I could feel a warm sensation, which seemed to drop from the top of my head and fall down my throat, as if someone were pouring a bucket of warm water over my head. Wherever Da Avabhasa's Hand would stay, this sensation, which was full and alive in ways that were clearly more than physical, would be drawn down into my body to that point. I felt Sri Da Avabhasa literally filling me and enlivening me with His Blessing and His Spirit, and this helped to draw me back into the physical body.

Sri Da Avabhasa also said wonderful things to keep my attention on Him. He said, "Do you love me? Do you really love me?" At one point, I rolled over and He held my face against His Belly and let me kiss His Stomach. The only thing that I could feel in that moment was that I wanted to be with Him forever. It was not just a thought, it was a <u>physical</u> sensation.

Then the doctors put a tourniquet on my arm and it caused incredible pain. I zipped out of my body again. This time, I had gone even further up, so that now I was outside the room. The space-time barrier changed in some way, and I could see, rather than doing things sequentially, Sri Da Avabhasa seemed to be maintaining a conversation with everyone in the room simultaneously—making many actions simultaneously.

The last image of the physical realm I remembered for a while was Heart-Master Da talking to some men outside the clinic about my situation. Then I drifted off further and further.

I started to get anxious. I was trying to get a physical reference—trying to feel my nose—but I realized I could not feel my body at all. All of a sudden, I lost the anchor to physical familiarity, and I began to have visual phenomena. I saw a dark background with silvery strands (much like what you see when you press your fingers into your eyes), and a matrix of light and dark and different shapes. Everything had the same patina and an ochre color.

Then I remember seeing a group of people that I had known throughout my life. I was standing around with these people. The meeting was very warm, and full of familial emotions. It was very happy and I felt relaxed again.

Next, I saw what might be described as a tunnel. I had the sensation of moving, and, as I entered the tunnel, the people drifted behind me. I looked up and I realized that I was suddenly in a totally different environment.

This new environment seemed to be a normal three-dimensional space at first, but I realized very quickly that it did not have the same physical laws. It had a different perspective, or a different dimension. It had a very familiar landscape, almost like the environment where I grew up in East Los Angeles! I felt comfortable, but there was also something odd about it.

Then I began shifting to many different experiences, and I had no control over any of it. It became terrifying. In daily life I am physically based, and I have some control of where my attention is because I can focus it. But, in this circumstance, because I had no bodily anchor, I went wherever my attention went. I had no capability to control attention. My attention was on one thing for one minute, and that was my total reality, and then the next moment my attention was somewhere else, and that became my reality.

When this happened, everything changed—I did not even have a memory of the previous experience or environment. I felt that all these experiences were in the same dimension, since they had a similar feeling to them, but I was very rapidly switching from one fantasy to another fantasy without any control. Later, I remembered what Sri Da Avabhasa has Said— "While you are alive, you make mind, but, after death, mind makes you". It may sound interesting, but it was actually completely horrific.

I became more and more terrified. At one point I had the general sense that the individuals, or entities, in this environment had an intention—to keep me in this bardo, this circumstance that they were in. They were trying to determine what experience would keep me most solidly fixed in this condition. There seemed to be an assumption that I would stay there forever.

During this whole experience, I had forgotten my relationship with Sri Da Avabhasa—or even any memory or experience of Him. I did not feel capable of resorting to Him and I was totally subject to this experience, which was constantly changing and quite disturbing.

In the midst of this, two people, a man and his son, began trying to help me. They felt very familiar to me, as if I had been close to them as I was growing up. This man and his son were trying to help me get back to where Sri Da Avabhasa was. I could see the realm where Sri Gurudev was—it had some of the qualities of a beautiful place in Hawaii I had visited once with Sri Da Avabhasa. These two individuals were trying to help me concentrate and feel towards Him and this place so that I could keep my attention there, and then I could stay there with my Sat-Guru.

While they were trying to help me, the other group of people finally hit upon the one experience which seemed to control my attention more strongly than anything else—the sense of being threatened. I was standing in the middle of a street, and a bakery truck would drive towards me. It would slam on its brakes and slide into me. Right before the truck would hit me, I could feel myself going into panic. Then the experience would repeat itself. It happened repetitively—hundreds, maybe thousands of times. I was stuck in that experience.

In the midst of this experience, I "shouted", but it was not a physical voice. Somehow, I could, just for a moment, remember and feel Heart-Master Da Avabhasa. Then the man and his son created a situation to help me get out of this endless cycle with the truck, back to where Sri Gurudev was.

Suddenly, I felt myself enter my body again, from the head down. I was back in the clinic, and Heart-Master Da Avabhasa was there. He was talking to me. When I saw Him, my heart burst with Happiness and relief. I had been so much in need of Him in that horrifying experience—more deeply and more profoundly than I had ever been in my entire life. I felt what an incredible opportunity it is to be physically embodied in a time and place where He is presently alive—and what a horror it is to pass through this life and not realize something greater than being completely controlled by your own mind and attention. I was weeping.

Sri Da Avabhasa was touching me. He was very gentle and humorous. He used whatever means necessary in any moment to keep me relating to Him directly. He would speak with me about the Witness-Position and He would address my sense of guilt. It was very amusing: There I was, very nearly dying, and He was addressing every way that I was self-contracted and defensive and emotionally-sexually retarded! I could feel His Help very directly, and I was so grateful to be back in His physical Company.

Sri Da Avabhasa told me that a helicopter was coming to take me off the island. He kept Saying, "Stay with Me." The helicopter arrived, and He looked after every aspect of getting me to the helicopter. He asked how long it would take to get me to the hospital.

I was fairly lucid at this point. They had me in a stretcher inside the helicopter. Daniel and Frans were on my right and beyond them was the pilot. My head was turned so I could look through a window in the helicopter. I stared at Naitauba as we flew away, and I felt that I could continue to remember Sri Da Avabhasa even at a physical distance or in a different environment. That was my practice—I had to continually feel Him, no matter what the experience was.

As soon as we arrived at the hospital in Suva, they took me to surgery. A big Fijian doctor and an Indian anesthesiologist introduced themselves. I was so tired I could not talk or move. But I could hear, and I responded through my eyes to indicate that I understood.

The Indian anesthesiologist wanted me to count out loud, if I could—starting from ten and going back to zero. He had a gas mask over my mouth. He explained that it was to make me unconscious so they could operate. I could not speak, but I counted in my mind, "Ten, nine. . ." to zero. He looked me in the eyes, and I looked back at him. He smiled and said, "Ok, do it again." I was trying to show him that I was counting, so I was blinking my eyes with each number—down to zero again.

My perception of everything was heightened. I could see in this doctor's eyes that he was becoming concerned. I could not understand what was wrong. He said, "Son, I am going to ask you to count one more time." His voice had started to tremble, and I became frightened. Again I counted, blinking my eyes as I did. When I got to zero, even though I was not unconscious, I kept my eyes closed.

They started the operation. I bore the pain as long as I could—but then I started gesturing, opening my eyes, and trying to shake my head. The nurse noticed that I was awake. They stopped and the anesthesiologist increased the anesthetic. I started to become really terrified because I felt I was going out of my body again.

I was afraid to lose consciousness—afraid that I would go back to this realm I had experienced before. People make a big deal of out-of-body experiences and near-death experiences as if it is all wonderful—you see God and your family. That was true in the beginning of my earlier experience, but the deeper I got in that state, it was just completely and totally horrific. There was nothing that I have ever experienced before or since that could possibly match the terror of being in that situation where you are just controlled by mind.

It was also clear to me that it is not just physical trauma that can knock you out of the body—any kind of emotional trauma can do this. I realized that that is what had occurred at the clinic on Naitauba—I had gone into emotional shock. I had lost a lot of blood, but that was not what sent me out of the body. I was in such a state of fear and anxiety that I was trying to remove myself from the circumstance. I was choosing not to be bodily incarnated rather than enduring and feeling through that strong emotion. Right in the middle of the operation, I remembered this about what had happened at the clinic on Naitauba, and I realized that it was happening again. I could feel myself retreating at the speed of light.

I woke up in the recovery room. Later that day and over the following days, the Fijian doctor and the Indian doctor came to see me many times, sometimes with four or five other doctors. They would huddle around me and speak in Fijian or Indian. Clearly they were curious, but also I felt their anxiety, as if something was wrong.

On the third day, I asked the nurse why everyone was so concerned. She called the two doctors to explain what had occurred in the operation. The Indian doctor indicated that they had given me a lot of anesthetic. In fact, He humorously said, I had gotten enough anesthetic to knock out a small Fijian village! They said they had never been in a situation quite like that and they were surprised at how much gas they had had to administer in order to knock me out. I tried to explain that I had been very anxious about losing consciousness—but they told me that that could not account for my resistance to the anesthetic. They asked if I had a history of this kind of thing when I had received anesthetics in the past, but I did not.

In that moment I remembered that when I was getting into the helicopter, Sri Da Avabhasa had asked exactly how long the helicopter trip would be, and had pressed His Spiritual Force into me repeatedly. I had felt this Force very physically and very powerfully. I felt like I was hyperenergized. It became obvious to me what had occurred. I explained to the doctors that I came from Naitauba, where my Spiritual Master was, and that He had Given me, while He was taking me to the helicopter, enough life-energy so that He would be certain that I had enough vitality to be transported. He Had Given the energy so that I could stay awake and alive. Immediately, the Fijian doctor understood what I was talking about. He said, "Mana" (the Fijian word for Spiritual force or power). Then the Indian doctor started speaking about Shaktipat (the Indian name for Spiritual force). "Yes!" I said. Here, in a third world country, these doctors were completely familiar with the Force I was talking about! I could feel that they had an appreciation of Who Sri Da Avabhasa Is.

During the days of my recovery, I tried to maintain remembrance of Sri Gurudev always. I would still slip in and out of consciousness, but I felt, when I would begin to lose bodily consciousness, that my only anchor was my remembrance of my Sat-Guru. If I did not intentionally remember Him, feel to Him, I would just end up free associating in the mind-realm. So I created ways to remember Sri Da Avabhasa. I could move my left arm, so I would trace the outline of His figure—as I remembered Him standing as I left Naitauba in the helicopter—over and over, thousands of times, just to stay associated with Him. It became a form of meditation for me.

Several weeks later, I returned to Naitauba. I heard from my friends there that on the evening I was having the most difficulty in the hospital, Heart-Master Da had met with everyone here and discussed my character with them. Clearly, He had been Giving me His Regard and keeping me associated with Him. He had also pointed out that, if I allowed myself to stay in the disposition of guilt—which is one of my primary emotions—I would literally create accidents and illnesses to punish myself. I saw that Sri Da Avabhasa was trying to help me see how I draw accidents to myself by dramatizing this sense of feeling guilty. He was showing this to me so I would not repeat this disaster for myself.

On the night I returned, we were called to gather with Heart-Master Da. I was incredibly weak, and incredibly happy to see Him, but I was also feeling guilty. I felt I had dishonored Him and ruined His celebration. But He dealt with me lovingly and joked with me a lot, relieving this chronic guilt of mine.

When He called me to show Him my cast, He put His leg against the cast. I could feel Him radiating His Heart-Force and healing energy sideways through my whole arm and into my chest. Then He Signed two names on my cast—mine ("Asshole", or "Narcissus") and His ("Da", or "The One Who Gives"). All I could feel was Him, His Happiness. I was ecstatic. Later, at the end of the evening, He shouted to me, "NEVER DO THAT AGAIN!" and walked out of the room.

CHAPTER 45

The Divine Gift

by Margot Soley

Judith Swaney

I praise my Beloved Heart-Master, Sri Da Avabhasa (The "Bright"), for the unbounded love that He showers upon each of His devotees. Through His great Compassion, my dear friend Judith Swaney was consistently Graced with His Help and Instruction during the final years of her life.

My service to Judith Swaney began shortly after she joined our regional community of Free Daists in Seattle, Washington, in 1983. Judith had been introduced to the Wisdom-Teaching of Sri Da Avabhasa by her husband earlier that year. Judith suffered from childhood diabetes, which was first diagnosed when she was five years old. Childhood diabetes is a very serious, life-threatening disease, and Judith continued to endure its complications (blindness at the age of twenty-one and a partial amputation of her leg at thirty-eight) until her death in 1990. She was forty years of age.

Judith was a very strong-willed and independent character who would not let her handicap slow her down. Thus, despite her serious health problems she always engaged life fully, and for years continued to teach preschool children, enjoy downhill skiing with a guide, and develop her musical skills.

Soon after I came to know Judith, she began to develop diabetic complications that required regular service from her friends. There were many details in her life that required our help, and I began to serve her regularly. Over time we became very good friends, but, even more importantly, our bond was really based on our mutual relationship with Sri Da Avabhasa. Even from the beginning this was a predominant aspect of our relationship. We did not spend a lot of time in unnecessary chitchat. Much of our time was spent in quiet feeling-Contemplation of Sri Da Avabhasa. This quality of our intimacy was very special and beautiful.

Judith brought great determination and stubborn will to her life and to overcoming and coping with the limitations that she faced because of her illness. Initially this made it hard for her to receive help from others, for she did not want to be a burden to her new friends. But as time went on she began to understand more and more that for her to receive our love and service was as much a gift to us as our service was to her. I felt tremendous gratitude in being able to serve her, and it was remarkable and inspiring for all of us who had this relationship with Judith (as well as our whole community of practitioners) to see her connection to Sri Da Avabhasa flourish even as her body failed.

In February 1989, Judith almost did not make it through a major heart attack. I was on retreat at Sri Love-Anandashram in Fiji at the time, and I had brought a mala (rosary) of Judith's with me in the hope that there would be an opportunity for our Beloved Heart-Master to Bless it. When Sri Da Avabhasa learned that I had Judith's mala, He requested that the mala be brought to Him. I was incredibly moved to hear later that Sat-Guru Da had taken the mala to His Sitting Room, oiled each bead individually, and worn it around His neck for a period of time before leaving it in His Sitting Room overnight.

I felt very blessed to be able to return to Seattle with this wonderful Gift for Judith from her Heart-Master. When she received the mala and heard the story of how Heart-Master Da had Blessed it, tears filled her eyes, her body visibly relaxed and softened, and her face radiated with a child-like joy. She confessed that the only means of getting through this terrible heart attack had been her Remembrance of, and resort to, Sri Da Avabhasa. I was very moved by Judith's confession and the obvious dropping away of her usual willfulness and independence into such sweet reception of her Sat-Guru's Blessing Gift. She wrote a response of simple thanks and heart-felt gratitude to Heart-Master Da, while also telling Him about her great desire to grow in practice, to feel her direct and personal relationship with her Beloved Heart-Master, and to be prepared, through Grace, for death whenever it came.

The final phase of Judith's life began on March 2, 1990, when she was once again hospitalized in critical condition with congestive heart failure. She fought for her life, confessing that she did not yet feel prepared for death. The crisis persisted for several weeks. At His request, daily reports on her condition were being sent to Heart-Master Da at Sri Love-Anandashram, while at the same time, Judith began to receive direct verbal Communications from Him, requiring responses in return. In one such response, Judith told Da Avabhasa that, although she had never seen Him because of her blindness, there was a figure that kept appearing to her in vision during meditation whom she knew to be Him, because He was Love.

Then, one day, Da Avabhasa asked Judith if she was sighted enough to make use of a Murti (a sacred photographic representation of Him) Blessed by Him. She responded with great joy with the following letter:

March 19, 1990

Beloved Heart-Master Da Love-Ananda Hridayam,[1]

I bow down at Your Blessing Feet and praise Your Great Gifts to all mankind. I am so grateful for my relationship with You. Even though this health crisis has been the worst so far, I have found it easier to be in Communion with You than ever before. This is because You have Instructed me in feeling-Contemplation of Your bodily (human) Form so well over the past year through The Love-Ananda Gita.[2]

The two most potent ways that I feel You are through feeling-Contemplation of You, and chanting with the "tongue of the mind". Even though I have no light perception, I would love to have a Blessed Murti. Many workers in the hospital asked about You when they saw Your Murti [one she already had] in my room. It was wonderful to share my love for my Sat-Guru with others.

1. The Sanskrit word "hridayam" means "heart". It refers not only to the physical organ but also to the True Heart, the Transcendental (and Inherently Spiritual) Divine Reality. "Hridayam" is one of Heart-Master Da's Divine Names, signifying that He Stands in, at, and as the True Heart of every being.

2. *The Love-Ananda Gita (The Wisdom-Song Of Non-Separateness)*, is Sri Da Avabhasa's "Simple Revelation Book" of the Way of the Heart. Please see "The Sacred Literature of Da Avabhasa" on pp. 408-19 of this book for a full description of all of Heart-Master Da's published literature.

Thank You for inviting me to Sri Love-Anandashram. I am sorry I am not able to travel. But I love You very much and feel Your Help Always. I am so grateful that You found me in this life. I feel that You will Guide me through the dying process and that is all I want. Thank You, Sri Gurudev,[3] for Your Love and Joy and Bliss.

Judith

Several days later, kidney failure made dialysis necessary for Judith, though it was a risky procedure because of her tendency to heart failure. When Heart-Master Da received word that dialysis and other life-saving measures were being discussed, He asked many questions about it, including whether dialysis might enable her to live long enough to come into His Company should He visit the United States in the next few months. This was deemed unlikely by her physicians. Heart-Master Da then asked Judith to inform Him of any further life-and-death decisions and to "leave it up to Me". This was a heart-opening message for Judith to receive, and she was now able to relax further into trusting the dying process through deeper surrender to her Sat-Guru. She felt so Graced by His intimate and personal Regard.

Judith did survive the dialysis procedure, and her condition began to stabilize over the next few days. She began to prepare to go home again, and she also became very humorous and bright. Her usual manner with the hospital staff changed from being characteristically demanding, or even curt, to being much more affable and less self-concerned. At one point with great humor she asked me if I noticed that she was no longer annoying the nurses! We had a good laugh over that. Through Grace she was surrendering to her circumstance and to everyone around her.

When her kidneys and her breathing had stabilized sufficiently, Judith went home. During this time she attended what turned out to be her last devotional occasion with all of us. Despite the intensely painful ordeal she had just been through, she was profoundly peaceful and radiant. She told us, "I came to show you what feeling-Contemplation of Sri Gurudev's Form and Spiritual Presence, and your prayers, can do." We were deeply moved by her obvious love and connection with Heart-Master Da.

---

3. "Gurudev" is a traditional Sanskrit term used as a designation for one's principal Guru. Thus, "Gurudev" is used by devotees of Sri Da Avabhasa, with other devotional Names, Titles, and Designations, as an appropriate and honorable form of address of Him.

Two days after she came home, Judith's condition worsened, and she returned to the hospital. At this time a retreatant returning from Sri Love-Anandashram arrived with Heart-Master Da's sublime Gift to her of the Blessed Murti. Judith had so looked forward to receiving this Gift, and we all felt an even greater depth of peace in her relationship with Him as she accepted His Great Love in the form of this Gift.

It was after receiving the Murti that Judith began to say that she did not want to hold on to life anymore, that she felt she was ready to die. There was a resolution in her prayers, and she began to show signs of a profound tiredness. It was clear she was given over to her Heart-Master and was no longer in the struggle to hold on to life. It was this capability to be prepared for death that was Sri Da Avabhasa's Graceful answer to her most passionate prayers.

Judith died the following day, March 30, 1990. Her death was very benign, which was a great relief to her doctors, who had feared that because of her complications she could have had a difficult time. This was another sign of Sri Da Avabhasa's incomprehensible Grace. She died in a private room with her mother and husband in attendance, confessing their love for her and urging her to "let go".

Over the following three days our community of practitioners of the Way of the Heart held a vigil for Judith in the funeral home that a few of us had selected. We purified the private room where her body was to be placed and prepared it for the vigil. Many devotees from our regional community attended the vigil. Through the unending Grace of Sri Da Avabhasa we were able to handle all of the practical details of the vigil very smoothly, which allowed our energy and attention to be concentrated on the process of Judith's transition for these three days. The room where the vigil was held became a place of Darshan (Sighting of the Spiritual Master). Sri Da Avabhasa's Perfect Help was obvious and tangible. We were being Instructed as a community to be happy even in the face of death.

During the vigil, many devotees reported that they could feel and even communicate with Judith as she went through the process of letting go. And it was completely obvious to us that death is not the end of one's relationship to Sat-Guru Da, nor of the sadhana lived in His Company. I thank Sri Da Avabhasa for this most sacred Heart-Intimacy that He freely Gives in Service to His devotees.

CHAPTER 46

The Life and Death
of a Temple Architect

by Deborah Fremont-Smith

Antonio Descamps

ntonio Descamps was an extraordinarily gifted artist, whose talents had been praised and nurtured by parents and teachers since his childhood. He graduated at twenty with a Master's degree from Princeton, and was one of the brightest architectural prodigies in the history of the school. Though many doors were open to him in the art world of New York City, he elected to travel West.

Living in the cultural ferment of San Francisco in the early 1970s, Antonio began to have a recurring dream in which a remarkable being, whom he knew to be a Spiritual Master, embraced him and said, "Come over here." After some time he discovered that the Guru in his dreams was Sri Da Avabhasa, then living and Teaching as "Bubba Free John" in northern California. Antonio described his first visits to see his Guru at Persimmon (the early name of the Mountain Of Attention Sanctuary) as "full of sensory responses, intense experiences, frightening jolts of Divine insight, and an understanding that I was involved in something extraordinary and something Blessed".

Heart-Master Da strongly urged Antonio to develop and expand his artistic talents by creating a career as a professional architect and helping with the many architectural design needs at the Sanctuary. Over the years, He often acknowledged that Antonio—in some ways uniquely among many people serving Him in professional capacities—had an intuitive understanding, in his own field, of what He was looking for. Antonio's service to Heart-Master Da, which involved intense collaboration through response to the Divine Master's requests for various designs, produced several of the most important—and extraordinarily harmonious and beautiful—Temples at the Mountain Of Attention Sanctuary (including Heart-Master Da's Residence there, the Manner of Flowers, and the Seventh Gate Shrine) and Da Avabhasa Chakra, Heart-Master Da's principal Residential Temple Complex at Sri Love-Anandashram.

Thus, Antonio provided exceptional personal service to Sat-Guru Da Love-Ananda. At the same time, however, he never could altogether overcome his reluctance to surrender more fully to his Sat-Guru by becoming a formal practitioner of the Way of the Heart. His resistance troubled and frustrated him, and he struggled with it for years.

Then, in June 1988, just after his fortieth birthday, Antonio Descamps was diagnosed as having AIDS.

For Antonio, the ensuing months were an intense trial of renunciation and surrender. Everything he had previously protected was falling away from him—physical appearance, friendships, career, social life, travel, physical activities he had enjoyed, sexual activity, even simple things like walking, eating, sleeping, and breathing normally.

With the realities of conditional destiny thus mercilessly bearing down upon him, Antonio turned to his Sat-Guru as he had not been able to turn before his illness. He felt that he was being Divinely Instructed and rapidly purified. Though the renunciation of his whole human life was difficult and sometimes extremely painful, both physically and emotionally, he told his intimates that he also valued it because it was requiring him to make the gesture of surrender he could never make in all those earlier years.

Antonio's intimate partner, Patrick Christopher, and many of their friends were either formally practicing devotees or long-time formal supporters of Sri Da Avabhasa's Work. Antonio was well served in a sacred manner by his friends, and he himself made good use of Sri Da

Avabhasa's Wisdom-Teaching and other forms of Good Company as he began to prepare for his death.

Patrick, who served Antonio throughout his illness, confessed that he feared this period would be morbid and sorrowful. But, as Antonio chose to speak almost exclusively about relationship and intimacy and the proven Truth of Sat-Guru Da's Wisdom-Teaching, his whole household was drawn into a remarkable period of Blessing. Patrick writes:

Frequent Darshan videos of Sri Da Love-Ananda and visits by practitioners of the Way of the Heart helped connect the household with the Sat-Guru's powerful Help. Even in Antonio's occasional periods of great discomfort he loved to watch these videos. In his bedroom were a few sacred objects, reminders of Sat-Guru Da. He loved to wear a brightly-colored tie-dyed silk scarf that had belonged to the Sat-Guru.

His health declined rapidly over the last few months. As he lay in bed with an emaciated upper body and head and terribly swollen stomach and legs, he never lost the energy to think creatively, and he continued to design for his Sat-Guru until literally a few days before he died. Those of us around him witnessed an explosion of his spirit in the last three months of his life—he simply became very happy and he could not contain it.

Da Avabhasa Paduka Mandir,[1] a small, beautiful Shrine at the Mountain Of Attention, was the last architectural project that Antonio completed for Sri Da Avabhasa. It was designed during the final months of his life and the most difficult days of his debilitating illness. Donovan Train, who was Sanctuary manager at the Mountain Of Attention at the time, tells of the ordeal Antonio endured in his commitment to that service:

I went to see Antonio just about every week during the final months of his illness to work with him on a number of designs for various Temples, including the Paduka Mandir.

He was always very grateful for this opportunity to serve Sri Gurudev. He very clearly understood it as a source of Grace and Blessing. And, in his deteriorating physical condition, he very intentionally embraced it as a potent source of Life and Happiness.

It was incredible to see his commitment to completing the designs. The

---

1. "Padukas", in Sanskrit, are the ceremonial sandals of the Sat-Guru, and are a sign of His bodily (human) Form. A "Mandir" is a temple. The Sri Da Avabhasa Paduka Mandirs are sacred temples that are available to practitioners of the Way of the Heart twenty-four hours a day for the purposes of sacramental worship of Sri Da Avabhasa via His Padukas. In addition to the Temple at the Mountain Of Attention which is described here, there is also a Paduka Mandir at Sri Love-Anandashram.

design for the Paduka Shrine, which he drew up in a single session of about four hours, was a particularly striking example of this. He was in great pain at the time, so much so that it would often take all his attention until it had passed.

On one occasion I was standing by his bed looking at a final set of drawings with him. He looked at them for a long time, and then he just said, "No, it's not right." And he scratched the whole plan and started all over again, changing the proportions of the building only very slightly. It was amazing to me that, in his condition, he found the energy to completely redraft the design.

But Antonio was right. I was with Sri Da Avabhasa when He opened the presentation of the plans for the temple. The design was so beautiful that I could feel how Antonio had poured himself into it. And that was basically the design that was used in the end, with the addition of a blue tile Japanese roof that Sri Da Avabhasa suggested.

On May 4, 1989, Ed Graham, then the minister of the Free Daist Communion in Marin County, California, and Malcolm Burke, a fellow minister, visited Antonio at his home. Sri Da Avabhasa was aware of Antonio's illness and, the ministers told him, He had invited Antonio to write to Him. Antonio told them that, reluctant to surrender, he had always kept his distance from Heart-Master Da. He had always found it difficult to write to Him, and, as a non-practitioner, had seen Him only very rarely through the years. He spoke with regret of his inability to make himself more visible and vulnerable to his Sat-Guru all that time.

Now, however, he felt such a dissolution of his resistance and fear, and such a deep heart-desire to express his long-standing love for his Sat-Guru, that he felt he could write and ask for His Instruction and Blessing.

On Friday, May 5, Antonio wrote to his Heart-Master. Stephanie Samuels (a long-time friend) and Patrick were with him as he composed his letter:

Friday 5-5-89

Sausalito, California

Sat-Guru Da Love-Ananda Hridayam
Loka[2] of Compassion and Blessing
    For the past fifteen years, through Your Gifts, I have had a Graceful and profound relationship to You, my Sat-Guru. You have shown me a

---

2. A "loka" is a world or realm of experience. The term often refers to places that are subtler than the gross physical world of Earth and that can be visited only in dreams or by mystical or esoteric means.

circumstance of devotion where I have been able to serve You. But all along, the process from my end has been one of avoidance. This is no longer the case nor the Truth. I am your devotee and confess that although I don't know You intimately, I long for Your Company more than anything. I now constantly miss Your physical Presence after years of fearfully fleeing the intensity of Your physical Company. This understanding is the true basis for developing my practice of feeling-Contemplation of Your Form, moment to moment. And so I ask for Your Guidance.

My reluctance to confront my avoidance of Your embodied human Form is no longer the case. My body is going through the fire of sadhana with no room for doubt or much consolation. I have been changed and transformed, at times painfully, from head to toe. It is hard and it is fine. Transcending conditional suffering has been a challenge when my breathing is difficult.

But Your Grace is what actually sustains this body. You sustain me. I have come to rightly understand Your true healing and Liberating work in my life. It is a great Blessing.

After all these years my mind is clear enough to appreciate Your Spiritual Vision in relation to Design. I am no longer concerned about worldly forms in design, but only in serving Your "Bright" Divine and Happy Vision for the sake of devotees. I would be honored to continue to help with Your Design Vision. Is there something special You would like?

Thank You for allowing me to be Your devotee in this life. Thank You for bringing such incredible Grace into my life and the lives of those loving people around me who also love You. You have so obviously created the harmony in this household with your devotee Patrick and my parents, Jorge and Josefina.

In the midst of these wild times and fierce winds which I have endured, only the intimacy of Heart-Love, Given by my Love-Blissful Sat-Guru, has remained standing. Thank You for Revealing this Truth to me.

You are my Source of life and harmony and Happiness, and I vow to go wherever You take me. I love You, Da Love-Ananda, and bow at Your Beautiful Feet.

Antonio

When Antonio's letter was received a few days later at Sri Love-Anandashram, Sri Gurudev Da Love-Ananda replied right away, through one of His most senior devotees, Kanya Tripura Rahasya. She wrote to Antonio as follows:

Dear Antonio,

As a preface to Sri Gurudev's Communications to you, I wanted to let you know that He read your letter over and over again for approximately ten minutes. He spent a great deal of time reading every word again and again, and then He responded.

First, in answer to your question asking if there is something special that Sri Gurudev would like to have designed, He listed a number of projects that needed to be done, and said that He would just allow others to "consider" with you what you would like to design.

He also asked specifically if you had done a design already for the Communion Hall at Tumomama Sanctuary. So, Sri Gurudev would like you to do more designs for Him.

Then, in answer to your question asking for Guidance relative to this matter of beginning to respond to His bodily (human) Form, Sat-Guru Da has this to Say to you:

> *Guidance in the practice of feeling-Contemplation of Me is already Given in the Scriptural text of* The Love-Ananda Gita *and in the Instructions that follow it in the section titled "I Am What you Require". You should really become involved in all My Instructions for student-beginner practice[3] in the Way of the Heart. The details of that real practice are My Recommendation to you. In this fashion, you will transcend your limitations relative to your devotion to Me. The process is a matter of truly engaging in feeling-Contemplation of Me. It is a process of surrendering and forgetting all aspects of egoic self and self-concern. In this manner, the karmic contents of the various levels of mind are released and purified.*

> *You should appreciate that death is simply the release of a peripheral aspect of form. The deeper aspects of personality continue, and they inevitably produce another embodiment. Therefore, the deeper aspects of the personality must be purified as much as possible, so that even death itself becomes a purifying event, and thus permits a future embodiment that is as auspicious as possible. So your work and your sadhana should be this purifying work of deep self-surrender and self-forgetting, through more and more profound feeling-Contemplation of My bodily (human) Form, My*

---

3. A student-beginner is a practitioner in the initial developmental stage of the Way of the Heart. In the course of student-beginner practice, the practitioner becomes stable in the foundation disciplines of the Way of the Heart, which are devotion, service, self-discipline, and meditation.

Spiritual (and Always Blessing) Presence, and My Very (and Inherently Perfect) State. You should enter into this feeling-Contemplation of Me more and more deeply and profoundly. Ultimately, you should enter into it to the point of releasing all forms of body and mind, so that the *Greater Reality may be Realized directly. (May 8, 1989)*

Antonio, I would like you to know that Sri Gurudev asks about you frequently, and He always has great attention on your life and on your death. In this moment also, His Regard was most Profound. May you be released and purified.

Kanya Tripura

Om Sri Da Love-Ananda Hridayam

Patrick Christopher writes:

Antonio's response to Sri Gurudev's letter was ecstatic. He was overwhelmed by Sri Gurudev's Grace. He cried. He said he could now relax his fear of death. We stayed up that night and read the Instruction in the letter and "I Am What you Require" from The Love-Ananda Gita. *Antonio was very moved, and he was convinced that Sri Gurudev was truly with him.*

On the night of May 15, Antonio Descamps died. Patrick writes:

The day Antonio died was a fine day of conversation, enjoying the bright sun of the Sonoma County hilltop house where we had so recently moved. We Installed Sat-Guru Da's Murti and performed the Sat-Guru-Murti Puja[4] that afternoon, which was a very beautiful occasion. That evening Antonio became very weak and remarked that it felt as if he was "falling apart". He lost consciousness for a few minutes, and this prompted me to call his doctor and eventually an ambulance. What arrived in fact was a helicopter to rush him from the hilltop to the Petaluma Valley Hospital.

He was fully conscious and cooperative. I stayed behind to pack a few sacred objects and books and phone numbers, and then drove his parents

---

4. A "Murti" is a sacred form or object through which the Divine Transmission may be contacted. "Sat-Guru-Murti Puja" refers to the sacred ceremony of worship performed on the Murti, or representation, of the Sat-Guru. During the Sat-Guru-Murti Puja, the Murti is anointed in sacred ceremony, expressing the devotional regard in which the devotee holds the Sat-Guru.

Practitioners of the Way of the Heart perform the Sat-Guru-Murti Puja daily, and through it they establish themselves in Communion with Sri Da Avabhasa. Typically, a photographic Murti of Sri Da Avabhasa is used.

down the winding road to the hospital. Upon arriving, we found him feeling cold but still alert.

After Patrick arrived at the hospital with Antonio's parents, he telephoned Connie Grisso, the worldwide director of Mate Moce, for instructions on serving Antonio's death. He also received news that Heart-Master Da was due to arrive in California within a few days. Patrick continues:

In that last hour before his death we were able to tell Antonio about Sat-Guru Da's upcoming travel to California, and he responded with a nod. We caressed him, confessed our love, massaged his cold feet, and encouraged him to surrender to the Great One completely. We talked about the importance of moving towards the Light. As we held his hands, he stopped breathing.

The hospital was quiet. Antonio's body was moved to an adjoining private room where his parents and I were allowed to sit with him for several hours. I anointed his body and scattered the entire room with an abundance of holy water. I applied sacred ash to his head and tied his favorite scarf that had been Sri Gurudev's around his neck. We continued to tell him to move toward the Light, to release us all and be transformed. I set a photograph of Sat-Guru Da against Antonio's chest and meditated quietly on the Blissfulness that pervaded the room.

Ed Graham and Deb Fremont-Smith (a representative of Mate Moce) arrived, and so began the outstanding service of Sri Da Avabhasa's devotees to this occasion. Antonio and his family and I were all given a remarkable Gift of the Sat-Guru's Guidance and Compassion.

Antonio's Vigil

Both Ed and I were aware that Antonio was in decline, so when we were informed at a late-night meeting that Antonio had died, we were not entirely taken by surprise. Ed and I were responsible for initiating the three-day vigil that Sat-Guru Da recommends after a death, so we hurried to the Petaluma Valley Hospital.

It was approximately 1:00 A.M. when we arrived at the Emergency Room. Patrick was there with Antonio's parents, and the funeral director from the nearby funeral home (where we had arranged to conduct the vigil) had also recently arrived. Under Connie Grisso's direction, Patrick, though obviously feeling the wound of his personal loss, had done a great deal towards ensuring that our needs for the vigil would be met. The funeral director was very willing to honor our request that Antonio's body not be embalmed or tampered with in any way, and we had his permission to maintain an around-the-clock vigil for the next three days at the funeral home.

When I first walked into the room where Antonio's body was lying, I felt two things simultaneously. The first was that I had literally walked into Sat-Guru Da's physical Company—the Force of His Love-Bliss struck me whole bodily and arrested my breath. At exactly the same moment I was halted by the sight of Antonio's body lying in rigor mortis, savagely wasted by his illness. Bliss and horror overcame me in a moment, but the Bliss of God far outweighed the "mortal show".

Once we arrived at the funeral home, the vigil formally began. We purified the room with holy water and re-anointed the body with ash. We performed the Sat-Guru-Murti Puja using a Murti that I had brought from home.

Patrick and Mr. and Mrs. Descamps stayed for a short while and then left for the rest of the night. Josefina stood by the body of her son and wept softly before we embraced. "Thank you so much," she said as she left. Sri Da Avabhasa's Blessing Presence was tangible to us all.

Anyone sensitive to the natural energies of human existence can feel a strong current of ascending energy around the body of a person who has just died. What characterizes the death of a devotee of Sri Da Avabhasa is the infusion of His Love-Bliss into this circumstance. A deep Sublimity fills the room, and our intuition of the "radical" Happiness that transcends both life and death is magnified. Sat-Guru Da has Instructed practitioners engaged in a vigil:

Sit quietly in feeling-Contemplation of Me, not of the dead person. Release the dead person and whatever arises. Persist in this releasing process and periodically formally recite from My Heart-Word, relating My Instruction to the dead and to the mourners. (April 8, 1989)

Once the vigil began, Sri Da Avabhasa's Compassion and Grace overwhelmed me, body and mind, so that I felt that I could not move. I felt Sat-Guru Da's Embrace of Antonio, me, and literally all beings in Perfect Love.

Ed wrote Sri Da Avabhasa the following letter later that morning:

Beloved Heart-Master Da,

Your Great Love permeates all existence and allows Your devotees to live and die in Blissful Peace. I am so grateful, my Lord, to have profoundly felt this truth as I sat with Antonio during the night. I was filled with overwhelming Happiness, and my love for You was magnified through feeling-Contemplation of You in the circumstance of Antonio's death.

Deb Fremont-Smith and I were blessed to be with Antonio as his body was transferred from the hospital to the funeral home, and we were able to ensure that it was treated gently and respectfully in the move. We then sat in feeling-Contemplation of You, absorbed in the depth of Your Love, which sweetly yet Powerfully filled the room. Both of us felt a deep trust in Your total Embrace of Antonio, and of all of us, as we surrender to You in the process of dying.

Sri Gurudev, I am overcome with love and devotion to You as I Contemplate You and serve You, for I feel Your Greatness, Magnificent beyond description, and more intimate than the beat of my heart.

I am eternally grateful to You.

Ed

Throughout the three-day vigil we read aloud Da Avabhasa's Instructions, reminding Antonio to release this body-mind and the world. As the days and nights progressed, there was clearly a change in the quality of the energy surrounding Antonio's body, and in the room itself. Twenty-four hours into the vigil, peace and stillness began to replace the more active sensations of ascent and bliss. By the time I returned on the third day, the room was still. I felt Antonio had gone.

That evening the vigil for Antonio was formally brought to a close. A final Puja was done on the Murti of Sat-Guru Da, the candles and incense were extinguished, and the body was taken from the room to await cremation.

A report was sent to Sri Da Avabhasa, who had arrived in California only hours before. On Friday morning, May 19, Antonio's body was cremated, and the following week his ashes were scattered in San Francisco Bay by Patrick and some intimate friends.

CHAPTER 47

Healed of Grief

Two Leelas of Retreat
in Sri Da Avabhasa's Company

Grieving is a natural part of the release process for all of us whenever we experience the death of those we love. Sometimes the grieving process can be delayed—as the shock of death can cause us to go numb in the moment—and only occurs when the initial shock has worn off. At other times the grieving process is not permitted at all, and the grief is locked in one's body and psyche. This often causes emotional difficulties of one kind or another, until the grieving process is allowed to occur or the suppressed emotions are otherwise released.

For years, devotees of the Divine World-Teacher Sri Da Avabhasa have attested to the fact that the Blessing Grace Transmitted in His Company opens their hearts, and also has a purifying effect at many levels of the being. Sometimes this purification occurs at the level of the deeper psyche, such that painful memories and emotions that have been suppressed, even for many years, are brought to the surface and, subsequently, released.

The two Leelas that follow, by Eileen Haight and Linda Focht, illustrate this purifying aspect of Heart-Master Da's Spiritual Heart-Transmission.

E ILEEN HAIGHT: In May 1970 my second grandchild was due, and I was invited to attend the birth. When my son-in-law called to tell me that my daughter, Helen, had gone into labor earlier than expected, I headed for the airport and took the first available flight.

During the flight I fell asleep and had a very strange experience. I left my body, and saw it sitting there as I flew out of the window and raced ahead of the plane to Big Sur, where I witnessed the birth of Dawn Eve. When I re-entered my body with a great jolt and found myself back on

Eileen Haight

the plane, I "knew" the baby had been born and that it was a girl. Later, I learned that the time of her birth coincided with this experience.

Dawn Eve was a very unusual child. She always seemed to be much wiser than her years, and even her voice was never childlike. She was a dear little friend and I loved her deeply. Tragically, several months after her third birthday, she died in a drowning accident.

Seventeen years later, in 1990, I was participating in a retreat at Sri Love-Anandashram, in Fiji, to receive Darshan and Instruction from Sri Da Avabhasa, my Spiritual Master for the past ten years. Of the many Gifts I received during this four-week retreat, perhaps the most important was a deep healing that took place in me regarding Dawn Eve's death.

Part of the retreat schedule included the practice of the laying on of hands.[1] On one such occasion, two or three ladies performed this healing prayer on me, after which an occasion of meditation was scheduled. I went into the Meditation Hall feeling relaxed and grateful, when suddenly, in the midst of what I thought was going to be a blissful meditation, I felt incredibly angry. I had a vision of Dawn Eve, and the circumstance of her death flashed before me.

I was living in Boulder, Colorado, at that time, and my daughter Helen called me from San Diego to tell me that Dawn Eve had drowned.

---

1. The laying on of hands, as practiced in the Way of the Heart, is a method of healing whereby an individual, in the disposition of self-surrender to Heart-Master Da's All-Accomplishing Power, effects positive changes in the condition of another individual's health or well-being, while placing hands on that individual's body. This healing process is coordinated with the breath, such that all negative conditions and presumptions are first released through the exhaled breath, and then, when this release is felt to be complete, positive changes are affirmed and magnified through inhalation. In general, the hands of the healer will be placed on the specific region of the body most needing to be healed.

She sounded so stoic and brave, and I felt I had to be brave for her. The truth of the matter is that we were both in shock and really did not know how to comfort one another. We talked rather philosophically about her death, and, remembering her particular qualities, remarked that perhaps she was not meant to be on this Earth very long but had only come as a temporary teacher. Clearly, we were not allowing ourselves to feel our grief.

Years later, after becoming a practitioner of the Way of the Heart, I learned to deal with many of my feelings, including my grief about Dawn Eve. But, as revealed to me on this retreat, I had not dealt with my anger, which had been deeply repressed. After meditation, we had a "Leelas and confessions" group,[2] and I began to confess the anger that had come up relative to Dawn Eve. Suddenly I was crying, screaming, and pounding the floor as I told the story of her death.

Dawn Eve's sister had gotten a steel shaving in her eye, and Helen had to take her to the hospital, leaving Dawn Eve in the care of house-mates. Dawn Eve, just three years old, went out to the swimming pool area to ride her tricycle around the pool. She cut one corner at the deep end of the pool too close, and fell in. When Helen arrived home, the fire department was there, but it was too late. Dawn Eve was already dead. The people who had agreed to be responsible for her care had been too busy watching television and smoking marijuana to care for her.

By the time I reached the last sentence of my story I was hysterical and gasping for breath. The anger I had harbored in my heart against these people for seventeen years, but never expressed or even felt, exploded from me. Then came an avalanche of sobs. With the anger released, I was able to feel my grief most profoundly.

Immediately after this event, we were invited to a Darshan occasion with Heart-Master Da Love-Ananda. The ladies in my group were very moved by my story and were loving and helpful as we prepared for Darshan. One lady gave me a lovely pale yellow flower. As I held the flower, it seemed to represent my little blonde grandchild. Before the Darshan occasion began, I offered the flower at Heart-Master Da's Chair, placing it near the place where He usually puts His Feet. In that moment,

---

2. "Leelas and confessions" groups were Given by Sri Da Avabhasa as a way for practitioners of the Way of the Heart to confess to other practitioners the ways in which they are living as "Narcissus", or the self-contraction. Such confession is then followed with a Leela of how Sri Da Avabhasa's Grace is transforming their life of practice, which serves their release of the self-contraction and their devotion to Heart-Master Da.

I consciously surrendered Dawn Eve to Him along with my anger and grief, and prayed for understanding, asking for whatever lesson I needed to be given.

When Sri Da Avabhasa entered the room, I gazed upon Him for a brief period of time, Contemplating His Form. Then my eyes closed spontaneously, and I fell into a very deep meditative state. I felt a strong pressure at the ajna center, my mind was quiet, and my head was bathed in light. After a while I had a vision of traveling through the tunnel of the Cosmic Mandala. A circle of light was around the edge of the tunnel, and I was being drawn to the brilliant Light at the Center. The thought arose that I was being prepared for death, and that I was being Instructed in the death process. I felt most grateful. Other devotees in the room made sounds and movements that were distracting, but I was Instructed to keep my attention on the Light at the Center. Thoughts would arise and dissolve. There was no fear. I realized I was not feeling anything in particular—not angry, not happy, not unhappy, not fearful, not doubtful, not distracted or attracted, not emotional or unemotional, not attached or detached—just rested and at peace. In that moment I felt free.

I stayed in this state for some time, probably forty-five minutes or more. When my eyes opened, the Darshan occasion was over and Da Avabhasa was leaving the Hall. I felt healed at the heart. Not only was I healed of Dawn Eve's death, but also of the repression and fear around death altogether, including my own inevitable death.

This was not a temporary healing. Although my ordinary state returned, there is an open space in my heart where fear, sorrow, and anger arise but are seen and felt from a different disposition. There remains this remembered feeling of Sublime Freedom. I am forever grateful to Sri Da Avabhasa for this Way of life and His Wisdom-Instruction.

◆ ◆ ◆

LINDA FOCHT: My first child was born in 1978, two months premature. The time of his birth was chaotic and confusing for me, as I did not really understand what was happening, and I was not at all educated about such matters as birth and death. He lived for about eight hours before my husband and I gave permission for him to be taken off the life-support systems, because it was clear to us that he was not going to live. The hospital technicians unhooked the machines and removed the tubes and needles invading his little body. Then they wrapped the tiny,

Linda Focht

three-pound, perfectly formed baby boy in a blue flannel blanket, and handed him to me.

My husband and I were ushered into a room to be alone with him for a time. After about five minutes of not really knowing how to deal with the situation, we handed him back to the doctors and went back to my room. We had no knowledge or sensitivity about the death process or the need for resolution or completion, so we just left the hospital the next day and went home.

I had no comprehension of the grief process that would try to unfold in me, and no one around me did either, so I just entered back into the game of my life, suppressing my feelings and trying to go on as if nothing profound had happened. Of course, this did not work very well, since such a powerful event will bring up many, many feelings and emotions. In trying to stay on top of it, however, I became a rather superficial and withdrawn character, never really at ease, and not able to fully participate in life.

About a year later I went to visit my brother, Steve, my only sibling, in Jackson, Wyoming. Not having seen each other in three years, we had a very full week together, catching up on everything and enjoying an intimacy we had shared since childhood. We discussed everything that was on our minds, including death, and how we would like our own deaths to be handled.

Two weeks later I returned home from work, where I had been thinking about him all day, and received a phone call from my mother, who chokingly delivered the news that Steve had been killed the night before in a motorcycle accident. Fortunately, to our minds, he had died instantly from a broken neck and had lain undisturbed in the mountains he had loved for eight hours before his body was discovered. My mother and I both began to perceive his presence immediately, a free and happy presence that we could feel to be his energy. We were very much affected and enlivened by this, feeling him often for the next three days. During this time Steve's friends came to Jackson from all over the country for his funeral, and while his best friends scaled the Grand Teton Mountains to scatter his ashes from the top at a designated time, the rest of his friends and family were in a meadow below, speaking about him and praising him and his life. After this uplifting occasion I went home, only to realize, over time, that the physical and emotional aspects of my being were way behind in facing the mortal reality of this great loss. I became more withdrawn and unhappy, heavy with sorrow and depression.

Thus, I did not believe it when, a year later, my husband got a phone call (no one wanted to report bad news to me anymore) informing us that my father, at 48 years of age, had just died of a massive heart attack. Boom! Like that, he was gone too. All I could feel in the moment of hearing the news was that I wanted to see him again, that I was not finished with our relationship.

The next morning I was out in the yard, yelling at the sky (fortunately we lived in the country), cursing God and telling Him to stop it! "I've had enough already!" I yelled. True to form, I was back on top of things in a day or two, unable to allow myself to feel anything, and invulnerable and superficial in all my relationships.

The first of my two living children was born six weeks later, and my second was born almost two years later. During the years that followed I simply and thoroughly involved myself in being a mother. I was protective, and always fearful that something dreadful would happen to my children, with whom I shared a deep, unspoken intimacy. The series of deaths I had experienced was not resolved but instead became like a pearl in my belly, a great burden of sorrow and depression that defined my being deeply. Thus, when I was Blessed to come to Sri Love-Anandashram in Fiji in October 1990 for a three-week meditation retreat in the Company of my Sat-Guru, Sri Da Avabhasa, my character was clearly defined by this history.

One afternoon on retreat, I was sitting in meditation when I suddenly had the vision of my tiny baby, wrapped in his blue blanket, floating in a dark space beside me. I was feeling very intimate with Sri Da Avabhasa, Who, in my heart, began to question me about the birth and death of the baby boy. As I "told" Him the story in my meditation, I began to cry and release some of the sadness I had kept bottled up inside me, and to feel quite relieved. In fact, when I left the meditation, I felt as if a great weight had been lifted, and I could feel my body filling with delight, happiness, and joy. I was ecstatic. I felt as if I had returned from a long bad dream. I would suddenly laugh out loud about something that struck me as humorous, and I was literally dancing all over the place.

At the Sat-Guru Arati Puja[3] that evening I was in the front of the Hall, dancing and singing and being ecstatic about how my Sat-Guru had relieved me of such an immense sorrow, when all of a sudden it hit me that it could happen again. At any time, my two children could be snuffed out, and I knew I would not be able to do anything about it. All of the life and light and happiness left my body, and I became frozen in a full-body death grip. I became paralyzed with the thought that something like this could happen again, no matter who Sri Da Avabhasa is. Leaving the Arati, I staggered to the Paduka Mandir, a beautiful and very potent Temple nearby, went in, and prostrated before Sri Da Avabhasa's Murti. I knew that I had no option other than to ask for His Divine Help. Through this prayer I felt restored in my relationship with Him, but the mortal fear was still there, bodily, like the grip of a vise.

By morning I felt extremely vulnerable in my powerlessness over the random affairs of life and death. I spoke to the woman who served as a guide for the female retreatants. She told me that one of Heart-Master Da's esoteric secrets is His vulnerability, that He feels everything without limitation. She also said that I had received a Gift by being able to feel my own vulnerability so profoundly, and thus able to feel the necessity for resort to the Divine, and she advised me to remain in that vulnerability and to begin to Contemplate Sri Da Avabhasa's vulnerable State.

That afternoon, we had a formal Darshan occasion with Sri Da Avabhasa. I sat in the back of the room and continued to feel this new sense of vulnerability. Then Heart-Master Da came in and sat down, and I was immediately moved beyond myself by the vulnerability I felt from Him. He was big and round and soft and totally open.

He looked at me right away, and it seemed to me that He motioned for me to close my eyes. I began to feel His Spiritual Heart-Transmission

3. Based upon a traditional Hindu ceremony, the Sat-Guru Arati Puja is a sacramental observance of waving lights around the body of the Sat-Guru (or a representation of his or her physical form, such as a photograph) to express devotion and gratitude. Practitioners of the Way of the Heart perform the Sat-Guru Arati Puja at the closing of each day by waving lights and incense around a Murti of Sri Da Avabhasa, making ecstatic sounds with musical instruments, and chanting.

descend through the top of my head, and then down to my throat, heart region, and solar plexus. At one point I realized that this descending Force had encountered an obstruction, and intuitively I felt moved to lie down, feeling that this would help. It did help, for a moment, but again I felt an obstruction, and was now moved to sit on my knees and lie arched back, with my feet and legs underneath me. It seemed ridiculous, so I sat up, but immediately my body knew it should lie back again, which it did.

I continued to breathe and remain open to the further descent of Spiritual Force while affirming my trust in this process and in my Sat-Guru, Sitting before me. I felt very much that He was with me, intimately, although He was Sitting in a Chair at the front of the room with His Eyes closed and there were thirty other people in the room also intimately involved with Him. At a certain point the Spirit-Force began to move through my belly and my (in this position) very open pelvic region. I began to release a great deal of emotion, anguish, sorrow, fear, and confusion, and suddenly I realized that I was going through the birth process! Something was literally moving down through my belly, about to be born. A moment later, I perceived my little baby on the floor in front of me. I spontaneously said out loud, "Please take him," and instantly had a vision of Sri Da Avabhasa, holding my tiny child, wrapped in the blue blanket. He was looking down at him, and both of their faces had an ancient, subtle quality to them. In that moment I had the sense they were together in a different realm.

Soon the Darshan occasion ended, and as my Beloved Sat-Guru walked past me, I knew Him as the Divine Being. His whole beautiful, vulnerable Body Radiated nothing but Love. I knew then that God is Prior to all else, and that birth and death and everything else are simply conditional Nature doing its work, but that Love, the Divine Being, is always Standing Prior to the crazy play of existence. After twelve years of suffering, my Sat-Guru had shown me this in an afternoon!

Following this occasion, while still on retreat, this process of releasing my grief continued. A couple of days later, moments before I awoke from sleep, I had a most vivid and significant dream in which I was with my brother again just after his accident. Through this dream, I was, for the first time, truly able to release him from this life. Then, a few days after this, while sitting in meditation, I spontaneously reconnected with the love I had felt for my father as a young girl, and, in that moment, fully felt and released the grief associated with his death. Through both of these incidents, as in the Darshan occasion, I realized that, once again, Sri Da Avabhasa had Gracefully led me through a process in which I could finally, happily, and energetically release my loved ones.

Since my retreat it has become clear to me that for twelve years I was terrified of bringing energy into life, frozen and unresolved over the loss of my intimates. When Sri Da Avabhasa Gracefully relieved me of these burdens, He Replaced them with His Heart-Transmission, enabling me to feel again, and to feel the life-energy moving in me again. Through this Gift, I have begun to grow again and enter into life in many ways which I had neglected or abandoned during my years of unresolved grief.

I am forever grateful to Sri Da Avabhasa for His Unconditional Love, His Profound Vulnerability, and His relentless commitment to the Liberation of all beings.

Afterword

In a Discourse Given during an informal gathering with His devotees on July 3, 1987, Sri Da Avabhasa clarified the phenomenon of delayed grieving. In the excerpt below, He Speaks with a devotee who had not gone through the process of grieving after his father's death, but who began to experience recurring dreams about his father some time later.

SRI DA AVABHASA: You felt guilty about your conflict with your father, could not let him go, and thus had to endure a natural psychic process of letting him go so that there could be a healing for you. Through these dreams, you were actually experiencing delayed mourning, a delayed process of letting your father go. By enduring that process, you also served him naturally, without any particular intention to do so.

It happens to many people when somebody dies that they do not mourn. They do not let the individual go. They become self-involved, full of grief and holding on. They endure the few days of the funeral, put the person's things away, and they think that if they just wait for a long period of time they will not have to feel anything. They do not really make use of the time when the body is still there to let the person go and to allow themselves to go through the process of relinquishment.

Therefore, they are still burdened with their mourning. You can experience the process of mourning, at least subjectively or subconsciously, for years. Even your entire life can be limited, even injured, by the inability to let someone go.

On the other hand, very often the letting go will take place naturally. Without the person intending to do something, mentally or in the waking state, the psyche itself erupts through imageries and associated emotions, and it does the letting go as a natural process.

CHAPTER 48

Allow Death to Occur
Two Dreams of Going beyond Fear

Most of us have probably had the experience of dreaming that we were about to die, and of resisting the impending threat with all our might. Typically, our fear and struggle in these dreams is so great that we wake up at the critical moment and do not go through the death itself. Two practitioners of the Way of the Heart, Raewyn Bowmar from New Zealand, and Connie Grisso from northern California, each write here of a "life-threatening" dream in which they were able to turn their attention to Sri Da Avabhasa and go through the "death experience" in Communion with Him.

RAEWYN BOWMAR: I frequently have dreams about death, but among them all, this one stands out. I was traveling in a large airplane with many people on board, when suddenly I realized that the plane was going to crash. I felt the plane falling and braced myself for the fatal impact. As we went down, I began to surrender to the inevitable. I breathed through my fear and gave my attention to my beloved Sat-Guru, Sri Da Avabhasa.

We crashed and my body died. I was certain of that. But it was equally obvious that "I" was still alive. And I felt no fear or sorrow because there was nothing to feel fearful or sorrowful about. In some sense, nothing had happened except that I had lost my body. But my body no longer held any significance or fascination for me. It was not a necessity, and I no longer put attention on it.

Two years later the dream is as vivid as ever—I can still see and feel the experience in its details, and my whole attitude toward death has changed. I understand that the body is just a temporary mechanism, not necessary to my continued existence. After the crash I did not even look

Raewyn Bowmar

back at the body. My new bodiless state seemed completely natural and ordinary, and this was an extremely liberating feeling. But to bring this understanding into life and have it affect my actual death is a matter of practice. I have since had many death dreams of a different nature, in which I have resisted and struggled and not allowed death to occur. This has been very sobering. It has shown me that my capability to surrender and feel Sri Da Avabhasa in the dream I have described was simply a Gift of His Grace. My responsibility now is to turn to Him constantly and do the practice He has Given, moment to moment, so that Remembrance of Him and surrender to Him is the gesture I can make under all circumstances, including the moment of death.

◆ ◆ ◆

CONNIE GRISSO: In 1980, when I had been in the Company of Sri Da Avabhasa for some years, I had the following dream. A group of us were swimming with Sri Da Avabhasa in an idyllic setting, a silvery lake surrounded by tall mountains. Everything seemed perfect at first, but then I looked more closely at the mountain sides. There was something strange about them. They seemed to be made of smooth, slippery gray slate. Suddenly I felt a sense of foreboding. Within moments a dull roar rose around the lake, and the mountain sides began to crash into the lake. I knew that we were all about to die in the landslide. As the rumbling grew louder across the lake, Sri Da Avabhasa swam by me. He looked directly into my eyes, Communicating the potency of His Love and of His relationship to me.

345

Connie Grisso

Soon I was underwater, buried by an avalanche of rocks and slate. My chest was crushed, and I felt I was suffocating. But somehow, in the midst of it all, I was also very alert and aware of what was occurring. Because of the Grace in the Glance of Sri Da Avabhasa a few moments before, I was able to allow the dream to continue and to surrender to the death process. Although I was dreaming, the whole experience was very vivid and "real".

I felt my breath and heartbeat subside, and for an instant "I" felt overwhelming panic, but then, remembering the Face of my Sat-Guru, I surrendered more deeply, right to the last heartbeat. Then, suddenly everything changed. I felt myself to be alive and conscious at a point outside my body. I no longer felt identified with my former body-mind, and I had an exhilarating feeling of freedom and bliss. Then I woke up.

Some time later I had the opportunity to relate this dream to Sri Da Avabhasa when He gathered with His devotees. He said that because of fear, few of us ever allow death to occur in our dreams. He said that we usually awaken ourselves in order to prevent the experience of it. He asked those who had experienced their own death in a dream to raise their hands, and there were not many. He went on to say that it is useful to go through a dream experience such as I had described so that we would have faith in the letting-go process and be able to use the experience in our lives of practice of the Way of the Heart as well as at death.

CHAPTER 49

Letting Go

by Ron Jensen

Ron Jensen

Ron Jensen is a practitioner of the Way of the Heart living in northern California. Ron's younger brother, David, struggled with cancer of the liver and the kidneys for several years and then died in the fall of 1989 at the age of 27. Although David was never a formal practitioner of the Way of the Heart, he became increasingly receptive to Sri Da Avabhasa's Grace and Instruction, and he chose to be Instructed and served by His Wisdom-Teaching as he died.

Sri Da Avabhasa has said that when we serve an individual who is dying, there should be no conflicts or confrontations with family members in the process. The service to the dying and deceased should be carried on in the disposition of release and equanimity, and, at times, the formalities of a vigil may need to be compromised in order to maintain harmony. Ron's service to his brother and family, which he describes in the following Leela, illustrates this principle.

I arrived in Salt Lake City, Utah, in September 1989, to serve my brother David in the last weeks of his life. From the moment I arrived, in meeting with family and friends, I noticed that everyone was denying the real possibility of David's death. There was an expected line of communication that David was going to make it somehow, that some miracle would save him. Of course, people do have miraculous remissions, so it was possible. David himself had experienced a remission earlier in his illness. But his body was ravaged at this point—his liver and kidneys practically destroyed. Nevertheless, there was this pervasive denial in the family, and even, I found, in me, which made real service to David very hard at first.

An important lesson I received during this time is that, in order to serve someone's death, I must truly feel this denial in myself, and continually move through it. When I did this, I was freely capable of serving David, and the family, and I could make a difference in the whole course of events. I was able to prepare for the three-day vigil and the memorial service, while at the same time helping David handle his affairs in this world and prepare for death.

David had thoroughly studied *Easy Death* (he must have read it three times) and had made a very strong connection to Heart-Master Da through *The Love-Ananda Gita*. His own desire to be served by the Wisdom of Sri Da Avabhasa's Teaching-Revelation on death and dying made serving his death much easier. Those of us who were serving David—my mother, my wife, myself, our friends who were also devotees or supporters of Heart-Master Da, and other friends of ours—did readings from Da Avabhasa's Wisdom-Teaching and talked with David about the death process. We also helped him wrap up his worldly affairs so he could relax into the process of dying.

In the midst of all of this, the relatives kept arriving. Like most people, my family just had a hard time with death. Many people came with their sorrow or guilt about his dying, and I could see that it drained David. Although David sometimes asked us not to let people in to see him, keeping them away was difficult, because they felt obliged to relieve themselves of their sorrow and guilt. Even though such people clearly did not serve David, letting people see him was one of those situations that could not be avoided.

Many relatives spent significant time with David trying to influence him with their religious beliefs and ideas about the afterlife. Although all of these people were sincere and meant well, David did not want any of this. He only wanted to tell them that he loved them, so that they could release him and he could release them.

What made the biggest difference for David was learning about the death process—the process in which he was involved in that moment and which would go on after his death. When he was engaged with that Wisdom, he responded very dramatically. But the attempts of people to engage him in simple belief systems and hopefulness about life after death did not touch the reality of his situation. Only the truth about the process he was involved in cut into his fear and anxiety. He would go through intense periods of pain and fear, but even when he was going through all of that, he would ask for readings from Sri Da Avabhasa's Wisdom-Teaching, or he would listen to audiotapes or watch videotapes of Heart-Master Da.

There was a full month of service to David before he died. During this time, we brought him home from the hospital. At our parents' home we had prepared a second-floor bedroom with a nice view of Salt Lake. David was in a steady decline, which arrested itself a few times when he would coast for a bit and then go into a greater decline. All the people who were involved in serving him with Sri Da Avabhasa's Wisdom were becoming very intimate. We were discovering that there was an ecstasy, a wonderful happiness and blissfulness, that was transforming David and attracting him more and more deeply. I could feel the Mystery of what was happening. I could feel that death could actually be an ecstatic occasion, a wonderful occasion of transformation, as my brother became more and more released from his body and mind.

Yet it was also true that the fear, the anxiety, and all the horror of losing someone you love was being felt by all of us. This was my younger brother dying, one of my closest intimates. There was the intense pain of watching him die from cancer. Nevertheless, there was always this other dimension to it that was powerful and potent. Everybody, even my aunts and uncles, staunch pillars of the mainstream churches, were eventually caught up in it. One uncle who serves as a bishop in a Christian denomination came to me and said that he had never been involved in a death and dying process of actually serving someone, talking about the technicalities of the death process with the person, and serving the person emotionally. He had never been involved in anything like what we were doing, and he was moved to tears many times by what was happening around my brother.

David dropped into a fairly deep coma early one morning. Those of us who were serving him at the time knew this was a sign that we had to enter into our service to him with much greater intensity. We also knew that our own process of releasing him into his transition had to be intensified. We observed that David was still responsive to Sri Da Avabhasa's Wisdom-Teaching even in the midst of his coma. We could feel him respond. Tears came from his eyes when we read to him from Heart-Master Da's Instructions.

That evening David came out of this comatose state. We felt that although he had said he was ready to go (he was even in a state of acute frustration about not being able to die when he felt that he was ready), there was clearly something unresolved for him. I felt that it was his concern for our mother. He felt uncomfortable about leaving her. I took my mother aside and encouraged her to really let David go, to really release him so he could go on. Then my mother went in and told David that he was free to go, free to die. She assured him that she would be fine without him. It was an incredible and powerful event to hear a mother release her son to death. She gave him permission to die. It broke my heart, because I knew how hard she had fought for his life. She had spent the last two years totally dedicated to helping David live. Now she was able to release all the time and energy she had put into this effort.

After the conversation with our mother, David became very calm. He did not want anybody to be close around him or to touch him. He was telling us goodbye. It was as if he were saying, "Stay away from me a bit so I can just relax and die." His outer awareness drifted. His breathing was rasping and difficult because of the fluid in his lungs. But he was not struggling. We quietly listened to the tape of Sri Da Avabhasa's Discourse "The Cosmic Mandala". At a certain point, all of us (there were about fifteen people in the room) realized that we were standing in the way of his death. Together we said that we were ready to let him go. There was great Help in the room at this point. We were all being helped by Heart-Master Da and His Wisdom-Teaching to release and let David go. A few minutes later, as David was looking at me, wide awake, he stopped breathing. I put my hand on his chest and told him to relax. David stopped struggling, and a moment later his heart stopped.

I stood by his bed and talked to him, describing to him how the Life-Current would move up and out of the top of his head. These moments were very intense for me, because even though his body had died, I could feel the concrete sensation of David still there with the body and moving out of it. It was not that he had died and that was the end.

I could feel a strong current of ascending energy in the room. Then, just moments after David had died, the feeling in the room changed. Now there was a very strong feeling of descending energy, and a deep silence came over the room. I felt the deep quality of stillness and heightened awareness that I have often felt just before seeing Sri Da Avabhasa. It was very dramatic; I could have heard a pin drop. The hair stood up on my body. Then I had a vision of Sri Da Avabhasa coming down the steps and walking into the room, His Arm swinging behind Him. He was wearing a beautiful blue shawl. He walked to the foot of the bed and Gave His Blessing to David. That was the vision I had. It was very powerful. The rest of that evening I could strongly feel our Heart-Master's Potent Blessing.

With Kelly, a friend who had been serving David all along, I had prepared another room, in a part of the house that was hardly ever used, with a Murti of Sri Da Avabhasa and everything we would need for a vigil, so that we could serve David's transition undisturbed. But after David's death, I felt we had to be sensitive to the people close to David. We could not move David's body without violating relationships with relatives, and the conflict this might create could also disturb the process of releasing David. We decided to leave his body in the bedroom where he had died and to keep the environment there as undisturbed as possible. The relatives came by and expressed their grief. They did not stay long, and we were soon able to anoint the body with ash and water, serve the Murti in David's room, and repeatedly read aloud Sat-Guru Da's Instructions on the death process.

I went through David's room and took out everything that was going to be given away. I cleaned up his wood shop and put away his projects. I found it helped me release him to finish things off in his life that he had not been able to get around to. We worked with his environment, giving things away, moving things, and completing everything. We felt how effective this was in the whole transitional process that was going on for David. It was an active form of release for everyone.

His body was not disturbed for about twenty-one hours. Then the mortician came and took his body to the funeral home. Before his death, one of the things I had promised David was that I would personally give instructions on how his body should be handled so that his transition would be as smooth as possible. We had made arrangements with the mortician to do as little embalming as legally possible.

This was another area where compromise was necessary. The family simply could not accept the idea of cremating the body. The idea was disturbing to them. And David had not accepted the concept of cremation either—he never came to a real understanding of it. Since this was the case, we did not cremate his body but we arranged for burial. When the body came back from the mortuary, we put a wreath on it. Then we put flowers in the coffin, including some flowers that had been Blessed by Da Avabhasa, and closed the coffin.

The funeral was a very positive occasion. So much had been worked through emotionally for people that everyone could just express their love for David. This is what people wanted to do anyway, just praise David and express their love. One of the most dramatic things about the funeral was that the family members who had witnessed the whole course of David's dying and our service to him came to us and told us how much they had also been served by the whole event. They said they had appreciated the Wisdom of Sri Da Avabhasa's Instruction, and they realized it had helped David as he died. My mother, who had been actively supportive throughout, was visibly relieved of her grief. After David's death, she was very peaceful and calm, because now she could feel that death was not just an end.

Throughout this whole event, I noticed that people can be open emotionally in confrontation with death, so that when I simply brought the Truth to them, or to a particular situation, they could make use of it. The Potency of Sri Da Avabhasa's Grace and Blessing transformed the whole event of my brother's death.

CHAPTER 50

King Vidor

by Toni Vidor

Toni Vidor

My father, the renowned Hollywood film director-producer King Vidor, died at 7:30 Monday morning, November 1, 1982. He suffered a sudden pain in the stomach and then passed away in fifteen minutes.

Especially in his later years, my father and I had been good friends. I loved him very much. When I received the phone call informing me of his death, I immediately collapsed emotionally and burst into tears. Shortly afterwards, I drove down the road to the Mountain Of Attention Sanctuary to ask Connie Grisso for help. As she explained Sri Da Avabhasa's Instructions for serving the death transition, I was heartened to feel that there was a way I could still do something for my father. The deep sorrow remained, but my mood of collapse vanished.

My husband, Kerwin, and I arrived around midnight at the small-town funeral home where my father's body had been taken. We secured a private room so we could be alone with him. We decided that I should start the vigil, so that Kerwin could recover from our long drive to the mortuary.

I began by reading aloud some of Sri Da Avabhasa's Essays on death, in order to orient myself to the death process. I noticed with surprise that I had no feeling of eeriness, although I had never been so close to a corpse before. The situation felt curiously natural to me. Then I just sat, relaxing into a meditative disposition.

I began to feel my father's presence in the room. There was no doubt about it. I got the clear feeling that he was totally confused, probably at having dropped the body so quickly and without preparation. I also picked up a sense of chaos from him: During his life my father had been involved in a series of difficult relationships with women; several of these relationships were still unresolved. As I sat with him I actually saw some of the "demons" of his mind-forms, and I felt in my own body the anger he held against his mother, his third wife, and another lady. I made a point of writing down whatever came to my notice about his anger, and then simply released everything as it came up to me.

I had brought with me holy water and ash that had been Blessed in a ceremony at the Mountain Of Attention Sanctuary. Every two hours or so I sprinkled holy water and ash on my father's body and around the room. I knew my father disliked ceremonies, but I explained to his presence that I felt moved to do this anyway. The first time I did this, I felt an overwhelming feeling of love sweep over me as if he was acknowledging me and was grateful that I was there. I was intuitively certain that I was definitely not imagining things, and his response confirmed to me the complete appropriateness and usefulness of what I was doing. At times I was overcome by a deep sorrow at the loss of him, and I would cry in those moments. But the necessity that I felt to serve him supported and strengthened me and kept me in relationship to the Divine and my Sat-Guru, Sri Da Avabhasa.

That night, while attending the vigil, I fell asleep for a short time, and, when I awoke at 5:00 a.m., I felt perfectly refreshed. A strong desire to meditate arose in me, and I sensed the strong Presence of Sri Da Avabhasa meditating me. A great peacefulness came over the room. My father was obviously affected by it, and I even imagined seeing his face relax. Yet, in the midst of this palpable peace I became again very much aware of my father's lingering earthly entanglements with women, money, properties, lawsuits, and so on. I knew that Spiritual practitioners spend months and years trying to disengage themselves from all of this. I could not see how my father could possibly release all these ties in a matter of two or three days.

At about 7:00 that morning Kerwin came to relieve me, and I went straight to a hotel to shower, eat, and rest. After only about an hour's sleep I heard a voice say: "Well, Kerwin is good, but where is Toni?" I realized that I should not be sleeping when I had this responsibility to serve my father. As I walked back to the mortuary, I felt a great happiness and joy well up in my heart at the thought of returning there. To my amazement, that tacky room in a small-town funeral home had temporarily become a holy site for me.

When I arrived, I learned that Kerwin, who never speaks of experiencing subtle energies, could very tangibly feel my father's presence. What is more, he too could feel my father's anxiety about those unresolved complications. Kerwin had spoken to my father about death and the Spiritual Process, using more my father's own language, that of Christian Science, with which my father had enjoyed a long familiarity during his life. Kerwin had told him to find the Source of the light all around him and to follow that Source.

I asked Kerwin to procure some candles, and continued to serve my father's transition, occasionally sprinkling ash and holy water, and reading from Heart-Master Da's Wisdom-Teaching. After a while, Kerwin returned with a few candles. I lit them, and, with one candle, did a kind of spontaneous ceremony over the whole body, offering it to the Divine. Again a powerful wave of love swept over me, and I began to weep, realizing that this was a form of goodbye.

Shortly after this I was again drawn into a meditative state. In a completely heart-felt prayer I asked Sri Da Avabhasa to do whatever was necessary to release this being to the Divine, and also to show me whatever I could do to help that release. At one point in meditation I became aware that my father could also experience the intensity of Sri Da Avabhasa's Divine Presence, and in that moment I began to feel a great relief. I felt intuitively that although my father would surely continue the work of releasing himself from the bondage of this life in the afterlife (or perhaps, in subsequent lifetimes), that a Power greater than his earthly entanglements and problems had also become known to him.

That was the last time I sensed my father's presence in the room. Within a couple of hours both Kerwin and I realized that he was no longer with us. We stayed a few more hours just to make sure, but he was obviously gone. The body now appeared to be just a piece of cold meat. I could hardly believe that my father's transition had been accomplished so swiftly and so gracefully.

I was overcome with gratitude for Sri Da Avabhasa, and at the same time I was humbled by how little I know of the whole mysterious death process. Every time I looked at that stiff, white corpse during the night or touched the cold, clammy skin I realized that no matter how famous, or beautiful, or wealthy we are in life, this is how we will inevitably end up. Even "kings" could not cheat death. My sacred practice was right there. Right there was the Mystery. Shortly before my father's death, I had prayed for an intensification of my practice. So I was and am ever grateful for this lesson, for the Presence of Heart-Master Da, and for the gracefulness of my father's transition out of life.

CHAPTER 51

The Touch of
"The Giver of Love"

*Sri Da Avabhasa's place of permanent Residence since 1983 has been
His Hermitage Sanctuary on the remote island of Naitauba, Fiji. Ciqomi
(pronounced "thing-GO-mee") is the village on the island where the Fijian
staff members live. "Ciqomi" means "great reception", a name Given by Sri
Da Avabhasa after He was first welcomed to the village in December 1983.
In the story told here, of events that took place on January 10, 1989, Sri Da
Avabhasa makes His second visit to Ciqomi, to attend Finau Solomani, an
aged Fijian who is dying. Finau is the father of Solo, another participant
in this Story, who has shown a strong devotional response to Sri Da
Avabhasa from the time He arrived on Naitauba. Since this time, Solo has
become a formal devotee of Sri Da Avabhasa.*

*Sri Da Avabhasa's coming to Ciqomi on this occasion was a unique
Gesture, a Gesture that moved and astonished everyone. Since the beginning of His Spiritual Work, Sri Da Avabhasa has Graced many dying individuals with His Blessing, but He had never before gone in Person to ease a
death transition. Sri Da Avabhasa's Compassionate attendance to Finau
in his final hours was a Mysterious sign of His Love for all beings and His
great desire to Bless the death transition of each one—to Bless each one
personally with an easy death.*

To the Fijian people of the island-Hermitage of Naitauba, Sri Da
Avabhasa is known as Tui Dau Loloma Vunirarama, "The Great
Chief Who Is the Giver of Love and the Source of 'Brightness'"
When He learned that Finau was in a coma and dying, Dau Loloma (the

This Leela is adapted from an article by William Tsiknas, which was first published in *Crazy Wisdom*
magazine (November 1988-February 1989).

Giver of Love) asked to be driven to the village of Ciqomi, and He sent word that two of His devotees, Dr. Charles Seage, who is His personal physician, and Mo Whiteside, a translator, should meet Him there.

Dr. Seage and Mo arrived ahead of Dau Loloma and found Solo sitting in the meeting house, drinking kava, a ceremonial Fijian drink, with some other men.

Mo told Solo, "Dau Loloma is coming to see Finau."

"Ah, vinaka (thanks)," said Solo.

Solo looked at Mo for a moment, and then it dawned on him. "Right now?" he asked.

"Yes. Tonight."

Dr. Seage helped Solo wash Finau while the family spread their most valuable mats on the floor and prepared their house for Dau Loloma's arrival.

Solo then stood in front of his home waiting to greet Dau Loloma. In the distance he could hear the engine of the Land Rover bringing Dau Loloma to Ciqomi. As Dau Loloma stepped out of the car, the villagers witnessed His gentle way. An orange shawl hung over His Shoulders. He walked by the four Kanyas[1] and the members of Finau's family to put His Arms around Solo and kiss him, and they walked together, arm in arm, into the house.

Finau lay on his side in a bed in a small room. Dau Loloma Stood next to the bed, His Staff in hand, looking intently on Finau. Finau's chest heaved, and he gasped for air as if he were about to die.

Dau Loloma handed Kanya Suprithi His Staff, and sat down on the edge of Finau's bed. He leaned down, His Face very close to the old man's. Softly, He took Finau's left hand and held it in His Lap. He placed His other Hand on Finau's small shoulder. Then very lightly, so as not to startle him, Dau Loloma massaged his emaciated, struggling body.

Finau's eyes opened, so beautifully slowly.

Traditions say that to die with the Name of God on your lips is auspicious, but to die in the Presence of a God-Realized Being is a Blessing without measure, for the Darshan, or sighting, of a Holy Man can transform a man's consciousness as he leaves the body.

Dau Loloma held Finau in His Arms. From the hallway, Solo and the

---

1. "Kanya" is the abbreviated Designation for one of the four members of the Da Avabhasa Gurukula Kanyadana Kumari Order. This Order is the unique sacred circle of women who have consecrated themselves to the service of Sri Da Avabhasa in "true intimacy" for the sake of their Divine Self-Realization and who, by virtue of that relationship, have the capability to serve the Spiritual growth of others by their inspiring devotional surrender to Heart-Master Da.

devotees watched. Each breath was a struggle for Finau. He seemed to be afraid and in pain. He tried to respond to Dau Loloma, but he could not speak or move. Yet Sri Dau Loloma responded to his feeble attempts to communicate. He understood Finau perfectly. Dau Loloma held Finau close and whispered, "Tcha",[2] and "Hmm".

A tear fell from the old man's sunken eyes down that long dark face. His lips parted, and his face widened with a fragile smile.

The Hands of Dau Loloma were kind to Finau's body, massaging and relaxing him. And Dau Loloma's Utterances, which are actually powerful Mantras, struck Finau's heart and Awakened his consciousness. By Touch, and by Speech, and by Glance, Dau Loloma had eased Finau toward his unavoidable transition from this life to the next.

Sri Da Avabhasa Says there is a secret to the death process: The right relationship to death is love-surrender to the Divine Person, not recoil or withdrawal. As Finau lay there struggling, Dau Loloma Worked to help him accomplish the Yoga of easy death.

Dau Loloma Says to the dying:

Release and relax all fear and simply surrender into cooperation with the death process, like a woman in labor—and, like a woman in labor, consciously and bodily accept and "feel through" even the more painful, embarrassing, unpleasant, or chaotic aspects of the total event. (p. 296)

As Finau's outer awareness subsided, Dau Loloma moved him into a more relaxed position, lying on his back in the "dead pose". Now Dau Loloma put His Hand on Finau's head. His Hand functioned like a magnet to draw Finau's attention upwards, releasing his body, emotion, and attention into the Divine Life-Current and toward the crown, so that he could emerge from the body-mind into the next or new dimension of existence. He placed His Thumb on Finau's forehead at the ajna chakra, or what is sometimes called the "Seat of the Guru". The ajna chakra is the Spiritual center located at the midbrain, where the life-force is said to enter the body and to leave it at death. As the life-force drove upwards at Da Avabhasa's Touch, Finau's eyes squinted closed, not in pain, but in a kriya,[3] a Spiritual sign that Finau's consciousness was ascending beyond

---

2. "Tcha" is a sacred sound that Heart-Master Da characteristically makes as a form of Blessing and Acknowledgement of a devotee's response to Him.

3. Kriyas (in Sanskrit, literally "actions") are spontaneous, self-purifying physical movements that arise when the natural bodily energies are stimulated by the Divine Spirit-Current, or as effects of a Sat-Guru's Spiritual Presence in and upon the body-mind of his or her devotee.

the agony of his fear and the dying mass of flesh.

Dau Loloma moved His right Hand over Finau's heart, and with the other Hand still on his head, Dau Loloma Meditated Finau, absorbing his pain and fear into His own Being. Dau Loloma breathed deeply and slowly, and finally the old man's breath became calm and even.

With Finau at peace, Sri Dau Loloma removed the orange shawl He was wearing, lifted Finau's body, and tucked the shawl around him. Finau Solomani lay calmly in Dau Loloma's care. The two were so peaceful together in the dimly lit room, they seemed in another world.

Dau Loloma stood, His Eyes still fixed on Finau. He stepped back and reached for His Staff.

Solo, Dr. Seage, and Mo had watched everything from the adjoining living room. Solo's young son, Pita, was there, too. And there were women huddled outside the house, peering in through the open windows. Dau Loloma embraced Solo again and held Him close in the space where they breathed. Dau Loloma's Love can draw out what a man otherwise conceals in his heart. The sorrow, the difficult thoughts, and the feelings of loss that the insult of death brings were all rising in Solo. Death's message to the living is that all who live will die. But Dau Loloma's Message, though He never Spoke a word, was that Finau's death was part of a living process, not an ending, but a mysterious transformation. Dau Loloma's body was a bridge of intimacy between a dying man, his grieving son, and the Supreme Reality that Eternally and everywhere Pervades and yet Perfectly Transcends the events of life and death.

Dau Loloma finally released Solo, and the Guru and Solo parted. Through tears of gratitude, Solo watched from the porch of his home as Dau Loloma stepped into the waiting vehicle. Dau Loloma called back, "Solo," and motioned him over to the window of the car. He took off His indigo hat and pressed it snugly on Solo's head. Minerva, Solo's daughter, came to the front door of the house, and Dau Loloma waved goodbye to her.

On the way up the hill and out onto the road leading back to His Residence, Da Avabhasa Chakra, Dau Loloma was quiet. The night was peaceful.

Finau died the following day, January 11, 1989, the third anniversary of the Event that initiated Sri Da Avabhasa's Divine Emergence.

The Heart
of
Understanding

Sri Da Avabhasa (The "Bright")
Sri Love-Anandashram, September 1991

The Heart
of Understanding

from The Knee Of Listening
by Da Avabhasa

Death is utterly acceptable to consciousness and life. There has been endless time of numberless deaths, but neither consciousness nor life has ceased to arise. The felt quantity and cycle to death has not modified the fragility of flowers, even the flowers within our human body. Therefore, our understanding of consciousness and life must be turned to that utter, inclusive quality, that clarity and wisdom, that power and untouchable gracefulness this evidence suggests. We must cease to live in our superficial and divided way, seeking and demanding only consciousness and life in the present form we grasp, avoiding and resisting what appears to be the end of consciousness and life in death.

The Heart is that understanding, that true consciousness, that true life that is under the extreme conditions of life and death. Therefore, it is said, that One that is is neither born nor come to death, not alive as the limitation of form, not rendered in what appears, and yet It is the Living One, than Which there is no other, appearing as all of this, but eternally the same.

There is only the constant knowledge and enjoyment of the Heart, moment to moment, through the instant of all conditions of appearance and disappearance. Of this I am perfectly certain. I am That.

Serving the Death Transition

*A Summary of Sri Da Avabhasa's Instruction
Presented by Connie Grisso, Director of Mate Moce*

S ome years ago I was caring for a man who was dying of lung cancer at a busy metropolitan hospital in the San Francisco Bay area. It was late at night, and my patient was resting quietly, so I sat reading nearby as he slept. All the while my attention kept being drawn to a commotion across the hall. There was another patient moaning and thrashing, and the nurses were rushing in and out of the patient's room. Wondering what was going on, I walked across the hall and saw a painful, though not unfamiliar, sight. There lay a woman, probably in her sixties, with short gray hair, pale, sweating profusely, and for the most part, unconscious. She was obviously near death and deeply comatose except for one leg and one arm that would heave violently from time to time. She was restrained, tied down to the bed even in her coma, and her labored breathing rang up and down the hallway.

Her disturbance was obvious even in the silence of her coma: She was trying to get someone's attention and hardly had any faculties left in her body to do so. I asked her nurse to tell me what had happened. She said this woman was from the Midwest and had come to California on vacation. She became ill that day and had come to the emergency room of the hospital to get some advice. While having a chest x-ray, she had suffered what is commonly called a massive stroke. Her medical history and the cause of the stroke were unknown, but now she was dying, with probably only hours to live. An attempt had been made to reach her family, but as yet no one had responded. This lady had no relations or friends here or anyone who knew her. She was just alone, and now suddenly dying. Ending her story, the nurse said sincerely, "Isn't it a shame?" and walked out of the room.

I had the same impulse, only I wanted to run. This lady's agitation and fear made the room feel oppressive. I wanted to go back to looking after my patient, who, by comparison, was relaxed in his dying. But feeling Sri Da Avabhasa's Compassion for all beings, I remembered His general Instructions on serving the death of another:

You must perform real service to a person while he or she is alive and preparing to die. . . . You must create an atmosphere that will release, bless, and calm the person so that he or she can be open and relaxed and able to observe and pass through the phenomena that arise. (November 9, 1980)

I realized it was possible to serve her and probably no accident that I was in the hospital that night.

I approached her bedside. Reading the name on her ID band, I addressed her as "Evelyn" and took hold of the hand that still had some movement and, I hoped, feeling. Sitting down, I spoke quietly near her ear, telling her what had happened today and that she was dying now. I told her that every attempt would be made to locate her family to be sure that someone would be found to make arrangements to take her home. I felt her relax as I put my hand on her chest and told her to breathe easy, that her fear could relax and her agitation could subside if she would start letting go. I read her this passage from the first edition of *Easy Death*, which I had brought with me that night, and I explained that my Spiritual Master was Instructing a devotee on how to help her dying mother. I read:

. . . she should have no fear that death will destroy her, that death is simply a transition into other experiences that also pass, that eventually she may resume a human existence, or at least perhaps a personal existence in an environment, and that as she passes through these stages of experience after she leaves this world, she will be given help. It is true that after your death people come to help you, telling you where you are and what is happening to you, just as people do in this realm. (from chapter 37, "How to Serve the Dying Person")

It was amazing to feel the immediacy of her response. She was right there with me, and her breathing calmed down to a natural rhythm. I went on to tell her that my Heart-Master has Said that at death it is good to meditate or remember the Divine Lord in whatever Form you have known and loved Him or Her in life. She seemed to take a deep breath and sigh. Further, I said, He has Instructed us to surrender into the death process as we do each night when going to sleep. I felt she was really listening. After speaking like this for a while, I said I would come back and check in on her later, and I returned to my room.

This dying process continued for the next several hours, and each hour or so I went in to talk with Evelyn and to support her, and each time she was further along. She was no longer moving about, and she was breathing softly and less often. A quiet calm and peace had entered the room, replacing her struggle and agitation of the previous hours. The staff nurses were amazed at the change in Evelyn, and I had the opportunity to share with them Sri Da Avabhasa's most basic Instruction on serving those who are dying. They were grateful and receptive, saying they too felt the need to support dying people, but they had never been taught how.

Finally, at 7:00 A.M., it was time for me to go home. I told Evelyn "goodbye", and I wished her God's Blessings. In the final moment, she pressed my hand with an almost imperceptible movement of her fingers. She was letting me know she understood, and I felt her appreciation.

After I arrived home and showered, I called the hospital nurses station to inquire about her condition. They told me she had died very peacefully just moments before. Shortly after I left, her sister had called from Chicago and they had been able to assure Evelyn that she was coming to take her home. The staff on the medical wing were very relieved to have such a difficult situation turn out so benignly. I attributed the Gracefulness of Evelyn's death entirely to Sri Da Avabhasa's Blessing Influence and to His Compassionate Instruction.

As this story illustrates, it is possible to serve an individual who is dying by creating an atmosphere that will "release, bless, and calm the person" and relieve him or her of the fear of letting go. Nevertheless, as Sri Da Avabhasa has clearly indicated in *Easy Death*, "The kind of destiny you experience [after death] is determined by the sadhana you have done during your lifetime and by your Realization at the time of death." Thus, to receive such service at death is useful in an ordinary human sense, but it is not a substitute for self-transcending practice in life.

For this reason, Sri Da Avabhasa's principal arguments in *Easy Death* are not so much about serving the dying as they are about the necessity for real practice in life. Sri Da Avabhasa's principles of preparation and relaxation into the death process can be used with anyone to the degree the person is able to receive this help. Yet the Greatest Help is available to those who enter into a true devotional relationship with Sri Da Avabhasa, Who is here to Guide us in life as well as in death. His immeasurably profound Help and Blessing have become obvious to all of us who have entered into this sacred relationship with Him. Heart-Master Da's principal Instructions for right participation in the death transition are, in fact, identical to His basic Instructions to practitioners of the Way of the Heart in all moments of practice. As He Says in *Easy Death* (chapter 22): "In whatever moment death begins, practice surrender of egoic self via the same form of the Way of the Heart that you were exercising up to that moment in life."

The Mate Moce Ministry

Sri Da Avabhasa has indicated that it is useful for practitioners of the Way of the Heart to serve other devotees at the time of their death, in order to create an appropriate and auspicious circumstance for the death transition. At the present time, particularly in the Western world, those who are dying are commonly served by outside professionals rather than in the context of an intimate devotional gathering. Thus, in order to respond to Sri Da Avabhasa's Instructions in this regard, and bring intimate and loving support to each other in the death process, a group of devotees of Sri Da Avabhasa came together in 1982 to form a death and dying ministry informed by His Divine Wisdom and practical Instruction. In 1983, Heart-Master Da Blessed this ministry with the name "Mate Moce" (pronounced MAH-tay MO-thay), a name with an unusual history.

On a tour of Naitauba Island (now also known as Sri Love-Anandashram, Da Avabhasa's Hermitage Sanctuary in Fiji) when Heart-Master Da first arrived there, He heard of a woman named Mate Moce, who had lived on the island some years earlier. She had been named in this way: Shortly before she was born, a resident in her village had died in sleep, and so the new baby was given the name Mate (death) Moce (sleep), in keeping with the Fijian custom of naming the newborn babies after noteworthy events occurring around the time of their birth. Dying in one's sleep implies to Fijians a peaceful death. Thus "Mate Moce" is the Fijian equivalent of "Easy Death".

Presently, Mate Moce, the death and dying ministry of the community of Free Daists, serves practitioners of the Way of the Heart who are dying, and their intimates, in the following ways:

■ By providing direct help with and service to the death of formal practitioners of the Way of the Heart, including the practical management of the three-day vigil that follows the death of a practitioner, the right orientation of those who serve this occasion, and the compassionate, formal guidance of the whole circumstance surrounding a death.

■ By providing general counseling to practitioners of the Way of the Heart in all matters related to death and dying.

■ By offering patrons, Friends of the Free Daist Communion, and participants in Da Avabhasa International[1] educational materials, courses, and audiotapes on the right understanding of death and dying, as Revealed by Heart-Master Da.

■ By developing educational materials and seminars for the public about understanding death from the point of view of the Way of the Heart.

Sri Da Avabhasa's Instructions on Serving the Death Transition

One of Heart-Master Da's principal Instructions for preparing for death is: "Settle your affairs in this world."[2] Mate Moce assists practitioners of the Way of the Heart in completing all the practical business related to the process of death and dying, in advance. Thus, each practitioner of the Way of the Heart is asked to complete and file several essential documents: a "Living Will"/"Durable Power of Attorney for Health Care", a "Testamentary Will", and a simple form called "Funeral Directions", which states the individual's wishes for how his or her body should be handled at death and afterwards. In addition, all practitioners are encouraged to keep with them at all times a wallet identification card that briefly states our religious principles discouraging autopsy, organ donation, and embalming or other invasive bodily procedures after death, so that the death transition is not disturbed.

In preparation for death, the practitioner of the Way of the Heart who is dying is told to intensify and deepen his or her practice of Guru-devotion, so that all activities become truly self-forgetting Remembrance of the Divine in the Form of Sri Da Avabhasa. While dying, as while living, each practitioner should fully embrace all the practices appropriate to

1. For a full description of the various forms of involvement available to anyone interested in entering into a formal relationship with Sri Da Avabhasa, see "'A Unique Advantage to Mankind': An Invitation to a Direct Relationship with Da Avabhasa", on pp. 389-402 of this book.

2. See chapter 43 of this book, "Surrender beyond Everything and Everyone", for a summary of Heart-Master Da's Instructions to practitioners of the Way of the Heart on how to prepare for, and practice during, the death transition.

his or her form and developmental stage of the Way of the Heart.

At the time of the death of a practitioner of the Way of the Heart, the focus of attention of all those in attendance is always feeling-Contemplation of Sri Da Avabhasa, in order to support the individual's release to the Divine. The dying individual may be reminded to keep surrendering attention to Heart-Master Da and to release the body in an upward manner along the spinal line toward the crown of the head.

In the earliest moments after death, periodically reading or reciting brief and specific passages designated from Sri Da Avabhasa's Wisdom-Teaching (available from Mate Moce) into the ear of the individual may be helpful, even though the individual seems to be unconscious. Such intensive service is primarily helpful in the earliest moments after death, since after a certain point no outer consciousness remains to be served in this manner.

Those who are serving the death process are responsible to help the dying practitioner find Sri Da Avabhasa through feeling-Contemplation of His bodily (human) Form, and, as Grace will have it, His Spiritual (and Always Blessing) Presence, and, as Grace will have it, His Very (and Inherently Perfect) State and to be released, thereby, beyond all conditional worlds and perceptions. It is through their own feeling-Contemplation of Sri Da Avabhasa that those who are serving the dying individual are to effectively support the most complete form of release in that individual.

To aid the practice of feeling-Contemplation, those in attendance may periodically chant Heart-Master Da Avabhasa's Principal Name, "Da", or the Sat-Guru-Naama Mantra,[3] at this time.

The intensive period of service continues for two to three hours following the cessation of the individual's heartbeat and breathing, until it is felt that the initial separation from the gross physical body has occurred. If possible, there should be no disturbance to the body during this critical period of time. For this reason, the Mate Moce ministry always tries to have a representative in attendance at the time of a practitioner's death to ensure that the body is not disturbed or moved during this most active time of the death transition.

---

3. Since ancient times, the Empowered Name of one's Sat-Guru has been used as an auspicious focus for Contemplation of the Divine Person. The Name "Da", meaning "the One Who Gives", is honored in many sacred traditions as a Name of the Divine Person, and it is the primary Name of God in the Way of the Heart. Sri Da Avabhasa's Name "Da" indicates His Most Perfect Realization of God and a sacred Function as Sat-Guru, "the One Who Gives or Transmits the Divine Influence and Awakening Grace-Power to all living beings".

The Sat-Guru-Naama Mantra, either in the form "Om Sri Da Avabhasa Hridayam" or in the form "Om Sri Da Love-Ananda Hridayam", is a sacred Mantra used by practitioners in the Way of the Heart.

At the conclusion of this initial phase of the death transition, the body is simply washed, dressed, and moved to the place selected for the three-day vigil. This may be a room in a private home, or a private space in a licensed mortuary. The room should be kept cool, and the environment around the body should be kept uncluttered, undisturbed, and calm at all times. A photographic Murti (or Representational Image) of Sri Da Avabhasa should be in the room, and a Sat-Guru Puja, or formal sacramental worship, should be performed on the Murti once each day. But there should be no photographs, artistic images, or memorabilia of the dead person, as these may tend to hinder the individual's process of release. Throughout the vigil, quiet formal chanting and formal recitations of Da Avabhasa's Wisdom-Teaching appropriate to the occasion may be done. All activities during the vigil should be done formally and in the disposition of release and surrender.

Optimally, the vigil should be served around the clock, twenty-four hours a day, for three to three-and-a-half days by representatives of Mate Moce and other practitioners of the Way of the Heart (although such a continuous vigil may not be possible in some settings). Each person who serves or attends the vigil is instructed about the importance of helping the individual who has died to pass on freely by maintaining the formalities of the vigil. The purpose of these formalities is to rightly focus the attention of each participant in the process of release. Thus, for example, the individual who has died is addressed compassionately, yet in a formal manner. If this is not done, those serving or attending the vigil may tend to lapse into their own cycle of sorrow and grief, or perhaps into fascination with the energy states or psychic phenomena that may be experienced during a vigil.

While grieving is a natural part of the release process, and those close to the individual are encouraged to feel and express their grief, it is important not to conduct this grieving in close proximity to the dead body. This is essential so the individual who has died is not drawn back to the physical body, and into the concerns pertaining to the former human life, by the emotional attachments of those who are left behind. Grieving individuals are encouraged to fully express their feelings, but in another location than that of the vigil, and they are helped to regain their balance before attending the site of the physical body. Sri Da Avabhasa has asked that Mate Moce also serve grieving family members and intimates by relieving them of all practical concerns or responsibilities relating to the vigil.

The vigil is brought to an end, generally from seventy-two to eighty-four hours after it began, when it is clearly felt that the individual who has died has transitioned fully. (The preceding description of service at the time of death presumes a conducive environment where the dying practitioner may be optimally served according to Sri Da Avabhasa's Instructions. However, even in emergencies when the circumstance of death cannot be optimally controlled, Sri Da Avabhasa's Wisdom-Teaching may still be applied. More complete Instructions for serving the dying practitioner are given in the literature from Mate Moce.)

At the end of the vigil, Mate Moce assists with planning for cremation, and with the scattering of ashes, according to the individual's wishes. In the Way of the Heart, cremation and the scattering of ashes is, in general, the recommended practice, rather than burial or the preserving of ashes. This is based on Heart-Master Da Love-Ananda's Instructions that such a practice can aid the process of releasing the individual who has died.

Either before or after the ashes are scattered, a memorial gathering of practitioners of the Way of the Heart, friends, and family may be held in order to provide an opportunity for all to express their love for the individual who has died, to confess their feelings of sorrow and loss, and to inspire and strengthen one another with a right understanding of life and death.

Contacting the Mate Moce Ministry

The Mate Moce ministry provides assistance free of charge to formal practitioners of the Way of the Heart and members of Da Avabhasa International, and is financially supported through donations and the sale of its publications.

If you would like more information about Mate Moce, or about the public education seminars it offers, or if you would like to make a donation toward the work of the ministry, please write to:

Mate Moce
P.O. Box 1076
Lower Lake, CA 95457
USA

The Seven Stages of Life

Sri Da Avabhasa has described the evolutionary development of the human individual and the process of self-transcending Spiritual, Transcendental, and Divine Realization in terms of seven stages of life. This unique Revelation of truly human evolution is one of the keys to a full appreciation of the Way of the Heart. Below is a brief description of each of the seven stages of life, which we are presenting here to aid your study of Heart-Master Da's Wisdom-Teaching.

The First Stage of Life—Individuation: The first stage of life is a process of individuation, or of becoming identified with the physical body in the waking state. In this stage, one gradually adapts functionally to physical existence and eventually achieves a basic sense of individual autonomy, or of personal independence from the mother and from all others.

The Second Stage of Life—Socialization: The second stage of life is a process of socialization, or social exploration and growth in relationships. In this stage, the individual adapts to the emotional-sexual, or feeling, dimension of the being and achieves basic integration of that dimension with the physical body.

The Third Stage of Life—Integration: The third stage of life is a process of integration as a fully differentiated, or autonomous, sexual and social human character. In this stage, one adapts to and develops the verbal mind, the faculty of discriminative intelligence, and the will. And one achieves basic adult integration of body, emotion, and mind in the context of the bodily-based point of view.

These first three stages are optimally developed in the context of authentic early-life devotion to the bodily (human) Form of the Sat-Guru and, thus and thereby, to the Divine Person.

The Fourth Stage of Life—Spiritualization: The fourth stage of life involves the cultivation of heart-felt surrender to and intimacy with the bodily (human) Form, and, eventually, and more and more profoundly, the Spiritual Presence, of a Spiritually Realized Sat-Guru and, through such explicit devotional self-surrender to the Sat-Guru, devotional intimacy and Union with the Divine Person. Secondarily, in the fourth stage of life, the gross body-mind of the Awakening devotee is adapted and submitted to, and harmonized in, the Living Spirit-Current of the Sat-Guru and, thus and thereby, of the Divine Person.

The Fifth Stage of Life—Higher Spiritual Evolution: The fifth stage of life, if it must be developed, involves the ascent of attention and self-awareness beyond the gross body-mind and into the subtler field of psyche and mind, outside and beyond the brain. Traditionally, the fifth stage of life, therefore, develops the esoteric Yogic and cosmic mysticism of the Spiritual Life-Current in its ascent to the Matrix of Light, Love-Bliss, and Spirit-Presence above the world, the body, and the mind. When that mysticism is followed to its eventual culminating Union with the Spiritual Divine Matrix of Love-Bliss, the individual enjoys fifth stage conditional Nirvikalpa Samadhi.

In the Way of the Heart, most practitioners are Graced to bypass some or all of the fifth stage Yogic process (and they may be Graced to bypass some or all of the "advanced" fourth stage Yogic process, which is the beginning of the Yoga of Spiritual ascent). This is possible by Sri Da Avabhasa's Grace, Whereby His devotee is Attracted by feeling-Contemplation of His bodily (human) Form and Spiritual (and Always Blessing) Presence directly into feeling-Contemplation of His Very (and Inherently Perfect) State, such that exhaustive (or even any) exploration of ascending Yogic processes is rendered unnecessary. Thus, for such practitioners, fifth stage conditional Nirvikalpa Samadhi and other "advanced" fourth stage or fifth stage states may or may not arise, but in any case the focus of practice is heart-felt Contemplation of Heart-Master Da's bodily (human) Form, His Spiritual (and Always Blessing) Presence, and His Divine State of Consciousness Itself, and, thus and thereby, Contemplation of the Divine Person.

The Sixth Stage of Life—Awakening to the Transcendental Self: In the conventional development of the sixth stage of life, the body-mind is simply relaxed into the Spiritual Current of Life, and attention (the root or base of mind) is inverted away from gross and subtle states and objects of the body-mind, and toward the Witness-Consciousness of attention, mind, body, and world. The ultimate possible expression of this inversion of attention is Jnana Samadhi, or the temporary and exclusive Realization of the Transcendental Self, or Consciousness Itself.

In the Way of the Heart, as in conventional developmental processes, the conscious being in the sixth stage of life enjoys fundamental freedom from and equanimity in relation to the conditions and states of the body-mind-self. But, by Sri Da Avabhasa's Grace, the sixth stage process develops without the strategic and stressful inversion of attention. Rather, by Grace of the Attractiveness of Sat-Guru Da's bodily (human) Form and His Spiritual (and Always Blessing) Presence, His devotee is drawn into sympathy with His Very (and Inherently Perfect) State of Consciousness Itself, the Self of the Divine Person. He or she Stands increasingly Free of the binding phenomena and illusions of psycho-physical existence, while observing and more and more profoundly and "radically" transcending the root-action of egoity, which is self-contraction, or the activity of primal separation that creates the fundamental sense of "difference", or the feeling of relatedness.

The Seventh Stage of Life—Divine Enlightenment: The seventh stage of life is neither the culmination of any conventional psycho-physical and Spiritual process of human developmental growth (which traditionally takes place in the fulfillment of the fifth stage of life) nor the end or goal of any process of the conventional inversion of attention and the exclusion of psycho-physical and Spiritual phenomena (which occupies traditional orientations toward the sixth stage of life). The seventh stage of life, rather, is the Free Condition of Inherently Perfect Divine Self-Realization that is, in the Way of the Heart, Awakened entirely and only by the Liberating Grace of Heart-Master Da Avabhasa, the Divine Sat-Guru. It is the State of Divinely Perfect Contemplative Identification, in the Way of the Heart, with Sat-Guru Da's Very (and Inherently Perfect) State of "Bright" Consciousness, the Uncaused, Unsupported, Unconditional, and Unqualified Realization of Being Itself, or Perfect Love-Blissful Unity with the Supreme Divine Person.

Thus, in Sahaj Samadhi in the seventh stage of life, the Divine Self, fully Awake, Recognizes all conditions of body, mind, and world as only modifications of Itself. In Moksha-Bhava Samadhi, the Radiance of that Divine Consciousness in Sahaj Samadhi Pervades and Outshines all phenomena so powerfully that the Awakened being ceases, temporarily, even to notice any phenomena at all. Divine Translation is final and conclusive Moksha-Bhava Samadhi, coinciding with the death of the human individual, in which the Awakened being is so Perfectly Translated into the Divine Self-Condition that future embodiment in the conditional worlds ceases to be necessary.

In the Way of the Heart, Sri Da Avabhasa Calls practitioners to transcend the first six stages of life rather than to fulfill them. This is made possible by the Grace of His unique Revelation of the Way of the Heart and by the Heart-Blessing of His Divine Transmission to His devotees practicing in the context of every stage of life. From His "Point of View" (of the seventh, or Divinely Awakened, stage of life), He addresses each of the first six stages of life as a stage of (generally) necessary psycho-physical development, with which we are chronically associated in an erroneous or egoically limited fashion.

The Way of the Heart is not strictly a passage through each of the first six stages of life, leading at the end to Perfect Divine Self-Realization and the great spontaneous Yoga of Divine Enlightenment that characterizes the seventh stage of life. Rather, the Way of the Heart is inherently a seventh stage practice. It is a Way of life founded from the beginning and in every moment in the inherently Free disposition, or seventh stage attitude, of total psycho-physical Communion with the Spiritual, Transcendental, and Divine Self-Condition, Which Is the Heart Itself. Thus, the Way of the Heart takes place in the context of the first six stages of life, but in every moment the devotee, practicing the Way of the Heart, effectively transcends the presumptions, motivations, and phenomena of conditional experience and conditional knowledge associated with those lesser or egoic stages of life.

The Secret of the Way of the Heart in every stage of life is devotional Communion with, or feeling-Contemplation of, the bodily (human) Form, Spiritual (and Always Blessing) Presence, and Very (and Inherently Perfect) State of Sri Da Avabhasa. By this Divine Means His devotee allows himself or herself to abide under all circumstances in Love-Blissful Unity with the Divine Person, the Heart, Whom he or she "Locates" in, as, and through Sri Da Avabhasa Himself as Adept Heart-Teacher and True Heart-Master. Heart-Master Da Writes in *The Dawn Horse Testament*:

In Truth, The Way Of The Heart Begins At birth and progresses Through (or Otherwise Directly Beyond) Each Of The Seven Stages Of Life, Until Divine Translation.

The Heart Is Mine. The Heart Is The Domain Of All My Work. The Heart Is Always In God, but Reaction To the conditions Associated With Apparent birth into the Cosmic planes Produces The Apparent conditional Destiny Of Retarded Growth and All The Suffering Of self-Contraction. Therefore, This self-Contracting Reaction To conditional or phenomenal states Must Be Transcended In The Context (or Otherwise In The Effective Transcendence) Of Every Stage Of Life. The Heart Must Awaken At (or In Relation To) Every Stage Of Life, and the individual being Must Grow To Be Attracted and Distracted By The Forms Of God, and Thus To Feel Beyond The Bond Of conditional events (or all that limits and Retards the conditionally Manifested being In God), and, Ultimately, To Feel Beyond (and Perfectly Prior To) all that is Not The Realization Of Divine Being Itself. (pp. 186-87)

Sri Da Avabhasa (The "Bright")
Sri Love-Anandashram, September 1991

"I Reveal
The Divine Person,
Who Is The Heart Itself"

A Brief Biography of
the Divine World-Teacher,
Da Avabhasa (The "Bright")

by Saniel Bonder

In his book *The Perennial Philosophy* (1945), Aldous Huxley, the English novelist and popularizer of Eastern and Western mysticism, spoke of the process whereby Divine Men and Women appear among us to Enlighten others:

The Logos [Divine Spirit-Word] passes out of eternity into time for no other purpose than to assist the beings, whose bodily form he takes, to pass out of time into eternity. If the Avatar's appearance upon the stage of history is enormously important, this is due to the fact that by his teaching he points out, and by his being a channel of grace and divine power he actually is, the means by which human beings may transcend the limitations of history. . . .

That men and women may be thus instructed and helped, the Godhead assumes the form of an ordinary human being, who has to earn deliverance and enlightenment in the way that is prescribed by the divine Nature of things—namely, by charity, by a total dying to self and a total, one-pointed awareness. Thus enlightened, the Avatar can reveal the way of enlightenment to others and help them actually to become what they already potentially are.[1]

---

1. Aldous Huxley, *The Perennial Philosophy* (New York: Harper & Row, 1970), pp. 51, 56.

A few short years before the publication of Aldous Huxley's book, just such a being had Appeared in the Western world.

Da Avabhasa was born as Franklin Albert Jones on November 3, 1939, on Long Island, New York, into an ordinary middle-class American family. For the first two years after His Birth, He continued to abide in the State of Infinite Divine Freedom and Joy that He knew prior to His physical Lifetime. Although aware of people and events around Him, He had only the barest association with the embodied state.

In the following extraordinary account, He describes the Purpose of His Birth and the mechanisms by which He "acquired" the body-mind at the age of two:

DA AVABHASA: For approximately the first two years after My Birth, I . . . allowed the gross vehicle to be gradually prepared for Me. Then, at approximately two years of age, I Spiritually descended to the region of the heart and thus established My basic association with . . . My manifested personality. . . .

This Spiritual descent into the gross body to the level of the heart occurred, when I was approximately two years old, on the basis of a sympathy or heart-response to those who were around Me at the moment. It was through this sympathetic response that I acquired the Vehicle of this body-mind.

Because I was Born to make this Submission, the decision to acquire the gross body-mind did not occur when I was two years old. The Vehicle of this body-mind had become sufficiently prepared at that point, but I had consciously decided to do this Work before I Incarnated. The descent was for the sake of the total world and all beings. I had Consciously decided to take a birth in the West. My Intention before this Birth was to take this Birth and to do My Work by complete Submission to the ordinary Western circumstance. (February 5, 1989)

No one around Da Avabhasa in His childhood sensed His Divine Nature and Destiny, so He grew up in many ways an ordinary American boy and youth of the mid-twentieth century. But He was always aware of the Spiritual process churning in His body and mind—though He could not give it a name, or predict its ultimate result. This process often produced precocious psychic, mystical, and Yogic phenomena of a sublime (and sometimes an extremely powerful and disorienting) kind.

By His late teenage years, His original Awareness had receded into unconscious latency. At that point (while in His first year at Columbia College in New York City), He determined to do whatever was necessary to regain the Divine Freedom and Happiness He had felt during His earliest years. He devoted His next thirteen years to this quest.

His odyssey of Divine Re-Awakening was a totally spontaneous and direct exploration of every aspect of Reality, both the apparently sacred and the apparently profane. He did not know where He would find Truth and God, and He refused to be limited by the conventional sanctions of people and doctrines that, to Him, were obviously bereft of love, wisdom, and happiness.

Eventually He became an exemplary Devotee of several Spiritual Masters, including Swami Rudrananda (or "Rudi"), Swami Muktananda, and Swami Nityananda,[2] in a great Hindu lineage of extraordinary Adepts. But His own Impulse to permanently regain unqualified Divine Freedom moved His own practice and Realization beyond that which was Transmitted by each of His human Teachers. Eventually, with the Blessings of Swami Nityananda, Da Avabhasa became for a time a devotee of the Divine Goddess, the infinite Source-Light or Radiant Energy appearing to Him in an archetypal female Form.[3] He enjoyed a paradoxical relationship to the Goddess as a concrete, living Personality. Such worship of the Goddess as Supreme Guru is the foundation and Spiritual Source of His Teachers' lineage, but at last Da Avabhasa's inherent

2. Da Avabhasa's first Spiritual Teacher was Swami Rudrananda (1928-1973), or Albert Rudolph, known as "Rudi", who was His Teacher from 1964 to 1968, in New York City. Rudi helped Da Avabhasa prepare the foundation for the advanced and the ultimate phases of His Spiritual life. Rudi's own Teachers included the Indonesian Pak Subuh (from whom Rudi learned a basic exercise of Spiritual receptivity), Swami Muktananda Paramahansa (with whom Rudi spent many years), and Swami Nityananda (the Indian Swami who was also Swami Muktananda's Spiritual Teacher, and who was Rudi's primary Guru).

The second Teacher in Da Avabhasa's Lineage of Blessing was Swami Muktananda (1908-1982), an Adept of Kundalini Yoga who served Heart-Master Da as Spiritual Teacher during the period from 1968 to 1970.

Swami Nityananda (d.1961), a great Yogi of South India, was Da Avabhasa's third Spiritual Teacher in His Lineage of Blessing. Although Heart-Master Da Love-Ananda did not meet Swami Nityananda in the flesh, He enjoyed his direct Spiritual Influence from the subtle plane, and He acknowledges Swami Nityananda as a direct and principal Source of Spiritual Instruction during His years with Swami Muktananda.

3. The Divine in Its active aspect, as the Living Divine Presence and Personality, may assume various female archetypes—the "Goddess" or "Mother Shakti" in the East, the "Virgin Mary" among Christians. Da Avabhasa first related to Her as the Virgin Mary, later as the Universal Goddess-Power. See *The Divine Emergence of The World-Teacher*, by Saniel Bonder, as well as Da Avabhasa's Spiritual autobiography, *The Knee of Listening*, for detailed accounts of this late period of Da Avabhasa's Sadhana before His Divine Re-Awakening.

Freedom Drew Him even beyond the Spiritual Blessings of the Goddess Herself, such that She ceased to function as His Guru and became, instead, His eternal Consort and Companion.

On the day following that Event, September 10, 1970, while Da Avabhasa was meditating in a small temple on the grounds of the Vedanta Society in Los Angeles, He Re-Awakened to immutable Oneness with the Consciousness, Happiness, and Love that is the Source and Substance of everyone and everything. He describes this State in His Spiritual autobiography, Written in the following year:

> . . . I remain in the unqualified state. There is a constant sensation of fullness permeating and surrounding all experiences, realms, and bodies. It is my own fullness, which is radically non-separate and includes all things. I am the form of space itself, in which all bodies, realms, and experiences occur. It is consciousness itself, which reality is your actual nature (or ultimate, and inherently perfect, Condition) now and now and now. (The Knee of Listening)

After that Great Event in the Vedanta Temple, Da Avabhasa became psychically aware of the body-minds of countless other persons and discovered that He was spontaneously "meditating" them. In time some of those individuals became associated with Him as His first "students" or "disciples". Finally, in April 1972, Da Avabhasa's formal Teaching Work was inaugurated when He opened a storefront Ashram in Los Angeles.

In His book Love of the Two-Armed Form (published in 1978), Da Avabhasa explained His method of Teaching in those years:

> The method of my Teaching Work with devotees is not common, although there are many traditional or ancient precedents for it. It is not merely a subjective, internal, or even verbal activity, but a matter of intense, full, and total consideration of any specific area of experience, in living confrontation with others, until the obvious and Lawful and Divine form and practice of it becomes both clear and necessary.
>
> . . . [Such "considerations"] always involved a period in which individuals were permitted to live through the whole matter and to be tested to the point of change.
>
> . . . Only a "consideration" entered as such a concrete discipline can proceed all the way to its true end, which is right adaptation and freedom, or natural transcendence, relative to its functional subject. (pp. 1-2)

Whatever outward activities Da Avabhasa generated in His Teaching theatre (and they ranged from the most worldly, even apparently self-indulgent, to the most mystical and even miraculous), He was always exposing the suffering inherent in the constant activity of self-contraction, which creates the sense of a separate, un-Happy self. He likened the activity of self-contraction to the chronic, painful clenching of a fist, but at every level of body, mind, and heart. And He patiently demonstrated that those who wish to understand and transcend the activity of self-contraction and thereby open up to the All-Pervading Life-Power of Reality must submit to an all-encompassing discipline.

Even in the midst of "consideration" and Teaching theatre, Da Avabhasa often reminded His devotees that He could not continue indefinitely to engage a method of Teaching that required Him to take on the human likeness of His devotees— that is, to conduct Himself among them in a sympathetic, brotherly way, often adopting their habits of speech and action, in order to allow them to become sympathetically Attracted to Him. In early 1978 He warned that at some point it would become impossible for Him to "hold on to the body-mind" and forestall "release into Inherently Perfect Energy". At last, that moment arrived in the pre-dawn darkness of January 11, 1986, at His Hermitage Ashram in Fiji. His devotees' failure to transcend the mind and habits of egoity and to become God-Realizing practitioners of His Way of the Heart had brought Him to the point of despair. In a sudden crisis of anguish, He entered into an extraordinary death-like Yogic state.

When He returned to bodily awareness some moments later, Da Avabhasa had spontaneously and completely relinquished the Impulse to Identify with others in order to reflect their egoity to them. The necessity and the ability to Teach in that unique manner had simply dissolved.

And, with that dissolution of His persona as Teacher, Da Avabhasa had fully "Emerged" as the Divine Self in bodily (human) Form. The change marked such an immense Spiritual descent and intensification that He later said of it, "In a sense that Event was My Birth Day." He has indicated that this Event, the initiation of His Divine Emergence, marks an even greater moment than His Re-Awakening in September 1970.

It was at this time that "Da Free John" (as He was then known) took the Name "Da Love-Ananda Hridayam". "Love-Ananda", a Name that had been Given to Him in 1969 by Swami Muktananda, means "Inherent Love-Bliss", and "Hridayam" means "the Heart". His principal Name, "Da", meaning "the One Who Gives", had been Revealed to Him some years earlier in vision and by other Spiritual means. Thus, the Name "Da Love-Ananda Hridayam" indicates that He is the Divine Giver of the Inherent Love-Bliss that is the Heart Itself.

Five years later, on April 30, 1991, this Great Adept Revealed a new Name—"Da Avabhasa (The 'Bright')"—in response to His devotees' confessed acknowledgements of His Radiant, bodily Revelation of God.

"Avabhasa", in Sanskrit, has a rich range of associations. As a noun it means "brightness", "appearance", "manifestation", "splendor", "lustre", "light", "knowledge". As a verb it may be interpreted as "shining toward", "shining down", "showing oneself". The Name "Da Avabhasa", then, praises the Mystery of Da, the Divine Being, "Brightly" Appearing as Man. It points to His Divine Emergence and the ever-growing Radiance of His bodily (human) Form that is apparent to all who have been Graced to see Him, particularly since the Great Event of 1986.

The Name "Da Avabhasa" also points to His role as Sat-Guru—meaning One who brings the light of Truth into the darkness of the human world.

The "Bright", as Da Avabhasa tells us in *The Knee of Listening,* was, in fact, His own earliest description of the sublime Condition He enjoyed at Birth. He speaks of this Condition as "an incredible sense of joy, light, and freedom". He was, He says, "a radiant form, a source of energy, bliss, and light. . . . the power of Reality, a direct enjoyment and communication. . . . the Heart who lightens the mind and all things." Even His entire life, as He once said, has been "an adventure and unfolding in the 'Bright'", the Radiance, Bliss, and Love of the God-State.

Da Avabhasa is not merely an extraordinary Teacher. He is not merely a man of uncommonly profound Spiritual experience who has managed to put together a remarkably comprehensive and insightful Teaching, and who can transmit vivid Spiritual experiences. He is, rather, a Realizer and Transmitter of the Source of all Being. This is what His devotees mean when we refer to Him as "Divine World-Teacher". The phrase "World-Teacher" comes from Sanskrit terms meaning "One Who Liberates everything that moves"—that is, all things and beings. Da Avabhasa's Wisdom-Teaching is a complete Revelation of the ultimate Wisdom relative to every aspect of existence and every stage of our possible growth and Realization. And His Grace is universally active and universally available.

All this has been confirmed to me through the vision Given in His physical Company—a whole bodily intuition that I have felt and seen face to face with Him. It is a deep and life-changing Revelation that has also been enjoyed by all kinds of ordinary people from all over the world, a vision of Him in physical Form that also Reveals the Divine Self and Love-Bliss of our very Being.

Da Avabhasa has come into this world to restore Wisdom and the Way of Truth, and to Bless all beings toward Divine Freedom, Happiness, Enlightenment, and Love. He excludes absolutely no one from His Blessing and His Help. As the Divine Self of all, He continuously Gives His Benediction to everyone, everywhere.

To learn more about this sacred opportunity, please see the invitation on the following pages.

Sri Da Avabhasa (The "Bright")
Sri Love-Anandashram, September 1991

"A Unique Advantage to Mankind"

An Invitation
to a Direct Relationship
with Da Avabhasa

by Carolyn Lee

The human Spiritual Master is an agent to the advantage of those in like form. When one enters into right relationship with a Spiritual Master, changes happen in the literal physics of one's existence. It is not just a matter of ideas. I am talking about transformations at the level of energy, at the level of the higher light of physics, at the level of mind beyond the physical limitations that people now presume, at the level of the absolute Speed of ultimate Light. The transforming process is enacted in devotees, duplicated in them in and through that Living Company. It is not a matter of conceptual symbolisms or emotional attachment to some extraordinary person. It is real physics. And it is to the advantage of people when someone among them has gone through the whole cycle of Transformation, because they can then make use of the Offering of that Process, that Company.

DA AVABHASA
*Scientific Proof of the Existence of God
Will Soon Be Announced by the White House!*

If you feel a heart-response to what you have read in this book, or if you simply feel moved to find out more about Da Avabhasa and the Way of the Heart, we invite you to explore the Sacred Literature of Da Avabhasa.

To focus your exploration we wish to draw your attention here to three of our publications by and about Da Avabhasa that will be especially useful introductions or overviews of the Way of the Heart. (More complete descriptions of these publications can be found on pages 408-19.)

Most important for your ongoing study are Da Avabhasa's "Source-Texts" or Scriptures, conclusively summarizing His Word of Instruction. We recommend that you begin with *The Love-Ananda Gita (The Wisdom-Song Of Non-Separateness)*, The Simple Revelation-Book Of The Divine World-Teacher and True Heart-Master, Da Avabhasa (The "Bright").

The Divine Emergence of the World-Teacher: The Realization, the Revelation, and the Revealing Ordeal of Da Avabhasa is a full-length "Biographical Celebration" of Da Avabhasa's Life and Work to date, by Saniel Bonder, a longtime practitioner of the Way of the Heart.

Divine Distraction: A Guide to the Guru-Devotee Relationship, the Supreme Means of God-Realization, as Fully Revealed for the First Time by the Divine World-Teacher and True Heart-Master, Da Avabhasa (The "Bright") is an introduction to the Guru-devotee relationship. It was written by James Steinberg, another longtime devotee of Da Avabhasa.

There are thousands of people all over the world today reading Da Avabhasa's books, and some people have been reading them for many years. But reading, while necessary and helpful, will only take you so far on its own. Once you acknowledge the greatness—the Truth—of Da Avabhasa's Wisdom-Revelation, it begins to require something of you.

Sri Da Avabhasa's literature is a Divine Gift, not to be treated casually. "Such Transmissions of Teaching do not occur arbitrarily," as Da Avabhasa says. "They are part of the higher scale of activity in the cosmos." Thus, it is only when you begin to participate in the practice and the sacred culture Da Avabhasa Offers that you really find out what it is about—Spiritual transformation and God-Realization never happened in an armchair! Therefore, in addition to reading, we urge you to attend the lectures, seminars, courses, and other events that our missionary institution, the Eleutherian Mission, makes available to the public in your area. At these events you will have the opportunity to see videotapes of Da Avabhasa and to meet practitioners of the Way of the Heart who can speak to you about His Wisdom and tell you Leelas (stories) of their own relationship with Him. You can also participate in a Way of the Heart Study Group in your area, joining others for a monthly evening meeting of recitations of Sri Da Avabhasa's Word and listening to or viewing audio-visual presentations about Da Avabhasa and the Way of the Heart.

All of this can lead to a deepening intuition of Who He Is and a deepening impulse to practice the Way of the Heart as His devotee.

Carol Mason, who lives in northern California, describes the process that brought her to the point of entering into a formal relationship with Da Avabhasa:

For over thirty years I sought Enlightenment. But despite profound Zen realizations and unusual Kundalini experiences, despite my teachers' acknowledgements of my attainment and good understanding, I realized that fundamentally I had not changed. I saw the failure of my search, and I despaired.

Then I read The Knee of Listening, *Da Avabhasa's Spiritual autobiography, and I began to have dreams of Him. In the dreams, He Instructed me, He laughed, He gave Talks at which many people gathered. He sat silently and escorted me to subtle realms. I was able to feel Him as a Spiritual Friend and Teacher during the day. I found through study that His Wisdom-Teaching had the power of mantra. The Truth of it became alive in me.*

Several months after I read The Knee of Listening *I saw a videotape of Da Avabhasa made during His Teaching years. At first sighting I acknowledged Him to be the True Master of Liberation, the One Whom all the world's religions await. I bowed down. I celebrated Him with thoughts of praise and soon He was all I thought about, all I wanted to talk about. For an entire year He was always available to me, but suddenly, one day, I no longer experienced Him, no longer felt His Influence or received His Instruction. Then one final time I heard His Voice: "Now, what will you do?"*

Realizing I must now approach Him in the traditional devotional manner, I soon became a student-novice, taking on the studies, disciplines, and meditation practices required of a novice, and consciously cultivating my devotional relationship with my Heart-Teacher. Even during this rudimentary stage of practice, Da Avabhasa has, on occasion, Blessed me with Heart-Bliss, with the purification of my karmic tendencies, and with a deepening sense of His Divine Form. I am ever grateful.

You should know that all of this has taken place without Carol's ever meeting Da Avabhasa in the flesh. The same is true for thousands of others around the world who, like Carol, are being drawn spontaneously into a sacred relationship with Da Avabhasa and are taking steps to honor that relationship in a formal way.

When you are clear in your intention to become a practitioner of the Way of the Heart, you may apply to become a **student-novice**. Student-novices take on in rudimentary form the range of devotional practices and disciplines that Da Avabhasa Offers to Free Daist practitioners. If, on the other hand, you feel you need to approach student-novice practice more gradually, you may become a **student** or a **tithing member** of Da Avabhasa International (the gathering of those who are formally preparing to practice the Way of the Heart). Students and tithing members engage a specific practice based on study and service, as I will describe in a moment. They pay a fixed fee for the educational and other services of Da Avabhasa International and, in addition, tithing members contribute 10% of their gross monthly income (or more, if they choose) in support of the Free Daist Communion.

If you are moved by the importance of Da Avabhasa's Work and would like to show your gratitude for His Presence in the world without becoming a practitioner of the Way of the Heart (at least for the time being), then you may wish to become a Friend of the Free Daist Communion. A Friend is essentially a patron, someone who accepts a level of responsibility for funding the missionary services of the Free Daist Communion and also for supporting the Treasures of Da Avabhasa's Work—principally His personal Circumstance and His Hermitage Ashram, in Fiji. All Friends contribute a minimum fixed fee each year. In addition, others tithe regularly, and some are able to offer major financial support. Friends also support the Dawn Horse Press and the missionary work of the Free Daist Communion by purchasing the new books published by or about Sri Da Avabhasa. Being a Friend is a very honorable way of associating with Da Avabhasa. At the same time, Friends are always invited and encouraged to take the further step of preparing to become a formal practitioner of the Way of the Heart.

For students, tithing members, and student-novices, who have already decided to practice the Way of the Heart, an intensive study of Da Avabhasa's Instruction is essential at the beginning of practice. As you do this day by day, in a guided way (using the study courses provided), you will be astonished at how your understanding of yourself and your response to Da Avabhasa will deepen and grow. I began my formal association with the practice as a correspondent living hundreds of miles from the closest gathering of devotees, and so study was my lifeline and the most exciting part of my life. Guided study, more than anything else, clarified

Students and tithing members engage a specific practice
based on study and service

Practitioners of the Free Daist Communion gathering at
the Mountain Of Attention Sanctuary

my intention to practice, instructed me in every aspect of my life, and placed my relationship to Da Avabhasa on a firm foundation.

Study, among other things, is a discipline of attention. Service is a more bodily-based discipline, but it is no different in principle. It is a way of actively bringing your energy and attention to Da Avabhasa. The discipline of service within the sphere of an Adept's Blessing is not about making yourself useful. It is a sacred matter. Traditionally the discipline of service was called "Karma Yoga", and it was understood to encompass the whole of one's life. Karma Yoga was the basic practice given to beginners, and especially to householders who had many obligations in the world. It was the great practice of devoting one's actions to God, of contemplating the Divine in the midst of all activity.

As a student or a tithing member, you will be invited to spend at least a few hours each week in some form of direct service to Da Avabhasa or the community of practitioners of the Way of the Heart. You may find yourself cleaning your local community bookstore or helping with the missionary work by putting up posters for our public events. If you have special skills in any area, we of Da Avabhasa International will help you find ways to use those skills to the maximum.

Whatever your form of service at any time, whether it is something you like doing or something you would not personally choose, the secret is to live it as a self-transcending gesture of devotion to Da Avabhasa. I recall with some amusement my first encounter with the discipline of service and all the resistance I felt. It was a wintry weekend early in 1986. I had made the journey to London from Ireland at considerable expense just to spend the weekend with devotees there. No sooner had I arrived from the airport than I found myself with a paint-scraper in one hand and sandpaper in the other. Everyone was busy around the clock renovating the newly-acquired missionary house associated with the London regional center. I still had on my professional clothes, I was developing a very uncomfortable sore throat, and I had been so tired before leaving Ireland that my friends there had begged me not to go.

Needless to say, I very nearly turned around and went back to the airport. But somehow I didn't. My dismay was so acute that it was interesting to me. I wanted to see what would happen if I actually stayed and participated. Would I die or develop bronchial pneumonia? And so I scraped, painted, cleaned, put up wallpaper with everyone else. For the first hour or two the only way I was able to stick at it was by concentrating with fierce intention on Da Avabhasa and remembering His Instruction about

... you will gradually adapt to further disciplines relative to meditation,
sacramental worship, exercise, diet and health, sexuality, child-rearing,
cooperative community, right use of money and energy, and other aspects
of daily living. . . . All of the disciplines simply support the primary
practice of Free Daism, which is Satsang (the "Company of Truth"),
or the cultivation of the relationship to Da Avabhasa.

Happiness ("You cannot <u>become</u> Happy, you can only <u>be</u> Happy"). This
was the most intense moment of practice I had ever been through, and it
bore fruit. As the evening wore on I ceased to be so concerned about
myself. There was a lot of laughter, and it did not seem to matter that I
hardly knew anyone when I walked in. By the time I emerged from the
plaster dust well after midnight, I was simply happy. I still had a sore
throat, but by the next morning it was almost gone. And I was not tired
anymore. I felt uncommonly alive, focused, and alert. All I could think
about was Da Avabhasa, how attractive He is, so attractive that I was
ready to transcend myself in response to Him and accomplish things I
would never have dreamed of attempting otherwise. Becoming a student-
novice is a crucial turning point, because it is the moment of committing
yourself unequivocally to Da Avabhasa in the eternal sacred bond of the
Guru-devotee relationship.

As a student-novice of Da Avabhasa International, and, later, as a formally acknowledged practitioner of the Free Daist Communion, you will
gradually adapt to further disciplines relative to meditation, sacramental

worship, exercise, diet and health, sexuality, child-rearing, cooperative community (including formal membership in the Free Daist Community Organization), right use of money and energy, and other aspects of daily living. These practices are necessary to develop bodily equanimity, free attention, and the capability for self-transcendence, without which nothing great can be Realized. But they are not an end in themselves. All of the disciplines simply support the primary practice of Free Daism, which is Satsang (the "Company of Truth"), or the cultivation of the relationship to Da Avabhasa. Devotees are Called to Remember Da Avabhasa at all times, not merely to think about Him, but to locate the feeling of Him, the feeling-sense of His Being that He Grants you when you sit in front of Him and regard His bodily (human) Form. While the great opportunity to come into Da Avabhasa's physical Company occurs only occasionally for most of His devotees, you can find the same feeling by His Grace in any moment of heart-felt resort to Him. Turning to His picture, Remembering His Image in the mind's eye, listening to recitations of His Word or Stories of His Work—all these and other means are potent aids to feeling-Contemplation of Him.

By reading in the tradition of Guru-devotion (which you will begin to do formally as a student-novice), by studying Da Avabhasa's own Wisdom-Teaching about the practice of feeling-Contemplation of Him, and especially by doing the practice of it according to His specific Instructions, you will discover why this form of sacred Remembrance is so potent, so revealing, and so Liberating. For the devotee, feeling-Contemplation becomes a literal life-support as basic as food and rest.

The best goad to practice is the possibility of coming into the physical Company of Sri Da Avabhasa. I was Graced to see Him bodily very soon after I committed myself to formal practice, and that sighting Revealed to me beyond any doubt that Da Avabhasa is Who He says He is, "The Realizer, The Revealer, and The Revelation Of The Divine Person". There is no greater Blessing than to come into the Company of His bodily (human) Form and feel His Regard face to face. To Contemplate the Divine Person, Compassionately Appearing in a human body, is an unfathomable, heart-breaking Mystery.

Whoever you are, wherever you live, whatever your apparent liabilities, this Grace could be yours in a relatively short period of time, if you fulfill the requirements of a student-novice and then rightly prepare yourself as a formally acknowledged practitioner of the Way of the Heart. The place you are most likely to see Da Avabhasa is Sri Love-Anandashram,

Da Avabhasa with
retreatants at Sri
Love-Anandashram

His Hermitage Sanctuary, in Fiji, and where He Offers retreats to qualified practitioners from all over the world.

Over the years Da Avabhasa has often pointed out in a vivid, humorous fashion that whoever is serious about practice in His Company is going to have to go through a fiery ordeal. The Way of the Heart is the Way of Grace, certainly, but it is not, as He has said, a "bliss-ride". This is how it has always been in the company of a genuine Adept, because there are Divine Laws involved in the Spiritual process, and the principal Law is the Law of sacrifice, the mutual sacrifice constantly enacted between the Guru and the devotee. The Guru Transmits the Divine Siddhi (or Power of Liberation), and the devotee renounces the egoic self, granting all feeling and attention, more and more profoundly, to the Guru.

This is an entire life-practice or Yoga, called by Sri Da Avabhasa "Ishta-Guru-Bhakti Yoga", the Way of devotion ("Bhakti") to one's "Ishta" or "Chosen" Guru, the Divine Beloved of one's heart. Because this Yoga is based on Attraction, or Distraction by the living Guru, it is possible for anyone who is so moved to practice it. It is a Divine Gift Given in response to the longing of the devotee. Great seriousness and great sacrifice are required, but in the midst of all of that there is the greatest imaginable joy. Ishta-Guru-Bhakti Yoga in its fullness is a life of Love, lived in Communion with the Divine in Person. Everyone, somewhere in the depths of his or her being, desires such a life.

For the devotee who gives himself or herself over fully to this great Guru Yoga in Sri Da Avabhasa's Company, growth in the Way of the

Heart is inevitable. And Sri Da Avabhasa has described in every detail the Spiritual, Transcendental, and Divine Awakenings that are the Graceful Gifts, over time, of Ishta-Guru-Bhakti Yoga. He has also established practicing orders—the Free Daist Lay Congregationist Order (or, simply, the Lay Congregationist Order), the Free Daist Lay Renunciate Order (or, simply, the Lay Renunciate Order), and the Naitauba (Free Daist) Order of Sannyasins (or, simply, the Free Renunciate Order)—the latter two of which have principal responsibilities in service to His Work, and all of which allow His devotees to intensify their devotional practice in the form and manner that is appropriate for them once they have basically developed their sacred practice.

When His devotee moves beyond the student-beginner stage (the first phase of formal practice in the Way of the Heart), he or she enters either the Lay Congregationist Order or the Lay Renunciate Order, depending on his or her demonstrated qualifications of practice.

The Lay Congregationist Order is a practical service order whose members perform the many supportive practical services necessary for the work of the institution, the culture, and the community of all Free Daists. "Lay congregationists" conform every aspect of their life and practice to the Wisdom and Blessings of Sri Da Avabhasa, but their practice is not as intensive, nor as intensely renunciate, an approach to Perfectly self-transcending God-Realization as the practice of "lay renunciates" or "free renunciates".

Any member of the Lay Congregationist Order who develops the required signs (at any point in his or her practice of the Way of the Heart) may be accepted into the Lay Renunciate Order.

The Lay Renunciate Order is a cultural service order composed of practitioners who are especially exemplary in their practice of devotion, service, self-discipline, and meditation. Members of the Lay Renunciate Order provide the inspirational and cultural leadership for the institution, the culture, and the community of Sri Da Avabhasa's devotees, and they also guide and participate in public missionary work. Their basic responsibility is to serve all practitioners of the Way of the Heart in their practice of Ishta-Guru-Bhakti Yoga and to attract others to a life of Guru-devotion. When they reach practicing stage three of the Way of the Heart (the first stage of full Spiritual Awakening), Sri Da Avabhasa has indicated that His "lay renunciates" will begin to function as His Instruments, or means by which His Divine Grace and Awakening Power are Magnified and Transmitted to other devotees and to all beings.

While members of the Lay Renunciate Order may be celibate practitioners, membership in the Lay Renunciate Order does not necessarily require celibacy, but only a truly renunciate and Yogic discipline of sexuality.

The Lay Renunciate Order is directly accountable to the senior practicing Order of the Way of the Heart, the Free Renunciate Order. The Free Renunciate Order is a retreat Order composed of devotees from the Lay Renunciate Order who have Awakened beyond the point of view of the body-mind to the Transcendental Position of Consciousness in the sixth stage of life, or to full Divine Self-Realization in the seventh stage of life.

Because of their extraordinary practice and Realization in the Company of Sri Da Avabhasa, "free renunciate" devotees are His principal human Instruments in the world. From among the seventh stage practitioners in the Free Renunciate Order, there will be selected after, and forever after, His human Lifetime, successive "Living Murtis", or Empowered Human Agents, who will serve the magnification of His Heart-Transmission to all beings universally and perpetually. "Murti" means "form", or "representational image". The "Living Murtis" of Sri Da Avabhasa (of which there will be only one in any then present-time) will not be Gurus in their own right. They will serve, rather, as a unique Living Link to Sri Da Avabhasa so that His Heart-Transmission will remain unbroken generation after generation.

Apart from its profound function to provide "Living Murtis" from among its membership, the Free Renunciate Order is the senior authority on all matters related to the culture of practice in the Way of the Heart and is completely essential to the perpetual continuation of authentic practice as Sri Da Avabhasa has Given it.

The members of the Free Renunciate Order generally reside at Sri Love-Anandashram. As in the Lay Renunciate Order, members of the Free Renunciate Order may be celibate or they may be sexually active in a truly renunciate and Yogic manner.

The original and principal members of the Free Renunciate Order are Sri Da Avabhasa Himself and the Da Avabhasa Gurukula Kanyadana Kumari Order, which consists of four women devotees who have for many years lived and served in Sri Da Avabhasa's intimate sphere and who have demonstrated the most exemplary practice of Ishta-Guru-Bhakti Yoga. Every practitioner who comes in contact with the Kanyas is deeply impressed by their radiant Happiness in the midst of all circumstances,

The Da Avabhasa Gurukula Kanyadana Kumari Order

and by their transformation as human beings. The Kanyas, who are presently practicing in the sixth stage of life, are a great sign of the Truth of Sri Da Avabhasa's Wisdom and the effectiveness of His Work.

The magnitude of the Gift Sri Da Avabhasa brings to humanity is being Revealed through the developing sacred culture of Free Daism. If you decide to participate in Da Avabhasa International and to proceed from there to become a formally acknowledged practitioner of the Way of the Heart, you will be collaborating in a unique experiment—the founding of a culture and a community whose sacred practice is always founded in direct enjoyment of the Happiness of the seventh stage of life, as Transmitted by a living, seventh stage Realizer, the Divine World-Teacher, Da Avabhasa.

How often has such a Being as Da Avabhasa Appeared? If such a One is here now, is there anything more worth doing than to enter into His Company? He is addressing you personally when He says:

SRI DA AVABHASA: Physical embodiment has the purpose of Enlightenment, the purpose of purification. . . . If you will receive My Teaching-Revelation, if you will "consider" it, if you will become responsive, then you become capable of making use of this lifetime for the purpose it inherently can serve. . . . You must submit the body-mind to the Great Purpose. . . . That is what I am Calling you to do. Accept the Dharma, the Law, inherent in your birth, the purpose that is inherent in your birth. Take up the Way of the Heart in My Company. (August 15, 1988)

If you are feeling the urge to move beyond your present level of human growth and are interested in what Da Avabhasa is Offering you, contact us at our Correspondence Department or at one of our regional centers (see the following page). We will be happy to send you a free brochure on the forms of participation available to you. We invite you to enter into this sacred relationship with Da Avabhasa, and be tempered and opened in God by His Grace. We look forward to hearing from you.

Correspondence Department
THE FREE DAIST COMMUNION
P.O. Box 3680
Clearlake, California 95422, USA

Phone: (707) 928-4936

The Regional Centers of the Free Daist Communion

UNITED STATES

NORTHERN CALIFORNIA
The Free Daist Communion
740 Adrian Way
San Rafael, CA 94903
(415) 492-0932

NORTHWEST USA
The Free Daist Communion
7214 Woodlawn Ave NE
Seattle, WA 98115
(206) 527-2751

SOUTHWEST USA
The Free Daist Communion
1043 Mesa Drive
Camarillo, CA 93010
(213) 391-8344
(805) 482-0854

NORTHEAST USA
The Free Daist Communion
28 West Central
Natick, MA 01760
(508) 650-0136
(508) 650-0424

SOUTHEAST USA
The Free Daist Communion
10301 South Glen Road
Potomac, MD 20875
(301) 983-0291

HAWAII
The Free Daist Communion
105 Kaholalele Road
Kapaa, HI 96746-9304
(808) 822-3386
(808) 822-0216

AUSTRALIA
The Free Daist Communion
173 Victoria Parade
Fitzroy, Victoria 3065
Australia
3-417-7069

EASTERN CANADA
The Free Daist Communion
108 Katimavik Road
Val-des-Monts, Quebec J0X 2R0
Canada
(819) 671-4397

THE NETHERLANDS
Da Avabhasa Ashram
Annendaalderweg 10
6105 AT Maria Hoop
The Netherlands
04743-1281
04743-1872

NEW ZEALAND
The Free Daist Communion
CPO Box 3185
21 High Street
Auckland
New Zealand
(09) 814-9272
(09) 390-0032

THE UNITED KINGDOM AND IRELAND
Da Avabhasa Ashram
Tasburgh Hall
Lower Tasburgh
Norwich NR15-ILT
England
0508-470-574
081-341-9329 (London Centre)

FURTHER NOTES TO THE READER

An Invitation to Responsibility

The Way of the Heart that Sri Da Avabhasa has Revealed is an invitation to everyone to assume real responsibility for his or her life. As Sri Da Avabhasa has Said in *The Dawn Horse Testament*, "If any one Is Interested In The Realization Of The Heart, Let him or her First Submit (Formally, and By Heart) To Me, and (Thereby) Commence The Ordeal Of self-Observation, self-Understanding, and self-Transcendence." Therefore, participation in the Way of the Heart requires a real struggle with oneself, and not at all a struggle with Sri Da Avabhasa, or with others.

All who study the Way of the Heart or take up its practice should remember that they are responding to a Call to become responsible for themselves. They should understand that they, not Sri Da Avabhasa or others, are responsible for any decision they may make or action they take in the course of their lives of study or practice. This has always been true, and it is true whatever the individual's involvement in the Way of the Heart, be it as one who studies Da Avabhasa's Wisdom-Teaching, or as a formal Friend of the Free Daist Communion, or as a participant in Da Avabhasa International, or as a formally acknowledged member of the Free Daist Communion.

Honoring and Protecting the Sacred Word through Perpetual Copyright

Since ancient times, practitioners of true religion and Spirituality have valued, above all, time spent in the Company of the Sat-Guru, or one who has Realized God, Truth, or Reality, and who Serves that same Realization in others. Such practitioners understand that the Sat-Guru literally Transmits his or her (Realized) State to every one (and every thing) with which he or she comes in contact. Through this Transmission, objects, environments, and rightly prepared individuals with which the Sat-Guru has contact can become Empowered, or Imbued with the Sat-Guru's Transforming Power. It is by this process of Empowerment that things and beings are made truly and literally sacred, and things so sanctified thereafter function as a Source of the Sat-Guru's Blessing for all who understand how to make right and sacred use of them.

The Sat-Guru and all that he Empowers are, therefore, truly Sacred Treasures, for they help draw the practitioner more quickly into the Realization of Perfect Identity with the Divine Self. Cultures of true Wisdom have always understood that such Sacred Treasures are precious (and fragile) Gifts to humanity, and that they should be honored, protected, and reserved for right sacred use. Indeed, the word "sacred" means "set apart", and thus protected, from the secular world. Sri Da Avabhasa is a Sat-Guru of the Most Perfect degree. He has Conformed His body-mind completely to the Divine Self, and He is thus a most Potent Source of Blessing-Transmission of God, Truth, or Reality. He has for many years Empowered, or made sacred, special places and things, and these now Serve as His Divine Agents, or as literal expressions and extensions of His Blessing-Transmission. Among these Empowered Sacred Treasures is His Wisdom-

403

Teaching, which is Full of His Transforming Power. This Blessed and Blessing Wisdom-Teaching has Mantric Force, or the literal Power to Serve God-Realization in those who are Graced to receive it.

Therefore, Sri Da Avabhasa's Wisdom-Teaching must be perpetually honored and protected, "set apart" from all possible interference and wrong use. The Free Daist Communion, which is the fellowship of devotees of Sri Da Avabhasa, is committed to the perpetual preservation and right honoring of the sacred Wisdom-Teaching of the Way of the Heart. But it is also true that in order to fully accomplish this we must find support in the world-society in which we live and from the laws under which we live. Thus, we call for a world-society and for laws that acknowledge the Sacred, and that permanently protect It from insensitive, secular interference and wrong use of any kind. We call for, among other things, a system of law that acknowledges that the Wisdom-Teaching of the Way of the Heart, in all Its forms, is, because of Its sacred nature, protected by perpetual copyright.

We invite others who respect the Sacred to join with us in this call and in working toward its realization. And, even in the meantime, we claim that all copyrights to the Wisdom-Teaching of Sri Da Avabhasa and the other sacred literature and recordings of the Way of the Heart are of perpetual duration.

We make this claim on behalf of Sri Love-Anandashram (Naitauba) Pty Ltd, which, acting as trustee of the Sri Love-Anandashram (Naitauba) Trust, is the holder of all such copyrights.

Da Avabhasa and the Sacred Treasures of Free Daism

Those who Realize God bring great Blessing and Divine Possibility for the world. As Free Adepts, they Accomplish universal Blessing Work that benefits everything and everyone. Such Realizers also Work very specifically and intentionally with individuals who approach them as their devotees, and with those places where they reside, and to which they Direct their specific Regard for the sake of perpetual Spiritual Empowerment. This was understood in traditional Spiritual cultures, and those cultures therefore found ways to honor Realizers, to provide circumstances for them where they were free to do their Divine Work without obstruction or interference.

Those who value Sri Da Avabhasa's Realization and Service have always endeavored to appropriately honor Him in this traditional way, to provide a circumstance where He is completely Free to Do His Divine Work. Since 1983, Sri Da Avabhasa has resided principally on the Island of Naitauba, Fiji, also known as Sri Love-Anandashram. This island has been set aside by Free Daists worldwide as a Place for Sri Da Avabhasa to Do His universal Blessing Work for the sake of everyone and His specific Work with those who pilgrimage to Sri Love-Anandashram to receive the special Blessing of coming into His physical Company.

Sri Da Avabhasa is a legal renunciate. He owns nothing and He has no secular or religious institutional function. He Functions only in Freedom. He, and the other members of the Naitauba (Free Daist) Order of Sannyasins, the senior renunciate order of Free Daism, are provided for by the Sri Love-Anandashram (Naitauba) Trust, which also provides for Sri Love-Anandashram altogether and ensures the permanent integrity of Sri Da Avabhasa's Wisdom-Teaching, both in its archival and in its published forms. This Trust, which functions only in Fiji, exists exclusively to provide for these Sacred Treasures of Free Daism.

Outside Fiji, the institution which has developed in response to Sri Da Avabhasa's Wisdom-Teaching and universal Blessing is known as "The Free Daist Communion". The Free Daist Communion is active worldwide in making Da Avabhasa's Wisdom-Teaching available to all, in offering guidance to all who are moved to respond to His Offering, and in providing for the other Sacred Treasures of Free Daism, including the Mountain Of Attention Sanctuary (in California) and Tumomama Sanctuary (in Hawaii). In addition to the central corporate entity of the Free Daist Communion, which is based in California, there are numerous regional entities which serve congregations of Sri Da Avabhasa's devotees in various places throughout the world.

Free Daists worldwide have also established numerous community organizations, through which they provide for many of their common and cooperative community needs, including needs relating to housing, food, businesses, medical care, schools, and death and dying. By attending to these and all other ordinary human concerns and affairs via self-transcending cooperation and mutual effort, Sri Da Avabhasa's devotees constantly free their energy and attention, both personally and collectively, for practice of the Way of the Heart and for service to Sri Da Avabhasa, to Sri Love-Anandashram, to the other Sacred Treasures of Free Daism, and to the Free Daist Communion.

All of the organizations that have evolved in response to Sri Da Avabhasa and His Offering are legally separate from one another, and each has its own purpose and function. He neither directs, nor bears responsibility for, the activities of these organizations. Again, He Functions only in Freedom. These organizations represent the collective intention of Free Daists worldwide not only to provide for the Sacred Treasures of Free Daism, but also to make Da Avabhasa's Offering of the Way of the Heart universally available to all.

An Invitation to Support the Way of the Heart

Just as association with a God-Realized Adept is the best kind of Company a man or woman can keep, so the practice of supporting the Work of such an Adept is the most auspicious form of financial giving.

A true Adept is a Free Renunciate and a Source of continuous Divine Grace. Therefore, he or she owns nothing, and everything given to support his or her Work is returned, both to the giver and to all beings, in many Blessings that are full of the Adept's healing, transforming, and Liberating Grace. At the same time, all tangible gifts of support help secure and nurture the Adept's Work in necessary and practical ways, thus benefiting the whole world.

All of this is immeasurably true for those who help provide financial gifts to the Work of the Divine World-Teacher and True Heart-Master, Da Avabhasa (The "Bright"). We therefore happily extend to you an invitation to serve the Way of the Heart through your financial support.

You may make a financial contribution in support of the Work of Da Avabhasa at any time. You may also, if you choose, request that your contribution be used for one or more specific purposes of Free Daism. For example, you may be moved to help support and develop Sri Love-Anandashram, Da Avabhasa's principal Hermitage Ashram and Empowered Retreat Sanctuary in Fiji, and the circumstance provided there for Da Avabhasa and the other members of the Free Renunciate Order (all of whom are renunciates, owning nothing).

You may make a contribution for this specific purpose directly to the Sri Love-Anandashram (Naitauba) Trust, the charitable trust that is responsible for Sri Love-Anandashram. To make such a contribution, simply mail your check to the Sri Love-Anandashram (Naitauba) Trust, P.O. Box 4744, Samabula, Fiji.

If you would like to make such a contribution and you are a U.S. taxpayer, we recommend that you make your contribution to the Free Daist Communion, so as to secure a tax-deduction for your contribution under U.S. tax laws. To do this, mail your contribution to the Advocacy Department of the Free Daist Communion, P.O. Box 3680, Clearlake, California 95422, and indicate that you would like it to be used in support of Sri Love-Anandashram.

You may also request that your contribution, or a part of it, be used for one or more of the other purposes of Free Daism. For example, you may request that your contribution be used to help publish the sacred Literature of Da Avabhasa, or to support either of the other two Sanctuaries He has Empowered, or to maintain the Sacred Archives that preserve Da Avabhasa's recorded Talks and Writings, or to publish audio and video recordings of Da Avabhasa.

If you would like your contribution to benefit one or more of these specific purposes, please mail your contribution to the Advocacy Department of the Free Daist Communion at the above address, and indicate how you would like your gift to be used.

If you would like more information about these and other gifting options, or if you would like assistance in describing or making a contribution, please contact the Advocacy Department of the Free Daist Communion, either by writing to the address shown above or by telephoning 707-928-4096 (FAX 707-928-4062).

Deferred Giving

We also invite you to consider making a deferred gift in support of the Work of Da Avabhasa. Many have found that through deferred giving they can make a far more significant gesture of support than they would otherwise be able to make. Many have also found that by making a deferred gift they are able to realize substantial tax advantages.

There are numerous ways to make a deferred gift, including making a gift in your Will, or in your life insurance, or in a charitable trust.

If you would like to make a gift in your Will in support of Sri Love-Anandashram, simply include in your Will the statement "I give the Sri Love-Anandashram (Naitauba) Trust, an Australian charitable trust, P.O. Box 4744, Samabula, Fiji, _____" [inserting in the blank the amount or description of your contribution].

If you would like to make a gift in your Will to benefit other purposes of Free Daism, simply include in your Will the statement "I give the Free Daist Communion, a California nonprofit corporation, 12040 Seigler Road North, Middletown, California 95461, _____" [inserting in the blank the amount or description of your contribution]. You may, if you choose, also describe in your

Will the specific Free Daist purpose or purposes you would like your gift to support. If you are a U.S. taxpayer, gifts made in your Will to the Free Daist Communion will be free of estate taxes and will also reduce any estate taxes payable on the remainder of your estate.

To make a gift in your life insurance, simply name as the beneficiary (or one of the beneficiaries) of your life insurance policy the Free Daist organization of your choice, according to the foregoing descriptions and addresses. If you are a U.S. taxpayer, you may receive significant tax benefits if you make a contribution to the Free Daist Communion through your life insurance.

We also invite you to consider establishing or participating in a charitable trust for the benefit of Free Daism. If you are a U.S. taxpayer, you may find that such a trust will provide you with immediate tax savings and assured income for life, while at the same time enabling you to provide for your family, for your other heirs, and for the Work of Da Avabhasa as well.

The Advocacy Department of the Free Daist Communion will be happy to provide you with further information about these and other deferred gifting options, and happy to provide you or your attorney with assistance in describing or making a deferred gift in support of the Work of Da Avabhasa.

The Sacred Literature
of Da Avabhasa
(The "Bright")

Heart-Master Da Love-Ananda provides a way in which Oneness may be experienced by anyone who is bold enough to follow his teachings. It is important to understand that his vision is neither Eastern nor Western, but it is the eternal spiritual pulse of the Great Wisdom which knows no cultural, temporal, or geographical locus; it represents the apex of awareness of our species.

Larry Dossey, M.D.
author, *Space, Time, and Medicine*
and *Beyond Illness*

The teachings of Heart-Master Da, embodied in an extraordinary collection of writings, provide an exquisite manual for transformation. . . . I feel at the most profound depth of my being that his work will be crucial to an evolution toward full-humanness.

Barbara Marx Hubbard
author, *The Evolutionary Journey*

Do you hunger for Spiritual Truth?

Do you long to know precisely why everything you seek, and everything you hold on to, never seems to give you lasting fulfillment?

Do you wish to see the whole process of Spiritual Awakening explained, and all the conflicting paths and doctrines of humanity clarified, by an all-illuminating Revelation of sacred understanding?

Are you ready for Wisdom that shows you exactly how you unconsciously cut yourself off from the Divine Reality—and exactly how to reconnect, and to always participate consciously in

that Reality, with every breath, in all relationships, in all action and meditation, even to the degree of Perfect Divine Self-Realization?

If your answer to any of these questions, or all of them, is "yes", then you need seek no further. We invite you to explore the Sacred Literature of Da Avabhasa.

SOURCE LITERATURE

THE LOVE-ANANDA GITA
(THE WISDOM-SONG OF NON-SEPARATENESS)
The "Simple" Revelation-Book Of Da Kalki (The Divine World-Teacher and True Heart-Master, Da Love-Ananda Hridayam)

The Love-Ananda Gita is Da Avabhasa's quintessential Revelation of His Way of the Heart, containing His basic Instructions on the fundamental practice of Satsang, or feeling-Contemplation of His bodily (human) Form, His Spiritual (and Always Blessing) Presence, and His Very (and Inherently Perfect) State of Free Being. The most basic Source-Text of His entire Word of Confession and Instruction. [The next edition of *The Love-Ananda Gita* will be published with the following attribution: *The Simple Revelation-Book Of The Divine World-Teacher and True Heart-Master, Da Avabhasa (The "Bright").*]
Standard Edition
$34.95* cloth, $19.95 paper

* All prices are in U.S. dollars

408

THE DAWN HORSE TESTAMENT
The Testament Of Secrets
Of The Divine World-Teacher
and True Heart-Master,
Da Avabhasa (The "Bright")

In this monumental text of over 800 pages (a substantial updating and enlargement of the original Work published in 1985), Da Avabhasa Reveals the Mysteries and devotional Secrets of every practice and developmental stage of the Way of the Heart. Ken Wilber, renowned scholar of Eastern and Western psychology and religion, was moved to write:

The Dawn Horse Testament *is the most ecstatic, most profound, most complete, most radical, and most comprehensive single spiritual text ever to be penned and confessed by the Human-Transcendental Spirit.*

New Standard Edition
$24.95 paper

THE DA UPANISHAD
THE SHORT DISCOURSES ON self-RENUNCIATION, GOD-REALIZATION, AND THE ILLUSION OF RELATEDNESS

Da Avabhasa's most concise Instruction relative to the forms of the Way of the Heart described in *The Dawn Horse Testament,* emphasizing the non-strategic, non-ascetical practice of renunciation in the Way of the Heart. (*The Da Upanishad* is an enlarged and updated edition of Da Avabhasa's Work formerly titled *The Illusion Of Relatedness.* The next edition will be titled *The Da Avabhasa Upanishad.*)
Standard Edition
$19.95 paper

THE ego-"I" is THE ILLUSION OF RELATEDNESS

Published here in book form, this central Essay from *The Da Avabhasa Upanishad* is an indispensable introduction to the esoteric Wisdom-Instruction of the Divine World-Teacher of our time. It includes Da Avabhasa's utterly extraordinary commentaries on diet and sexual Yoga, His Divinely Enlightened secrets on how to responsibly master and transcend all of the psycho-physical "sheaths" or bodies, and passage after passage that exposes the very core of our suffering, the illusion of relatedness.
$8.95 paper

THE BASKET OF TOLERANCE

A GUIDE TO PERFECT UNDERSTANDING
OF THE ONE AND GREAT TRADITION
OF MANKIND

Never before in history has it been possible for a seventh stage Adept to Give the world such a Gift: a comprehensive bibliography (listing more than 2,500 publications) of the world's historical traditions of truly human culture, practical self-discipline, perennial religion, universal religious mysticism, "esoteric" (but now openly communicated) Spirituality, Transcendental Wisdom, and Perfect (or Divine) Enlightenment, compiled, presented, and extensively annotated by Da Avabhasa Himself. The summary of His Instruction on the Great Tradition of human Wisdom and the Sacred ordeal of Spiritual practice and Realization.
New Standard Edition
(forthcoming, late 1992)

THE LION SUTRA

(ON PERFECT TRANSCENDENCE OF
THE PRIMAL ACT, WHICH IS THE ego-"I",
THE self-CONTRACTION, OR attention
itself, AND ALL THE ILLUSIONS OF
SEPARATION, OTHERNESS, RELATEDNESS,
AND "DIFFERENCE")
The Perfect Revelation-Book
Of The Divine World-Teacher
and True Heart-Master, Da
Avabhasa (The "Bright")

A poetic Exposition of the "Perfect Practice" of the Way of the Heart—the final stages of Transcendental, Inherently Spiritual, and Divine Self-Realization. Of all Da Avabhasa's Works, *The Lion Sutra* is the most concentrated Call and Instruction to Realize the Consciousness that Stands prior to body, mind, individual self, and objective world. (First published in 1986 under the title *Love-Ananda Gita*.)
New Standard Edition
(forthcoming, early 1992)

THE LIBERATOR (ELEUTHERIOS)

AN EPITOME OF PERFECT WISDOM
AND THE PERFECT PRACTICE

In compelling, lucid prose, Da Avabhasa distills the essence of the ultimate processes leading to Divine Self-Realization in the Way of the Heart— the "Perfect Practice", which involves the direct transcendence of all experience via identification with Consciousness Itself, through feeling-Contemplation of His Form, His Presence, and (most crucial in these stages of practice) His Infinite State.
New Standard Edition
(forthcoming, early 1992)

THE HYMN OF THE
TRUE HEART-MASTER

The New Revelation-Book Of The Ancient
and Eternal Religion Of Devotion To The
God-Realized Adept

The Hymn Of The True Heart-Master is Da Avabhasa's ecstatic proclamation of the Sat-Guru as the supreme Means for Divine Self-Realization. In 108 poetic verses, Da Avabhasa extols the Way of Divine Unity through Ishta-Guru-Bhakti Yoga, or worshipful service and devotion to the Ishta-Guru or "Chosen" and "Most Beloved" Master of one's heart. This volume also includes many of Da Avabhasa's primary Essays and Discourses on the principle of Guru-devotion in His Company as well as moving Leelas (or Stories) by His devotees that demonstrate the supreme transforming power of this Yoga.
New Standard Edition
(forthcoming, early 1992)

INTRODUCTORY TEXTS

FREE DAISM

THE ETERNAL, ANCIENT, AND NEW
RELIGION OF GOD-REALIZATION
An Introduction to the Blessing Work
of the Divine World-Teacher and
True Heart-Master, Da Avabhasa
(The "Bright") and the Spiritual Process
Lived in His Company
by Richard Schorske

Addressed to new readers and written in a highly accessible style,
Free Daism thoroughly introduces Da Avabhasa and the sacred orders of His most exemplary devotees, the stages and disciplines of the Way of the Heart, and the unique features of the institution, the sacred devotional culture, and the worldwide community of His devotees.
(forthcoming, early 1992)

LOVE OF THE GOD-MAN

A COMPREHENSIVE GUIDE TO THE
TRADITIONAL AND TIME-HONORED
GURU-DEVOTEE RELATIONSHIP, THE
SUPREME MEANS OF GOD-REALIZATION,
AS FULLY REVEALED FOR THE FIRST
TIME BY THE DIVINE WORLD-TEACHER
AND TRUE HEART-MASTER, DA
AVABHASA (THE "BRIGHT")
by James Steinberg

Love of the God Man is a full-length (over 800-page) discussion of the profound laws and virtues of the Guru-devotee relationship as practiced in the Way of the Heart. Nowhere else in the literature of sacred life does such an encyclopedic treatment of the Guru-devotee relationship exist. *Love of the God-Man* is an inexhaustible resource, full of Da Avabhasa's Wisdom and His Leelas (inspiring stories) and many stories from the Great Tradition.
Second Edition (forthcoming, late 1992)

DIVINE DISTRACTION

A GUIDE TO THE GURU-DEVOTEE
RELATIONSHIP, THE SUPREME MEANS
OF GOD-REALIZATION, AS FULLY
REVEALED FOR THE FIRST TIME BY
THE DIVINE WORLD-TEACHER AND
TRUE HEART-MASTER, DA AVABHASA
(THE "BRIGHT")
by James Steinberg

Presented by a longtime devotee of Da Avabhasa, this shorter version of *Love of the God-Man* describes, illustrates, and extols the Guru-devotee relationship. *Divine Distraction* features compelling stories of Da Avabhasa's Work with His devotees, and illuminating passages from His Wisdom-Teaching, along with instruction and stories from great Masters and disciples in the world's religious and Spiritual traditions.
$12.95 paper

FEELING WITHOUT LIMITATION
AWAKENING TO THE TRUTH BEYOND
FEAR, SORROW, AND ANGER
A Spiritual Discourse by The Divine
World-Teacher and True Heart-Master,
Da Avabhasa (The "Bright")

A brief introductory volume featuring a Discourse from Da Avabhasa's Teaching years that presents in simplest terms His fundamental Argument about human suffering, seeking, and freedom. Also includes remarkable Leelas and testimonies by three devotees.
$4.95 paper

THE PERFECT ALTERNATIVE
A TESTIMONY TO THE POWER OF
THE TRANSFORMING GRACE OF
SRI DA AVABHASA (THE "BRIGHT")
by Kanya Samatva Suprithi

A gem of a book by one of the four most mature practitioners of the Way of the Heart, a woman who has entered the sixth stage of life through Da Avabhasa's Grace. Kanya Samatva Suprithi presents here a very readable summary of Da Avabhasa's basic Arguments about seeking and Happiness, and she includes some of her own story as a Daist practitioner. An excellent and very concise introduction to Da Avabhasa and His Work.
$4.95 paper

AVADHOOTS, MAD LAMAS, AND FOOLS
by James Steinberg

A brief and lively account of the "Crazy Wisdom" style of sacred Instruction employed by Adepts in many traditions, times, and cultures, including Leelas of Da Avabhasa's Teaching years and His Divine Emergence Work.
(forthcoming, early 1992)

THE WISDOM-LITERATURE OF DA AVABHASA'S TEACHING WORK

THE KNEE OF LISTENING
THE EARLY LIFE AND EARLIEST
"RADICAL" SPIRITUAL TEACHINGS OF
THE DIVINE WORLD-TEACHER AND
TRUE HEART-MASTER, DA AVABHASA
(THE "BRIGHT")

VOLUME I
THE LIFE OF UNDERSTANDING

Da Avabhasa's autobiographical record of the very human—as well as Spiritual, Transcendental, and Divine—Ordeal of His Illumined birth and His boyhood in America, His Spiritual insights, practice, and growth as a Devotee of great modern Yogic Adepts, and His Divine Re-Awakening or Enlightenment.
New Standard Edition (forthcoming)

VOLUME II
THE WISDOM OF UNDERSTANDING

Da Avabhasa's earliest Essays on the practice and Realization of "Radical" Understanding.

(These first two volumes of *The Knee of Listening*, taken from the original, unabridged manuscript and including recent commentary by Da Avabhasa and His devotees, are nearly twice the length of the previously published edition of *The Knee of Listening*.)
New Standard Edition (forthcoming)

VOLUME III
THE METHOD OF THE SIDDHAS:
TALKS ON THE SPIRITUAL TECHNIQUE
OF THE SAVIORS OF MANKIND

In this book of powerful and often extremely humorous Talks with His devotees in 1972 and 1973, the first year of His formal Teaching Work, Da Avabhasa Reveals the Secret of the Way of Satsang—the profound and transforming relationship between the Sat-Guru and His devotee.
New Standard Edition (forthcoming)

SCIENTIFIC PROOF OF THE EXISTENCE OF GOD WILL SOON BE ANNOUNCED BY THE WHITE HOUSE!
PROPHETIC WISDOM ABOUT THE MYTHS AND IDOLS OF MASS CULTURE AND POPULAR RELIGIOUS CULTISM, THE NEW PRIESTHOOD OF SCIENTIFIC AND POLITICAL MATERIALISM, AND THE SECRETS OF ENLIGHTENMENT HIDDEN IN THE BODY OF MAN

Speaking as a modern Prophet, Da Avabhasa combines His urgent critique of present-day society with a challenge to create true sacred community based on actual Divine Communion and a Spiritual and Transcendental Vision of human Destiny.
New Standard Edition
(forthcoming)

THE TRANSMISSION OF DOUBT
TALKS AND ESSAYS ON THE TRANSCENDENCE OF SCIENTIFIC MATERIALISM THROUGH "RADICAL" UNDERSTANDING

Da Avabhasa's principal critique of scientific materialism, the dominant philosophy and world-view of modern humanity that suppresses our native impulse to Liberation, and His Revelation of the ancient and ever-new Way that is the true sacred science of Life, or of Divine Being Itself.
New Standard Edition
(forthcoming)

THE ENLIGHTENMENT OF THE WHOLE BODY
A RATIONAL AND NEW PROPHETIC REVELATION OF THE TRUTH OF RELIGION, ESOTERIC SPIRITUALITY, AND THE DIVINE DESTINY OF MAN

One of Da Avabhasa's early Revelations of the Way of Eternal Life that He Offers to beings everywhere, including Ecstatic Confessions of His own Enlightened Realization of the Divine Person, and sublime Instruction in the practices of the Way of the Heart. When initially published in 1978, this Text was a comprehensive summary of His Way of the Heart. Includes a unique section, with illustrations, on the esoteric anatomy of the advanced and the ultimate stages of Spiritual transformation.
New Standard Edition
(forthcoming)

NIRVANASARA
Da Avabhasa critically appraises the sacred Wisdom-Culture of mankind, particularly focusing on the two most sublime traditions of sacred life and practice—Buddhism and Hindu non-dualism (Advaita Vedanta). Here He also announces and expounds upon His own Way of the Heart as the continuation and fulfillment of the most exalted Teachings of Buddhism and Hinduism.
New Standard Edition
(forthcoming)

THE DREADED GOM-BOO, OR THE IMAGINARY DISEASE THAT RELIGION SEEKS TO CURE

In this remarkable book, Da Avabhasa Offers a startling and humorous insight: All religion seeks to cure us of an unreal or fundamentally imaginary disease, which He calls "the Dreaded Gom-Boo". This disease is our constant assumption that we have fallen from Grace and are thus in need of the salvatory "cure" of religious belief.

The good news of Da Avabhasa's Way of the Heart is that we need not seek to be cured but need only feel, observe, understand, and renounce (through the real ordeal of sacred practice) the very activity of seeking itself, and thus be restored to our native Happiness and Freedom.
New Standard Edition (forthcoming)

CRAZY DA MUST SING, INCLINED TO HIS WEAKER SIDE
CONFESSIONAL POEMS OF LIBERATION AND LOVE

Composed principally in the early 1970s and expressed spontaneously with the ardor of continuous, Divinely Awakened Identification with all beings, these remarkable poems proclaim Da Avabhasa's vulnerable human Love and His Mysterious, "Crazy" passion to Liberate others from ego-bondage.
$9.95 paper

THE SONG OF THE SELF SUPREME
ASHTAVAKRA GITA
The Classical Text of Atmadvaita by Ashtavakra

An authoritative translation of the *Ashtavakra Gita*, a text Da Avabhasa has described as "among the greatest (and most senior) communications of all the religious and Spiritual traditions of mankind". His illuminating Preface is a unique commentary on this grand classic of Advaita Vedanta, discussing the *Ashtavakra Gita* in the context of the total Great Tradition of Spiritual and Transcendental Wisdom. Da Avabhasa also identifies and discusses the characteristics of those rare texts and traditions that fully communicate the Realization and "Point of View" of the seventh, or fully Enlightened, stage of life.
New Standard Edition (forthcoming)

PRACTICAL TEXTS

THE EATING GORILLA COMES IN PEACE
THE TRANSCENDENTAL PRINCIPLE OF LIFE APPLIED TO DIET AND THE REGENERATIVE DISCIPLINE OF TRUE HEALTH

In a substantial reworking of the first edition of this text, Da Avabhasa Offers a practical manual of Divinely Inspired Wisdom about diet, health and healing, and the sacred approach to birthing and dying.
New Standard Edition
(forthcoming, late 1992)

CONSCIOUS EXERCISE AND THE TRANSCENDENTAL SUN
THE PRINCIPLE OF LOVE APPLIED TO EXERCISE AND THE METHOD OF COMMON PHYSICAL ACTION. A SCIENCE OF WHOLE BODY WISDOM, OR TRUE EMOTION, INTENDED MOST ESPECIALLY FOR THOSE ENGAGED IN RELIGIOUS OR SPIRITUAL LIFE

Conscious exercise is a "technology of love"—which transforms physical exercise, play, and all ordinary activity into an embrace of the infinite energy of the cosmos, always in the conscious context of feeling-Contemplation of Da Avabhasa Himself as Divine Heart-Master. Greatly enlarged and updated from earlier editions.
New Standard Edition
(forthcoming, early 1992)

LOVE OF THE TWO-ARMED FORM

THE FREE AND REGENERATIVE
FUNCTION OF SEXUALITY
IN ORDINARY LIFE, AND THE
TRANSCENDENCE OF SEXUALITY
IN TRUE RELIGIOUS OR SPIRITUAL
PRACTICE

Da Avabhasa's Instruction on the cultivation of "true intimacy" and the Realization of truly ecstatic, Spiritualized sexuality—a profound critique of both worldly exploitation of sex and ascetical, anti-sexual religious messages. As an alternative to these errors of West and East, Da Avabhasa proposes the specific practices of sexual "conscious exercise" and "sexual communion" (for sexually active individuals who practice in Satsang with Him). His Enlightened Wisdom-Teaching on emotion and sexuality Calls and inspires all men and women to a new and compassionate union of love, desire, and Spiritual consciousness.
New Standard Edition
(forthcoming)

EASY DEATH

TALKS AND ESSAYS ON THE INHERENT
AND ULTIMATE TRANSCENDENCE OF
DEATH AND EVERYTHING ELSE

In this major expansion of the popular first edition of His Talks and Essays on death, Da Avabhasa Reveals the esoteric secrets of the death process and Offers a wealth of practical Instruction on how to prepare for a God-Conscious and ecstatic transition from physical embodiment. Elisabeth Kübler-Ross wrote: "An exciting, stimulating, and thought-provoking book that adds immensely to the literature on the phenomena of life and death. Thank you for this masterpiece."
New Standard Edition
$24.95 cloth, $14.95 paper

LEELAS

The Sanskrit term "leela" (sometimes "lila") traditionally refers to the Divine Play of the Sat-Guru with his (or her) devotees, whereby he Instructs and Liberates the world. Da Avabhasa has said that Leelas of His Instructional Play with His devotees are part of His own Word of Instruction, and they are, therefore, Potent with the Blessing and Awakening-Power of His Heart-Transmission.

THE DIVINE EMERGENCE OF THE WORLD-TEACHER
THE REALIZATION, THE REVELATION, AND THE REVEALING ORDEAL OF DA KALKI
A Biographical Celebration of Heart-Master Da Love-Ananda
by Saniel Bonder

Never before have the Life and Work of a seventh stage Divine Incarnation been so carefully documented. This lively narrative focuses on Da Avabhasa's life-long Ordeal of Divine transformation, which finally culminated, on January 11, 1986, in the Great Event that inaugurated His Divine Emergence as the World-Teacher and His ongoing Blessing Work.

Richly illustrated with more than 100 photographs of Da Avabhasa and full of the often dramatic Stories of His Teaching years and His Divine Emergence Work, as well as His own unique Confessions of Divine Incarnation, Realization, and Service to all beings. [The next edition of *The Divine Emergence of the World-Teacher* will be subtitled *The Realization, the Revelation, and the Revealing Ordeal of Da Avabhasa (The "Bright")*].
$14.95 paper

THE CALLING OF THE KANYAS
CONFESSIONS OF SPIRITUAL AWAKENING AND PERFECT PRACTICE THROUGH THE LIBERATING GRACE OF THE DIVINE WORLD-TEACHER AND TRUE HEART-MASTER, DA AVABHASA (THE "BRIGHT")
by Meg McDonnell
with the Da Avabhasa Gurukula Kanyadana Kumari Order
(Kanya Tripura Rahasya, Kanya Samarpana Remembrance, Kanya Kaivalya Navaneeta, and Kanya Samatva Suprithi)

The story of the Graceful ordeal of sacred practice and transformation embraced by the formal renunciate order of four women devotees who personally serve Da Avabhasa. The confessions and the example of the Kanyas call everyone to deeply understand and heartily respond to the Supremely Blessed Event that has made their own Spiritual transformation possible: Da Avabhasa's Great Divine Emergence, beginning in early 1986 and continuing ever since. (forthcoming)

FOR AND ABOUT CHILDREN

WHAT AND WHERE AND WHO TO REMEMBER TO BE HAPPY

A SIMPLE EXPLANATION OF THE WAY OF THE HEART (FOR CHILDREN, AND EVERYONE ELSE)

A new edition of Da Avabhasa's essential Teaching-Revelation on the religious principles and practices appropriate for children. In Words easily understood and enjoyed by children and adults, Da Avabhasa tells children (and adults) how to "feel and breathe and Behold and Be the Mystery".

New Standard Edition, fully illustrated (forthcoming)

THE TWO SECRETS (yours, AND MINE)

A STORY OF HOW THE WORLD-TEACHER, DA KALKI, GAVE GREAT WISDOM AND BLESSING HELP TO YOUNG PEOPLE (AND EVEN OLDER PEOPLE, TOO) ABOUT HOW TO REMEMBER WHAT AND WHERE AND WHO TO REMEMBER TO BE HAPPY A Gift (Forever) from Da Kalki (The World-Teacher, Heart-Master Da Love-Ananda), as told by Kanya Remembrance, Brahmacharini Shawnee Free Jones, and their friends

A moving account of a young girl's confrontation with the real demands of sacred practice, and how Da Avabhasa lovingly Instructed and Served her in her transition through a crisis of commitment to practice that every devotee must, at some point, endure.

$12.95 paper

VEGETABLE SURRENDER,

OR HAPPINESS IS NOT BLUE by Heart-Master Da and two little girls

The humorous tale of Onion One-Yin and his vegetable friends, who embark on a search for someone who can teach them about happiness and love, and end up learning a great lesson about seeking. Beautifully illustrated with original line drawings.

$12.95 cloth, oversize

LOOK AT THE SUNLIGHT ON THE WATER

EDUCATING CHILDREN FOR A LIFE OF SELF-TRANSCENDING LOVE AND HAPPINESS: AN INTRODUCTION

Full of eminently practical guidance for the "whole bodily" and sacred education of children and young people, this simple, straightforward, informative text is also perhaps the best available brief summation of Da Avabhasa's Wisdom on the first three stages of life, or the period from infancy to adulthood.

$12.95 paper

THE TRANSCENDENCE OF CHILDHOOD AND ADOLESCENCE

Compiled from Da Avabhasa's previously unpublished Instructions, this book comprehensively addresses the conscious education of young people in their teenage years, providing for the modern age an Enlightened vision of the ancient principle and way of life called "brahmacharya". In this approach, as practiced in the communities of Free Daists, young people (typically between the ages of 11 and 15) make a free and conscious choice to devote their lives to the Realization of the Divine Reality, under the direct tutelage of their "brahmacharya master" or Guru. This book presents a "radical" vision of education that is virtually unknown in the modern West.

(forthcoming, late 1992)

PERIODICALS

THE FREE DAIST

The Bi-Monthly Journal of the Heart-Word and Blessing Work of the Divine World-Teacher and True Heart-Master, Da Avabhasa (The "Bright")

The Free Daist chronicles the Leelas of the Teaching Work and the Divine Emergence Work of Da Avabhasa, and describes the practice and process of devotion, self-discipline, self-understanding, service, and meditation in the Way of the Heart. In addition, the magazine reports on the cultural and missionary activities of the Free Daist Communion and the cooperative community of Da Avabhasa's devotees. Of special interest is the regular "Hermitage Chronicle" offering current news of Da Avabhasa's Life and Work.

Subscriptions are $44.00 per year for six issues. Please send your check or money order (payable to The Dawn Horse Press) to: The Free Daist, P.O. Box 3680, Clearlake, CA 95422, USA.

THE "BRIGHT"

Celebrations of the Divine World-Teacher, Da Avabhasa (The "Bright")

A brief bi-monthly periodical, oriented to the general reader, introducing the Good News of Da Avabhasa and His Work and countering the trends of scientific materialism, religious provincialism, and anti-guruism in present-day society.

Subscriptions are $12.00 per year for six issues. Please send your check or money order (payable to The Dawn Horse Press) to: The "Bright", P.O. Box 3680, Clearlake, CA 95422, USA.

A subscription to both *The "Bright"* and *The Free Daist* is only $48.00.

THE GARDEN OF LIONS MAGAZINE

The Worldwide Voice of Young Free Daists

This unique magazine is the voice of the worldwide culture of children and young people who practice the Way of the Heart under the Enlightened Guidance of the living Sat-Guru, Da Avabhasa. *The Garden of Lions Magazine* includes published Instruction on various aspects of sacred practice for young people, Discourses Given by Da Avabhasa, personal accounts and inspiring stories from the lives of young devotees, and a great variety of articles and artwork from young people of all ages from all over the world. Themes have included: an introduction to the practice of Brahmacharya, or the study of God, the Spiritual practice of Ecstasy and Guru-devotion, and the Enlightened practice of sexuality for young people.

The Garden of Lions Magazine is a truly extraordinary celebration of the unprecedented Wisdom-Teaching and Way of life Given by Da Avabhasa.

Subscriptions are $16.00 per year for three issues. Please send your check or money order (payable to *The Garden of Lions Magazine*) to: The Garden of Lions Magazine, Subscription Department, P.O. Box 1737, Lower Lake, CA 95457, USA.

VIDEOTAPES

THE WAY OF THE HEART

On the "Radical" Spiritual Teaching and Universal Blessing Work of the Western-Born Adept, Heart-Master Da Love-Ananda

Incorporating rare segments of recent and historical footage, Part One tells the Story of Sri Da Avabhasa's Illumined Birth and His Ordeal of Divine Re-Awakening for others, and celebrates the Emergence of His Work of World Blessing. Part Two (which includes Talk excerpts by Da Avabhasa and testimonials by longtime practitioners) describes the Gifts and forms of practice that are Given to all who take up the Way of the

Heart as Da Avabhasa's devotees. Part Three introduces the sacred culture of the Way of the Heart.
$29.95, 2 hours,
VHS, NTSC, or PAL format

The Way of the Heart is also available in a modified form, which includes recent footage of Da Avabhasa in Darshan with devotees and other material not included in the full-length version. A brief, summary audiovisual introduction to His Life and Divine Work as the World-Teacher in a world addicted to egoic suffering and seeking.
$19.95, 76 minutes,
VHS, NTSC or PAL format

ORDERING THE BOOKS AND VIDEOTAPES OF DA AVABHASA

The books and videotapes of Da Avabhasa are available at local bookstores and by mail from the Dawn Horse Book Depot.

Please write to us at the address below for a complete catalogue of books and audiovisual publications on the Way of the Heart and traditional sacred literature.

In the USA please add $3.00 for the first book or videotape ($5.00 for each *Dawn Horse Testament*) and $1.00 for each additional book or videotape. California residents add 7¼% sales tax.

Outside the USA please add $5.00 for the first book or videotape ($6.00 for each *Dawn Horse Testament*) and $1.50 for each additional book or videotape.

To order the books and videotapes listed above, and to receive your copy of the Dawn Horse Press Catalogue, please write:

The Dawn Horse Book Depot
P.O. Box 3680
Clearlake, CA 95422, USA
(707) 928-4936

Y

An Invitation

Of all the means for Spiritual growth and ultimate Liberation offered in the sacred traditions of humankind, the most treasured is the Way of Satsang, or the Way lived in the Blessing Company of One Who has Realized the Truth. The Divine World-Teacher and True Heart-Master, Da Avabhasa (The "Bright"), Offers just such a rare and graceful Opportunity.

The Transformative relationship to Da Avabhasa is the foundation of the Way of the Heart that He Offers. Through a whole personal and collective life of self-transcending practice in His Company, ordinary men and women may be purified of their egoic suffering and enjoy the Blessings of a God-Realizing destiny.

If you would like to receive a free introductory brochure or talk to a practicing devotee about forms of participation in the Way of the Heart, please write or call our Correspondence Department:

Correspondence Department
The Free Daist Communion
P.O. Box 3680
Clearlake, California 95422, USA
(707) 928-4936